Both the English Civil War and the French Revolution produced in England an outpouring of literature reflecting intense belief in the arrival of a better world, and new philosophies of the relationship between mind, language, and cosmos. *Milton, the metaphysicals, and romanticism* is the first book to explore the significance of the connections between the literature of these two periods. The book analyzes Milton's influence on Romantic writers including Blake, Beckford, Wordsworth, Shelley, Radcliffe, and Keats, and examines the relationships between other seventeenth-century poets – Donne, Marvell, Vaughan, Herrick, Cowley, Rochester, and Dryden – and Romantic writers. Representing a wide range of theoretical approaches, and including original contributions by leading British, American, and Canadian scholars, this is a provocative and challenging assessment of the relationship between two of the richest periods of British literary history.

Milton, the metaphysicals, and romanticism

Milton, the metaphysicals, and romanticism

EDITED BY

LISA LOW

Pace University, New York

and

ANTHONY JOHN HARDING

University of Saskatchewan

CAMBRIDGE
UNIVERSITY PRESS

Published by the Press Syndicate of the University of Cambridge
The Pitt Building, Trumpington Street, Cambridge, CB2 1RP
40 West 20th Street, New York, NY 10011-4211, USA
10 Stamford Road, Oakleigh, Melbourne 3166, Australia

First published 1994

Printed in Great Britain at the University Press, Cambridge

A catalogue record for this book is available from the British Library

Library of Congress cataloguing in publication data

Milton, the metaphysicals, and romanticism / edited by Lisa Low and Anthony John Harding.
p. cm.
Includes bibliographical references and index.
ISBN 0-521-44414-4
1. English poetry – 19th century – History and criticism.   2. English poetry – Early modern,
1500–1700 – History and criticism.   3. English poetry – Appreciation – Great Britain.
4. Influence (Literary, artistic, etc.)   5. Milton, John, 1608–1674 – Influence.
6. Romanticism – Great Britain.   7. Metaphysics in literature.
I. Low, Lisa.   II. Harding, Anthony John.
PR590.M55   1994
821′.4 – dc20   93-41033   CIP

ISBN 0 521 44414 4 hardback

UP

Contents

———

Notes on contributors

FREDERICK BURWICK is Professor of English and Comparative Literature at the University of California, Los Angeles. He is the author of many books, including *De Quincey's Essays on Rhetoric* (Carbondale: Southern Illinois University Press, 1967) and *The Damnation of Newton* (Berlin and New York: Walter de Gruyter, 1986), and has edited several, including a recent facsimile edition of Byron's *Hebrew Melodies* (Tuscaloosa: University of Alabama Press, 1988).

ANNETTE WHEELER CAFARELLI, Associate Professor of English and Comparative Literature at Columbia University, is the author of *Prose in the Age of Poets: Romanticism and Biographical Narrative* (University of Pennsylvania Press, 1990), and *Women and the Formation of Romanticism* (Cambridge University Press, forthcoming), and is currently working on a book about the British literary marketplace entitled *Romanticism and Patronage*.

MICHAEL CHAPPELL is a doctoral candidate at Fordham University. His dissertation is on the literary relationship between Samuel Johnson and Charlotte Lennox.

ANTHONY JOHN HARDING is Professor of English at the University of Saskatchewan and author of *Coleridge and the Idea of Love* (Cambridge: Cambridge University Press, 1975) and *Coleridge and the Inspired Word* (Kingston and Montreal: McGill-Queen's University Press, 1985). He is presently completing the editing of volume 5 of the Notebooks of Samuel Taylor Coleridge, to be published by Princeton University Press under the editorship of Kathleen Coburn.

BETH LAU is Associate Professor of English at California State University, Long Beach. She is the author of *Keats's Reading of the Romantic Poets* (Ann

Arbor: University of Michigan Press, 1991) and co-editor of *Approaches to Teaching Brontë's Jane Eyre* (Modern Language Association, 1993).

LISA LOW is Associate Professor of English at Pace University, New York. She is the author of "Ridding Ourselves of Macbeth" in *Macbeth*, ed. Harold Bloom (New York: Chelsea House, 1991) and has published in *The Massachusetts Review*, *Massachusetts Studies in English*, *Cross Currents*, and *Kritikon Litterarum*.

TILOTTAMA RAJAN is Professor in the Department of English and the Centre for Criticism and Theory at the University of Western Ontario. She is the author of *Dark Interpreter: The Discourse of Romanticism* (Ithaca: Cornell University Press, 1980) and *The Supplement of Reading: Figures of Understanding in Romantic Theory and Practice* (Ithaca: Cornell University Press, 1990), and is editing *Intersections: Nineteenth-Century Philosophy and Contemporary Theory* with David Clark (State University of New York Press, forthcoming). She is working on two studies: *Romantic Narrative* and *Deconstruction Before and After Post-Structuralism*.

GEORGE ANTHONY ROSSO, JR., is Associate Professor of English at Southern Connecticut State University. He has published *Blake's Prophetic Workshop: A Study of "The Four Zoas"* (Bucknell University Press, 1993) and co-edited with Daniel Watkins *Spirits of Fire: English Romantic Writers and Contemporary Historical Methods* (Fairleigh Dickinson University Press, 1990). He is currently co-editing with Jacqueline Di Salvo an anthology titled *Blake, Politics, and History*.

E. S. SHAFFER is the author of *"Kubla Khan" and the Fall of Jerusalem: The Mythological School in Biblical Criticism and Secular Literature, 1770–1880* (Cambridge University Press, 1975), and of a number of articles on Coleridge and Beckford. She is Editor of *Comparative Criticism*, an annual journal published by Cambridge University Press (1979–), of which volume 4 was "The Languages of the Arts." She is currently working on a book on literature and the visual arts in the Romantic period.

JOHN T. SHAWCROSS is Professor of English at the University of Kentucky. He is the distinguished editor and author of many books including *The Complete Poetry of John Donne* (New York: New York University Press, 1968), *The Complete Poetry of John Milton* (New York: Doubleday, 1963), and *Milton 1732–1801: The Critical Heritage* (London: Routledge and Kegan Paul, 1972).

ANYA TAYLOR is Professor of English at John Jay College of Criminal Justice of the City University of New York. She is the author of *Coleridge's Defense of the Human* (Columbus: Ohio State University Press, 1986) and of *Magic and English Romanticism* (Athens: University of Georgia Press, 1979).

NICOLA ZOE TROTT holds a British Academy Postdoctoral Fellowship at St. Catherine's College, Oxford. Her monograph, *Wordsworth's Second Sight*, is to be published by Oxford University Press, and she is co-editor, with Jonathan Wordsworth and Duncan Wu, of the forthcoming Longman Annotated *Wordsworth: Selected Poetry and Prose*.

Acknowledgements

This book began as a group of papers written for a special session which Lisa Low chaired at MLA in 1986 called "Marvell and the Romantics." The editors would like to thank Frederick Burwick for suggesting that these papers become the nucleus of a book, and Joseph Anthony Wittreich, Jr., for invaluable assistance given over the past several years.

Kevin Taylor, English Literature editor at Cambridge University Press, has been supportive and encouraging from the first involvement of the Press in the project: we should like to thank him for his tact and patience, and his interest in the idea of this volume. We would also like to thank the librarians at our respective universities – especially Elizabeth Birnbaum at Pace University – and the ever-helpful staff of the New York Public and Bobst libraries and the British Library, London.

Lisa Low is grateful to Pace University for the Provost-sponsored Summer Research Grant and for awards from the Scholarly Research Committee, both of which helped finance this project. She would also like to thank her research assistant, Raphael Guay, for devoted and uncomplaining labor over the past two years. During the last phase of the editing, Camille Slights, William Slights, and Ron Cooley, at the University of Saskatchewan, cheerfully and patiently shared their knowledge of existing scholarship on Milton and the seventeenth century.

The editors would like to make further specific acknowledgements as follows:
Extracts reprinted from Samuel Taylor Coleridge: *Notebooks*, v. 3, *Marginalia*, *Lectures 1808–1819*, *Biographia Literaria*. Copyright © Princeton University Press. Used by permission of Princeton University Press.
Extracts reprinted from William Wordsworth: *Poems, in Two Volumes, and*

Other Poems, 1800–1807, edited by Jared Curtis. Copyright © 1983 by Cornell University Press. Used by permission of the publisher.

Extracts reprinted from William Wordsworth: *Descriptive Sketches 1793*, edited by Eric Birdsall, with the assistance of Paul M. Zall. Copyright © 1984 by Cornell University Press. Used by permission of the publisher.

Extracts reprinted from William Wordsworth: *An Evening Walk*, edited by James Averill. Copyright © 1984 by Cornell University Press. Used by permission of the publisher.

Extracts reprinted from William Wordsworth: *Home at Grasmere, Part First, Book First of The Recluse*, edited by Beth Darlington. Copyright © 1977 by Cornell University. Used by permission of the publisher, Cornell University Press.

A note on texts and abbreviations

Unless otherwise stated, *The Prelude* is quoted from the Norton parallel text. Other poetry by Wordsworth is quoted from the de Selincourt edition. The three editions of the letters of Wordsworth are abbreviated as *Early Years*, *Middle Years*, and *Later Years*. Milton's prose is taken, where possible, from Hughes; otherwise, from Wolfe. The following editions are used unless otherwise stated:

Blake, William. *The Complete Poetry and Prose of William Blake*. Edited by David Erdman. Berkeley and Los Angeles: University of California Press, 1982.

Coleridge, Samuel Taylor. *The Collected Works of Samuel Taylor Coleridge*. General Editor Kathleen Coburn. Bollingen Series LXXV. Princeton: Princeton University Press, 1969– .

Donne, John. *The Complete Poetry of John Donne*. Edited by John T. Shawcross. New York: New York University Press, 1968.

Hazlitt, William. *The Complete Works of William Hazlitt*. Edited by P. P. Howe. 21 vols. London: J. M. Dent, 1930–34.

Herrick, Robert. *The Poetical Works of Robert Herrick*. Edited by L. C. Martin. Oxford: Oxford University Press, 1956.

Keats, John. *The Poems of John Keats*. Edited by Jack Stillinger. Cambridge: The Belknap Press of Harvard University Press, 1978.

Keats, John. *The Letters of John Keats*. Edited by Hyder E. Rollins. 2 vols. Cambridge: Harvard University Press, 1958.

Lamb, Charles and Mary. *The Works of Charles and Mary Lamb*. Edited by E. V. Lucas. 7 vols. London: Methuen, 1903.

Marvell, Andrew. *The Poems and Letters of Andrew Marvell*. Edited by H. M. Margoliouth. 2 vols. 2nd edition. Oxford: Clarendon Press, 1967.

Milton, John. *Complete Poems and Major Prose*. Edited by Merritt Y. Hughes. Indianapolis: Odyssey, 1957.

Milton, John. *Complete Prose Works of John Milton*. Edited by Don M. Wolfe. 8 vols. New Haven: Yale University Press, 1953–82.

Shelley, Percy Bysshe. *Shelley's Poetry and Prose*. Edited by Donald Reiman and Sharon Powers. New York: Norton, 1977.

Vaughan, Henry. *The Complete Poetry of Henry Vaughan*. Edited by Ernest Sirluck. New York: Anchor Books, 1964.

Wordsworth, William. *The Letters of William and Dorothy Wordsworth. The Early Years, 1787–1805*. Edited by Ernest de Selincourt, revised by Chester L. Shaver. Oxford: Clarendon Press, 1967.

Wordsworth, William. *The Letters of William and Dorothy Wordsworth. The Middle Years, 1806–1820*. Edited by Ernest de Selincourt. 2 vols. 2nd edition. Part 1, *1806–11*, revised by Mary Moorman. Oxford: Clarendon Press, 1969. Part 2, *1812–1820*, revised by Mary Moorman and Alan G. Hill. Oxford: Clarendon Press, 1970.

Wordsworth, William. *The Letters of William and Dorothy Wordsworth: The Later Years, 1821–1850*. Edited by Ernest de Selincourt. 2nd edition. Parts 1–3 revised, arranged, and edited by Alan G. Hill. Oxford: Clarendon Press, 1978–82.

Wordsworth, William. *The Poetical Works of William Wordsworth*. Edited by Ernest de Selincourt, revised by Helen Darbishire. 5 vols. Oxford: Clarendon Press, 1940–49; revised 1952–59.

Wordsworth, William. *The Prelude: 1799, 1805, 1850*. Edited by Jonathan Wordsworth, M. H. Abrams, and Stephen Gill. New York: Norton, 1979.

Wordsworth, William. *The Prose Works of William Wordsworth*. Edited by W. J. B. Owen and Jane Worthington Smyser. 3 vols. Oxford: Clarendon Press, 1974.

Milton, the metaphysicals, and romanticism: reading the past, reflecting the present

LISA LOW *and* ANTHONY JOHN HARDING

━━━

WHEN WE REMAKE THE CANON, to paraphrase Yeats, it is ourselves that we remake. The critic's desire to see affinities between writers belonging to different literary periods is as persistent and perhaps as irresistible as the contrary impulse to separate literature into periods in the first place. Such negotiations of the canon, often fiercely debated, are part of the normal traffic of critical inquiry.

Yet negotiations of and around the canon have probably never been as controversial as they are at present, when cultural materialism, new historicism, and feminism, as well as other critical movements, are directing our attention to the ideological interests that lie behind both the received canons themselves, and all proposed alterations or additions to them. The very grounds of the debate have changed radically and, it seems, irrevocably. In 1954 Louis Martz could argue that there was such a thing as the meditative style (defined as "'current language heightened,' molded, to express the unique being of an individual who has learned, by intense mental discipline, to live his life in the presence of divinity"), that this style was present in the poetry of Southwell, Donne, Herbert, Vaughan, Crashaw, Marvell, Blake, Wordsworth, Hopkins, Dickinson, late Yeats and late Eliot, and that it "forms a tight link between the seventeenth and the twentieth centuries."[1] If this claim now seems extraordinary it is not so much because of any inherent deficiencies in Martz's argument, but rather because very different questions are now being asked. Our sense of what is significant in the literature of the last two centuries (it is safe to say) is profoundly different from Martz's. As Martz pointed out, for example, Donne and Hopkins were both schooled in Jesuit methods of meditation, and this common factor in their backgrounds undoubtedly has a bearing on the poetry they both wrote. What has changed is not the *evidence* for such affinities between the poets, but our sense of the

I

relative importance of such evidence. Few critics now would argue that a poet's language expressed her or his unique being as an individual, and those who did would couch the argument in terms rather different from those used by Martz. It is no dishonor to Martz's book to observe that his critical agenda, and his sense of what is valuable in poetry, were strongly influenced by his proximity to Hopkins, Yeats, and Eliot.

On the whole, questions of value were in Martz's book second to questions of historical continuity. Even so, by including Blake and Wordsworth in his list of the poets in whom "the meditative style" could be found, and invoking the Milton of *Paradise Lost* Book VII and *Paradise Regained* as a further example, Martz was implicitly going against the hostile value-judgments on Milton and the Romantics pronounced by both Eliot himself and later by F. R. Leavis. Martz saw affinities – and, more, saw several kinds of affinity, constituting a "line" or canon – where Eliot and Leavis saw only a falling-off, a surrendering of intellectual rigor for impressionistic description and of "felt life" for narcissistic posturing. Both strategies – constructing "lines" of descent, as if appreciating poetry meant determining who were the true inheritors of the mantle, the true successors to an original master, and the opposite strategy of trumpeting the virtues supposedly unique to an earlier period while decrying the qualities of a later one – now seem naive and ill-informed. (John T. Shawcross, in an essay in this volume, takes issue with both approaches, on historical and other grounds.) Criticism has learned to be a good deal more precise about both the nature of the Romantic project and the historical reality which provided the enabling conditions for that project, if not absolutely determining it.

At the same time, however, new historicism has sometimes given the appearance of tending to isolate the Romantic poets from all their literary precursors, canonical or not, and to relocate them in a very narrowly defined historical moment, as if any appeal to a purely literary antecedent, stylistic affinity, or other transhistorical relationship might lead straight to the ideologically-suspect process of canon-formation – which, it goes without saying, serves only entrenched academic interests. But even new historicism has to find some way to deal with moments such as Wordsworth's "Milton, thou shouldst be living at this hour" – with the image of the seventeenth century reflected in and constructed by Romantic writing, with the reception history of Donne, Milton, and other seventeenth-century poets in the early nineteenth century, with the reappropriation of totemic figures such as Milton by culturally-marginalized writers of a later period (Keats, Beckford, Ann Radcliffe), not to mention deeper affinities arising out of the needs that poet and reader shared in the seventeenth century and the nineteenth. The very availability of *Paradise Lost* as a vernacular poetic resource which was not restricted to a classically-educated readership changed the way in which poetic allusion was practiced, as Lucy Newlyn has argued:

Milton's reception ... can be seen to have made more accessible the process of allusion itself. No longer associated only with learned reference to the ancients (and therefore precluding the understanding of less educated readers), allusion depended more and more on the vernacular. Milton's epic provided literary material which was available to readers of vastly differing classes and educational backgrounds: it levelled hierarchical distinctions, both within the literary canon and within the readership itself.[2]

Such inquiries into the process of canon-formation as it operated in the Romantic period inevitably reflect the needs and priorities of our own time: for one of the lessons of the new historicism is that we should view with suspicion the privilege scholarship has sometimes too easily claimed, of being untouched by the present.[3] This volume is concerned not only with those aspects of the seventeenth century that were visible to the Romantics, but with what from both periods is visible to us now – and not merely what can be "made available," as in an archive.

All this is merely to point out that, as Tilottama Rajan proposes in the first essay in this volume, literary traditions and theoretical positions intergenerate one another. Rajan is particularly concerned with what she judges to be an important structural feature of both *Paradise Lost* and key texts of Wordsworth and Blake: the non-determinative positioning of the reader, or the "reading-function," discernible in both – a function which she carefully distinguishes from the "implied" reader and "ideal" reader of reader-response theorists. Where these hypostatized readers carry a certain weight of ideological determination, enforcing a certain kind of reading (though not necessarily a specific "meaning") on the text, the "reading-function" as inscribed within *Paradise Lost* and certain Romantic works creates "a position within the text which can and will be occupied differently by different readers." Such questions as these raise once again, and more acutely, the problematic nature of literary relationships, whether or not we choose to deal in such loaded terms as "canon" and "tradition." By discovering how Milton and the Romantics develop in parallel a new kind of text which in its very structure is open to interpretive difference, Rajan's essay prefigures a new literary history that does not have to isolate its texts either from historical reality or from the phenomenological, from readers' actual experiences of literature.

Milton, the Metaphysicals, and Romanticism begins, then, a long overdue revaluation of the interrelationship between romanticism and the seventeenth century, especially in the context of new strategies of reading. Not all our essays raise the question of the positioning of the reader in the text in the way that Rajan's does, of course, but all of them do address in one way or another the issue of the reader's "constitutive role in the making of the text," and the assumptions which the reader brings to the text. Our essays put forward a variety of views on the vital first principle of whether it is legitimate to read author A "through" author B – or whether on the other hand *any* reading of A is bound to be affected by the gravitational pull of B, so that the best we can hope to do is to understand this effect and compensate for it, or alternatively to place the two texts in a mutually illuminating dialectic.

The debate about reading A through B, or comparing A with B, as applied to the relations between seventeenth-century poets and the Romantics, has a long history, of course, going back at least to the 1920s, and William Empson's challenge to T. S. Eliot's theory of the "dissociation of sensibility." In Eliot's view the stronger line of English poetry followed not from the Romantic but from the metaphysical school, a school which for Eliot included Donne, Herbert, Bishop King, Lord Herbert of Cherbury, and Marvell among others. According to Eliot, these were the last practitioners of the fusion of thought and feeling. This fusion, consummated in "wit," enabled the metaphysical poets to "feel their thought as immediately as the odour of a rose." But after the metaphysicals, and, tellingly, just prior to the English Civil War, a disabling "dissociation of sensibility set in, from which we have never recovered."[4] This dissociation forced poets into either thinking too much (the Augustans), or feeling too much (the Romantics). In *Seven Types of Ambiguity* (1930) Empson challenged Eliot's "dissociation of sensibility" thesis. Where Eliot had argued that the metaphysicals practiced a poetry invariably superior to that of the Romantics, and that Marvell's in particular was wholly different in kind from theirs, Empson argued the opposite: that, while pursuing further the metaphysicals' poetic program, Romantic poetry achieved more, because it was polysemous, predicated not on one-to-one but on multiple and ultimately indeterminate correspondences. Thus the later metaphysicals were read as having anticipated romanticism, as well as improving upon Donne.

Empson's view was attacked and has never been widely accepted. For example, Merritt Y. Hughes and Ruth Wallerstein complained against the "kidnapping" of Donne and Marvell; Rosemond Tuve countered Empson by analyzing Marvell's poetry in the context of Ramistic rhetorical practices; Joseph Summers argued that despite some similarities Marvell's vision is "finally unlike" that of the Romantics; and for Frank Kermode, "The Garden" does not celebrate but rather deliberately rejects an arboreal sensuousness that only *seems* to us Romantic in character.[5] These 1940s-to-1960s views of the metaphysicals remain influential. Thus, for Donald Friedman, writing in 1970, nineteenth-century critics erred in seeing Marvell as a pantheist; for Barbara K. Lewalski and Andrew J. Sabol, Vaughan's love of nature was generally "overemphasized"; and as recently as 1986 John T.

Shawcross has argued, like Wallerstein, that "Donne needs to be rescued from too close an association with romanticism" and that "the false specter of Romantic effusion has blighted poetic criticism for a long time."[6]

If Eliot and his followers had shown how to read the metaphysicals, F. R. Leavis, in *Revaluation* (1935), did the same for the cavalier poets and the Augustans, once again at the expense of Milton and the Romantics. Leavis named the metaphysical-Augustan school the "line of wit." Leavis's poetic, based on qualities he perceived in Jonson, Carew, Marvell, Dryden, and Pope, was what would now be called masculinist: he praised "tough reasonableness," "native robustness," "racy vigour," and "impersonal urbanity." On the other hand Milton, Shelley, and (interestingly) Herrick came in for severe criticism. "Milton's dislodgement," Leavis wrote provocatively, "in the past decade, after his two centuries of predominance, was effected with remarkably little fuss." Shelley was "in some ways a very intelligent man," Leavis reported, but "peculiarly emotional," and his poetry unlike Donne's becomes "unreadable" in maturity.[7]

In the 1960s and 1970s some of the assumptions behind these influential critics' views were brought into question. In the 1970 preface to the revised edition of *The Visionary Company* Harold Bloom targeted Eliot and his followers in particular, rejecting the appearance of political neutrality which their criticism assumed. "English culture," he argued, "has been divided between those who have accepted the Puritan religious revolution of the late sixteenth and seventeenth century and those who have fought against it." Eliot's critical judgments were guided by a conservative political and religious agenda rather than by purely aesthetic principles. In claiming that Eliot's Anglo-Catholicism "accounts finally for *all* of Eliot's judgements on English poetry" Bloom not only called those judgments into question but permitted a revaluation of the line in the light of his and others' particular political and religious affiliations.[8]

The politicization of English romanticism was a relatively new phenomenon. Until the 1960s, at least according to M. H. Abrams, the connection between romanticism and the French Revolution, or for that matter, between the Romantics and the English Civil War, had been almost wholly ignored. In the 1960s and 1970s Abrams and Bloom joined Christopher Hill in offering a revisionary reading of Milton and the Romantics as fellow-laborers in a progressive political movement. Thus for Bloom, "the French Revolution ... is the single most important external factor that conditions Romantic poetry" (xiv); similarly, Abrams writes that, far from constructing Eliot's "dream world," the Romantics were "to a degree without parallel ... obsessed with the realities of their era."[9] Equally important was Bloom and Abrams's sense that romanticism was a reemergence of the ideals that impelled the republican side in the English Civil War. For Abrams, the Romantics were non-conformists who looked back past the eighteenth century and Augustan moderation to find in the left-wing activists of the seventeenth century the source of their own version of Puritan radicalism. For Bloom, pointing out the descent of the English Romantics from the "Left Wing of England's Puritan movement" was the "most important point to be made about English Romantic poetry ... particularly since it has been deliberately obscured by most modern criticism" (xvii).

Joseph Anthony Wittreich, Jr. continued this radical revision of the canon, arguing that the Romantics' vision of Milton had been "much neglected, often misrepresented and generally misunderstood," and pointing out that the New Miltonists' exclusive focus on Satan had distorted the complexity of the Romantic response to Milton. Wittreich argued that Milton was for the Romantics a hero of political and religious radicalism, and "chief spokesman for a version of Christianity that the Romantics sought to establish as a 'new orthodoxy.'"[10] The Miltonic image of the poet as a God-like creator, prophetically reshaping a world, informed the Romantic experiment. For Wittreich, the Miltonic–Romantic school was essentially democratic and utopian: while the Catholic–classicizing line was predominantly elitist and conservative, the Romantics, like the republican Milton, looked forward to a reformed society.

Wittreich's view of Milton as a republican hero has been modified in more recent years by critics such as Jackie Di Salvo and Leslie Tannenbaum, who see the Romantic poets, especially Blake and Shelley, as revising rather than simply extending Milton's program. Di Salvo emphasizes that Blake and Shelley democratized and feminized Milton's elitist republicanism.[11] Others have followed Bloom's lead in seeing the Romantics as, in comparison with Milton, failed revolutionaries, who turned away from outward forms of revolution to the ever-fading interior light. Nicholas Roe, for example, has traced Wordsworth's withdrawal from the political sphere as far back as 1794, in an addition to *An Evening Walk*.[12] Nicola Trott, in an essay in this volume, agrees with Roe in seeing Wordsworth as moving to the interior "surprisingly soon" in a mental revolution which "replaces – rather than precedes – a material revolution."

In the 1980s, new historicists including Marjorie Levinson, Marilyn Butler, and Jerome J. McGann attacked Bloom and Abrams for too readily accepting the Romantics' own claims to progressive and democratic sympathies. For Levinson, such claims suppress the fact that Wordsworth exploited the poor as a poetic subject, while turning away from them in his own political praxis.[13] For McGann, Abrams's brand of criticism betrayed "an uncritical absorption in Romanticism's own self-representations." If in Abrams's view the

Romantics were politically engaged, for McGann the Romantics practiced more self-flattery than actual democratic politics. Far from sustaining engagement in the cause of revolution or even democratic reform, the Romantics disengaged from the political; in fact, the poetry they wrote, recommending withdrawal into the inner paradise, confesses that disengagement. In the end, for McGann as for T. S. Eliot, the Romantic myth was a "mere" myth, as precarious as it was delusionary: "Blake fell silent. Wordsworth fell asleep, and Coleridge fell into his late Christian contemptus." As for the second-generation Romantics, they escaped from political engagement as well, Shelley into idealism, Keats into aestheticism, and Byron into sensationalism.[14]

A similar reaction has taken place in the feminist revaluation of the Romantics. In the 1970s and 1980s, feminist criticism of romanticism has taken at least three principal tacks. In the first place, feminists have begun to demonstrate how far the emphasis on male Romantic writers has distorted our perception of romanticism. The low status academic critics give the gothic novel, for example, unfairly disqualifies writers like Ann Radcliffe and Mary Shelley from serious consideration. Similarly, some feminists have argued that periods have been defined in such a way as to exclude women: Jane Austen has been read as more conservative than she really is, with the result that she is considered irrelevant to romanticism and taught alongside the Victorian novelists instead.[15] Similarly, the critics themselves have been called to account. Bloom's neo-Freudian theory of influence, based on a father-to-son line of descent and an oedipal model of the poet's relation to the precursor, has come to be seen as objectionably masculinist. A second line of attack has been the recuperation of the little-read women poets of the Romantic period – many of whom were in their lifetimes much better known than any male Romantic except Byron. Poets such as Charlotte Smith, Mary Robinson, "L. E. L." and Felicia Hemans have been brought forward as writers vital to the culture of the time, and who have their own claims to our attention.[16] In a third revisionary move, feminist critics have begun to revaluate the "canonical" male Romantics themselves, examining for example their treatment of women. Is their view of woman only superficially more positive than (say) Herrick's or Milton's? Do they patronize women while practicing a division of labor, a doctrine of separate spheres, which relegates women to service roles? Under such scrutiny, the sympathy some male Romantic poets express toward women has been exposed as compromised, ambivalent, and far distant from "feminism" as we understand it today.[17]

Feminists have called just as persuasively for a revaluation of the seventeenth century. Whether and to what extent Milton was sexist, or misogynist, has been debated since Milton's own times. It is safe to say that many feminists regard Milton as Virginia Woolf did, as a maddeningly male-centered poet who required of women submission to men, a submission all the more horrible for its having been called *love*. Donne, on the other hand, is according to Janel Mueller the last metaphysical poet able to carry off masculine bravura, and even Donne could not sustain it past the early period of his secular love poetry.[18] According to Leah S. Marcus, the metaphysicals turned away from women altogether when they turned to God.[19] In the cultural despair brought on by the new science and the collapse of the established church, the metaphysicals retreated to the transcendental sphere where they had themselves to become the " other " – they had, in effect, to become children (and in effect, women as well). Whether this transformation was a good thing, in feminist terms, is a question too complicated to address here. But it is important to draw attention to this issue, especially as we embark on a reconsideration of the relationship between the metaphysicals and the Romantics. For both the Romantics and the metaphysicals were lyric poets who arguably practiced the idealization of childhood and, perhaps, the feminization of the self.

If it seems inevitable that in some sense or other we have to see Milton, however reconstructed or misread, as a major presence in Romantic writing, the presence of the metaphysical poets in, to, or behind the Romantics remains a question that somehow refuses to be settled. Romantic writers are much less likely to claim an affinity with the metaphysicals than with Milton, of course, since their poetry, by comparison with Milton's, was nearly invisible. Herbert was known to the Romantics as a divine, but not as a poet; Marvell was known chiefly as a prose satirist and republican hero; Vaughan was known only in scattered poems in anthologies; and the Dobell manuscript of Traherne's poems was not uncovered until the early 1900s. Even Donne was relatively obscure. "Do you know Donne?" Leigh Hunt asked Shelley in a letter in 1821.[20] Nevertheless the temptation to see affinities between Marvell's paradise imagery and Wordsworth's, or between the innocence of childhood vision in Herbert or Traherne and the evocations of the child's visionary power in Blake and in *Lyrical Ballads*, remains strong; and the case has been made that the superficial similarities do reflect more than just the modern reader's telescoping of historical difference or the projection of decadent Romantic taste back into the seventeenth century. If it is true, as scholars working on the seventeenth century have long indicated, that we cannot claim influence, what explains the similarities?[21]

Partial answers, at least, have been suggested by Christopher Hill and Leah S. Marcus. For Hill, if the political and social tensions of the English Civil War subsided during the Restoration and eighteenth century, they reemerged in the Romantic period. The eighteenth century, for Hill, was in effect an interruption in what otherwise would have been a continuous movement toward a more egalitarian society. Where the neoclassical poets were "disturbed by none of the doubts which have tormented the sensitive since the days of Shakespeare," the metaphysicals and the Romantics, troubled by doubt and "internal conflict," charged their lyrics with "the most intense feeling of their age."[22] Thus for Hill it is a mistake to identify the metaphysicals, as New Criticism traditionally has, exclusively with medieval scholasticism and Anglicanism; rather, metaphysical poetry is transitional, its paradoxes representing, if nothing else, the conflict between medieval and modern in an age of transition.

More recently Leah S. Marcus has argued that both the metaphysical and the Romantic poets retreated to childhood as a way to find unity in periods of cultural despair. For example, she writes,

William Blake's *Songs of Innocence* and Book Second of the *Prelude* are as concerned with the unity of infant vision as the writings of Thomas Traherne. Sexual innocence and experience and their relationship to artistic creativity are as constant a theme in Blake's poetry as they are in Andrew Marvell's. Coleridge's notebooks indicate that he planned a whole series of poems on the subject of infancy. The traditional association of childhood with the ideals of humility and simplicity was as central to the *Lyrical Ballads* as it was to the verse of Herbert and Herrick. (*Childhood and Cultural Despair*, 245).

Following Marcus, Janel Mueller has suggested that in Traherne "the child is erotically self-cognizant," and that this has significant implications for subsequent "representations of poetic subjectivity and femininity." Traherne's "open sensibility and ostensible artlessness" anticipate Blake's child speakers, both suggesting "revolutionary articulations of sexual freedom and equality" ("Among the Metaphysicals," 156).

It is important to point out, however, that such claims go against New Critical as well as new historicist practice. We may take Ruth Wallerstein as representative of a view of history which harmonized well with the New Critic's estimation of seventeenth-century poetry. In *Studies in Seventeenth-Century Poetic* (1950), Wallerstein argued that Marvell's "habit of thought had deep roots not in Hegelian but in Mediaeval and Renaissance logic"; thus, Marvell should be studied in the context of Plato, Plotinus, and Tertullian rather than of Freud, Marx, or Darwin. Readings which saw "modern" concerns already emerging in seventeenth-century poets constituted for Wallerstein a "barbarous" kidnapping of men who were schooled since youth in the "great concinnities and ornaments of rhetoric" (152–53).

Wallerstein's book was enormously influential. From it followed a spate of works of an even more scholastic kind, pursuing still more remote ancient and medieval theological and philosophical sources. But there are several problems with Wallerstein's method. In the first place, as Colie points out, Wallerstein pursues her investigations into Marvell without considering whether Marvell actually knew the tradition she delineates.[23] The emphasis on intellectual background in some ways places Marvell in the same category (as "thinker") with Tertullian and St. Bonaventure, and leads to a neglect of the poetry itself. It could also be argued that Wallerstein underestimates the extent to which the Romantics shared the metaphysicals' admiration for Platonic and neo-Platonic traditions, and similarly profited from them. But the most obvious short-coming of Wallerstein's method, from a new historical standpoint, is that it ignores the social and political realities of Marvell's age. For the new historicist, it is absurd to claim, as Wallerstein does, that Marvell remained aloof from his contemporary milieu, or that the scholastic approach is more "consistently historical" than the political one (*Studies in Seventeenth-Century Poetic*, 152).

Still, the new historicist McGann is just as rigorous as Wallerstein in his opposition to constructing "modernist" connections, cautioning us against comparing periods as radically divergent as the seventeenth, nineteenth, and twentieth centuries. For McGann such inter-period comparisons are likely to fail because they will overlook relevant "historical differentials." Thus, McGann derides the current received view that "romanticism comprises all significant literature from Blake to the present," just as he views with suspicion comparisons between Renaissance and Romantic poetry. Curiously, in a phrase that almost word-for-word recalls Wallerstein's, McGann argues that Donne's "self-awareness is more Plutarchian than Hegelian" (*Romantic Ideology*, 56, 20, 75). But is this true? Or is McGann here merely replacing the neoromantic views of a Bloom or an Abrams with a different kind of taste, one that (ironically) he shares with Wallerstein, a far more traditionalist critic?

Wallerstein's and McGann's observations are sanative and even liberating, but may underestimate continuities between the metaphysicals and the Romantics by confining "the modern" too narrowly to our own era. Some scholars are much less ready to believe that the divide between one period and another might be absolute and unbridgeable. The historian Lawrence Stone describes the "*early* Modern period" (italics ours) in English culture (from 1500 to 1800) as undergoing "massive shifts in world views and value systems."[24] Do such shifts undermine Wallerstein's claim of continuity between medieval scholasticism and metaphysical poetry? Similarly, Basil Willey has argued that the transfer of interest from God to the self, and particularly to the self-in-nature, began as early as Bacon's *Advancement of Learning*, which proposed the scientific method as the key to the acquisition of knowledge. For Willey, the "submission of the whole self to 'things'" which underpins Baconian scientific method anticipates both Wordsworth's idea of a union of mind with external world, and Keats's idea of negative capability.[25]

If Willey is even partially right claims for affinities between seventeenth- and nineteenth-century poetry are neither naive nor crass, and McGann's more narrowly-drawn historical differentials may need to be questioned or at least qualified.

In his essay "The Dead-End of Formalist Criticism" Paul de Man pursues a similar line of argument.[26] According to de Man, Marvell (like Keats) is chiefly concerned with the problem of nature and consciousness. In arguing this de Man challenges most twentieth-century scholarship on the metaphysicals. Joseph Summers, for example, mounts his whole case against reading Marvell as a proto-Romantic by arguing that while the Romantics are close to, Marvell is absolutely separated from nature ("Marvell's 'Nature,'" 137–50). But according to de Man, Marvell and Keats are both separated from nature. For both, the connection with nature is longed-for, but immediately it is thought of, it turns into conflict. The ironic relation to nature, then, is not – as Summers has argued – the special relation of the theologically secure seventeenth-century poet, it is simply the *modern* relation to nature. In his garden retreat, in other words, Marvell may have stumbled upon what de Man identifies as the dilemma of the modern lyric, the relation of self to nature, and this may be the crucial moment of seventeenth-century poetry. If for the Jonson of "To Penshurst" nature in its infinite plenty offers itself up gladly to the wealthy – fish run into the net, deer run upon the arrow, and peasants are pleased to feed their masters – in Marvell, a different description of nature emerges. It may be that during and after the Civil War, as a result of the visible degradation of the landscape which the first modern technological war caused, seventeenth-century poets began to perceive nature as something sacred that needs to be protected. Certainly this view was being put forward by the eighteenth century. But if de Man is right the modern attitude to nature – that it must be defended against science, technology, and capitalism, as well as against medieval *contemptus mundi* – has its analogue in the time of Marvell. In this sense, Vaughan, Traherne, and Marvell, no less than Milton, the Romantics, and Wallace Stevens, may be seen as belonging in the "line of vision": in the line, that is, of the modern attempt to recover the connection between nature and mind.

If Marvell places a new kind of value on nature in order to reestablish a harmony that is seen as threatened, destabilized, or lost, it could be argued that this crisis of perception itself originates in an antecedent, urgent, and equally "modern" crisis, that "sense of psychic dislocation" which Leah S. Marcus identifies as common to both the seventeenth-century poets and the first-generation Romantics (*Childhood and Cultural Despair*, 245). Donne is perhaps the most important case in point, and as Harvey and Maus have argued "the received view of Donne as politically and religiously conservative is seriously incomplete" (*Soliciting Interpretation*, xvi). Perhaps of most relevance to his relation to romanticism in this context is Anne Ferry's argument that already in the Renaissance sonnet, and supremely in Donne's Holy Sonnets, something like the modern sense of self has been developed. Ferry's close study of sixteenth-century poetry brought her to the interesting conclusion that even though a systematic, philosophic vocabulary for the description and analysis of psychological states does not appear until the time of Locke, it is no falsification of Shakespeare's sonnets, or of Donne's Holy Sonnets, to see their speakers as voicing "a kind of modern consciousness." That is, Ferry argues, "some poets of this period held conceptions of internal experience comparable to those implied by our language about an *inner life* or a *real self*," even though the vocabulary available to us was not available to them.[27]

At least by the time of Donne, the hold that medieval theology exercised on people's minds was weakened, religious beliefs were more diverse, and the private decisions of the individual conscience were beginning to acquire a new importance.[28] If these conflicts were modified and contained after the Restoration, they emerged again at the outbreak of the French Revolution. Perhaps Leah S. Marcus's view of things is correct: that the kind of cultural breakdown which shook the seventeenth century had itself become a norm in the Romantic period. And the way intertextual reference is used in the Romantic period both reflects and helps to disseminate the sense of cultural crisis, by locating the reader's subjectivity in the apparent power to choose between readings of the indeterminate text. Lucy Newlyn makes this point, suggesting that "The Rime of the Ancient Mariner" (like *Paradise Lost*, to which it alludes) creates a Miltonic "overlapping" of the "fallen" and "unfallen" perspectives. Such intertextuality "puts the reader 'between' texts, creating at the rhetorical level also an illusion of suspended choice."[29]

This is *not* to say that the seventeenth-century poets were Romantics or proto-Romantics; there are important differences, as Marcus points out. By 1790, for example, the idealization of childhood had lost its association with conservatism and had acquired newly radical implications; and the Romantics were more "interested in the possibility of... reinvesting [nature] with spiritual significance." Still, the similarities cannot be entirely dismissed as illusions caused by our foreshortened twentieth-century perspective. Referring to parallels between seventeenth-century and Romantic images of childhood, Marcus enquires: "why limit comparisons to Vaughan and Wordsworth? 'The Retreate' and the 'Intimations Ode' are only the two most obvious of many points of contact" (*Childhood and Cultural Despair*, 245–46). In a similar spirit this book assumes that many more "points of contact" between seventeenth-century and Romantic poetry need to be explored, and more finely discriminated.

Can we, for example, manage to see a Donne poem as resonating with a Romantic poem, in the kind of context we have just outlined, without falling into the error of anachronistically referring to it as Romantic (as Legouis and Cazamian once referred to Marvell's "Upon Appleton House" as Romantic)?[30] Like Wordsworth, it could be argued, Donne responds to crisis by a kind of reality-testing, trying to fix experience to a specific moment. "Goodfriday, 1613. Riding Westward," with its specific location in space and time, its spiritual quest against the inward-corroding pressure of guilt, and its Wordsworth-like reliance on memory for salvation, is closer to Wordsworth than mere chronology might have suggested. In some lines that almost exactly parallel Wordsworth's "These beauteous forms, / Through a long absence, have not been to me / As is a landscape to a blind man's eye," Donne describes the crucifixion as a still point for his fixation through memory: "Though these things," he writes, "as I ride, be from mine eye, / They're present yet unto my memory."[31] Donne's poem resembles Wordsworth's in tone as well. Donne speaks to Christ as passionately and as filially as Wordsworth speaks to Dorothy in "Tintern Abbey": "thou look'st towards mee," he writes,

> O Saviour, as thou hang'st upon the tree;
> I turn my backe to thee, but to receive
> Corrections, till thy mercies bid thee leave.
> O thinke mee worth thine anger, punish mee,
> Burne off my rusts, and my deformity;
> Restore thine Image, so much, by thy grace,
> That thou may'st know mee, and I'll turne my face.

How far is this homely and colloquial but urgent petition for salvation from Wordsworth's "For thou art with me here upon the banks / Of this fair river; thou my dearest Friend, / My dear, dear Friend; and in thy voice I catch / The language of my former heart," or his, "If solitude, or fear, or pain, or grief, / Should be thy portion, with what healing thoughts / Of tender joy wilt thou remember me, / And these my exhortations"?

In both poems there is intense self-consciousness. In both the speaker's "self" is guilty. Both employ an intensely religious vocabulary. Both exhort. Both poets are "dying" for salvation. Both poets wish to be remembered, and both rely on memory to call to mind what must not be forgotten. The major difference is that God is more present to one poet than to the other, or perhaps that the nature of God's presence/absence has changed. Feeling as filially and as faithfully toward him as Wordsworth does toward Dorothy, Donne relies on Christ for protection against the storm of himself as Wordsworth must rely perforce on Dorothy. But the high and petitioning tone of personal meditation, the immediacy and candor of the diction, the violence of feeling, and the sense of the frail self on the verge of disaster appear from our perspective very similar.

The twelve essays in this volume address the issues we have discussed here: revolution and retreat, the place of the self in nature, the breakdown (both personal and social) caused by the weakening of Christian certainties, and the new myths – including the myth of the reading self – created in response to this breakdown. We have put Tilottama Rajan's essay first because, as this introduction has already suggested, she teaches us in the most comprehensive way that periods intergenerate one another, and that the nature of the relationships between modern reader, Romantic epigone, and seventeenth-century predecessor cannot be settled by commonsensical appeals for "objectivity" in place of "subjectivity." For the very way we read is historically-conditioned and even pre-formed to some extent by the Romantics themselves, with their practice of inscribing the reader-function integrally within the text, and our way of reading therefore needs to be placed in a more consciously-theorized historical relationship with the texts rather than treated as a perfectly transparent medium.

Continuing the emphasis on the triple relationship between Milton, the Romantics, and the modern reader, in "Newton's pantocrator and Blake's recovery of Miltonic prophecy" George Anthony Rosso, Jr. shows how Milton's prophetic strain becomes overlaid and contained within a Newtonian Anglicanism, the disruptive elements of revelation stabilized by unholy marriage with natural philosophy, until Blake's reading releases it again, calling up a "Milton" to overthrow and slay Milton's own miscreated God. There is also, Rosso argues, a sense in which Milton is himself responsible for the Newtonians' move to contain him, and, therefore, for Blake's reaction to it, since his anti-prelatism was qualified and limited by his distrust of anarchistic tendencies among the radical sectaries of his time. Rosso's essay is less a "Blakean" reading of Milton, however, than an attempt to show how much of Blake's Milton is constructed under the shadow of Newton's "pantocrator," and in reaction to him.

Next follow two essays dealing with writers outside the traditional canon. In "Milton's Hell: William Beckford's place in the graphic and the literary tradition," E. S. Shaffer claims for Beckford a "pivotal position" in the development of Romantic readings of Milton's Hell. For Shaffer, it is with Beckford, not Byron nor even "Monk" Lewis, that the "movement towards the revision of a conventional cultic hell into a personal hell" begins. Annette Wheeler Cafarelli's "How theories of romanticism exclude women: Radcliffe, Milton, and the legitimation of the gothic novel" starts from the innocuous-seeming statement that "One typical measure of the significance of a work of literature is its communication with monuments of the artistic past," but then sets out to show how by this test Ann Radcliffe's work, so long excluded from the canon, is not only closely linked with the writings of the "mainstream" Romantics, but through a "program of implicit and explicit references to Milton's works" positively sets out to claim a "legitimate ancestry" for gothic writing. This makes the critical and institutional blindness to Radcliffe, and other women writers whose work appeared mainly in the 1790s and mainly in prose, all the more culpable.

One of the key images through which Wordsworth laid claim to a Miltonic role and simultaneously attempted to justify a lapse from revolutionary enthusiasm into his mature poetic quietism is that of the "inward light." This is the subject of Nicola Zoe Trott's essay "Wordsworth, Milton, and the inward light," which traces the links between Wordsworth's self-identification with Milton and his cultivation of the poetic and spiritual security promised by the "inward light" image. Trott shows that in the poems he wrote between 1794 and 1814 there is a considered and consciously ideological (rather than a concealed, denied, and suppressed) kind of self-making at work.

The assumption by poets of a superior role, and the way it contradicts the committed poet's urge to break down barriers between classes and individuals, is also a topic of Michael Chappell's "De-fencing the poet: the political dilemma of the poet and the people in Milton's *Second Defense* and Shelley's *Defence of Poetry*." Chappell focuses on the way Shelley repeats a number of the rhetorical moments of Milton's treatise, justifying the poet as fully entitled to join ranks with the republican soldier and statesman in a progressive cause, while simultaneously placing the poet on a superior plane, as one whose ultimate loyalty is to higher considerations of "truth" and "reason" rather than to force.

Although the notes that Keats wrote in his copy of *Paradise Lost* have been studied, very little attention has been paid to the "extensive underscorings and marginal lines" which, Beth Lau argues in "Keats's marginalia in *Paradise Lost*," tell us a great deal about Keats's tastes and reading habits that is not apparent merely from the few margin notes. In particular, Lau analyzes the comparative "neglect of speeches and dialogue" evident in these markings, and suggests how this has a bearing on Keats's own poetic practice.

Following this series of essays on the Romantics' relationship to Milton we have grouped five essays which examine their relationship to the metaphysical poets. First, Frederick Burwick contrasts Wordsworth's response to the problem of whether to choose political engagement over private contemplation, the active life over the contemplative life, with Marvell's. Wordsworth's "Reply to Mathetes" honors Marvell as one of the "glorious Patriots" of his age, and Wordsworth evidently hoped to emulate Marvell in responding to political crises of his own time, yet Burwick shows that while

Marvell could maintain an undivided poetic self, not separating the "contemplative" from the "active," Wordsworth prescinds the poetry of political consciousness, treating it as a different *kind* of poetry and thereby inevitably putting it into conflict with the reflective mode which came more easily to him.

Pursuing the careful discrimination of the different characteristics of poets in the two periods, John T. Shawcross's "Kidnapping the poets: the Romantics and Henry Vaughan" is a radical challenge to the view that there are important and revealing affinities between Vaughan's poetry and that of the Romantics, particularly Wordsworth. Shawcross questions not only the "incompetent understanding of romanticism" which underwrites this mistaken view of Vaughan as a Wordsworthian before his time, but also the opposite kind of misreading, foisted on Vaughan by "would-be 'classicists,' adherents of a 'line of wit.'" Paying close attention to such questions as what texts of Vaughan were actually in existence and available to the Romantics in the early 1800s, Shawcross's essay is a reminder of the dangers of projecting on to the poets of the last three centuries the poetic taste (and oversimplified categorizations) of the present.

The conventional reading of the relationship between the Romantics and the metaphysical poets also fails to explain Coleridge's admiration for John Donne, Anthony John Harding finds in his essay "'Against the stream upwards': Coleridge's recovery of John Donne." His inquiry into the reasons for Coleridge's championing of Donne proposes that Coleridge did not look to Donne for the quasi-Romantic effusion of feeling, or even for arcane learning. Rather, particularly after 1815, in the effort to construct a distinctly English poetic tradition, Coleridge needed to find a worthy successor to Shakespeare, a poet to inherit the qualities of ruggedness and vigor which he saw as characterizing English accentual verse, in contrast to the enfeebled accentual-syllabic verse that drove English poetry off course in the eighteenth century.

One unexpected and generally ignored point of contact between the Romantics and the seventeenth century, Anya Taylor argues in "Coleridge, Keats, Lamb, and seventeenth-century drinking songs," is the persistence among certain Romantic poets of a *carpe diem* topos, evident in poems on the simple pleasures of tavern and table that hark back to Anacreon, Catullus, and their seventeenth-century epigones. Coleridge and Keats in particular, Taylor shows, wrote many such poems, and while differences need to be carefully delineated (such as the more problematic nature of belief in an afterlife in the later period), there are also many points of resemblance, and some evidence for direct influence.

Finally, Lisa Low challenges the narrowness of the currently-dominant periodization of the canon which (she argues) tends to obscure important historical continuities and aesthetic resemblances between the work of seventeenth-century poets like Marvell and that of nineteenth-century poets like Keats. Low takes issue with those who assume that the differences are all-important while the continuities are illusory, or at best trivial. She argues that the deepest cultural and existential crises of the seventeenth century have persisted into our own period, and moreover that we value Marvell and Keats along with Wallace Stevens precisely because their cultural dilemmas are to a large extent still our own.

Taken together, the twelve essays in this volume address – for an audience armed with a new vocabulary and conscious of a new kind of criticism – the long-debated and too often misconstrued relationship between Milton, the metaphysicals, and romanticism.

NOTES

1 Louis Martz, *The Poetry of Meditation* (1954; reprint, New Haven: Yale University Press, 1966), 324–25.
2 Lucy Newlyn, *"Paradise Lost" and the Romantic Reader* (Oxford: Clarendon Press, 1993), 42.
3 A similar point is made by Lauro Martines, *Society and History in English Renaissance Verse* (Oxford: Basil Blackwell, 1987), 51.
4 *Selected Essays*, third edition (London: Faber and Faber, 1951), 288.
5 Merritt Y. Hughes, "Kidnapping Donne," *University of California Publications in English* 4 (1934): 61–89; Ruth Wallerstein, *Studies in Seventeenth-Century Poetic* (Madison: University of Wisconsin Press, 1950), 152; Rosemond Tuve, *Elizabethan and Metaphysical Imagery* (Chicago: University of Chicago Press, 1947); Joseph Summers, "Marvell's 'Nature,'" in *Andrew Marvell*, ed. John Carey (Baltimore: Penguin, 1967), 137–50; Frank Kermode, "The Argument of Marvell's Garden," in *Andrew Marvell*, 250–65.
6 Friedman, *Marvell's Pastoral Art* (Berkeley: University of California Press, 1970), 124; Barbara K. Lewalski and Andrew J. Sabol, eds., *Major Poets of the Earlier Seventeenth Century* (New York: Odyssey Press, 1973), 394; John T. Shawcross, "Poetry, Personal and Impersonal: The Case of Donne," in *The Eagle and the Dove: Reassessing John Donne*, ed. Claude J. Summers and Ted-Larry Pebworth (Columbia: University of Missouri Press, 1986), 57.
7 *Revaluation: Tradition and Development in English Poetry* (1935; reprint, London: Chatto & Windus, 1956), 19–21, 24, 42, 207–8, 204.
8 Harold Bloom, *The Visionary Company: A Reading of English Romantic Poetry*, revised edition (Ithaca: Cornell University Press, 1971), xvii–xviii.
9 M. H. Abrams, "English Romanticism: The Spirit of the Age," in *Romanticism and Consciousness*, ed. Harold Bloom (New York: Norton, 1970), 93.
10 Joseph Anthony Wittreich, Jr., ed., *The Romantics on Milton: Formal Essays and Critical Asides* (Cleveland: The Press of Case Western Reserve University, 1970), xi, 11.

11 See for example "Fear of Flying: Milton on the Boundaries Between Witchcraft and Inspiration," *English Literary Renaissance* 18 (1988): 114–37, and *War of Titans: Blake's Critique of Milton and the Politics of Religion* (Pittsburgh: University of Pittsburgh Press, 1983).

12 Nicholas Roe, "Wordsworth, Milton, and the Politics of Poetic Influence," *The Yearbook of English Studies* 19 (1989): 112–26.

13 *Wordsworth's Great Period Poems: Four Essays* (Cambridge: Cambridge University Press, 1986), 92.

14 Jerome J. McGann, *The Romantic Ideology: A Critical Investigation* (Chicago: University of Chicago Press, 1983), 1, 116, 117.

15 McGann begins *Romantic Ideology* with criticism of the attempt by the journal *The Wordsworth Circle* to consider Austen as a Romantic.

16 See Stuart Curran, "The 'I' Altered," in *Romanticism and Feminism*, ed. Anne K. Mellor (Bloomington: Indiana University Press, 1988); and *British Romantic Women Writers*, ed. Paula R. Feldman, Theresa M. Kelley, and Susan J. Wolfson (Hanover, New Hampshire: University Press of New England, 1994).

17 On such "understanding" as a disguised form of appropriation see Julie Ellison, *Delicate Subjects: Romanticism, Gender, and the Ethics of Understanding* (Ithaca and London: Cornell University Press, 1990).

18 Janel Mueller, "Among the Metaphysicals: A Case, Mostly, Of Being Donne For!" *Modern Philology* 87 (1989): 142–58.

19 Leah S. Marcus, *Childhood and Cultural Despair: A Theme and Variations in Seventeenth-Century Literature* (Pittsburgh: University of Pittsburgh Press, 1978).

20 A. J. Smith, ed., *John Donne: The Critical Heritage* (London: Routledge and Kegan Paul, 1975), 313.

21 As long ago as 1925 Arthur H. Nethercot made a case for seeing more than merely surface similarities between the poetry of the metaphysicals and that of the Romantics. Nethercot claimed that the metaphysicals did enjoy something of a revival in the Romantic period, though it was not their wit so much as their experiments in form which interested the Romantics. The "higher and more varied rhythms" of the metaphysicals appealed to the Romantics above the "arithmetical 'smoothness'" of the neoclassicists. See "The Reputation of the 'Metaphysical Poets' During the Age of Johnson and the 'Romantic Revival,'" *Studies in Philology* 22 (1925): 81–132.

22 "Society and Andrew Marvell," in *Andrew Marvell*, 76. For Hill's comments on Vaughan and Traherne in relation to the romantics see *Collected Essays*, 1: *Writing and Revolution in Seventeenth-Century England* (Amherst: University of Massachusetts Press, 1985), 207–25 and 226–46. Rosemary Kegl writes that for many Marxists, the English Civil War was "one moment within a more general *structural* change in English society," but the picture of a continuous bourgeois revolution has been questioned by revisionist historians who describe the English Civil War as a "punctual event." See "The Politics of Labor in Marvell's Mower Poems," in Elizabeth D. Harvey and Katharine Eisaman Maus, eds., *Soliciting Interpretation: Literary Theory and Seventeenth Century English Poetry* (Chicago: University of Chicago Press, 1990), 91.

23 Rosalie L. Colie, "*My Ecchoing Song*": *Andrew Marvell's Poetry of Criticism* (Princeton: Princeton University Press, 1970), 142–43.

24 *The Family, Sex, and Marriage in England 1500–1800* (New York: Harper and Row, 1979), 21. See also Leah S. Marcus in *Childhood and Cultural Despair*, 32.

25 See *The Seventeenth Century Background. Studies in the Thought of the Age in Relation to Poetry and Religion* (1935; reprint, New York: Doubleday Anchor, 1953), 33ff., 44, 43. For a more recent and systematic argument for the modernization of a metaphysical poet see A. Leigh DeNeef, *Traherne in Dialogue: Heidegger, Lacan, and Derrida* (Durham and London: Duke University Press, 1988).

26 See *Blindness and Insight: Essays in the Rhetoric of Contemporary Criticism*, revised edition, Theory and History of Literature, 7 (Minneapolis: University of Minnesota Press, 1983), 229–45.

27 *The Inward Language: Sonnets of Wyatt, Sidney, Shakespeare, Donne* (Chicago: University of Chicago Press, 1983), 215–46, 7.

28 On the importance of casuistry in this connection see Camille Wells Slights, *The Casuistical Tradition* (Princeton: Princeton University Press, 1981).

29 *"Paradise Lost" and the Romantic Reader*, 195.

30 Emile Legouis and Louis Cazamian, *A History of English Literature*, revised edition (London: J. M. Dent and Sons, 1971), 557.

31 "Goodfriday, 1613. Riding Westward" quoted from *Complete Poetry*, 366–68; "Tintern Abbey" from *Poetical Works*, 2: 259–63.

CHAPTER ONE

The other reading: transactional epic in Milton, Blake, and Wordsworth

TILOTTAMA RAJAN

DISCUSSIONS OF THE RELATIONSHIP between Milton and the Romantics have often focused on lines of thematic influence. Even where those connections have been treated in a more "intertextual" way, as in essays by Robin Jarvis and Kenneth Gross in the recent *Re-Membering Milton*, the emphasis has remained thematic. Alternatively, in the essay by David Riede in the same collection, intertextual relationship has been used largely to reread Blake through his reading of Milton. The present essay tries to make the connection in a more equal and somewhat different way, by arguing that both Milton and the Romantics wrote a certain kind of text, which inscribes the activity of reading within itself so as to open itself to interpretive and historical difference.[1] Such a text renounces what H. R. Jauss calls the "substantialist conception of a work" as a container with a fixed content,[2] in favor of the idea that literature is a transaction between the text and its readers. It does not simply concede that the text is open to interpretation. It allows that the text's meaning is to some extent developed in its appropriation by the reader, and it thus grants what the hermeneutic tradition describes as "applicative reading" a constitutive role in the making of the text.

I have described elsewhere how "the supplement of reading" develops in the Romantic period in literary and theoretical traditions that intergenerate one another.[3] Forms such as the conversation poem, the dialogue, and the fragment coexist with an increasing theoretical focus on the reader evident in the rise of secular hermeneutics. In making the reader an internal constituent of the text, these forms sometimes figure their desired reader in the form of a sister, a friend, or a child, so as to coopt the extratextual reader into a sympathetic or recuperative reading of the text, or into a continuation of its unfinished project. But whether or not they seek to lay out a decorum of reading, such texts necessarily open themselves to interpretive difference by including what we can call "the reading-function": by creating a position within the text which can and will be occupied differently by different readers. The reading-function must be distinguished from concepts like the "designated reader," the "implied reader," or the "superreader," in that it is a structural position within the text, rather than an ideological position identified with a certain category of person and thus given a specific content. *Paradise Lost*, constructed as it is around dialogues between Raphael, Michael, and Adam, is one of the earlier instances of the transactional text that is the major transgeneric form of the Romantic period.

We can only speculate on why it is that Milton anticipates a characteristically Romantic form. It may be that Puritanism anticipates a shift of emphasis from the institution to the individual that will be further developed by the Romantics. It is surely significant that Wolfgang Iser's account of the implied reader begins with *Pilgrim's Progress* and thus locates the rise of the reader on a threshold between allegory and epic on the one hand and the novel on the other hand.[4] The rise of the novel as a form constructed around the reader is thus associated by Iser (at least initially) with a Puritan hermeneutic. But there is no reason why we must see that hermeneutic as beginning with Bunyan or as confined to the novel. We can also hazard a different answer to our question. The Romantic emphasis on the reader can be linked to a replacement of spatial by temporal paradigms evident in the stress on such categories as "experience," "process," and "history." To conceive of the text as historical is to unfix it from its own reproduction of things as they are, but also to concede that it cannot prescribe the form of things as they should be. It may be that this new sense of history, not as a static repetition of *exempla* but as a site of development and/or unpredictable change and contingency, was just beginning in the seventeenth century.

The transactional text can be distinguished from another kind of text that exists in the Renaissance, and exists at least as a theoretical possibility in the Romantic period. We can follow M. H. Abrams in referring to this variety of text as "heterocosmic." In a heterocosmic aesthetics art is seen as an autonomous second creation, a well-wrought urn, validated by its internal coherence and structural complexity. Abrams associates the term with the metaphor of the poet as a second creator, who repeats the totalizing act of God but is subject to laws that are aesthetic rather than empirical, so that poetic probability is "freed from all reference to outer reality and made entirely a matter of inner coherence and non-contradiction."[5] Where the allegorical or otherwise non-organicist style of the Middle Ages marks the status of the text as mere sign, the heterocosmic text presents a possible world in which art improves on nature. We can cite as an example *The Tempest*, where Prospero as demiurge and artist-surrogate stages the perfect romance in the controlled environment of his island laboratory. In a very different genre, Donne's poems of mutual love arrogate to love the power to create its own autonomous world. Metaphors of globes and hemispheres are frequent in these poems, and set the lover up as a rival creator, by making the poem a place where nature is hyperbolically transformed through art. On a vaster scale an encyclopedic romance like Spenser's *The Faerie Queene* tacitly makes a heterocosmic claim in including a range of problems similar to that which exists in the real world, but resolving its various narratives in the idealized setting of the Arthurian world. Characteristic of the heterocosmic text is a certain intricacy of narrative or metaphoric structure. Such intricacy replicates the complexity of the real world, so that when the artist dissolves and dissipates the elements of his or her world in order to recreate them, his or her contrivances can seem justified if not in terms of "nature," then at least in terms of the dialectic of proof.

It is important to note that the heterocosmic text in Abrams's terms is neither expressive nor mimetic, neither a lamp nor a mirror. If it claims for itself an objectivity and structural coherence that transcends the nebulousness of the visionary, it is also not an imitation of reality. It is rather an imitation of an illusionist parallel world not entangled in the complexities of the real world, but by the same token unreal. Thus Jacopo Mazzoni distinguishes between icastic imitation, which represents things that already exist, and phantastic imitation, which is the creation of poetic artifice.[6] Tasso on one level goes further, in conflating or crossing the terms of Mazzoni's opposition. Reluctant to denigrate poetry in any way, Tasso defines it as icastic, while retaining the phantastic notion of the poet as superior to reality by virtue of the prominence he gives to the metaphor of the artist as god creating his own cosmos that is infinitely complex yet finally unified. But although the fact that the text is a "world" naturalizes its artifice and gives it a structural authority that signifies or stands in place of the empirical reality it lacks, Tasso still claims that poetic creation is "verisimilar" and not true.[7] Best known, of course, is Sidney's double use of Plato to concede that the poet "never affirmeth," and thus to claim that "therefore though he recount things not true, yet because he telleth them not for true, he lieth not." Turning Plato on his head, Sidney argues that it is precisely this exemption from truth that allows the poet to range "within the Zodiack of his owne wit," and thus to represent a golden world superior to the brazen world of nature and immune from being dismissed as false.[8]

Given that romanticism is virtually synonymous with the unfinished, the heterocosmic text tends to have no more than a theoretical or projected existence for the Romantics. As project it has an intentional existence in Coleridge's complete "logosophia," in the larger structure to which *The Prelude* was to have been an antechapel, and in the secular scripture to which

Blake contributes *Jerusalem* as work-in-progress. The most famous theoretical example of the heterocosmic hyperbole is of course Coleridge's definition of the imagination in *Biographia Literaria* as "a repetition in the finite mind of the eternal act of creation in the infinite I AM."[9] The hyperbole obviously becomes possible in the sixteenth century because of the humanist discourse generated by Florentine neoplatonism. Post-Kantian idealism is on one level a resumption of that discourse, and enters Coleridge's work by way of his borrowings from Schelling. We might want to say that while the sixteenth century retains a Platonic caution that restrains art from representing the transcendence of representation, Coleridge's notion of the "consubstantiality" of art and nature crosses the threshold between image and reality so as to make profoundly metaphysical claims for art. But those claims are already present in Tasso's linking of poetry to dialectic and theology.[10] And here we encounter what is perhaps most problematical about the heterocosmic construct. On the one hand, it exchanges a "correspondence" model of truth for a "coherence" model that emancipates art from things as they are. On the other hand, it resists the resulting separation of the imaginary from the real, and therefore tries to give aesthetic structures a pseudo-referential status, by making coherence a signifier that stands in place of correspondence.

Yet correspondence, as a point of contamination between the ideal and the real, is precisely what the heterocosmic text wants to avoid. This "contamination," moreover, enters the text as a structural principle through the insistence on intricacy and inclusiveness. In a description of the heroic poem that anticipates Coleridge's emphasis on multeity-in-unity, Tasso argues for a "variety ... so much the more marvellous as it brings with it a measure of difficulty, almost of impossibility," and he provides a list of what the poem must include in order to parallel God's world: a catalogue almost impossibly forced into a single sentence that is virtually a page long.[11] This inclusiveness renders virtually impossible the creation of a self-identical world of illusion that is at no point different from itself, deferring one element of the text by way of another. The more such texts attempt to be inclusive totalities, the more they also risk multiplying the points at which the ideal and the brazen worlds intermix. Or to put it differently, extended narrative structures like *The Faerie Queene* or intensively intricate metaphoric structures like the lyrics in Donne's *Songs and Sonets* almost inevitably tend to become self-complicating. The inability of the verbal icon to remain self-identical frequently leads in these texts to a self-correction, in which the text interrupts or retrospectively cancels its own metaphysical claims. Prospero's ending of his revels provides an example of this self-correction, motivated as it is by the fact that his aesthetic island includes Caliban as well as Ariel. "The Mutabilitie Cantos" provide a coda that cancels the heterocosmic claims of *The Faerie*

Queene and defers its project to a higher realm, while Coleridge's interruption of his discussion of the imagination by a letter from the "friend" who advises him to reduce it from a hundred pages to two paragraphs serves a similar purpose in the *Biographia*.

Insofar as these gestures of self-cancellation or theological deferral are completely at odds with the humanism that motivates the heterocosmic text, such texts are locked in a cycle of illusion-making and illusion-breaking. We can argue that the cycle is precipitated by the anxiety of Platonic influence, an influence from which a heterocosmic aesthetic attempts to swerve away. In using its imaginary structure as a way of transcending the limits of mimesis, the text remains haunted by its status as a representation that does not correspond to reality. But in attempting to make inclusiveness a signifier that stands in place of reference, it loses its autonomy from a world that it merely repeats in finer tone. Thus an impasse occurs in which *Paradise Lost* creates a significant opening, by making the text part of a transaction with history and the reader. For the aporia between autonomy and authority arises from an assumption that it is only through non-contradiction that coherence can be made to take the place of correspondence and reference. The introduction of the reader into the literary equation mediates this aporia, by allowing the text's difference from itself to be the stimulus for a correspondence between text and world that is constantly being revised: in other words by allowing difference to be a transaction rather than a denial of coherence or correspondence. This transaction, moreover, is no longer felt as a contamination of illusion, because the text no longer claims to enclose a meaning that is fully self-present.

Although the parallel involves a simplification, the Platonic attack on art raises from an opposite perspective problems that are not dissimilar to those raised by the deconstructive readings of texts that have become so common in Romantic studies. Plato's critique of the image and his consequent expulsion of art from the metaphysical domain of philosophy becomes in our own time a critique of language as unable to achieve self-identity and thus "presence." Although post-structuralism ostensibly aims at a deconstruction of metaphysics, the work of de Man at least is inversely metaphysical in making "identity" or non-contradiction into the absent criterion which allows us to name the impossibility of presence. Implicit in de Man's deconstruction is the assumption that presence occurs through an attempt at denomination or designation that collapses into aporia: in other words through a single linguistic act that proves impossible, rather than through an activity in which aporia is dialogically related to the attempt to reread it. The introduction of the reading-function into the process of signification redefines reference (which is necessary for presence) as an activity rather than an act. It enables us to approach the problem of reference in phenomenological rather than (post)metaphysical terms. Reference is no longer the single act of designating a meaning outside words, but the ongoing activity of realizing that meaning in the language of events. It is the implication of the text in the world that gives ideas an existence but also allows them to be shifted by experience.

This paper suggests that the inclusion of the reading-function within the text results in a discursive formation that is characteristically Romantic, but which Milton in some ways anticipates. I associate the supplement of reading with romanticism not because it is unique to that period, but because it is pervasive, because reading is an object of increasingly problematic theoretical speculation from Schleiermacher to Kierkegaard, and because the interest in the reader can be linked to other Romantic discourses such as the historicizing of the "real" in the work of Hegel and more generally the shift from products to processes. As against the Foucauldian view that the classical episteme is synchronic and taxonomic, Gerald MacLean has already argued that the genre of historical poetry begins in the seventeenth century, which is the scene of a major shift in the idea of the historical.[12] In addition, the narrative of *Paradise Lost* after the third book unfolds not as mimesis or direct presentation but as a reported or predicted narrative communicated to Adam by Raphael and then Michael. Not only does Milton thereby place his theodicy within two extended scenes of reading; he also puts Adam as recipient of the angels' narratives in the position of a reader, going so far as to reverse the relationship between the inscribed reader and the figure of authority in allowing Adam to tell his own story to Raphael in Book VIII. As importantly, Adam's role is almost equally that of a participant in the poem's action and a reader of it. These two roles cannot be separated. Their conflation, moreover, creates a place for the extratextual reader that is best described by Rousseau's injunction to "Shelley" in *The Triumph of Life*: "But follow thou, and from spectator turn / Actor or victim in this wretchedness, / And what thou wouldst be taught I then may learn / From thee" (lines 305–8). *Paradise Lost*, in other words, stands on the verge of Shelley's recognition that the text is not a constative utterance which records history and then transmits it to a reader. Reading is not simply the interpretation of what has already happened, but also involves participation in a history that is yet to be written and that is partly written through its reading.

In suggesting a parallel between the inscription of the reader in *Paradise Lost* and in various Romantic texts, I am not concerned to argue for Milton's influence (although that argument is easily made), but rather for an *intertextual* relationship between Milton and his successors. The problem with the model of influence lies not in its tracing of parallels, but in the fact that as an *exegetical* principle it has been used to limit reading by recourse to an authorial "intention" which is often specified in ways that reflect canonical conventions of *reading*. "Influence" allows us to note verbal and formal parallels between Milton and the Romantics: to point out that Wordsworth and Blake inherited the project of constructing a providential history, or to observe that *Paradise Lost* anticipated certain Romantic texts both in placing itself in the middle of an ongoing historical process and in making the reader an internal constituent of the text. But it then obliges us to interpret these parallels in certain ways. Thus we will probably argue that the Romantic inscription of the reader must be read in terms of Milton, and that because Milton was in turn "influenced" by Dante his inscription of the reader cannot reflect an internalized skepticism but must serve the largely expository purpose it serves in *The Divine Comedy*. By contrast the model of intertextuality allows us to read Milton and the Romantics through each other. We can argue that whatever Milton may have "intended," his thematizing of reading puts the "implied reader" that the text may want to construct in relation to what Jauss calls the "explicit" or extratextual reader, who in some sense is *not* simply extratextual but is a dialogical presence within the text.[13] "Intention" is in any case a problematic term, and is better conceived of as what Kristeva calls a "trans-position," something that cannot be posited in any simple way because it is the shifting product of a transfer from "one signifying material ... into another," in this case from the psyche into the text.[14] If Milton "intended" to construct through Adam a reader who would be the passive recipient of "his" wisdom as represented by Michael and Raphael, the role of the reader is a trans-position that is already in the process of changing as Milton writes it into the text. Indeed the (post)Miltonic epic itself is probably a trans-position between heterocosmic and transactional models of textuality.

Although the term intertextuality, like the term trans-position, is Kristeva's, its first exponent may well be the Romantic hermeneuticist Friedrich Schleiermacher. Schleiermacher distinguishes between "objective–historical" and "objective–divinatory" reading. The former, which conforms to the assumptions of traditional philology, concerns itself with the text or discourse as a finished product to be understood in terms of the existing system of language and generic conventions, while the latter deals with the text as part of an ongoing historical process and is concerned with how "the discourse itself developed the language."[15] Objective–divinatory reading, in other words, focuses on the text as developing further, and as further developed by, a system of linguistic and generic conventions that cannot be conceived statically as a synchrony or a temporal succession of synchronies. While Kristeva's vocabulary was not yet available to him, it is clear that Schleiermacher's notion of divinatory reading depends upon a conception of the "existing system" of language and convention as already a trans-position. If we use the tools of objective–historical reading to reconstruct this system as a static rather than a moving object, that is largely a heuristic convenience. What this paper attempts, then, is an intertextual discussion of Miltonic and Romantic inscriptions of reading, such that Milton's view of reading as worked out in *Paradise Lost* is seen as already a trans-position rather than a fixed set of rules and practices which the Romantics radicalized, and which can be described in clear separation from that radicalization.

Lest an intertextual reading of *Paradise Lost* should seem anachronistic, we can make two related points: one with reference to Romantic readings of Milton, and the other with reference to Milton's theory of reading itself. In the first place writers like Blake and Shelley were already reading *Paradise Lost* as a trans-position when they suggested that Milton was of the devil's party without knowing it. Crucial to Shelley's antinomian reading of *Paradise Lost* in *A Defence of Poetry* is his father-in-law William Godwin's distinction, in his seminal, if neglected, essay "Of Choice in Reading," between the "moral" and the "tendency" of a text.[16] The moral is "that ethical sentence to the illustration of which the work may most aptly be applied," where the tendency is "the actual effect [the text] is calculated to produce upon the reader and cannot be completely ascertained but by the experiment." Authors often "show themselves superlatively ignorant of the tendency of their own writings."[17] The Romantic view that *Paradise Lost* is articulated around a tension between moral and tendency that makes Milton his own rereader focuses on the relationship between Satan and God. More accurately, it focuses on the relation of God as a sign for authority and the *status quo* to Satan as a sign for the Other. In our time the position of the Other has come to be occupied by Eve, and I shall be concerned neither with Satan nor with Eve but with the "Other" reading of human and divine history. But however we specify the thematic site of the poem's dialogue with itself, the point is that the Romantics saw the effect of the poem on its readers as exceeding or differing from its "intention" as stated in such places as the proems or the speeches of God and his angels. My choice of the term trans-position to reconceive an approach that sees the text as rereading itself in its writing is a deliberate one. Godwin's terms "moral" and "tendency" operate in terms of a historicized model of surface and depth that devalues the manifest content in favour of a latent content which emerges in the history of the text's reading. In opening the text to rereading he also closes off the reading process by referring to a "true" tendency that has "often lain concealed for ages"[18] until uncovered presumably by Godwin. The word trans-position does not specify the text's difference from itself in terms of residual, dominant, and emergent elements, and does not attribute a direction to the transformations occurring in the text, as does the word "tendency." It would allow us, for instance, to read *Paradise Lost* as a dialogue between authoritarian and revolutionary modes of thought, instead of as a movement from one to the other.

Secondly and more importantly, the Romantics did not see themselves as reading *Paradise Lost* against the grain. They thought they were reading it in accord with the spirit, if not the letter, of Milton's own life and writings. If Milton has now become a figure for patriarchal author(ity), the Romantic Milton was an upholder of liberty. One suspects that Wordsworth might have wanted to attribute a specific ideological content to "liberty," but for Shelley it was the very process that allowed us to generate different ideological contents. Milton's republicanism is necessarily a hermeneutics as well as a politics, and has ramifications for the licensing of interpretation. Those ramifications are assumed in *Milton*, as David Riede points out in arguing for the importance of *Areopagitica* to Blake.[19] They are also assumed by Shelley as licensing his rereading of Milton in the *Defence*. But they are more explicit in Godwin, whose essay on reading is essentially a rewriting of *Areopagitica*. Godwin translates Milton's concern with licensing into a concern with censorship in education, and with the problem of whether young readers should be prevented from reading certain books. He argues that because the "tendency" of the text is often different from its "moral," a text we may censor as pernicious can actually be put to good use by a reader. While he might seem to be assuming a "proper" reading, Godwin is more concerned to argue that readers will interpret texts in radically different ways, and that truth cannot be dogmatically imposed but can be ascertained only by "experiment." *Areopagitica* is structured around a tension between the interpretive pluralism that follows from Milton's argument against licensing, and a belief that through dialectic the scattered limbs of Osiris will be reassembled and "Truth" will be reestablished at the end of time. Godwin similarly holds on to a belief in "truth" despite his insistence on interpretive difference, but defers the achievement of this truth in such a way that it becomes no more than a heuristic construct. The affinities between *Areopagitica* and "Of Choice in Reading" thus allow us to go beyond simply saying that Milton anticipated the Romantics in the construction of a transactional text. We can also argue that such a view of Milton goes back to the more radical Romantics – Blake, Godwin and Shelley, as opposed to Keats and Wordsworth – and that their reading of Milton is theoretically underwritten by their understanding of his own theory of reading.

Paradise Lost at first seems to be the most ambitious of the heterocosmic texts. The encyclopedic claim of the epic to encompass all of human and divine history, the description of the Holy Spirit brooding over the vast abyss and creating the universe (I.20–22), and the parallel account of the blind poet struggling to conjure light out of his own darkness (III.13–26), all combine to recall the familiar topos of the poet as second creator which Milton significantly avoids. They also claim a transcendental ground for the illusion of aesthetic totality, for the providential patterns that the poet cannot literally see and can only figuratively represent. Indeed epic – particularly Christian epic – would seem to be a profoundly metaphysical mode that claims to know the grounds of things. As such it would seem to stand in contrast to masque and theatre, which in works like *The Tempest* unmask themselves as spectacle, or to the lyric from Catullus to Donne, which recognizes itself as nugatory.

As Milton's representation of his narrative in epic rather than novelistic form seems to inscribe providential history as true, so critical representations of the poem as pattern rather than process, as architecturally symmetrical or as balanced around a numerological centre, claim for it the structural intricacy and internal coherence crucial to the heterocosmic text. But not surprisingly there are gaps in the vast design that draw attention to its status as asserted rather than justified. To give a minor example, the poem wavers between describing the number of rebel angels as a third of the total in the early books (II.692, V.710), and suggesting in Book VI that they come close to being equal in strength (245–46). Evident in this discrepancy is an uncertainty as to whether evil is powerful but numerically subordinate, or is actually the Manichean equal of good. This uncertainty is apparent also in the oscillating depiction of evil. Sometimes it is projected and contained in the figure of Satan, who is demonically or allegorically characterized so as to typecast and reduce what he represents. Sometimes, as in the account of human history in the last books, evil, though equally unseductive, is dispersed and therefore insidious in its workings, granted a real and empirical power. Where Dante represents evil in purely allegorical terms, constructing a taxonomy of error that is mapped onto a spatial and synchronic cosmos, Milton represents evil both allegorically and realistically within a world that unfolds diachronically, and he thus dialogizes or re-cites Dante. The shift between allegory and realism places the poem on the threshold between a world of theological guarantees, in which the forces of disturbance are mere signifiers to be understood within a preestablished language, and a more open-ended world in which one must cope with their literal existence as what they are. Insofar as the "nature" of evil shifts according to the style in which it is depicted, the text suggests that truth is partly an effect of its representation and that changing generic conventions disclose different ways of seeing the nature of things. Epic itself may be no more than another convention: one whose datedness is marked by its dependence on a classical muse as the mediator between "truth" and its representation. Indeed in the genesis of Milton's poem epic is a diacritical rather than a positive term, a difference from and a deferral of the tragedy he did not write.

Although the vast sweep of *Paradise Lost* makes it seem to disclose the *arche* and *telos* of the human condition, the poem raises profound questions about whether evil was initially avoidable, and, more importantly for our purposes, what the outcome of human history will be. In part the poem's difference from itself arises from a recursiveness intrinsic to encyclopedic forms, which try to encompass all perspectives and levels of action from the human to the divine, and which mirror and repeat themselves so as to reflect on what they are saying. Thus evil is portrayed grotesquely and allegorically in the account of Satan, Sin, and Death, psychologically in the temptation, and historically in the last books. In a segment of the poem we shall consider later, the story of how heaven and earth are made one at the end of time is told in two different ways. The excess or heteroglossia of the heroic poem, described by Tasso himself, can easily defeat the text's attempt at representation.[20] But Milton uses it instead to place *Paradise Lost* in the space of interpretation, and to involve the reader in a dialectic with his poem.

To put it differently, *Paradise Lost* does not aim to contain an authoritative meaning, the notions of encyclopedic knowledge and poetic authority being themselves figures within the text. Since the poem is written on the threshold between scholasticism and empiricism, any deductive construction of the total shape of things that it offers must be tested against experience, both individual and historical. The panoptic vision we are afforded in the first proem and the council in heaven must be made valid through personal and historical narrative. The importance given to experience relates in turn to the greater role that Milton allows the reader in being persuaded by the interpretation he gives to events. This empirical emphasis on the reader is nowhere more evident than in the prominence assumed by dialogue. In the central and final books the plan of the universe and of universal history is expounded not through authoritative monologue but in a series of dialogues between Adam, Raphael, and then Michael. The dialogue between the angel and his human student can be seen as an intratextual allegory of the relationship between the inspired poet and his human readers. As the angels cannot simply intone but must present their account of things in a way that answers Adam's questions, so too the author must think of his text as addressed to the experience of his reader. Nor is the relativizing of truth inherent in dialogue confined to the angels. Even God himself in Book III must engage in dialogue, so that his providential point of view becomes only one voice in a plurivocal text.

The extent to which the poem is opened up by the inscription of the reader in the person of Adam is most evident in the final books. For it is there that reading – or rather its analogues, interpretation and listening – is thematized so as to make it not just a mode of exposition but also the site of a certain self-reflexiveness. In *The Divine Comedy* too there is a characterized listener who functions as a surrogate for the reader. Virgil takes Dante on a guided tour through the book of the world, in such a way that the reader functions as no more than a way of unfolding a preestablished meaning. One can argue similarly that Milton's use of the reader as a rhetorical device rather than a dialectical stimulus in the conversation between Adam and Raphael in the central books prescribes a passive role for the reader, and includes us only to forestall a more active and critical reading. For the "dialogue" here consists largely of two long monologues by Raphael, with Adam obediently asking all the right questions. Already, however, Milton is beginning to unsettle the authoritarian hermeneutic to which one side of him is committed. The theory of accommodated metaphor which introduces the War in Heaven, and which argues that spiritual events must be represented in physical terms if human understanding is to grasp them, supports such a hermeneutic by arguing for an absolute division between divine and human knowledge. But the curious (and extensively detailed) fact that the angels need food undermines the division of matter and spirit, and lays the groundwork for Raphael's surprising concession that man may actually be much closer to the angels than we think:

> though what if Earth
> Be but the shadow of Heav'n, and things therein
> Each to other like, more than on Earth is thought? (V.574–76)

Raphael's concession is a metaphysical one, but it has the hermeneutic ramification of reducing the distance between angel and man, authority and its interpretation. As significantly, it is also a concrete instance of how the dialogue between question and answer at the heart of the reading process actually produces revisions to truth, not because of the questions Adam actually asks, but because of the question he causes Raphael to ask himself: because of the question*ing* his presence inscribes in the text.

That Milton gives Adam as reader rather more authority than Dante gives himself is borne out by other details. Adam, who usually assumes the off-stage role of a secondary narrator in relation to Eve (VIII.50–52), is allowed to be principal narrator in the story of his own creation. Indeed he knows something that his guide does not, Raphael having been absent from heaven on that day (VIII.229–31). Moreover, it is in the same book that Adam asks cosmological questions about whether the universe is geocentric or heliocentric. Although he accepts Raphael's statement that he does not need to know such things (VIII.159–87), the very raising of such questions reminds us of the contemporary controversies that made knowledge a matter of debate, and places us on an unstable boundary between a theocentric and a scientific universe. Adam's knowledge of the Copernican theory is of course an anachronism: a curious surfacing of Renaissance science in a world where the

Renaissance has not yet happened. In thus marking its own historical moment by making conspicuous the temporal disjunction between the time of its narrative and the time of its writing, the poem (whether intentionally or not) creates a strange effect. It seems to admit anachronism as an interpretive possibility through a kind of metalepsis in which it is the poem itself that is later than itself. Anachronism is a way of figuring the possibility that the text may, in Mary Nyquist's phrase, lose itself to history: that the truths in terms of which it is understood may themselves be historical. In reflecting on the historicity of interpretation Nyquist raises the question of whether losing *Paradise Lost* to "the history of its reception necessarily means losing its contact with the historical moment of its production," and she concludes that reception aesthetics and literary history are not incompatible, because it is the overdetermined nature of the text at the moment of its production that makes it the "site of conflicting and historically variable readings."[21] The inscription of the reader in the text, we can suggest, is both the symptom and the acknowledgment of this overdetermination.

Milton's inclusion of the reader has its origins in the rise of empiricism and also in his particular brand of Puritanism, with its emphasis on the individual will and on the understanding as something that each man must achieve for himself. The radical indeterminacy of *Paradise Lost*, the fact that it allows us to read human history in more than one way, is tied to the role given to the human will, which may write history in more than one way. The paradox, at once moral and hermeneutic, in Milton's doctrine of free will, is unstably articulated in God's famous lines to Christ, lines whose verbal symmetry masks a certain undecidability:

> Man shall not quite be lost, but sav'd who will,
> Yet not of will in him, but grace in me
> Freely voutsaf't ...   (III.173–75)

Is man's will a mere auxiliary verb, aiding God's design but finally contained within it, or is it a substantive with powers of its own? God raises the second possibility only to defer it with a syntactic sleight-of-hand. But the problem remains and also has hermeneutic ramifications. One cannot claim authoritative understanding of history and of the text that conveys it when history itself may have more than one narrator, and indeed more than one author. This is not a simple matter of admitting that there are limits to human understanding. It is because the history that God has written in some sense remains to be written that Milton's poem is paradoxically encyclopedic and yet open, as encyclopedias often are, to the addition of further supplements by future readers. Milton's most explicit reflections on the relationship between reading, authority, and freedom are found in *Areopagitica*. Here the notion of an authoritative truth is nominally protected through the myth of Osiris, and of an original body whose fragments we are trying to reassemble. Nevertheless, Milton's refusal to advocate licensing, his insistence that we have the freedom to read and interpret, allows for differences in the way people see things that may not always be resolved within the ideal of a single body. Committed to the ideal of a transcendent and atemporal truth like that outlined by God in Book III, Milton, as Balachandra Rajan has argued, is equally committed to the notion of truth as something that shifts and evolves historically, as it is written by the human will.[22] Thus literature must paradoxically be both the articulation of a totality and the constant revision of that totality. In his critique of licensing Milton defends not only the freedom of the reader, but also the freedom of the author to change his mind:

And what if the author shall be one so copious of fancy as to have many things well worth the adding, come into his mind after licensing, while the book is yet under the press, which not seldom happens to the best and diligentest writers; and that perhaps a dozen times in one book. (735)

Perhaps the greatest challenge to any authoritative reading of the text comes in the final books, where Michael represents divine author(ity). Michael's argument for the providential outcome of human history is based on that most conservative of exegetical methods, typological reading. Such reading asserts a unity of purpose across vastly different epochs, suppressing the differential pressure of history, the fact that historical events are autonomous occurrences that do not all promise the same meaning and that may even revise our sense of that meaning. But from the seventeenth and eighteenth centuries onwards the reading of the Bible was undergoing crucial shifts. Hans Frei traces to Spinoza what was to become far more pervasive in eighteenth- and nineteenth-century hermeneutics: namely a widening gap between narrative depiction and subject matter, such that the alleged "true" meaning of events is no longer seen as realistically embodied in the events but seems arbitrarily and allegorically imposed on them. This meaning, in turn, is no longer beyond question. The interpretation of scripture must obey the same rules of logic and reason as the reading of any other text, and the meaning of the sacred texts must seem valid in terms of the experience of a contemporary reader.[23] To put it differently, in the new hermeneutics the typological reading of events begins to disclose its supplementary structure, and appears as belated and compensatory, only hypothetically integrated with the original event. Understanding also emerges as something that is historical and not fixed. The final books of *Paradise Lost* are caught in a double movement that resists but also invites the erosion of authoritative reading. Against Michael's upholding of authority in these books, we must set Milton's incorporation of a historicizing

33

perspective elsewhere. For in establishing a distance between himself and the world of classical epic, while repeatedly invoking the classical muse, Milton allows us to establish a further distance between ourselves and the world of typology, to see typological reading itself as another instance of accommodated metaphor. That the radical Milton revered by the Romantics was not insensitive to the relativizing critical currents described here is well known. In *Eikonoklastes* he argues against the canonization of the king's book, and by implication for a culture of texts rather than books.[24] In the divorce tracts his interpretation of crucial passages in scriptural law is liberal rather than literal. Its justification in terms of a hermeneutics of charity enabled by the progress from law to gospel is in a sense a justification of historical reading: of changes in understanding brought about by changing customs. This is not to argue that we should identify Milton with the more radical tendencies of nineteenth-century hermeneutics. Rather we should recognize that the issue of interpretation in *Paradise Lost* is itself overdetermined, caught within contradictory pressures that allow us to read Milton's thematization of reading in different ways.

Crucial to the unsettling of authoritative meaning is the representation of providential history in the form of a dialogue between Adam and Michael. Focusing on the role of Adam as reader, Robert Crosman argues that the poem enacts the process by which Adam learns to read correctly, and finally to internalize Michael's instruction as part of his own experience.[25] But Adam's function is not merely rhetorical, it is incipiently dialectical. Or to put it differently, although Adam is respectful in his questions and accepts Michael's answers, his presence as interlocutor opens a space for the explicit reader to enter and question the world of Milton's text. The first two tableaux in Michael's exposition provide relevant examples. In the first of these Adam sees a man who is offering up a sacrifice brutally and irrationally slain by another man. His initial reaction is to question a world in which piety and devotion are thus rewarded (XI.450–52). Michael explains that this is the story of Cain and Abel, and that despite the temporary appearance of injustice the good man will ultimately receive what he deserves. Two objections may occur to the skeptical reader. To begin with, Michael's promise of eventual justice is no more than that. Where the murder of Abel has visual force, Adam does not similarly see the rewarding of Abel, for in the latter case Michael does not have the power, in Adam's words, to represent "future things ... as present" (XI.870–71). Secondly, there is nothing in the original scene to explain why one man's sacrifice is accepted and the other's rejected in a quite arbitrary and provocative way. Michael's claim that Cain "was not sincere" (XI.443) is an editorial interpolation, and the tableau itself might well be interpreted in the way Byron reads it in *Cain*. In Byron's play Abel's altar catches "propitious

Fire" (XI.441) more quickly than Cain's simply because the former is burning animal fat; the vegetarian Cain, who rejects animal sacrifice, is thus a man pushed by an unjust God into further injustice. We may not go as far as Byron, but it is by no means certain that the first tableau presents a just world, nor were orthodox readings of episodes from the Bible uncontested by heresies that the Romantics were not the first to promulgate. The heretical reading is not solicited by the poem, but it is deferred, dialogically present at the margins of the text.[26]

The problem of another side to interpretation, of reading itself as the Other of belief, arises partly from the way the poem combines different modes of representation so as to draw attention to the status of representation itself. Michael's visual presentation of history before the Flood, in contrast to his narrative presentation of events thereafter, is often interpreted as making his message in Book XI that much more immediate and convincing. But one can also argue that the tableaux are radically ambiguous, and that the shift from visual presentation to moralizing explanation emphasizes the gap between depiction and subject matter, between the literal appearance of events (which is far from clear) and the true significance (which is no more than an assertion). The disjunction between visual and verbal, between showing and telling, is augmented in the second tableau by the cultural distance betweeen pre-Christian and modern times. Here Adam sees a lazar-house full of people suffering from various diseases. Michael's assurance that this is not an instance of undeserved suffering because disease is the just punishment for intemperance, is surely one of the most difficult rationalizations for a modern reader to accept. Nor is this reaction wholly anachronistic. For as we have seen in Book VIII Milton stands on the verge of recognizing that the answers we provide to fundamental questions about the universe may not be timeless and incontrovertible.

The scene of reading in the final books is constructed around the contrast between the literal meaning of the events depicted and the very different meaning attributed to these events when they are understood in the framework of Christian history. On a literal level the world seems to go from bad to worse. On a typological level a providential outcome is assured by a deduction from first principles. The stark disjunction between the two levels creates a certain indeterminacy and invites us to raise a variety of questions about whether it really is a just world in which we suffer for the sins of others, in which culpability is inherited, and in which the suffering seems so out of proportion to Adam and Eve's original deed. On the other hand, given the massive evidence of moral corruption, we can also question whether mankind is capable of collective regeneration. Are the few examples of uprightness in men like Noah and Abraham tokens that truth has survived, or indications that justice is fighting a losing battle in a world whose historical rhythm is endlessly repetitive rather than progressive? We are invited to ask such questions not only by the dialogical structure of the books, which introduces the formal possibility of the question, but also by the gap between visual text and verbal gloss, which raises the question of narrative as interpretation and of interpretation otherwise.

Beginning in Book XII Michael shifts from visual to purely narrative presentation, so that the text disappears entirely and we are left only with the gloss. The typological representation of history after the Flood, as critics like Martz have noted, is increasingly doctrinal and abstract, lacking in dramatic embodiment.[27] The problems of embodiment and presence raised by the poem's metaphors of sight and insight come to a head in a curious passage in the middle of Book XII. Adam asks enthusiastically about the climactic fight between Christ and the serpent earlier promised by Michael, and Michael replies:

> Dream not of thir fight,
> As of a Duel, or the local wounds
> Of head or heel: not therefore joins the Son
> Manhood to Godhead, with more strength to foil
> Thy enemy; nor so is overcome
> *Satan*, whose fall from Heav'n, a deadlier bruise,
> Disabl'd not to give thee thy death's wound:
> Which hee, who comes thy Saviour, shall recure,
> Not by destroying *Satan*, but his works
> In thee and in thy Seed   (XII.386–95)

It is striking that Michael, a major participant in the War in Heaven, should here dismiss physical victory as meaningless. It is true, of course, that Raphael has prepared us for this dismissal in describing the War as an accommodated metaphor, necessary to make tangible what surpasses the reach of human sense. Yet the effect here is to give Christ's victory over Satan no more than a ghostly existence, where the effect of Raphael's narration had been precisely the contrary: to make the defeat of Satan seem real within the terms of this world. Or to put it differently, Michael's response makes us suddenly and anxiously aware of the status of the poem's providential narrative as representation, and of the epic paraphernalia so necessary to the text's high argument as mere figures. The positioning of the epic world between outside and inside is abruptly reversed, displacing it from the sublime to the hermeneutic, as when Keats tells us that the triumph of Psyche is something that happens in some untrodden region of the mind. The problem is not so much that Michael designates Christ's victory as spiritual rather than physical, as that he thereby describes it as individual and private. If there is to be no external victory over Satan because the true enemy is within, there is no guarantee that "Satan" will be defeated in the hearts of a sufficient number of individuals for the collective regeneration of mankind to be symbolically consolidated in a victory of Christ over Satan. And if the victory must occur in each person individually, in what sense can it be final, since the battle will have to be fought over and over again in each generation? Michael's strange answer leaves us wondering when and where this victory will happen, given what may be its deferral from the literal to the figurative level. Even more importantly, it may leave us asking what "Christ" is. If there is no serpent, no literal Satan, these names being figures for things within us, then Christ himself may be (as he is for Blake) a metaphor for some power of action within us. Indeed Milton's poem itself may be an accommodated metaphor that each of us must appropriate and demythologize for ourselves.

As characterized reader Adam does not raise these questions. But the contrast between the straightforward expectations in his question and Michael's complex answer, filled as it is with double negatives and litotes, creates an effect of deferral, as though the answer to the question is a further question. The resulting uncertainty as to how the providential outcome will occur comes to a head in Michael's concluding account of how at the end of time heaven and earth will be made one. For in effect he tells the story of what happens between the resurrection and the Last Judgment twice over, thus displacing it from story to discourse. Michael's first account of this long interregnum is highly positive (XII.436–65). He describes how Christ leaves the world in the charge of his disciples, ascends triumphantly to heaven, drags Satan around in chains, and then returns

> When this world's dissolution shall be ripe,
> With glory and power to judge both quick and dead,
> To judge th' unfaithful dead, but to reward
> His faithful, and receive them into bliss,
> Whether in Heav'n or Earth, for then the Earth
> Shall all be Paradise   (XII.459–64)

Adam replies with what may be mandatory enthusiasm: "Oh goodness infinite, goodness immense!" (XII.469). But a discrepancy may have struck him between this happy ending and Michael's previous bitterly negative accounts of the state of the world. At any rate he tactfully asks for more details about what precisely happens to the disciples after Christ's departure: "what will betide the few / His faithful, left among th' unfaithful herd" (XII.480–81). In the final book, abandoning visual presentation for an off-stage narration that catalogues rather than dramatizes events, Michael has been all too inclined to avoid narrative and emotional detail so as to fit the individual event into his author's palpable design. Now as he looks more closely at the interregnum he completely changes his emphasis, and describes how the apostles of the early church are succeeded by "Wolves" (XII.508), and how the world grows steadily more degenerate, until Christ returns

> to dissolve
> *Satan* with his perverted World, then raise
> From the conflagrant mass, purg'd and refin'd,
> New Heav'ns, new Earth, Ages of endless date
> Founded in righteousness and peace and love,
> To bring forth fruits Joy and eternal Bliss. (XII.546–51)

The conclusion is the same as in the first account of the Last Judgment: eternal bliss and the union of heaven and earth. But where the world had previously grown better and better until it was "ripe" for dissolution by a process of natural maturation, it now grows worse and worse until Christ in apocalyptic frustration destroys it by fire. Between the first account, in which earth is subsumed into heaven, and the second account, in which it is purged as something rotten, there is a world of difference. The first account assumes that humankind earns its deliverance; the second dualistically rejects everything associated with humanity. Both accounts affirm the presence of providence in history. But in the second case we might well feel that "providence" is a dubious blessing.

The more pessimistic account is not necessarily true. Rather the doubling of the narration makes us aware that history is narrative, interpretation. It consolidates our sense that the poem does not contain a meaning because it is also the site of our discovery that a text can be written otherwise. This awareness of representation occurs precisely because of the role played by the reader in Milton's poem. It is Adam's questions that cause Michael to reconsider his version of events and to include previously omitted information that slants the story in a different direction. These questions, in turn, allow the explicit reader to ask further questions that result in the text being lost to history.

The heterocosmic authority of the text is not complicated only by the presence of Adam as reader. Equally important is the fact that God's plot is not directly revealed, but mediated through angels whose knowledge is partial. Eve had been absent from the dialogue between Adam and Raphael, supposedly because she preferred Adam's mixture of pleasure and usefulness to the angel's high philosophy, and less euphemistically because of a gender hierarchy Milton tactfully questions when he raises and drops the possibility that "her ear" was unsuited to "what was high" (VIII.49–50). At the end of the final book and without the angel's knowledge she turns out to have learned everything that Adam has been told by Michael, but intuitively in a dream rather than discursively, and not by way of her husband playing the role of "the Relater" (VIII.52). The revelation to Eve suggests not only that the hierarchies around which the poem is built are not canonical, but also that man's fallen part may be less impure and the road to salvation less impossible than we think.[28] Indeed the different explanations Milton provides for Eve's absence (as well as the varying pattern of these absences) suggest that he himself sees gender hierarchy with all its attendant philosophical ramifications as overdetermined, while the parenthetical way in which he explains her absences indicates his hesitation about dogmatically urging any one explanation.[29] The revelation to Eve, combined with the doubling of Michael's final account, suggests that angelic prejudices and angelic knowledge are far from authoritative. But whether that means that our future holds less or more promise than Michael implies remains unclear, as does the issue of what exactly it is that he implies. The inconsistencies that inhabit the poem have no uniform effect. In the dialogue with Michael the questions posed by Adam lead to a bleaker revision of the angel's account of the Last Judgment. In the dialogue with Raphael they lead to the concession that heaven and earth may be more similar than we have hitherto thought. Indeed the effect of making Adam the inscribed reader, rather than giving that position to a character like Eve who has since come to be identified with a definite (that is, feminist) ideological position, may well be to maintain reading as the "other" side of writing. For Adam's questions come from no particular perspective. Instead they open the poem to further reading, as the truth in God's narrative is itself open to being written by the human will, if not in its final outcome, then in those details that determine how the outcome will be interpreted.

Milton's inclusion of the reader as an essential constituent not only in the interpretation but also in the action of his poem has broad affinities with a number of Romantic texts that similarly inscribe the reader as a dialogical component of the textual process. They include works as different as the conversation poems, the political novels of Godwin, Wollstonecraft and Hays, and the Romantic fragment. It is more useful, however, to place *Paradise Lost* in the context of one particular genre: the providential epic which returns in secularized form as a national or cultural epic in the work of Blake and Wordsworth.

It is well known that the later Blake retrospectively constructed his texts as a secular scripture modelled on the Bible as the great code of art. In so doing he tried to contain the negative force of poems like *The [First] Book of Urizen*, by making them dialectical moments in the progress from a gospel of wrath to one of love. Milton is at the heart of Blake's epic project in ways too complex to describe here. On the one hand, Blake imaginatively refigures him in *Milton*, using a Milton who resembles the original in little more than name to give supplementary authority to the *Aufhebung* of tragedy and irony in epic attempted in *Jerusalem*. On the other hand, one can argue that Blake never really overcomes the spectre of the actual Milton: that *Europe* and *Urizen* (which he continued to reengrave alongside the later prophecies) deconstruct the earlier poet's system of salvation by making it the cause of the fall it is supposed to correct, but do not succeed in writing their way out of Milton's myth of the fall itself. "Milton" in other words is a figure for the problematic at the heart of Blake's corpus, a problematic that is formal as well as intellectual. For Blake is also linked to him in a very different way: in his periodic undoing of his own salvationist narrative and in his deferral of providential epic from the mimetic to the hermeneutic.

This deferral is most obvious in the early texts up to and including *Urizen*. In poems like *The Book of Thel* and *Visions of the Daughters of Albion*, "Blake" tries to use his female characters as figures in an argument for a providential design that makes "experience" a fortunate fall which leads to "organized innocence." But by choosing protagonists whose experience is en-gendered differently from the en-gendering of the category "experience" in Blake's "system," and by giving a voice to those characters, he creates a space from which we can read the gaps in his myth. The opening of the text to the reader is even more obvious in *Songs of Innocence and of Experience*, where Blake gives us a heteroglossia of poems unassembled into a narrative, somewhat like a sentence without a syntax. The title of the collection may ask us to read the poems in terms of Blake's later myth of a progress from experience to organized innocence, and the famous statement from *The Marriage of Heaven and Hell* that there is no progression without contraries may suggest that that progress is to be accomplished through a dialectic between the songs of experience and those of (un)organized innocence. But the poems are not organized so as to generate a dialectical progression, such an organization being left to the inference of the reader. As I have argued elsewhere, they form a network of combinatorial possibilities, amongst which chiasmus and aporia are as likely as dialectic.[30] Moreover, for the reader who chooses to use the contents of the collection dialectically, the synthesis of the two contrary states is unembodied by any specific poem in the collection, and remains something that must be brought into being in our own minds. If the fact that organized innocence is not represented allows us to conceive of Eden as a process rather than a fixed entity, it also concedes the difficulty of embodying the utopian impulse within the historical world. The end of history, the form that this end will take, and indeed whether there will be an end at all, are questions that are left to interpretation. Interpretation, moreover, is participation. It is not simply that we must imagine a synthesis which is not represented; what is not represented will not exist if we do not imagine it, and what we do imagine through our reading will determine how we write our history.

The later prophecies are attempts to sublate the forces of negativity and fragmentation in the early texts by absorbing them into the teleology of Blake's canon conceived as epic project. In *Milton* Blake begins this project as a specifically hermeneutic act by re-citing parts of *Urizen* so as to reread irony as a pre-text for epic. As the antechapel to *Jerusalem*, *Milton* is in fact structured as a scene of reading in which the extratextual reader too is implicated. "Milton" rereads his past after hearing the Bard's song and then enters the body of "Blake," who functions both as the poem's author and as its implied reader, in a doubling that either confirms authority or marks its claims as vertiginously circular. Blake's canonical epic gives priority to the late over the early texts, and this self-canonization has been privileged by criticism written in the wake of Frye. But because he continued to engrave the early texts alongside *Milton* and *Jerusalem*, the early texts also provide lenses through which to revision both the epic subsumption of the parts of the canon into a whole, and the heterocosmic vision of epic itself. In other words the intertextual connections between the early and later work transform a canonical epic based on the internal coherence of the system into a transactional epic in which the differences between and within texts are the very conditions of possibility for the reading of epic.

This transformation is related to another point of connection between Blake's corpus and Milton's: the problematizing of any distinction between story and discourse. Criticism in the wake of Frye has attributed to Blake a "system," which consists of recurring characters, episodes and concepts, combined into a master-narrative that is most fully worked out in *Jerusalem*, and in relation to which other versions of cosmic history (such as *Urizen*) are to be seen as partial or deviant. The fiction of a system presupposes a correct "story," that can be distinguished from discourse, from the way(s) in which it is told. But given the difficulty of discerning what actually "happens" in the prophecies, it may be more accurate to think of the system as a collection of what Lévi-Strauss calls "mythemes" or "gross constituent units": characters and configurations of events that recur in narratives of a certain type, but not always in the same order or in the same relationships. According to this model, the "system" would no longer be a providential arche-narrative: a fully organized structure testifying to the possibility of organized innocence. It would be a collection of mythemes, of unorganized mythic material that is reprocessed differently in texts such as *Urizen* and *Jerusalem*, or even in readings of texts like *Urizen* and *Europe* which have yielded no critical consensus. In *Paradise Lost* there were two versions of the end of history. Blake's work contains and elicits several different organizations of its gross constituent units.

Blake's canon can be seen as a radicalization of Milton in more ways than one. On one level, as is well known, Blake presses beyond the pessimism of *Paradise Lost* and transforms the Puritan poet into a Romantic prophet. But this mythopoeic radicalism is suspended by the far more radical direction in which Blake takes the role of the reader and the reduction of story to discourse. For the realization of Blake's epic project, more obviously than in Milton, depends on the reader, and Blake's early texts more explicitly offer us a choice in reading that makes the thematic radicalization of Milton subject to an autocritique generated by his radicalization of Miltonic form. But Blake's texts do not resemble *Paradise Lost* stylistically, although "Milton" is central to his struggle with his spectre, and more obliquely to his struggle with an epic vision that is open to historical re-vision.

By contrast *The Excursion* is the Romantic text that comes closest in mode and style to Milton's poem, being modelled on the last two books of *Paradise Lost*. As Milton writes in the aftermath of the Puritan Revolution, so Wordsworth writes in the wake of the French Revolution and its failure, to correct the despondency of that part of himself represented by the Solitary. Wordsworth too is concerned to produce a theodicy: an assertion that there exists a providential design in things, despite the suffering of characters like Margaret in Book I, and despite the errors of the modern European governments castigated in Book IX. His arguments for design are strangely immanent and transcendent: they take the form both of a program of national education explicitly intended as an intervention in the political arena, and of the Pastor's address to the Supreme Being, which seems necessary to supplement the possible vanity and futility of Wordsworth's belatedly Enlightenment project. Wordsworth is said to have known *Paradise Lost* by heart, and Miltonic echoes are ubiquitous in the final book of what purports to be a secular and not a Christian epic. For instance there is the reference to "paradise, the lost abode of man" being raised again, and to the Atonement as a "marvellous advance / Of good from evil" (IX.717–18, 722–23), a line that recalls Adam's words, "O goodness infinite, goodness immense! / That all this good of evil shall produce" (XII.469–70). What is most striking, however, is the discursive form of Wordsworth's national epic. The poem begins as a conversation between the Wanderer, the "Author," and the Solitary, in which the Wanderer voices what we can take to be Wordsworth's "creed," and in which the other two characters occupy the position of the reader. In Book V they are joined by the Pastor, who plays an instructional role not unlike that of Michael. The next two books consist of epitaphic accounts of the lives of various people interred in the churchyard: equivalents to the visual and narrative tableaux that comprise Milton's account of history in the last books. But it is in the final book of *The Excursion* that the Miltonic parallel becomes explicit. The Lake Country pilgrims ascend a hill where the

Wanderer expounds his program of national education. When he has finished they descend from their "exalted station" to the "plain," and pursue their "homeward course / In mute composure" (IX.756–58), like Adam and Eve at the end of *Paradise Lost* descending from the hill to the "subjected Plain" and proceeding through Eden with "wand'ring steps and slow" (XII.640, 649).

If the early Blake radicalizes Milton's transactional poetics, the later Wordsworth reproduces the more conservative impulses behind the inscription of the reader in *Paradise Lost*. However, in constructing an implied reader as a way of containing doubt, he not only finds his own intentions unsettled by the complexity of the paradigm he borrows, he also shifts and unsettles the paradigm itself. To begin with, he foregrounds what is only one element in Milton's text. *Paradise Lost* intersperses narrative with dialogue and does not make the latter its predominant mode until the final books; *The Excursion* places narrative within conversation from the very beginning. It thus acknowledges a shift from mimesis to discourse that suspends, more radically than Milton's poem, the project of intervening in history, and that makes the last book of the poem an elegy upon the text it re-cites in order to augment its own authority. This shift from mimesis to discourse is recognized in one of the text's most striking images, the image of the ram reflected in a pool of water. Commenting on this "twofold" image, in which the snow-white ram on the grassy bank has a "shadowy counterpart" in the water, the Author describes two worlds "unconscious of each other" yet exactly homologous in their internal completeness (IX.439–51). The ram simile sums up a heterocosmic aesthetic in which illusion repeats reality in finer tone, claiming an ideological authority that is based not on a correspondence between sign and truth but on the internal coherence of the sign. But the Pastor's wife goes on to abjure such magic in pointing out how easily the world of illusion can be disturbed by a mere breath of air (IX.452–473). Because she also comments sadly on the limits of rhetoric and voice (IX.459–73), what she dismantles is not only a heterocosmic aesthetic but also a transactional aesthetic conceived simply as a supplement to the former, such that the failure of imagination to achieve presence can be recovered in the power of the author to construct the right reader.

Moreover, if the conversation between Wordsworth's characters is modelled on the dialogue between Michael and Adam, there is a curious doubling of the structure used by Milton that can be read intertextually with *Paradise Lost* to bring out the deconstruction of authority already implicit in Milton's inscription of the reader. As there are two subjects in Wordsworth's poem who speak from a position of author(ity), so too the reading-function is divided between two characters, one of them being the Author, who figures himself as the recipient rather than the origin of his own discourse. The first book of *The Excursion* consists of an interchange between the Wanderer and the Author, in which Wordsworth's earlier poem "The Ruined Cottage" is re-cited, in an attempted subl(im)ation of Margaret's story into the Wanderer's theodicy that is not unlike Milton's transposition of tragedy into epic or Blake's reworking of *Urizen* in *Milton*. The relative silence of the Author may seem to mark the implied reader's consent to the Wanderer's rewriting of Margaret's story. But the anxiety about this rewriting that was present as early as MS B of "The Ruined Cottage" is simply displaced onto the Solitary, who joins the conversation in Book II and uses his own experience to argue against the Wanderer's creed. The introduction of the Solitary does not simply create a space for the resisting reader. It also brings back the figure of Margaret, whose socioeconomic position had allowed the Wanderer to speak for her, but whose experience now finds parallels in that of a character whose education and gender make him harder to silence, and whose grief is spoken in a historical and not simply a private voice. The troubling presence of the Solitary leads Wordsworth to introduce the Pastor in the second half of the poem, as a supplement to the increasingly contested position of the Wanderer. At the same time the arrival of the Pastor also splits the position of authority, dividing it between a voice that argues for earthly perfectibility (through a program of national education) and a transcendental voice that acknowledges the vanity of human wishes.

The discourse of authority, moreover, is not spoken by Wordsworth, who writes himself into the poem as a character who spends most of his time listening.[31] This displacement of the author to the marginal position of reader is a secularized but also more ironic version of a pattern already in *Paradise Lost*: namely Milton's figuration of himself as the recipient rather than the origin of the Muse's discourse, and his self-fictionalizing division of authority between Christian God and classical Muse. The division and displacement of authority is paralleled by an equally troubling split in Wordsworth's figuration of the reader, a split that persists despite the poem's attempt to homogenize its own reading. As the Solitary proves less and less amenable to persuasion by the voice(s) of authority, the text tries to "forget" him, and the Author, who has been relatively silent, begins more assertively to fill the space left by the author's withdrawal, making himself into the text's desired reader. The Solitary, however, is still present at the very end as a sign that the position of the reader will be occupied in more than one way. Wordsworth's division of the receptive position between a desired and a resisting reader makes explicit what is only potential in *Paradise Lost*. As an intertextual supplement to the earlier poem, it is thus one possible sub-version of the future to which Milton opens the epic in the very act of writing it as a transactional epic.

NOTES

1 Robin Jarvis, "Love between Milton and Wordsworth"; Kenneth Gross, "Satan and the Romantic Satan: a notebook"; David Riede, "Blake's *Milton*: on membership in the Church Paul"; in *Re-Membering Milton: Essays on the Texts and Traditions*, ed. Mary Nyquist and Margaret W. Ferguson (New York: Methuen, 1987), 301–17, 318–41, 255–77.

2 H. R. Jauss, "Theses on the Transition from the Aesthetics of Literary Works to a Theory of Aesthetic Experience," in *Interpretation of Narrative*, ed. Mario J. Valdes and Owen Miller (Toronto: University of Toronto Press, 1978), 138.

3 Tilottama Rajan, *The Supplement of Reading: Figures of Understanding in Romantic Theory and Practice* (Ithaca: Cornell University Press, 1990).

4 Wolfgang Iser, *The Implied Reader: Patterns of Communication in Prose Fiction from Bunyan to Beckett* (Baltimore: Johns Hopkins University Press, 1974), 1–28.

5 M. H. Abrams, *The Mirror and The Lamp: Romantic Theory and the Critical Tradition* (New York: Oxford University Press, 1953), 278.

6 Jacopo Mazzoni, "On the Defense of the Comedy (selections)," in *Literary Criticism: Plato to Dryden*, ed. Allan H. Gilbert (Detroit: Wayne State University Press, 1962), 360.

7 Torquato Tasso, *Discourses on the Heroic Poem*, trans. Mariella Cavalchini and Irene Samuel (Oxford: Clarendon Press, 1973), 29, 77–78, 61.

8 Sir Philip Sidney, "The Defence of Poesie," in *The Prose Works of Sir Philip Sidney*, ed. Albert Feuillerat (Cambridge: Cambridge University Press, 1912), 3: 1–46.

9 Samuel Taylor Coleridge, *Biographia Literaria*, ed. James Engell and W. Jackson Bate, 2 vols., *Collected Coleridge*, vol. 7 (Princeton: Princeton University Press, 1983), 1: 304.

10 Tasso, *Discourses*, 29.

11 Tasso, *Discourses*, 78–79.

12 Gerald MacLean, *Time's Witness: Historical Representation in English Poetry, 1603–1660* (Madison: University of Wisconsin Press, 1990).

13 Jauss, "Theses," 142.

14 Julia Kristeva, *Revolution in Poetic Language*, trans. Margaret Waller (New York: Columbia University Press, 1984), 59–60.

15 Friedrich Schleiermacher, "The Hermeneutics: The Outline of the 1819 Lectures," trans. Jan Wocjik and Roland Haas, *New Literary History* 10 (1978): 9.

16 See *Shelley's Poetry and Prose*, 498.

17 William Godwin, "Of Choice in Reading," in *The Enquirer: Reflections on Education, Manners and Literature in a Series of Essays* (1797; reprint, New York: Augustus M. Kelley, 1965), 136, 132.

18 Godwin, "Of Choice," 134.

19 Riede, "Blake's *Milton*," 259–60.

20 Tasso, *Discourses*, 77–78.

21 Mary Nyquist, "Fallen Differences, Phallogocentric Discourses: Losing *Paradise Lost* to History," in *Post-structuralism and the Question of History*, ed. Derek Attridge, Geoff Bennington, and Robert Young (Cambridge: Cambridge University Press, 1987), 234.

22 Balachandra Rajan, *The Form of the Unfinished: English Poetics From Spenser to Pound* (Princeton: Princeton University Press, 1985), 99–101.

23 Hans Frei, *The Eclipse of Biblical Narrative: A Study in Eighteenth and Nineteenth Century Hermeneutics* (New Haven: Yale University Press, 1974), 7, 42–50.

24 Derrida's distrust of the visual as a form of "presence" can be seen as a displaced version of a much earlier suspicion of icons and graven images.

25 Robert Crosman, *Reading Paradise Lost* (Bloomington: Indiana University Press, 1980), 205ff.

26 On the question of "other" readings that are part of the archeological substructure of the poem, see most recently Jacqueline Di Salvo's *War of Titans: Blake's Critique of Milton and the Politics of Religion* (Pittsburgh: University of Pittsburgh Press, 1983), 101–38. Writing from a Marxist-feminist perspective that is theoretically simpler than Nyquist's, Di Salvo suggests that "within the constructs of his poem, Milton and his God win the debate. If Milton's materials backfire for a modern reader, the problem lies with what is buried in those materials" (138). However, if the buried material already predates Milton, he can scarcely have been unaware of it, nor can we continue to see the text as a static object confronted by a resisting contemporary reader. My argument is that it is precisely his inclusion of the reader that marks Milton's awareness of Michael's interpretation as a potentially contested one.

27 Louis Martz, *The Paradise Within: Studies in Vaughan, Traherne, and Milton* (New Haven: Yale University Press, 1964), 150–52.

28 Northrop Frye discusses the revelation to Eve, but reads the episode archetypically and not in such a way as to unsettle the hierarchy of gender in the poem. Thus Eve has her revelation in a dream because Adam is no longer "trustworthy as a medium of revelation," and Frye also emphasizes the fact that while Adam's dialogue with Michael occurs on a hill, Eve "is placed on a much lower level to receive her dreams" ("The Revelation to Eve," in *Paradise Lost: A Tercentenary Tribute*, ed. Balachandra Rajan [Toronto: University of Toronto Press, 1969], 19, 25).

29 The fact that in VIII.39–40 Eve is represented as withdrawing out of tact (because Adam "seem'd / Ent'ring on studious thoughts abstruse") suggests that the discourse of masculine superiority may well be woman's tolerant concession to man's gendering of thought and rationality. On another occasion, Eve is actually present to hear of "things high and strange" (VII.53), while on yet another she is present when Adam and Michael imagine her to be absent (XI.265–66).

30 Tilottama Rajan, *The Supplement of Reading*, 222–34. For a more detailed discussion of Blake's use of female figures see 238–52.

31 On Wordsworth's resignation of a position of authority in *The Excursion*, see William Galperin, *Revision and Authority in Wordsworth: The Interpretation of a Career* (Philadelphia: University of Pennsylvania Press, 1989), 32–33.

CHAPTER TWO

Newton's pantocrator and Blake's recovery of Miltonic prophecy

GEORGE ANTHONY ROSSO, JR.

This Being governs all things, not as the soul of the world but as Lord over all; and on account of his dominion he is wont to be called *Lord God [pantocrator] or Universal Ruler.*

(Newton)

WHEN IN BLAKE'S *MILTON* the hero returns to earth after a century of pondering providence among the elect in heaven, Blake informs us that a "Bard's prophetic Song" moves him to this unexampled deed. What in the hundred-year interim provokes the Bard's song and Milton's return? The answer is bound up with the fate of Christian prophecy in Britain between the English and French revolutions. While a thoroughgoing investigation would exceed the scope of this essay, I will trace, in an admittedly schematic fashion, the Puritan source, Newtonian critique, and Blakean recovery of Milton's prophetic legacy.

Between 1641 and 1789, prophecy is linked to a cluster of related concepts – reason, vision, revolution – whose handling determines in large part how writers approach the subject. Miltonic prophecy embraces inspired vision yet posits right reason as the supreme human faculty. Milton's visionary rationalism is complicated further by the English revolution: with the radical sectaries he attacks the "impertinent yoke of prelaty," the bulwark of the state church; yet, despite affinity for their "enthusiasm," he accuses the sectaries of anarchy. After 1660, Milton projects the rational triumph of reformation into the future, which belongs ironically to those Anglican elites of the restored state church whose religion, while nominally based on revealed scripture, takes its cue from Newton's natural philosophy. Associating the *Principia* (1687) with the Settlement of 1689, the Newtonians redesign the whole scheme of prophecy: they transpose providence from the messy terrain of

47

history to the more stable ground of nature, a move that enables them to discard the visionary and revolutionary aspects of sectarian prophecy. The radical Puritan threat contained, Christian liberalism advances on a global scale, sanctioned by Newtonian natural religion and supported by an emergent capitalism, which breeds the conditions of democratic revolt. Enter William Blake. Blakean prophecy champions visionary imagination against the heritage of rationalism – in religion, politics, aesthetics – and rescues Milton from his Augustan heirs by having "Milton" slay his own God, or the Newtonian version of this deity, the pantocrator of order and dominion.[1] Like Milton, Blake is forced by history to project a utopian victory into the future; but he mixes the Jacobin principle of *fraternité* with the Christian ethic of brotherhood to herald the "Vox Populi" as the key to democratic change. Blake recovers in Miltonic prophecy a republican consciousness and oppositional stance, with roots in sectarian independency, that challenges the hegemonic order of the ruling Anglican elites. Yet forged in the dissenting artisan culture of the 1790s, Blakean prophecy moves beyond Milton's elitist republicanism to deliver a powerful critique of empire and dominion, a critique that Blake derives, ultimately, from the Book of Revelation.

In what follows, I build on studies of the Milton–Blake alliance by Joseph Anthony Wittreich, Jr. and Jacqueline Di Salvo while diverging from recent work on Blake and Newton.[2] I draw on Wittreich's construction of Milton's visionary legacy, which connects Renaissance and Romantic poetry through the genre of prophecy, but with Di Salvo I emphasize Milton's dialogue with the radical sectaries of the English revolution. The Miltonists, however, tend to leap over Newton (and the eighteenth century), leaving it to Blakeans such as Donald Ault to demonstrate Newton's importance to Blake's poetry.[3] Yet Ault, in turn, concentrates primarily on the narrative and ontological aspects of Blake's relationship to Newton, shunting its social features. An adequate approach to the Milton–Newton–Blake connection must engage the social meaning of Newtonianism, charting narratological and cultural changes as "Milton" passes through Augustan and Romantic contexts.

While Miltonic prophecy develops from the early poetry, through the prose of the revolutionary period, to the epic poems written during the Restoration, I will focus on the final books of *Paradise Lost* as Milton's response to the defeat of Puritan reformation. These books present Milton's account of providential history, embodied in the complex figure of the Son, who, as bearer of divine judgment and deliverer of human mercy, effects an uneasy balance between the rational and visionary aspects of Milton's prophetic art.

Although Milton retains a lifelong ambivalence toward his sectarian brethren, he shares their visionary enthusiasm, apocalyptic hopes, and rationalist ideology. Milton subscribes to two key principles of rationalism:

that truths can be grasped directly by the intellect *a priori*, or prior to experience; and that discrete individuals act reasonably insofar as they are free of internal and external constraints. This freedom gathers an ideological charge when plugged into the "inner light" epistemology of the Puritan reformers, who wield their polemics against state religion and aristocratic privilege, invoking the "light" most radically in a personal interpretation of the Bible. Reading contemporary history in terms of the Bible's typological code, Puritans identify the Author of the Book with the Lord of history narrated in it and insert a dangerous immediacy into the interpretive process. As that keen critic of the Puritans, Thomas Edwards, laments in his *Gangreana* (1646): "Some of the Sectaries in London do hold that in Suffolk there is a Prophet raised up to come and Preach the everlasting Gospel," a gospel "which is expected daily."[4] The political arm of the sectaries, the Independents, push this idea to a revolutionary conclusion: in their enthusiasm to establish a Godly kingdom, they execute the king and overthrow monarchy and episcopacy. In his prose tracts, Milton articulates his poetic function in these apocalyptic terms, in which he facilitates reformation by singing "at high *strains*" of God's judgments and mercies "in this Land," the land of militant Christians awaiting the millennial arrival of their "shortly-expected King."[5]

Yet Milton's rationalism is in creative tension with his enthusiasm for the sectaries, a tension exacerbated by the defeat of the Independents and the collapse of the republic. Defeat forces Milton to rethink his prophetic function: how to justify the deferral of the "shortly-expected King"? Milton's response, in the final books of *Paradise Lost*, is to shift the political focus of his prophecy from the level of content – direct attacks on bishops and kings – to that of form.

In *Paradise Lost* generic subversion becomes the agent of prophetic transformation. Milton deploys the narrative method of crypsis or concealment to make this point: the method, analyzed by Joseph Mede, of introducing a vision "in brief" and only gradually unfolding its meaning.[6] While in *Areopagitica* (748) this method is both historical and theological – God orders the enlightenment of his church "to dispense and deal out by degrees his beam, so as our earthly eyes may best sustain it" – in *Paradise Lost* Milton transforms it into a narrative strategy. Crypsis is designed to lift readers to new levels of awareness and teach them to reject the mental habits, corrupt customs, and cultural values associated with classical epic.[7]

In Books XI and XII Milton foregrounds the figure of God's Son, who enacts the narrative strategy through the prophecy of the "woman's seed," the *protoevangelium* or first anticipation of the Gospels. Milton introduces the prophecy in Book X, when God delivers judgment on Satan, Adam and Eve "in mysterious terms, judg'd as then best" (X.173). In banishing Adam and Eve from the garden, Milton's God cryptically forecasts that he will put enmity between Satan and Eve, that while Satan's seed will bruise her heel, her "Seed" will bruise his head (X.179–81). That this bruising, however, will not occur until the Last Judgment enables God the Father to mitigate the severity of his judgment on Adam and Eve. God commands Michael before he sends him on his mission to earth:

> Dismiss them not disconsolate; reveal
> To *Adam* what shall come in future days,
> As I shall thee enlighten, intermix
> My Cov'nant in the woman's seed renew'd. (XI.113–16)

Two elements of the passage – the judgment or expulsion and the promise of the woman's seed – embody the tension between Milton's rationalist and visionary sides. For, on the one hand, God argues that judgment is as inevitable as natural process: "But longer in that Paradise to dwell, / The Law I gave to Nature him forbids" (XI.48–49).[8] Yet, on the other hand, God ties the judgment to vision and history. When Eve suggests that they commit suicide to avert passing "certain woe" onto the human race, Adam realizes that this sabotages God's provident scheme: "which methinks / I have in view, calling to mind ... that thy Seed shall bruise / The Serpent's head" (X.1029–32). The effect of their decision is dramatized throughout Michael's narrative in Books XI and XII.

In the Restoration context, these books expose Milton's uneasy mingling of rational and visionary structures. Michael presents a series of incidents in which Israel–England's national failure is offset by the actions of exemplary men of vision, Old Testament "types" of the woman's seed. Michael retains the Puritan tenet of immediate personal interpretation: Adam must individualize the Angel's narrative, advance from a dependence on the shadowy types of Israelite history to an enactment of the Christ within. Yet Michael also rationalizes national failure as individual failure: reformation is deferred because of the irrationality of the saints. The few good men that persevere, while types of the seed, remain obedient to right reason, to the law of nature ingrafted on their hearts. Each type – Enoch, Noah, Moses, Abraham, and David – resembles the beleaguered Milton, the one just man "daring singular to be just," "denouncing wrath to come" on his apostate contemporaries (XI.703, 815).

While in Book XII Michael shifts from vision to commentary, he preserves the narrative strategy and thematic structure of Book XI. By identifying himself with Noah (described as the "second source of men"), Adam shows that he has begun to internalize the seed prophecy. Michael highlights his cryptic strategy in the story of Abraham, the first figure he explicitly affiliates with the woman's seed. "All Nations of the Earth / Shall in his Seed be blessed," Michael announces, although he withholds information: "whereof to thee anon / Plainlier shall be reveal'd" (XII.147–48, 150–51). In the next frame, Moses prefigures the seed and illustrates the typological method and design of Milton's providence: "informing them, by types / And shadows, of that destin'd Seed to bruise / The Serpent" (XII.232–34). But only when he hears the tale of David, type of Christ the king, does Adam finally discern the deliverer in the figure: "O Prophet ... now clear I understand ... Why our great expectation should be called / The seed of Woman" (XII.375–79). Yet all is not clear. Anticipating a long-awaited revenge, Adam expects the "capital bruise" to be a revolutionary blow to the head and wants to know when and where it will occur. With Mede, Milton avoids setting a precise date for Armageddon – "When is not set" (X.499) – yet having labored twenty years to bring about a literal kingdom, Milton reaches a critical moment in his prophetic development. Satan, he admits, will not be destroyed: inwardly, yes, his works in Adam's offspring will be overcome. But the divinely rational law of "high Justice" demands also that Adam and Eve's progeny must die, including the seed itself, by "his own Nation" slain for obedience to God. On the approach to the apocalypse (and full disclosure of the seed's identity), Michael pauses "at the World's great period." Adam seizes the opportunity to ask what will happen to the just few when the deliverer ascends to heaven – a question that penetrates to the crux of Milton's grim predicament in Restoration England.

Michael's response embodies the full range and power of Milton's prophetic poetry. The anger of the anti-episcopal tracts is fused with hard-won insight into the higher heroism of love and spiritual warfare, yet it is war nonetheless. Once "the Lord" ascends and the disciples record his story, "grievous Wolves" succeed as teachers, hireling clergy who, driven by "lucre and ambition," seek "vile advantage" in a state-sponsored religion (XII.505–16). Indeed, such leaders – understandably associated by Milton with Restoration divines – join their cause with "Secular power" and institute "heavy persecution" on sectaries and regicides. The good old cause and its doctrine of inner light reformation is displaced, yet once more, by the "outward Rites and specious forms" of the established church. In such a clime, Michael brings his cryptic method to a close:

so shall the World go on,
To good malignant, to bad men benign,
Under her own weight groaning, till the day
Appear of respiration to the just,
And vengeance to the wicked, at return
Of him so lately promis'd to thy aid,

> The Woman's seed, obscurely then foretold,
> Now amplier known thy Saviour and thy Lord. (XII.537-44)

Michael offers Adam visionary consolation and guarantees a fortunate end to history. The woman's seed *will* at last dissolve the satanic world and raise from its ashes the utopia promised in Revelation. Yet in the context of the Restoration, *only* the future can secure the rational triumph of the faithful. Thus, while the *protoevangelium* represents Milton's mature prophetic response to the defeat of radical Reformation, it is, as Andrew Milner has it, "essentially formal" and relegates political victory to the future.[9]

Milton's experience in the English Civil War taught him that prophecy divorced from history must abandon all hope of effecting social change. Yet it is precisely this marriage that the Restoration divines annul. The Anglican clergy and their cultural allies undermine Puritan prophecy by inserting the rational category of "nature" between the scriptural promise and its historical realization. Milton's potent mix of wrath and vision looks suspicious in the new society, which hails the stable values of natural law and social order as former royalists and republicans collude to form a new ruling and religious elite. But Milton's own Christian rationalist perspective contributes to this situation, as his treatment of the Son suggests. The fault line in Miltonic prophecy lies in the duality of the poet's rational judge and visionary seed, both of whom take on a decidedly bourgeois cast in the post-1688 order.

Two elements are particularly important: the singular "types" that prefigure the woman's seed and the Father's transfer of power to the Son. The "types" evince something of Milton's elitist conception of heroism, his reduction of moral stature to the fit few, fortunate enough to be free of external constraint. The latter suggests the meritocratic or liberal character of his politics in *Paradise Lost*.[10]

Indeed the narrative transfer of power from Father to Son approximates, allegorically, the political compromise of 1688. The basic issue concerns the mechanism of change, the way the Son earns or merits his title: he avenges God upon those enemies to right reason, those who break the "great Hierarchal Standard," driving them into the utter deep. Upon completion of his task, all the saints sing him "Victorious King, / Son, Heir, and Lord, to him Dominion giv'n / Worthiest to reign" (VI.886–88). Dominion, as we will see, is the defining characteristic of Newton's God. But the point is that the transfer of power avoids the feudal trappings of divine right legitimacy, replacing the absolutist with the power-sharing model of government. Needless to say, this is the model of the liberal Anglican faction that assumes control of Reformation after 1688. Puritan demands for a kingdom of saints diminish as

England's cultural leaders turn their attention to a more worldly, less severe, reformist program.

It may seem unfair to sandwich Newton between two poets and trumpet his shortcomings regarding prophetic narrative. But Newton's natural philosophy helps eclipse the biblical cosmos and heralds the demise of prophecy in the eighteenth century. Newton also extends the critique of Puritan ideas of providence mounted quietly amidst the English Civil War by moderate Christian virtuosi such as Robert Boyle, John Wilkins, and Henry More, who took a "middle way" between royalist and sectarian positions.[11] Situated between high-church Anglicanism and deism, Newton fashions a liberal stance on prophecy that, combining empiricism with a gradualist political strategy, supplies a justification for the Glorious Revolution of 1688.[12]

Yet Newton's interest in Joseph Mede complicates his approach. Mede's *Clavis Apocalyptica* (1627) – translated by order of Parliament in 1643 as *Key of the Revelation* – was the most influential millenarian tract of the seventeenth century. During the Civil War, Mede was hailed as a champion of apocalyptic thought, a prophet who not only unravelled the difficult "synchronistic" structure of Revelation, but who worked out a chronology placing the fall of Antichrist sometime in the 1600s. Sectaries adopted Mede's historicist approach in their effort to turn the world upside down. Yet, during the Restoration, as millenarianism is appropriated by the crown and established church, Mede's work is turned against the apocalyptic fervor of the radical Puritans. Mede becomes in effect an Anglican apologist, the exemplar of a philosophical method that "stresses the rigorous rational and moral preparation of the prophet rather than his wild ecstasy."[13] The true prophet, as Newton also will argue, avoids enthusiasm and eschews personal claims to inspiration. Newton and the Restoration divines find in Mede's work a system that regulates the deity's partisan involvement in history.

Little more than a decade separates *Paradise Lost* from Newton's earliest commentaries on Revelation, but the temporal distance is all-important. Newton's primary challenge is to frame a cosmology that accommodates both God and science: thus his Mede is not the champion of millenarian enthusiasm, but the architect of a "calculus" for interpreting prophetic symbolism. In a short "Treatise on Revelation," Newton acknowledges that Mede laid "the foundation" of contemporary prophetic interpretation by disclosing the "design of the Apocalypse," yet he alleges that even Mede made some mistakes, "chiefly in his Clavis." Apparently because Mede failed to "adjust" perfectly some "parts and periods" in the complex structure of the text of the Book of Revelation, Newton proposes a system or hermeneutic of "Rules" for more carefully "methodising the Apocalyps."[14] Drawing on his expertise in mechanics, Newton compares the internal structure of Revelation with that of an "engin" whose parts can be "right set together." The "true opening of scripture by scripture" (Mede's phrase) turns on a "philosophic understanding" of the "God of order," who prefers simplicity to multiplicity in all things:

> Tis true that an Articifer may make an Engin capable of being with equal congruity set together more ways than one, and that a sentence may be ambiguous: but this Objection can have no place in the Apocalyps, becaus God who knew how to frame it without ambiguity intended it for a rule of faith.[15]

Newton's metaphor of "framing" underpins both his scientific and theological writings. While he cautions that it is *not* God's purpose to make prophecy as "perspicuous" as a mathematical demonstration, Newton articulates a formula held in common by Christian rationalists: that truth lies in "the wisdom of God in the contrivance of creation."

This formula is diffused in the work of the Boyle lecturers, who apply the natural philosophy of the *Principia* to alter the debate on prophecy. By arguing that the very design of Newton's cosmos *demonstrates* the wisdom of God, Newton's followers effectively shift providence from the human sphere of history to the mechanical realm of nature. The die is cast by Richard Bentley, first Boyle lecturer, who claims that the order and harmony displayed in the universe supply proof of a rational creator. Newton, corresponding with Bentley during the lectures, praises him for using the *Principia* in such a forum: "When I wrote my treatise about our system," Newton opens his first letter, "I had an eye upon such principles as might work with considering men for the belief of a Deity."[16] The key phrase – it echoes throughout their letters – is "contrivance or design," which points to creation by an "intelligent Agent." Although he refrains from defining this agent as either "natural or supernatural," Newton asserts that such a "cause" or agent must be "very well skilled in mechanics and geometry."[17] The debate has moved away from Raphael's warning – "be thou lowly wise" – concerning celestial dynamics.

Milton may have directed Raphael's warning toward Newton's precursors, the virtuosi of Boyle's ilk, men like Wilkins and Bishop Tillotson, who attempt to naturalize providential history. Yet the more they identify God with intelligent design, with his creation, the more they bind "Him" to natural laws. Newton and his compeers struggle to escape this conclusion, arguing that the universe is no mere machine, that spirit dominates matter, that their theories of natural philosophy prove the compatibility of revelation and science. Nonetheless the Boyle lecturers could not dispel criticism that the mechanistic world view led, by fatal steps, to deism, skepticism, and ultimately atheism.

Newton and his theological lieutenants Samuel Clarke and William

Whiston encounter no less an intellectual foe than Gottfried Wilhelm Leibniz, who ridicules their version of natural providence. Leibniz objects to a specific point in Newton's cosmology.[18] In his third letter to Bentley, Newton discusses the idea of other worlds or "systems" that by force of gravity could "descend toward the middlemost" of our own system and destroy it. Newton returns to this problem in the thirty-first Query to his *Optics* (1706), where he points out certain orbital irregularities "which may have arisen from the mutual actions of comets and planets upon one another, and which will be apt to increase till this system wants a reformation."[19] "Reformation" is no arbitrary choice of words in context: for Newton asserts that these irregularities prove that "this frame of things could not always subsist without a divine power to conserve it."[20] Unconvinced by this conservative-liberal rationale, both Leibniz and orthodox Christians dismiss this conception of providence, charging that if God has to tinker periodically with the universe to keep it running, he lacks either the foresight or the skill to contrive a perfect cosmos. In reaction, Bentley and Roger Cotes, editor of the second edition of the *Principia* (1713), encourage Newton to compose a rebuttal explaining the nature and function of divine providence in his system of the world.

Newton's response, the General Scholium to Book III of the *Principia*, does not so much answer his critics as overpower them with his concept of the pantocrator. The defining attributes of this being are law, order, and "dominion." Qualifying his earlier sense of cosmic irregularity, Newton claims that the "Supreme God" shapes and governs creation through natural law, which, on the argument from design, *manifests* his providence: "This most beautiful system of the sun, planets, and comets," Newton insists, "could only proceed from the counsel and dominion of an intelligent agent and powerful Being." The deity's providential function, however, is fixed from the beginning, as Newton reveals in the next sentence: "and lest the systems of the fixed stars should, by their gravity, fall on each other, he hath placed those systems at immense distances from one another."[21] Yet, by the sheer force of his inhuman power, Newton's God effectively replaces the need for providence in his system. The absolutely transcendent deity no longer plays an active role in history, or in personal life, so that the special providence of Milton and the radical Puritans disappears. Newton reduces God's providential activity to sustaining, with minor adjustments, the mechanical order of his original act of creation.

Newton of course does not draw this conclusion. In theory he studiously avoids collapsing religion and science – "We are not to introduce divine revelations into philosophy nor philosophical opinions into religion."[22] Yet the age demands that he reconcile the two. That Newton did not fulfill this task is symptomatic not of his inability or lack of knowledge, but rather of the problems of Christian rationalism. A God lacking human attributes cannot link the terrestrial and celestial spheres without mediation, a point that brings us to Newton's treatment of the Son.

Two passages from Newton's theological work indicate his position. In the first, he argues that since the titles assigned to Jesus – Messiah, Lamb of God, Son of God, Son of Man – derive from the Old Testament, this book supplies the proper context for interpreting Jesus's mission. Newton is not advancing typological exegesis. He warns that even though such titles are useful, worshiping them constitutes idolatry.[23] The Son's defining attribute is sacrificial obedience:

> Christ, by His obedience to God and particularly by His submitting to God's will even to die an ignominious and painful death upon the cross as an example to teach us absolute obedience in all things to God's will, has so far pleased God as to merit of Him a kingdom ... [and] to have ... satisfied God's wrath and ... made us kings and priests.[24]

Those familiar with Blake may find compressed here much that he abhors about the Christian tradition: submission to authority, subordination of Jesus to the Father, respect for priests and kings. The passage also ignores the visionary and features the pantocratic aspect of Milton's Son. In the second passage, from the "Short Scheme of the True Religion," Newton diminishes the Son's role to the point of exclusion, asserting that all must "acknowledge one God, infinite, eternal, omnipresent, omniscient, omnipotent, the Creator of all things," a God whom we must love, honor, praise, and obey: "And these things we must do not to any mediators between him and us, but to him alone ... And this is the first and principal part of religion."[25] Newton's account of the Son bears importantly on his view of providence and especially on his notion of the prophet, the interpreter of God's design and government of the world.

This view figures in his last work, the *Observations upon the Prophecies of Daniel, and the Apocalypse of St. John* (1733), where Newton excoriates those who attempt to interpret Revelation without proper credentials. In particular, Newton chastises those who act as if "God designed to make them Prophets" – the "design of God was much otherwise." God spoke his word in prophecies so that "after they were fulfilled they might be interpreted *by the event*, and his own Providence, not the Interpreters, be then manifested thereby to the world." The attack derives from Newton's mistrust of enthusiastic visionaries who, donning the prophetic mantle, presume to understand God's historical intentions: it is part of "this Prophecy [Revelation], that it should not be understood before the last age of the world." Contemporary prophets are anathema: the Almighty established Christianity through the sanction of Old Testament prophecy; once the Christian writings were codified, "Prophecy ceased a second time."[26]

Newton's successor at Cambridge, William Whiston, attests to the demise of prophecy in the eighteenth century. In a review of Newton's *Observations*, Whiston places this work in the context of Reformation and observes: "the study of Prophecies is, among the polite World, generally in a low, or rather an ill esteem, for which Newton's reputation will suffer."[27] As his theological manuscripts were suppressed for two hundred years, Newton's reputation did not suffer: he remained the symbol of science in a Christian society. Yet Whiston's point is apt: in the polite world of ascendent Whig politics, Anglican elites institute their version of rational reformation in opposition to visionary, particularly sectarian, prophecy. And they do so without overt bloodshed. How they manage this coup brings us to the politics of Newton's scientific theism, or to the influence of Newtonianism in the new social order.

Like the Restoration divines who educated him, Newton uses science as a model for political and ecclesiastical stability, based on an analogy between the "worlds natural and politic."[28] As it discloses the regular, predictable, orderly processes of nature, science affords the proper method for building a stable polity. Newton's theory of universal order arising from the mutual interaction of isolated, self-contained atoms is applied by his followers to the social sphere, where human atoms act according to *their* nature, characterized by the pursuit of individual gain.[29] The Newtonians – from pulpit and coffeehouse to Parliament and the Royal Society – argue that since Britain survived the transition from feudalism to constitutional monarchy, discrete self-interests evidently could harmonize to bring about stability. This ideological rationale for economic egoism associates the Newtonians "with the rise of the Whig oligarchy and with the difficult adjustments which followed the Revolution of 1687–89."[30]

But the Newtonians faced a complex task: how to spread the new gospel of wealth, order, and stability in terms that might suggest beneficence to all? The answer was to herald the new order as providentially sanctioned and, therefore, as in the common interest. Surely, Britain's cultural leaders viewed the compromise between monarchy and parliament, landed and commercial interests, as the *natural* solution to civil strife. In a certain sense, Newtonianism did offer the most complete and reliable "world picture" to date. But the goal of the new rulers was to cast their ideas as universal, to represent these ideas as the only reasonable and valid ones, so that they could imbue the changing status quo with the rationality and permanence of nature itself. Thus, in opposition to feudal absolutism, Christian men of business applied Newtonian mechanics to the problems of industry and trade, claiming that God wisely assigns nations the production of certain commodities according to their natural resources. Joseph Addison catches the essence of this "natural" providence in his encomium to the Royal Exchange:

Nature seems to have taken particular Care to disseminate her Blessings among the different Regions of the World, with an Eye to this mutual Intercourse and Traffick among Mankind, that ... the several Parts of the Globe might ... be united together by their common Interest.[31]

While the common interest may serve as the social equivalent of gravity, the discourse of nature authorizes *laissez-faire* and free competition for the spoils of the world. Grasping the far-reaching social consequences of Newtonian science, eighteenth-century liberal intellectuals promulgate a new creed: they teach the men of the new age the importance of thinking mechanically. The political and cultural leaders who attend lectures on applied Newtonian mechanics in the 1720s rear the sons who invest heavily in industry in the 1760s.

As it promotes the self-interest of Britain's new liberal establishment, Newtonianism aids and abets the development of capitalistic enterprise.[32] Such enterprise does bring prosperity to England and helps assure peace and stability through the reign of Walpole. But two points need to be emphasized: that the chief beneficiaries of this prosperity were Whig merchants, "men of large landed property, and the intellectuals whom they employed or subsidized"; and that peace and stability did not endure.[33] Blake lived for seventy years (1757–1827) and England was at war for half of them. Furthermore, Britain's successful overseas "traffick" hinged on the African slave trade and on its own accelerating industrialization, which impoverished large segments of the population, forcing them into the cities, factories, and mills where they labored in abject conditions. These conditions, in turn, fomented the democratic movements of the later eighteenth century, the era in which the bardic Blake came to maturity.

In an effort to make sense of the vast social and cultural changes in Europe since Milton's age, Blake returns to the source-book of Christian prophecy, the Book of Revelation. Drawing on the mythological symbolism and political perspective of John, Blake identifies Britain's colonial trade with Roman imperialism, lumping both under the inclusive banner of "natural religion." He also condenses Milton's and Newton's God in the figure of Satan and critiques that part of Miltonic prophecy appropriated by eighteenth-century Anglican apologists: namely, the universal ruler, bound to his own laws of nature by Milton's successors, who, guided by the "invisible hand" of Adam Smith's market economy, align providence with the dominions gained by the elect. This version of providence provokes the Bard's song, which moves "Milton" to descend from the transcendent regions of heaven to reclaim his discarded prophetic heritage on earth.

> "O Satan my youngest born, art thou not Prince
> ... of the Wheels of Heaven, to turn the Mills day & night?
> Art thou not Newtons Pantocrator"   (*Milton*, 4.9–11)[34]

Blakean prophecy evolves in several stages that remarkably parallel Milton's own development. Blake writes visionary poetry at an early age, is compelled by historical events to mix vision and politics, and is forced to deal with the experience of defeat. Blake responds to the "failure" of the French Revolution in a typically complex way: he retains its critical attack on Christendom but rejects its militant rationalism. As the revolution is ensnared in the web of imperial intrigue, Blake views its ambition as satanic pride and scorns its deification of reason as state religion, a modern type of Christian collusion with pagan Rome. Pinned between the rock of British reaction and the whirlpool of French aggression, Blake searches Revelation for signs to help navigate the turbulent currents of his age.

Blake draws on chapters 17 and 18, which describe the opening of the seventh seal and "the judgment of the great whore that sitteth upon many waters" (17.1). As John harangues the local churches for "fornicating" with the merchants of Rome, Blake inveighs against the London and Paris liberals for their worldly "intercourse," which he interprets, after John, as the "hire" paid to a prostitute. "Babylon" symbolizes the goddess Roma and the Roman empire, the great red dragon of the Augustan imperial cult, whose dominion is augmented by religious idolatry – often extracted by economic oppression and retaliation. Blake updates John's symbol, yoking Britain's international "traffick" with French imperial conquest: "Babylon again in Infancy Calld Natural Religion."

Recasting the debate in terms of John's Revelation, Blake offers the British public a clear-cut apocalyptic choice between the (regenerated) Miltonic and Newtonian versions of prophecy. He does so by overturning Milton's individualist conception of heroism. In the Lambeth works – *The Book of Urizen, The Book of Ahania, The Book of Los* – Blake's hero is a collective force of cosmic, political, and sexual change named Orc. While he functions as the metamorphic power of the American and French revolutions, Orc's fierce energy entraps him in the folds of his reactionary opponent, Urizen, a composite mythic figure playing the roles of Jehovah, Milton's God, and Newton's pantocrator. As Orc fails to liberate Europe from Urizen's grip, Blake (compelled like Milton to rethink his prophetic function) develops the enigmatic figure of Los – "the spirit of prophecy" – who in the epic prophecies bears the heroic task of stopping the bloodshed of the Urizen–Orc wars. In the Lambeth poems Los is implicated in the wars for adopting Urizen's tactics in his treatment of Orc; but in *Milton* he transmutes Orcian violence into "intellectual war" through the visionary medium of the Lamb, Blake's symbolic Jesus, who enters the state of Orc to protect him from Urizen's dominion. Through the Lamb, Los teaches "Milton" to humanize Urizen's mathematical holiness and to spiritualize Orc's wrath, enabling "Milton" to distinguish the rationalist and visionary tendencies of British prophecy.

From Blake's late eighteenth-century standpoint, Christian rationalists build on the iconoclastic work of the reformers but leave reformation incomplete. The Newtonians (who now include Rousseau and Voltaire), in turn, throw out the baby of revelation with the bathwater of superstition, sacrificing the Son – Blake's "Lamb" – to holy war and nature worship. One of Blake's symbols of natural religion, Tirzah (Urizen's counterpart, the whore of Revelation), mocks Milton's "sons": "Where is the Lamb of God? where is the promise of his coming?... His images are born for War! for Sacrifice to Tirzah! / To Natural Religion" (19.50, 53–54). Blake here exposes the theology of the Son's ransom (to God's law) as a mystified rationale for the ritual slaughter of the Anglo-French war: "Between South Molton Street & Stratford Place: Calvarys foot" (4.21) is where prisoners, soldiers, and workers are sacrificed to glut the maw of the "elect," the elites who engineer such policies. In *Milton*, it is only through the posthumous power of the Lamb that Milton redeems himself: the Lamb's resurrection contravenes natural law, showing that self-sacrifice, not sacrifice of others, is the true mode of Christian reformation. Milton, however, cannot save himself until he conquers his rational specter and embraces the "Vox Populi."

Despite his ambivalence toward the revolution, Blake rescues Milton from his elitist and rationalist errors (heirs) through the ideology of brotherhood, the *fraternité* of the Jacobins. This concept measures the distance between 1641 and 1789: Blake writes at a moment when the lower orders reject both feudal and liberal disdain for democracy and the common man. In the penultimate scene, when Milton finally confronts Satan in Blake's garden at Felpham, Milton renounces the rationalist creed, identifying Satan as his own specter. Satan thunders back in the language of Newton's pantocrator: "Saying I am God the judge of all ... Fall therefore down & worship me. Submit ... to my eternal Will" (38.51–53). But this exposure of Satan as Newton's God ushers in a moment of visionary clarity. Blake sees Milton on his path, flooded with the sun's radiance, as angels of providence trumpet "human forms" that announce dramatically: "Awake Albion awake! reclaim thy Reasoning Specter. Subdue / Him to the Divine Mercy. Cast him down into the Lake / Of Los" (39.10–12). Albion as the British people awakens to the apocalyptic rumblings of a renewed revolutionary consciousness, aroused as Satan (the "Specter of Albion") is defeated by a collective power. This power, feared and distrusted by both Milton and Newton, is the voice of the people "combind in Freedom & holy Brotherhood" (32.15).

Blake associates both British and French natural religion with the "baseness" of the Greeks and Romans, with the martial virtues of classical epic. As these virtues advance the satanic agenda of sacrificing people to war, they become tools of Antichrist. In Blake's view, both Orcian and Urizenic forces seize "laws from Plato and his Greeks to renew the Trojan Gods ... to deny the value of the Saviours blood" (22.53–54). That is why Blake subjects Milton to what he calls "self annihilation": "Milton said I go to Eternal Death! The Nations still / Follow after the detestable Gods of Priam; in pomp / Of warlike selfhood" (14.14–16). To Blake, Augustan England is a replica of imperial Rome, a culture that not only "imitates" the warrior ethos of Greece, but crucifies the visionary "Lamb of God," the fount of all spiritual and imaginative activity. Demoting biblical while promoting classical values, "Augustan" intellectuals depress mental and prolong corporeal war. Pursuing Milton's lead while rejecting his neoclassicism, Blake overturns the "silly Latin and Greek slaves of the Sword" to rescue Milton from his Augustan heirs, and to restore an anti-hegemonic stance to his lost prophetic art.

This brief overview suggests that what incites the Bard's wrath and prompts Milton's return is the emergence of a view that associates prophecy with the fulfillment of reformation by Christian capitalists. Theirs is a God of dominion, the world ruler of the merchant and manufacturing classes. The fate of prophecy in such a culture is shaped by these classes and their literary and religious allies, who adopt that aspect of Miltonic prophecy – its elite rationalism – that both preserves the "great Hierarchal Standard" and serves the new liberal political agenda. If Newtonianism merits the distinction of a rational alternative to sectarian strife, the social policies made in its name plant the seeds that lead to democratic unrest. Augustan society legitimates the building of a political economy based on colonial and domestic slavery, one that not only tolerates the back-breaking millennial labor of millions, but that ruthlessly dispossesses the artisans of Blake's own social class, ultimately driving him out of work. Such government, such providence, could only draw the ire of a man like Blake, who, as Raymond Williams puts it, suffers the changes of industrial capitalism, and the misery it induces, "on the ground."[35]

When Blake asks, "Are not Religion & Politics the Same Thing?" he is being more than rhetorical. He answers: "Religion is Brotherhood" (*Jerusalem* 57.10). This concept, forged in the cauldron of the French Revolution, demands that "Los listens to the Cry of the Poor Man," his cloud over

London "low bended in anger." While Blake recovers he also advances Miltonic prophecy by exposing its link to the genteel rationalism of Newtonian natural religion and by restoring its integrity as a collective endeavor. Although the democratic revolutions of the eighteenth century succumbed to imperialist enterprise, Blake prophesies the day when people will go forth to the great harvest and vintage of the nations, turn the old world upside down, and finally take control of their own history.

NOTES

1 While space does not permit an examination of the important role that Blake's engraved illuminations play in his conception of prophecy, the full-page design on plate 18 of *Milton* is relevant here: it depicts the God of the Decalogue sitting on his throne, hands resting on the tablets of law, as a young figure ("Milton"?) reaches for his neck to strangle him.

2 See Joseph Anthony Wittreich, Jr., *Visionary Poetics: Milton's Tradition and His Legacy* (San Marino: Huntington Library, 1979); Jacqueline Di Salvo, *War of Titans: Blake's Critique of Milton and the Politics of Religion* (Pittsburgh: University of Pittsburgh Press, 1983); Donald Ault, *Narrative Unbound: Re-Visioning William Blake's "The Four Zoas"* (Barrytown: Station Hill Press, 1987); and Stuart Peterfreund, "Blake and Newton: Argument as Art, Argument as Science," *Studies in Eighteenth-Century Culture* 10 (1981): 205–26.

3 Exceptions are Florence Sandler, "The Iconoclastic Enterprise: Blake's Critique of 'Milton's Religion'," *Blake Studies* 5 (1972): 13–57, and Jean H. Hagstrum, "William Blake Rejects the Enlightenment," in *Blake: A Collection of Critical Essays*, ed. Northrop Frye (Englewood Cliffs: Prentice-Hall, 1966), 142–55. See also Joseph Anthony Wittreich, Jr., "The Poetry of the Rainbow: Milton and Newton among the Prophets," in *Poetic Prophecy in Western Literature*, ed. Jan Wojcik and Raymond-Jean Fontain (Rutherford: Fairleigh Dickinson University Press, 1984), 94–105.

4 In A. L. Morton, *The Everlasting Gospel: A Study in the Sources of William Blake* (New York: Lawrence & Wishart, 1958), 11.

5 *Complete Prose Works of John Milton*, 8 vols., ed. Don M. Wolfe (New Haven: Yale University Press, 1953–82), 1: 616.

6 In *The Art of Logic* Milton defines "crypsis" as a method of concealment in which something implied is left unsaid: "while crypsis is, strictly speaking, a technical principle, it ... has affinities with the traditional attitude toward scriptural obscurity," writes Michael Fixler. See "The Apocalypse within *Paradise Lost*," in *New Essays on Paradise Lost*, ed. Thomas Kranidas (Berkeley: University of California Press, 1971), 147–48.

7 Wittreich, *Visionary Poetics*, 42–43.

8 For a divergent view of Milton's providence in *Paradise Lost* see John Rogers, "Milton and the Mysterious Terms of History," *English Literary History* 57 (1990): 281–305. Rogers does not mention the "woman's seed," an omission that detracts from an otherwise solid account of Miltonic prophecy.

9 Andrew Milner, *John Milton and the English Revolution: A Study in the Sociology of Literature* (London: Macmillan, 1981), 166.

10 Although she cautions against critics "encrypting" or reading their own politics into Milton's work, Mary Ann Radzinowicz views Milton as a liberal. See "The Politics of *Paradise Lost*," in *Politics of Discourse: The Literature and History of Seventeenth-Century England*, ed. Kevin Sharpe and Steven N. Zwicker (Berkeley: University of California Press, 1987), 204–29.

11 I take the term "Christian virtuoso" from Richard Westfall's astute *Science and Religion in Seventeenth-Century England* (1958; reprint, Ann Arbor: University of Michigan Press, 1973), 13–22.

12 James E. Force and Richard H. Popkin excavate some crucial contexts for the study of Newton's religion: see especially Force's essay, "The Newtonians and Deism," in *Essays on the Context, Nature, and Influence of Sir Isaac Newton's Theology*, ed. James E. Force and Richard H. Popkin (London: Klumer Academic Publishers, 1990), 43–73.

13 Frank Manuel, *A Portrait of Isaac Newton* (Cambridge: Harvard University Press, 1968), 121.

14 In Frank Manuel, *The Religion of Isaac Newton* (Oxford: Clarendon Press, 1974), 119.

15 Quoted in Manuel, *The Religion of Isaac Newton*, 121.

16 H. S. Thayer, *Newton's Philosophy of Nature: Selections from his Writing* (New York: Haffner Press, 1974), 46.

17 Thayer, *Newton's Philosophy of Nature*, 47–49, 54.

18 According to David Kubrin, Leibniz objected to Newton's sense of the world's ultimate decay: see "Newton and the Cyclical Cosmos: Providence and the Mechanical Philosophy," *Journal of the History of Ideas* 28 (1967): 325–46.

19 Thayer, *Newton's Philosophy of Nature*, 177.

20 Thayer, *Newton's Philosophy of Nature*, 56.

21 Isaac Newton, *Sir Isaac Newton's Mathematical Principles of Natural Philosophy and his System of the World*, trans. Andrew Motte, revised by Florian Cajori (Berkeley: University of California Press, 1966), 2: 544.

22 H. McLachlan, ed., *Sir Isaac Newton: Theological Manuscripts* (Liverpool: Liverpool University Press, 1950), 58.

23 John Maynard Keynes, who made public nearly half of Newton's theological manuscripts, argues that idolatry constitutes the great sin in Newton's system. He says of Newton: "He was rather a Judaic monotheist of the school of Maimonides." See Manuel, *A Portrait of Isaac Newton*, chapter 6 for a discussion of Newton and Maimonides.

24 Quoted in Westfall, *Science and Religion*, 211.

25 Thayer, *Newton's Philosophy of Nature*, 66.

26 Isaac Newton, *Observations Upon the Prophecies of Daniel and the Apocalypse of St. John* (London: J. Darby and T. Browne, 1733), 251–52, 13.

27 William Whiston, *Six Dissertations* (London: John Whiston, 1734), 269.

28 McLachlan, *Theological Manuscripts*, 120. See also Margaret Jacob, *The Newtonians and the English Revolution, 1689–1720* (Ithaca: Cornell University Press, 1976), 135–37.

29 Alexander Koyre, *Newtonian Studies* (Chicago: University of Chicago Press, 1965), 22.

30 Larry Stewart, "Samuel Clarke, Newtonianism, and the Factions of Post-Revolutionary England," *Journal of the History of Ideas* 42 (1981): 53.

31 Joseph Addison, *Selections from "The Tatler" and "The Spectator"*, ed. Robert J. Allen (New York: Rinehart, 1960), 119.

32 Marx and Engels argue that England's global trade not only fostered the development of "big industry" but "made natural science subservient to capital." Ironically in regard to Addison, this subservience took from "the division of labor the last semblance of its natural character"; see *The German Ideology*, ed. C. J. Arthur (New York: International Publishers, 1970), 78.

33 Jacob Viner, *The Role of Providence in the Social Order: An Essay in Intellectual History* (Princeton: Princeton University Press, 1972), 97. See also the erudite book by Peter Linebaugh, *The London Hanged: Crime and Civil Society in the Eighteenth Century* (Cambridge: Cambridge University Press, 1992).

34 All Blake quotations are cited according to the plate and line number of each specific work.

35 Raymond Williams, *Politics and Letters: Interviews with New Left Review* (London: Verso, 1981), 115.

CHAPTER THREE

Milton's Hell: William Beckford's place in the graphic and the literary tradition

E. S. SHAFFER

A RECENT WRITER ON MILTON and the eighteenth century has suggested:

Satan was after all not very interesting to the eighteenth century except as a polemical image in political satire and (as in Cowper) as a figure for the damned and lost soul ... Mid-eighteenth-century critics found Satan sublime, but primarily as arousing terror, not admiration.[1]

This seems wrong-headed. The critic's own statement poses the intensely interesting question, how did the eighteenth century move from a Satan who was "a polemical image in political satire" to a Satan who was "a figure for the damned and lost soul"? The whole subject of Milton and the Romantics may be discussed in these terms. I shall suggest that light may thereby also be thrown on the relation of the metaphysical style to both Milton and the Romantics.

To show this shift in progress, no figure can be more crucial than the early or proto-Romantic William Beckford (1760–1844). The recent emergence of his manuscripts from family custody into relative availability (though still largely in manuscript form) is the first step in the release of a very considerable *oeuvre* from the obscurity and innuendo in which it has so long been concealed.

A major topic of dispute has always been the Romantics' understanding of Milton's Satan. I shall argue that Beckford occupies a pivotal position, and that his understanding of Milton is not only extraordinarily interesting in itself, but that it prepares several major themes that were to be further explored by poets – Blake (his contemporary), Byron (his most avowed disciple), Shelley, and Coleridge – and by prose writers (both essayists and novelists) and painters. Some of Beckford's work was too extreme for publication (or so his family thought, and so he himself came to believe after being exposed to public scandal); as a consequence, we shall be looking in part at unpublished

65

manuscripts that are only now seeing the light of day, at material written in French or published only in France (where his reputation has always stood higher than in England), and at material which, although published in English, has remained difficult of access. The history of the suppression or partial suppression of Beckford's work, complex and fascinating, calls for a lengthy critical reassessment. In order properly to estimate the extent of his influence, much needs to be done, too, on its subterranean reception during his lifetime and after. In the manuscripts (and in the semi-suppressed Episodes to *Vathek*, originally intended to be published as part of *Vathek*, written in French and published several times in French, but in English translation published only in 1912 in an edition separate from *Vathek* itself) much is made more explicit, especially those themes that became influential through Beckford's best-known work, *Vathek* (1786), in which the Miltonic echoes of his underworld have long been recognized. Here we can only pick out a few relevant themes.

Beckford is also of vital importance because of his full awareness of and lifelong participation in the growing tradition of visual illustration of Milton. A major collector, connoisseur, and patron of the arts throughout his life, he was, unlike many writers and critics, fully aware of both Milton's poetic texts and the graphic tradition which was accumulating around them throughout his own lifetime and on which he himself may be said to have had an influence. Again, a great deal of work needs to be done, for his activities in this as in the literary field have been ignored or dismissed with the label "eccentric."[2]

It is often forgotten how long and how rich a period Beckford's productive life spanned. He began his career as a writer of fiction and critic of the arts with the publication of the unduly neglected, finely ironic, lives of imaginary painters, *Biographical Memoirs of Extraordinary Painters* (1780), in which he does much not merely to parody the form but to establish a lineage and a tradition for gothic art, and so for English art as part of the Northern European tradition. As in much else, he may have been stimulated in this by his tutors, who included his art master, Alexander Cozens, the innovative water-colorist. In 1834 Beckford published a carefully revised and expanded version, *Italy; with Sketches of Spain and Portugal*, of his brilliant early travel book, *Dreams, Waking Thoughts and Incidents* (1783), which had been suppressed after publication by his family (leaving only a handful of extant copies). *Italy* includes his splendid descriptive piece on his visit, following, as he thought, in Milton's footsteps, to Vallombrosa. Edward Chaney has argued that Milton never in fact visited Vallombrosa, and that Beckford's brilliant evocation of it as a Miltonic topos began the long series of writers' pilgrimages there.[3] Beckford is, of course, well known for his contributions to gothic architecture, but Fonthill is too often treated in isolation as evidence of "eccentricity" rather than seen in connection with his redefinitions of the gothic across several fields.

Of particular importance for the visual tradition of the representations of Hell was Beckford's role in the vogue for Piranesi. Piranesi's *Le Carceri d'invenzione* or *Imaginary Prisons*, etchings reworked and extended in the 1760s from the 1745 *Invenzioni capric[ciose] di Carceri*, were interpreted in terms of themes of imprisonment, labyrinthine enclosures, and the classical, Dantesque, and Miltonic hells. In particular, the fantastic and grandiose architecture of Piranesi became closely linked with representations of Milton's Pandemonium. For Beckford, whose father, Member of Parliament and twice Lord Mayor of London, and, through his Jamaican holdings, an extremely wealthy man, had already been a collector of Piranesi, the latter's championship of Etruscan and Egyptian art had already suggested, in the interior furnishings of Fonthill Splendens (his father's mansion), a number of aspects of his later imagined hells. Of particular importance in our present connection is Beckford's close association with the painter and theatrical designer Philippe de Loutherbourg, whose eidophusikon scenes, especially his Hell from *Paradise Lost* (1782), exploited the popular sense of the sublime and hence were immensely popular in London. *Satan Arraying his Troops on the Bank of the Fiery Lake, with the Palace of Pandemonium: from Milton* came as the climax to London evenings. The eidophusikon, a kind of precursor to the cinema, involved the use of colored lights, colored glass, and varied sounds. Joshua Reynolds and Gainsborough were both delighted spectators of such displays. Beckford brought de Loutherbourg to Fonthill Splendens to put on private performances.[4] This aspect of Beckford's wide-ranging and lifelong connection with the art world is more often mentioned than others, simply because it bears out his reputation for spectacular extravagance; but its importance for his own handling of Miltonic materials, and for the alteration in the image of Milton, is considerable.

Beckford appears again as a patron of the first importance in his travels in Italy with the young painter J. R. Cozens, son of his art master, Alexander Cozens. As Ronald Paulson has remarked, "First J. R. Cozens and then Turner developed the simple light–dark, high–low contrasts of *Paradise Lost* in paintings of demonic landscapes (Lakes Albano, Nemi, and Avernus)."[5] In fact, Cozens contributed Miltonic illustrations which may help to suggest a date for Beckford's early prose, with its clearly visualized references to Milton's Hell. Cozens's three early Miltonic roundels in a sublime manner – *A Figure on the Edge of an Inferno*, probably the earliest, *Satan Passing through the Gulf between Heaven and Hell*, the first illustration in England of this passage in *Paradise Lost*, and *Satan directing his Legions* – may antedate his first trip to Italy in 1776, drawing not on the Alps but on the mountainous and cavernous landscape of Matlock, Derby; or they may follow his meeting in Rome with J. H. Fuseli who had completed his "beautiful and heroic" Satan in that year.[6] Fuseli's drawing, *Satan und Tod, von der Sünde getrennt*, in which the fine fair Satan, turning his amorous gaze on Sin, is contrasted with dark Death, is often seen as a turning-point in the depiction of Satan.[7] In either case, the Miltonic imagery in the work of both Cozens and Beckford in the mid-1770s presages their journey to Italy together in 1782 which resulted in Beckford's little masterpiece of a travel book, *Dreams, Waking Thoughts and Episodes* and some of the finest of Cozens's work, commissioned by Beckford; and both were influenced by Alexander Cozens's teaching that certain emotional effects could be produced by particular landscape compositions. Cozens supplies another link between Piranesi and the "demonic landscape," for at Beckford's behest he travelled to Paestum to paint the massive ruins in the manner of Piranesi's late engravings of that site.[8] This transfer to landscape was a decisive turning-point: the "amplification of architecture by pictorial means was introduced into English art through the inspired topographical work of painters such as John Robert Cozens and Turner."[9] Paulson has argued that "landscape was the solution to the problem of the powerful English burlesque tradition – the Hogarthian mode in which the Michelangelo or Old Master remains as a mock-heroic vestige rather than as a primary precursor of the graphic tradition" (*Book and Painting*, 102). But Beckford suggests another solution, in which the architectural fantasy became a projection of an inner landscape.

One of the major episodes developed in the visual arts was "Satan, Sin and Death" from the end of Book II of *Paradise Lost*. The painter Jonathan Richardson in *Explanatory Notes and Remarks on Milton's "Paradise Lost"* (1734), drew Hogarth's attention to "Satan, Sin and Death," which he thought the best thing in *Paradise Lost*. As a result, Hogarth initiated a long line of major treatments of the topic, running down through James Barry, Fuseli, and political interpretations of the theme in the 1790s (*Book and Painting*, 106ff.). This was certainly of great importance in the literary reinterpretations as well, for a major critical battle was fought over it, focusing the differences between the Augustans and the proto-Romantics not only on Miltonic but on metaphysical style.

In Beckford's own collection (as his sales catalogues tell us) we find Blake's engraved *Paradise Lost* and two drawings of the "Gates to Paradise." Beckford was also the patron of John Martin and thus of the later Romantic aspects of the illustration of *Paradise Lost* and the apocalyptic religious epic. Beckford, admiring Martin's work, which he had several times seen, invited him to visit Fonthill and to paint the gothic pile. Martin did so, and used Beckford's vast walled gardens at Fonthill as a model for Milton's Eden, painting *Adam and Eve Entertaining the Angel Raphael* in 1823. His splendid series of twenty-four mezzotints from *Paradise Lost* begun in the following year stresses the Eden *versus* Underworld, or Paradise *versus* Hell themes. The mezzotint is especially well suited to rendering the Underworld of *Paradise Lost*. As William Feaver puts it, Martin "concentrated almost exclusively on the epic–pastoral landscapes of Eden and on the vast industrial complexes of the nether regions."[10] Critics such as Feaver find Martin's original contribution to Milton illustration in this architectural contrast; but clearly it owes much to Beckford. The frontispiece to the 1815 edition of *Vathek*, of *Satan presiding at the Infernal Council*, by Isaac Taylor, was a model for Martin's treatment of the same theme. As late as 1835 Beckford commissioned a painting based on *Paradise Lost, Adam and Eve at their Orisons*, from William Etty.[11] These are merely a few indications of Beckford's rich involvement in this history. In his own writing the visual analogues play an equally large role with the written text of Milton's poem.

However, Beckford's handling of the theme of Milton's Hell, remarkably original and rich, is not merely a precursor to or an anticipation of later Romantic work. Rather, Beckford's writing on Milton and Miltonic themes absorbs and utilizes the graphic tradition, affecting landscape description, gothic fiction, and fantasy. Beckford was steeped in the French literary sources which supplied him with a potential form, the *conte orientale*, which had been so flexible and diverse an instrument both of political, religious, and social controversy and of erotic exploration throughout the century.[12] *Vathek*, the oriental tale (or short novel) for which Beckford is best known, has always seemed something of a "sport" in England; behind it lay a formidable proliferation of debate, skeptical, even blasphemous inquiry into the grounds of religion, and provocation, often disguised in satirical and ironic forms, from Crébillon fils to Voltaire. That Beckford often wrote in French reflects both his emulation of his admired relative, the writer Antoine Hamilton (1646–1720), the author of light, witty *contes* like the *Histoire de Fleur d'épine*, and his sense that in France the *conte* had been developed into a freer and more supple instrument.

I shall argue that Beckford's use of Milton shows the movement towards the revision of a conventional cultic hell into a personal hell which characterizes Romantic poetry. Beckford develops the Edenic or paradisal theme followed by an elective fall, in which an exploration of an authentic experience of evil is cast in new terms. Beckford's creation of landscapes of paradisal vision and of infernal loss on a grand scale, and his employment of an architectural fantasy that finds fruition in Coleridge, De Quincey, and Baudelaire, breaks the mold of the *conte* form. The Miltonic sources are clearly visible even while being mingled with others and transformed into a new mode. Finally, the lines of satire, mockery, wit, and metaphysical imagery, as well as those of the sublime, that are present in Milton himself, are carried through Beckford down into romanticism in fresh guises.

I shall treat here primarily one tale (or suite of tales) of hell – "Histoire de Darianoc" – together with its linked tales, "Histoire de Messac" and "Histoire de la jeune indienne de Visapour," and some further fragments (for each of the linked tales helps to convey the way Beckford intended to develop and conclude "Histoire de Darianoc"). The tales come from a larger manuscript collection of *Suite de contes arabes*, some of which have recently been published in France.[13] The date is unknown, but Beckford's best informed critics have conjectured that this suite is an early work, which, with the precocious Beckford, means it was written between *A Vision* and the publication of *Vathek*, or between 1777 and 1786.[14] Beckford appears to have written it rapidly in uncorrected French; a fair copy of the opening pages shows his process of correction and polishing.[15] The brilliant and strange story of Darianoc, while still in the form of a *conte*, nevertheless suggests a *Bildungsroman* of evil, with its extraordinary successive landscapes of corruption and damnation, in which an inward experience is projected onto a fantastic architecture. The tale creates its own universe. It begins in the paradise of Gou-Gou, an exotic African (or "oriental" in the terms of the day) setting, and follows the progressive downfall through the macabre gothic cave of witches and sorcerers, the initiation into the rites of Moloch, and the large-scale procession of the worshippers of the Serpent to the Palace of the Abyss. The grandeur of the external settings is matched by the growth of the propensity to evil in the boy Darianoc; as the settings gain a grip on him they are projected into external powers which reflect desires hitherto concealed even from himself and from which he cannot escape. Darianoc's progress may be compared with *Vathek*'s study of evil, but it is still more interesting, because young Darianoc with his bold skepticism and radical propensity to question is a partly sympathetic character, for whom the reader fears, whereas Vathek is certainly not. Darianoc's rashness, his subsequent hesitations, and his ambivalences, his genuine shock at the evil he has let himself in for and his increasing inability to extricate himself, have a wider application. Such a progress suggests a study of the Enlightenment skeptic as devil which antedates Goethe's Mephistopheles, but in fact "Darianoc" shifts the focus from the devil to human forms of evil. In this persuasive symbolic landscape of Darianoc's daring perversity and its consequences Milton's Satan is again playing a role; the displacement of superhuman defiance into a human being who cannot sustain it has an authentic moving power. We may see the imprint of Burke's influential argument about Milton's Satan: that long perseverance in evil is sublime.

A number of Beckford's pieces deal with paradises or the Golden Age, from a variety of different cultures and periods, but nearly all oriental or non-European. "Darianoc" opens in the land of Gou-Gou, the legendary African country where all violence is abjured, where humans and animals live in mutual harmony (the human race is vegetarian), and where people believe in a God known simply as "Le Grand," the Great One, who is in "le vaste bleu," the blue vastness, and who looks after them. Into this peaceful and happy society is born the boy Darianoc. From childhood a bold skeptic, he persistently questions and doubts the platitudes and shibboleths of his parents. He begins to hunt and shoot birds with his little bow and arrow. He has a pastoral and innocent amour with a young girl, Dhulkianouz; but in order to impress her he tears one wing off each of his captive butterflies to immobilize them so that he can present them as a love-offering to his half-admiring, half-horrified friend: "Dhulkianouz fut donc consterné de cette espèce de sacrilège, mais elle n'eût pas la force de blâmer une témérité dont elle était la cause" ("Dhulkianouz was appalled by this kind of sacrilege, but she had not the strength to reproach a temerity of which she was the cause").[16]

This impiety has a real shock value in the pastoral paradise. We already sense what Parreaux (speaking of *Vathek*) calls the "equivocal savour of sacrilege" (192). It is the Enlightenment story, and Darianoc is an ambiguous figure. The satiric probings of the free spirit arouse sympathy and excite awe; yet the danger is palpable and present, for after a love idyl with the young girl, in which Darianoc and the girl wander far from their usual flowery playgrounds, Darianoc in a sense entices her, leading her away; in another sense, they are equally innocent playmate-lovers (a recurrent theme in Beckford). In trying to persuade her to ride a beast the long way home (using an animal as a beast of burden is against the precepts of Gou-Gou), he mounts the animal himself and finds himself climbing a precipice and entering a dark cave belonging to the witch or sorceress Messac.

In the "Histoire de Messac" Beckford describes a strange and grotesque episode which introduces Darianoc to the powers of witchcraft and sorcery. But there is still a satiric note, as if he cannot yet believe in these dark powers any more than he believed in the good. This episode, together with the next (when having expressed a great wish to see the Serpent whose arrival is said to be imminent, Darianoc – still with a boy's natural curiosity – is sent on into the infernal regions to be initiated and prepared for the vision of the Serpent), is closely tied both to the graphic representations of "Satan, Sin, and Death" and to the strong negative critique of Milton's poetry most vigorously expressed by Voltaire and Dr. Johnson.

Messac and her sorcerers are the "small fry" of the Devil's party. As such they are presented with the paraphernalia of current low "gothick" trappings and Arabian *contes*, bringing Milton's miscellaneous inhabitants of Pandemonium up to date. When Darianoc is handed on to the next station of hell his initiation takes the form of helping to feed the babes who are being fattened for sacrifice; thus, the rites of Moloch (Satan's companion in Hell) are being carried out. It is characteristic of Darianoc's descent that at each stage he consents yet does not fully understand to what he is consenting; the terms change once he is inveigled. So here he is turned over by Messac to the "nurse" in charge of the victims, a dwarf with pendulous dugs which leave tracks in the sand ("une Naine, dont les mamelles pendantes marquaient leurs traces sur le sable ")[17] – a clear literary analogue to James Barry's *Satan, Sin and Death*. Barry's monumental compositions on Miltonic themes became well known in the 1770s. There is considerable complexity in the visual representations of Sin, who is sometimes presented as sexually alluring, as in Hogarth's version (1764), and sometimes as monstrous, as in Barry's; but a fixed element is her squatness, which is brought about by an attempt to represent Milton's lines describing Sin, the Portress of Hell:

> The one seem'd Woman to the waist, and fair,
> But ended foul in many a scaly fold
> Voluminous and vast, a Serpent arm'd
> With mortal sting: about her middle round
> A cry of Hell Hounds never ceasing bark'd
> With wide *Cerberean* mouths full loud, and rung
> A hideous Peal   (II.650–56)

Below the loins (in Barry's version) she is serpentine, and thus she is depicted as only half human, with the bottom half of her body curling away behind her in serpentine folds.

The reckless Darianoc is forbidden nourishment and sleep during the nine days of his initiation. He now weeps to return to his native hills and vales. The experience of initiation is treated in different ways throughout Beckford's work, and it becomes a central theme in romanticism; in Beckford it most probably refers in a variety of veiled terms to a homosexual initiation. A constant feature of his initiation scenes is a powerful magus figure with arcane knowledge who holds sway over an underworld imagined in oriental terms. In "Darianoc" it is clearly related to Milton's Hell, ruled by the Serpent, who represents Lucifer at his lowest point; the fallen Archangel, who still retains his splendor when he voluntarily assumes the Serpent's form in order to tempt Eve in Eden, turns involuntarily into a crawling beast on his return to tell the good news in Pandemonium:

> His Visage drawn he felt to sharp and spare,
> His Arms clung to his Ribs, his Legs entwining
> Each other, till supplanted down he fell

> A monstrous Serpent on his Belly prone,
> Reluctant, but in vain: a greater power
> Now rul'd him, punisht in the shape he sinn'd,
> According to his doom   (X.511–17)

The allegory of Satan, Sin, and Death in *Paradise Lost* was the element of the poem that drew the harshest criticism. Beckford was undoubtedly familiar with Voltaire's barbed but shrewd comments, and Voltaire's analysis itself plays a role in isolating and highlighting the elements Beckford chooses to make use of. It is in this context that the negative or metaphysical elements are linked with the eighteenth-century gothic in Beckford's hands.

Voltaire had written his critique of Milton in 1727 with a view to defending Milton against the aspersions of his countrymen; he had made a similar case for Shakespeare, while giving the English a notion of French taste; in both cases, he became more critical of the English writers later. His witty rendering of what the French would find objectionable in *Paradise Lost*, which supplied grounds for their refusal to bestow epic status on it, gives a sufficiently strong taste of the negative view of Milton however.

Voltaire's two main objections are to just those elements Beckford enlarges upon: the "contrivance of the *Pandaemonium*," that is, its combination of solid, specific architectural realization, and fanciful size-and-shape-shifting to fit the infinite crews of Hell into it; and "the Fiction of Death and Sin." The first refers, of course, to Milton's description of the building of "the high capital of Satan and his peers":

> Anon out of the earth a Fabric huge
> Rose like an Exhalation, with the sound
> Of Dulcet Symphonies and voices sweet,
> Built like a Temple, where *Pilasters* round
> Were set, and Doric pillars overlaid
> With Golden Architrave; nor did there want
> Cornice or Frieze, with bossy Sculptures grav'n;
> The Roof was fretted Gold   (I.710–17)

Voltaire remarks of this hellish architecture:

The Poet seems to delight in building his *Pandaemonium* in *Doric* Order with Freeze and Cornice, and a Roof of Gold. Such a Contrivance savours more of the wild Fancy of our Father *le Moine* then of the serious Spirit of *Milton*. But when afterwards the Devils turn dwarfs to fill their Places in the House, as if it was impracticable to build a Room large enough to contain them in their natural Size; it is an idle Story which would match the most extravagant Tales. And to crown all, Satan and the chief Lords preserving their own monstrous Forms, while the rabble of the Devils shrink into Pigmees, heightens the Ridicule of the whole Contrivance to an unexpressible Degree. Methinks the true Criterion for discerning what is really ridiculous in an *Epick Poem* is to examine if the same Thing would not fit exactly the Mock heroick. Then I dare say that no-thing is so adapted to that ludicrous way of Writing, as the Metamorphosis of the Devils into Dwarfs.

It is clear how similar these remarks are to the objections made to incongruities in metaphysical poetry: both the concretizing of abstract or mental entities and the mere ingenious fancy employed inappropriately on a serious topic.

In treating "Satan, Sin and Death" Voltaire is even more categorical in his condemnation:

We must first lay down that such shadowy Beings, as *Death, Sin, Chaos*, are intolerable, when they are not allegorical. For Fiction is nothing but Truth in Disguise ... An Allegory is a long Metaphor; and to speak too long in Metaphor's must be tiresom, because unnatural ...

Then *Sin* springing out of the Head of Satan, seems a beautiful Allegory of Pride, which is look'd upon as the first Offence committed against God. But I question if *Satan*, getting his Daughter with Child, is an Invention to be approv'd of. I am afraid that Fiction is but a meer Quibble; for if Sin was of a masculine Gender in English, *as it is in all the other Languages*, that whole Affair Drops, and the Fiction vanishes away. But suppose we are not so nice, and we allow Satan to be in Love with *Sin* because this Word is made feminine in English (as Death passes also for masculine) what a horrid and loathsome Idea does *Milton* present to the Mind, in this Fiction? *Sin* brings forth Death, this Monster inflam'd with Lust and Rage, lies with his Mother, as she had done with her Father. From that new Commerce, springs a Swarm of Serpents, which creep in and out of their Mother's Womb, and gnaw and tear the Bowels they are born from.

Let such a Picture be never so beautifully drawn, let the Allegory be never so obvious, and so clear, still it will be intolerable, on the Account of its Foulness. That Complication of Horrors, that Mixture of Incest, that Heap of Monsters, that Loathsomeness so far fetch'd, cannot but shock a Reader of delicate Taste.[18]

Voltaire also effectively questions the significance of "the communication between Sin and Death" – if the allegory doesn't work, we are left with the gruesomeness: "the filthy Abomination of the Thing is certainly more obvious than the Allegory." He goes on to point out that the French would laugh at such "low comical Imaginations" as "the Paradise of Fools, at the Hermits, Fryars, Cowles, Beads, Indulgences, Bulls, Reliques, toss'd by the Winds, at St *Peter*'s waiting with his Keys at the Wicket of Heaven" ("Milton," 255). Voltaire's slur on Ariosto, who indulged in such "low, comical Imaginations," would not have pleased Beckford, for Ariosto was one of his favorite authors, and he had already drawn on him to good effect in *Biographical Memoirs of Extraordinary Painters*.

Voltaire also singles out the bridge for particular dispraise, both because it is again a literal engineering feat in a supernatural setting, and because it is the grotesque realization of an allegory. As he says finely, the "nice Criticks" of

France would find it useless; for "Men's Souls want no paved Way, to be thrown into Hell, after their Separation from the Body" ("Milton," 255).

These passages go far to explain both why the perception of "mock" epic, low comedy, and metaphysical incongruity were still strong in the eighteenth-century reception of Milton; but Beckford deliberately embraces these traits, incorporating them into a new landscape of evil.

The landscape of hell Beckford depicts is a grandiose architectural fantasy of the kind Voltaire condemned in *Paradise Lost*. Not only is there an equivalent of Pandemonium in the Serpent's Palace of Smoke, but he picks especially on the bridge over the abyss that Voltaire singles out for dispraise as the scene of Darianoc's advance towards the Serpent. In Milton the bridge is built by Sin and Death:

> So he with difficulty and labor hard
> Mov'd on, with difficulty and labor hee;
> But hee once past, soon after when man fell,
> Strange alteration! Sin and Death amain
> Following his track, such was the will of Heav'n,
> Pav'd after him a broad and beat'n way
> Over the dark Abyss, whose boiling Gulf
> Tamely endur'd a Bridge of wondrous length
> From Hell continu'd reaching th' utmost Orb
> Of this frail World (II.1021–30)

Collecting examples from oriental travels, Beckford often used the element of the grand procession or ceremonial reception or ritual, usually in an exotic architectural setting.

In the continuation of the story in "Histoire de la jeune indienne de Visapour," the great Caravan of worshippers of the Serpent approach his Palace of Smoke from afar, Darianoc among them. They pass a number of extraordinary monuments: an immense building where pheasants have been nailed by their wings to the walls (presumably a reminder of Darianoc's crimes against birds and butterflies), with a grand gate that opens onto a valley paved with marble and filled with pyramids, columns, and colossal statues identified as "les Idoles des toutes les Nations" ("the Idols of all the Nations").

The bridge appears as the last phase of their approach to the Palace. They see the bridge first from the edge of a precipice:

ils arrivèrent sur la marge d'un précipice. Darianoc, jêtant les yeux en bas distingua non sans horreur un torrent qui coulait à grands flots dans un gouffre embelli de roches scabreuses. Sur ces eaux fatales, l'esprit malfaisant avait construit un pont dont les arcades avaient au moins quatre cents pieds de hauteur. Le grand chemin qui traversait cette masse énorme, était couvert de plaques d'airain et les murs étaient enduits de couvre rouge qui réflechissait la lumière de mille brasiers érigés sur les bords de la cataracte. Une foule de victimes toutes nues y couraient en remplissant l'air de leurs cris. Mais malgré leur agilité, des sacrificateurs d'une taille gigantesque armés de massues d'ébène, les saisirent l'un après l'autre et les trâinèrent aux brasiers, puis les précipitèrent dans la braise ardente.[19]

They arrived at the edge of a precipice. Darianoc, casting his eyes below, made out not without horror a torrent which rushed in great waves in an abyss bordered by jagged rocks. Over these fatal waters, the evil-minded spirit had constructed a bridge whose arches were at least four hundred feet high. The grand avenue which traversed this enormous mass was covered with bronze tiles and the walls were dressed with red coverings which reflected the light of a thousand braziers set up on the banks of the cataract. A crowd of completely naked victims ran up and down there, filling the air with their cries. But despite their agility, sacrificial priests of gigantic stature armed with clubs of ebony seized them one after another and dragged them to the braziers, then threw them into the burning embers.

A group of black horses in a vast field on the side of the mountain now gallop towards the bridge:

Les chevaux, après avoir fait mille évolutions dans le pré, prirent tous à la fois la route du pont et traversèrent le plancher d'airain au grand galop. Le bruit de tant de pieds surpassa de beaucoup le fracas du tonnerre.   ("Histoire de la jeune indienne," 233)

The horses, after having executed a thousand manoeuvres in the meadow, took all at once the road to the bridge and crossed the brazen highway at full gallop. The noise of so many feet was louder by far than the din of thunder.

The Palace of Smoke with the Globe of Fire above it has been hidden in the mist; but as the procession reaches the first steps of a staircase of black marble, a wind rises, and the mist clears:

L'obscurité fit place à une lumière assez vive et Darianoc vit avec une sensation d'admiration melée de crainte, la vaste perspective de l'escalier traversant les rochers d'albâtre. Sur la pointe la plus exhaussé [sic] de la montagne, le jeune homme distingua clairement le Palais de l'Abime avec mille portails et cent fois plus de croisés dont les vitraux de cristal éblouissaient la vue.   ("Histoire de la jeune indienne," 233)

The obscurity gave way to a bright light and Darianoc saw with a feeling of admiration mixed with fear the vast perspective of the staircase climbing the alabaster rocks. On the highest point of the mountain, the young man could make out clearly the Palace of the Abyss with a thousand portals and a hundred times more casement windows whose crystal panes dazzled the sight.

This vision of the high capital of hell is repeated many times in the graphic tradition surrounding Milton. Cozens's *A Figure on the Edge of an Inferno*, an attractive young figure on the edge of an abyss, may not represent Satan himself (as indeed the title suggests), but a Darianoc, a youth looking into the Serpent's Abyss.[20] This is the vital Romantic turn, from a sublime Satan, to a human affected by satanic experiences. Later images of the capital of the underworld become more grandiose, as in Martin's treatments. Darianoc has seen the Palace of the Abyss, but at the cost of prostrating himself before the Serpent (although still he has a hidden reservation, for he retains his dislike of all sects).

These scenes of hell were undoubtedly affected also by the monumental architecture of Piranesi and the great light shows of Milton's Hell staged by de Louterbourg in the early 1780s.

Piranesi is of prime importance for the landscape of hell and for Beckford's links with later romanticism, especially Coleridge and De Quincey, and their French counterparts. This is a complex topic, and I can only touch on the immediately relevant heads here.[21] Beckford's *Dreams, Waking Thoughts and Incidents* gives an account of his experiences in Venice, Piranesi's birthplace, and the site of the fearsome prisons inside the Doge's Palace, which he links explicitly to Piranesi's engravings:

I left the courts; and stepping into my bark, was rowed down a canal, over which the lofty vaults of the palace cast a tremendous shade. Beneath these fatal waters, the dungeons I have been speaking of, are situated. There, the wretches lie marking the sound of the oars, and counting the free passage of every gondola. Above, a marble bridge, of bold majestic architecture, joins the highest part of the prisons to the secret galleries of the palace; from whence criminals are conducted over the arch, to a cruel and mysterious death. I shuddered whilst passing below; and believe it is not without cause, this structure is named PONTE DEI SOSPIRI [Bridge of Sighs]. Horrors and dismal prospects haunted my fancy upon my return. I could not dine in peace, so strongly was my imagination affected; but, snatching my pencil, I drew chasms and subterraneous hollows, the domain of fear and torture, with chains, racks, wheels, and dreadful engines in the style of Piranesi.[22]

Beckford's description, often quoted, of his infamous twenty-first birthday party in the Egyptian Hall at Fonthill Splendens, contains architectural images clearly linked to Piranesi, in particular the "interminable staircase" whose top and bottom are undiscoverable, and which was so important in Coleridge and De Quincey's account of *Carceri*, published in the *Confessions of an English Opium Eater* (1821), and passed on to the French Romantics through Musset's translation (1828):

The solid Egyptian Hall looked as if hewn out of a living rock – the line of apartments and apparently endless passages extending from it on either side were all vaulted – an interminable stair case, which when you looked down it – appeared as deep as the well in the pyramid – and when you looked up – was lost in vapour, led to suites of stately apartments gleaming with marble pavements – as polished as glass – and gawdy ceilings.[23]

Here not only the interminable staircase of Piranesi's *Carceri*, but the vapor, the pyramid, and the marble floor have their parallels in "Darianoc." Piranesi's *capriccio* from the *Antichità romane* (frontispiece to Volume 2) of the numerous buildings in different styles – temples, pyramids, towers, obelisk, rotundas – crowded together at an imaginary crossroads in Rome conveys the impression Beckford achieves in his prose.

Darianoc's arrival at the Palace of the Abyss is not the end of his story. Rather, the story continues in another fragment belonging to "Darianoc", *L'Isle de Saîlah*. The island of Saîlah is another paradise, but now a highly ambiguous one, a place, according to Arab tradition, so seductive that strangers can never tear themselves away from it: "le moment qu'on met le pied sur les fleurs dont cette Isle abonde une douce langueur s'empare de vos sens" ("the moment that one sets foot on the flowers in which this Isle abounds a soft languor takes possession of your senses").[24] On this happy Muslim isle where there are many women (and access to sensuous pleasures of other kinds), and where the Infidels tempt all comers from their faith, the impious Darianoc is offered the chance to become a priest, with all the power and pleasures of the office. But his encounter with the Serpent has left a permanent mark on him, and he refuses the levities of the Isle. Beckford is markedly "Byronic" here, Byron having drawn a number of the attributes of what became known as "the Byronic hero" from Beckford. Darianoc becomes gloomy and melancholic, scarred by an encounter with evil, but having acquired a kind of dignity. Darianoc's servant runs to him to give him the good news, but finds him in a corner "bien sombre du temple pâle & frissonant" ("pale and trembling in a dark corner of the temple"):

Le Serpent que le Pro: de Gougou avoit lancé dans son coeur le ronga sans miséricorde – une sensation intérieure – de crainte & de désespoir ne lui laissait pas un instant en repos – quelque chose lui manquoit – il ne reconnoissoit point d'être suprême à qui s'adresser – devant qui se prosterner & les larmes aux yeux implorer du secours.

The Serpent that the ruler of Gou-Gou had cast into his heart gnawed at it without pity – an interior sensation – of fear and despair left him not an instant's repose – something was lacking in him – he did not recognize any supreme being to whom to address himself – before whom to prostrate himself and with tears in his eyes to beg for help.

The implication is that another over-simple religion – like faith in "Le Grand" in his native country (Parreaux suggests this faith may be conventional religion, or it may be eighteenth-century Deism, the faith of Voltaire and of Rousseau's Savoyard vicar) – no longer attracts Darianoc, even though, perhaps because he can never return, he feels intense nostalgia for this native religion. But there is a new note here: the Serpent's realm is now clearly within him.

By a profound irony, it is the impious one – the one who has been scarred by the Serpent – who is able to reject the temptation of false religion and thereby save his companions. We begin to see the Byronic heroism of the outsider, and the state of permanent exile and wandering which is his fate:

Dans cet état deplorable il n'étoit plus sensible aux charmes séduisantes de l'Isle qu'il méditoit de quitter le plus tôt possible – Changer de situation – c'est le principal desir des Impies & des malheureux.

In this deplorable state he became insensible of the seductive charms of the Isle that he planned to leave as soon as possible – To change one's place – that is the principal desire of the impious and the unhappy.

We say "Byronic" – but Byron was scarcely born when this was written, and as the context has made abundantly clear, it is "Miltonic."

It is this kind of irony that Tillyard found to be Miltonic, a form of wit that was analogous to metaphysical wit, though more profound and far-reaching.[25] This he found not in the shorter Miltonic poems, where more usually metaphysical wit has been located – in, for example, the "Ode on Christ's Nativity," or even "Lycidas" – but in the great religious paradoxes of *Paradise Lost*. Though weakened by his persistent denigration of Donne, Tillyard's argument has force. If the greatest irony is that Satan never learns that by opposing God he forwards his purposes, perhaps closest to Beckford's theme is the human discovery that Eve and Adam do not rise in the hierarchy of beings by transgressing, as the Serpent seemed to promise, but instead fall within their own order. The evolution into evil of Milton's fallen archangel is transferred to humankind, and, as the Enlightenment gives way to romanticism, Adam, or Cain, wanderer and founder of the corrupt cities of the plain, is at the center.

The descriptions of hell in "Darianoc," an outward hell expressive of an inward one, augmented Miltonic structures with contemporary Piranesian monumentality; Beckford's underlining of that monumentality with personal experiences of terror contributed to the perception in England of Piranesi as "gothic," despite his origins in the baroque *capriccio*. One more event of the early 1770s confirmed this shift: George Dance produced plans for Newgate prison which borrowed openly from Piranesi, whom he had met while studying in Rome in the 1760s, and other prison designers such as Jean-Charles Delafosse drew on him for "the symbolism of penal retribution."[26] The prison building was designed to inspire terror: "This style, now considered part of the phenomenon known as *architecture parlante*, stressed the capacity of architecture to foster emotion in its spectators as much as painting did."[27] In fact, the direct borrowing from Piranesi for this purpose antedates the formal development of the *architecture parlante* of Boullée and Ledoux. The definition of Piranesi's prisons as "gothic" was confirmed in Coleridge's reading of *Carceri*. Thus, some of the metaphysical elements in Milton so brilliantly analyzed by Voltaire were absorbed into the late eighteenth-century conception of the gothic as embracing gruesome, grotesque, and contradictory emotional tones (such as the coexistence of the terrible and the comic).

De Loutherbourg's effects of light and fire undoubtedly played a role for Beckford's hell, as well as for later scenography and painting, although his influence was less far-reaching than Piranesi's. The best description of de Loutherbourg's Eidophusikon of 1782 (it was destroyed by fire early in the nineteenth century) featuring the Hell from *Paradise Lost* in *Satan Arraying his Troops on the Bank of the Fiery Lake, with the Palace of Pandemonium: from Milton* is the following:

But the most impressive scene which formed the finale of the exhibition, was that representing the region of the fallen angels ... de Loutherbourg had already displayed his graphic powers, in his scenes of fire, upon a great scale at the public theatre – scenes which had astonished and terrified the audience; but in this he astonished himself – for he had not conceived the power of light that might be thrown upon a scenic display, until he made the experiment on his own circumscribed stage. Here, in the foreground of a vista, stretching an immeasurable length between mountains, ignited from the bases to their lofty summits, with many-coloured flame, a chaotic mass arose in dark majesty, which gradually assumed form until it stood, the interior of a vast temple of gorgeous architecture, bright as molten brass, seemingly composed of unquenchable fire. In this tremendous scene, the effect of coloured glasses before the lamps was fully displayed, which being hidden from the audience threw their whole influence on the scene, as it rapidly changed, now to a sulphurous blue, then to a lurid red, and then again to a pale vivid light, and ultimately to a mysterious combination of the glasses, such as a bright furnace exhibits in fusing various metals. The sounds which accompanied the wondrous picture, struck the astonished ear of the spectator as no less preternatural; for to add a more awful character to peals of thunder and the accompaniments of all the hollow machinery that hurled balls and stones with indescribable rumbling and noise, an expert assistant swept his thumb over the surface of the tambourine which produced a variety of groans that struck the imagination as issuing from infernal spirits.[28]

The later Milton illustrations, especially the work of John Martin, display the combined influences of Piranesian monumentality and the de Loutherbourg sublime, as well as the spectacular elements of the eidophusikon. Pointon has commented that "Artists like Gandy, Papworth and Danby were all painting in a similar vein, and, among writers, Maturin and Beckford exhibit the same predilection for the sepulchral, the extraordinary and the vast" (*Milton and English Art*, 176). This is vague enough, and omits all mention of Beckford's patronage of Martin. The direct influence of *Vathek*, the 1815 edition of which used an engraving of Martin's stupendous *Satan presiding over the Council of Hell* as a frontispiece, is highly probable. Martin couched his prospectus of the *Paradise Lost* illustrations in terms of the sublime, but Seznec has pointed to his theatricality as in the line of de Loutherbourg.[29] Charles Lamb in his perspicacious criticism of Martin called Martin's phenomenally popular painting in the grandiose Biblical style, *The Feast of Belshazzar*, a "phantasmagoric trick" in the manner of de Loutherbourg.

Thus, the apparent difference between the "sublime" Milton tradition and the "mock or satiric" Milton tradition narrows in the course of the eighteenth century, and Beckford is both an innovator of and an important influence on that shift.

In conclusion, then, Beckford, both as a writer and as a patron of the visual arts, played an important role in the transformation of the interpretation of Milton's Satan, and the Hell he dwelt in, from the polemical and satirical mode of the earlier eighteenth century, to the Romantic figure of the damned and lost soul. Beckford was not merely a wealthy patron; his own practice as a writer, reflecting his own strongly visual imagination, was intimately related to and helped to shape that of the artists he patronized. This was the case over a long career, from his decisive early association with Alexander Cozens, through his fruitful collaboration with Cozens's son John Robert, and his furtherance of the work of de Loutherbourg, John Martin, Etty, and others. The crucial moment came in the decade 1776–85, when his own landscape of damnation took form, in close conjunction with the landscape art of J. R. Cozens. The fantastic architecture of Piranesi enabled a projection of inner states onto an external world, creating an expressive landscape. The hitherto unpublished story of *Darianoc* shows clearly how the literary and the graphic treatment of Miltonic themes and imagery developed in a shared context and direction. In our present frame of reference, the metaphysical mode so criticized by Voltaire in Milton, with its concretizing of allegorical abstractions, was understood and acclimatized first as political satire, passing into Enlightenment mockery of religious literalism, and thence into a Romantic perception of the grotesque and sublime aspects of the satanic power lodged in man himself.

NOTES

1 Dustin Griffin, *Regaining Paradise: Milton and the Eighteenth Century* (Cambridge: Cambridge University Press, 1986), x.

2 Some recent criticism has begun to redress the balance. See Clive Wainwright, *The Romantic Interior: The British Collector at Home 1750–1850* (New Haven: Yale University Press, 1989).

3 Edward Chaney, "The Visit to Vallombrosa: A Literary Tradition," in *Milton in Italy*, ed. Mario di Cesare (Binghamton, NY: n.p., 1991), 113–37.

4 Marcia R. Pointon, *Milton and English Art* (Manchester: Manchester University Press, 1970), 105.

5 *Book and Painting: Shakespeare, Milton, and the Bible: Literary Texts and the Emergence of English Painting* (Knoxville: University of Tennessee Press, 1982), 102, hereafter cited as *Book and Painting* in text. Paulson does not at any point mention Beckford.

6 The date is still controversial. Kim Sloan, in *Alexander and John Robert Cozens, The Poetry of Landscape* (New Haven: Yale University Press, 1986) suggests the earlier date;

Andrew Wilton holds them to be in Cozens's post-Alps style (*Alexander and John Robert Cozens*, 103 and 107; and figs. 119, 121, and 122).

7 Gert Schiff, *Johann Heinrich Füsslis Milton-Galerie* (Zurich/Stuttgart: Fretz und Wasmuth Verlag, 1963), 49–50; and fig. 13. Fuseli's drawing is now in the Ashmolean Museum, Oxford.

8 John Wilton-Ely, *Piranesi* (catalogue) (London: Arts Council, 1978), 47.

9 John Wilton-Ely, *The Mind and Art of Giambattista Piranesi* (London: Thames and Hudson, 1978), 124.

10 William Feaver, *The Art of John Martin* (Oxford: Clarendon Press, 1975), 73–74.

11 "Unfortunately, all that remains of this picture is a sketch in York City Art Gallery in a totally ruined condition" (*Milton and English Art*, 211). Etty had painted a number of paintings based on Milton, including the large-scale *The World before the Flood*, a bacchanalian orgy in the manner of Poussin, taken from *Paradise Lost*, Book XI. The painting is now in the Southampton City Art Gallery.

12 E. S. Shaffer, "William Beckford's Transformation of Chinese and Pseudo-Chinese Tales," in *Concepts of Literary Theory East and West*, ed. Han-liang Chang, Proceedings of the Third International Comparative Literature Association Colloquium on Literary Theory (Taiwan: National Taiwan University Press, 1993), 399–440.

13 William Beckford, *Suite de contes arabes*, ed. Didier Girard (Paris: José Corti, 1992). Girard includes "Histoire de Darianoc," "Histoire de Messac," and the (unfinished) "Histoire de la jeune indienne de Visapour," but not the other fragments.

14 André Parreaux, *William Beckford, auteur de Vathek (1760–1844)* (Paris: A. G. Nizet, 1960), 178, confirms Guy Chapman's judgment.

15 Roger Lonsdale in his Introduction to *Vathek* uses the example of "Darianoc" to describe Beckford's probable mode of composition (Oxford: Oxford University Press, 1983), xiii.

16 Beckford, "Histoire de Darianoc" in *Suite de contes arabes*, 190. My translation.

17 "Histoire de Messac" in *Suite de contes arabes*, 210.

18 François-Marie Arouet de Voltaire, "Milton," *An Essay Upon the Civil Wars of France …And also Upon the Epick Poetry of the European Nations From Homer to Milton* (1727), 102–21; quoted in *Milton 1732–1801: The Critical Heritage*, ed. John T. Shawcross (London: Routledge and Kegan Paul, 1972), 254. Hereafter cited in text as "Milton."

19 "Histoire de la jeune indienne de Visapour" in *Suite de contes arabes*, 232. Hereafter cited in text as "Histoire de la jeune indienne."

20 Sloan argues that this figure represents the new trend towards attractive Satans (*Alexander and John Robert Cozens*, 107).

21 E. S. Shaffer, "Coleridge and the Object of Art," *The Wordsworth Circle* 24 (1993): 117–28, includes a discussion of Beckford's precedence to, and probable influence on, Coleridge's and De Quincey's interpretation of Piranesi's *Carceri*, plate VII.

22 *Travel-Diaries*, ed. Guy Chapman (Cambridge: Cambridge University Press, 1938), 1: 98.

23 Roger Lonsdale, Introduction to *Vathek*, iii.

24 The continuations of "Histoire de Darianoc" are discussed in Parreaux, *William Beckford*, 188–93. Parreaux retains Beckford's orthography, whereas Girard silently corrects the minor mistakes in French and modernizes spelling, though keeping any "maladresses" in vocabulary or turn of phrase.

25 E. M. W. Tillyard, *The Metaphysicals and Milton* (London: Chatto and Windus, 1956), 71–73.

26 Wilton-Ely, *Piranesi*, 73.

27 On Piranesi's influence on prison architecture, see also Wilton-Ely, *The Mind and Art of Giambattista Piranesi*, 90, and John Bender, *Imagining the Penitentiary: Fiction and the Architecture of Mind in Eighteenth-century England* (Chicago and London: University of Chicago Press, 1987), 241. Bender nowhere mentions Beckford.

28 W. H. Pyne, *Wine and Walnuts*, quoted in Pointon, *Milton and English Art*, 105. Hereafter cited in text as *Milton and English Art*.

29 Jean Seznec, *John Martin en France* (London: Faber & Faber, 1964), 48.

CHAPTER FOUR

How theories of romanticism exclude women: Radcliffe, Milton, and the legitimation of the gothic novel

ANNETTE WHEELER CAFARELLI

When an architect examines a Gothic structure by Grecian rules, he finds nothing but deformity. But the Gothic architecture has its own rules, by which when it comes to be examined, it is seen to have its merit, as well as the Grecian.

(Richard Hurd, *Letters on Chivalry and Romance*, 1762)

There is frequently a striking resemblance between works of high and low estimation, which prejudice only, hinders us from discerning, and which when seen, we do not care to acknowledge.

(Clara Reeve, *The Progress of Romance*, 1785)

FOR THE TWENTIETH CENTURY, the British Romantic canon has chiefly comprised five or six "major" poets, excluding women and most genres, and fostering a reductive and detrimental construction of late eighteenth- and early nineteenth-century literature. In examining why women's writing of this period has been excluded from the definition of romanticism, this paper will explore the transfiguration of inherited tradition as a status indicator. One typical measure of the significance of a work of literature is its communication with monuments of the artistic past, whether voluntary or unawares, whether in imitation or in transgression. The task of this project is to reconsider the work of Ann Radcliffe in the context of the Romantic canon and the uses of the Miltonic past.[1]

In this regard, we need not only to be reminded that the gothic novel is connected with the mainstream of Romantic literature, but newly to examine how Radcliffe's novels attempted to define the gothic as a literary genre inheriting the same intellectual lineage as male texts. Her program of implicit and explicit references to Milton's works sought to provide an intellectual pedigree for gothic description and plot, and, like other Romantic writers, to illuminate the nature of perception and what the mind might "half-create and what perceive."

While the so-called "new eighteenth century" has ambitiously annexed figures such as Austen and Edgeworth, and Victorian studies have edged backward into the Regency years, the twentieth-century construct of the Romantic canon has remained exceptionally hidebound. The dominant epistemology of romanticism still regularly invokes the conventional centurial periodization of literature to exclude female authors, but not male. Even as critical fashions privilege the early Wordsworth, the *Lyrical Ballads*, and the 1799 *Prelude*, women writers of the nineties are disowned as not truly, thoroughly, or authentically Romantic. Wordsworth, born 1770, and Coleridge, Scott, Hazlitt, Lamb, and Southey, all born within the decade following, are unconditionally Romantic. Yet Austen, born five years after Wordsworth, and Radcliffe, born six years before, are deemed peripheral to the definition of the era. The same inconsistency permits Blake, born thirteen years before Wordsworth, and such incompatible male writers of the turbulent 1790s as Burke, Paine, Malthus, and Godwin, to be incorporated as useful or significant formative voices, but resists viewing women writers across the political spectrum in the same light.

Calendrical rationalizations for excluding women have gone hand in hand with conceptual ones. A skewed emphasis on poetry to the neglect of all other genres has impeded modern understanding of women writers and the era as a whole. In reinstating women writers (and readers) into literary history and the definition of romanticism, we must be especially wary of the superstitious belief that the Romantic spirit is most purely expressed in a single genre. Needless to say, the reintegration of prose fiction and nonfiction into the concept of romanticism means a new visibility for many neglected male writers as well. Some scholars have recently sought to expand the Romantic classroom by reviving once-popular women poets in the search for collateral expressions of romanticism. As commendable as this is from the perspective of gender, it has regrettably perpetuated the narrow twentieth-century equation of romanticism with poetry. It is worth remembering that the era itself construed literature – belles lettres – in the broadest sense, as the eclectic gallery of Hazlitt's *The Spirit of the Age* and similar compendia illustrate. Twentieth-century privilegers of the five-man Romantic canon resist women writers with the preemptive notion that they don't and won't fit in with existing definitions; the same desire to affirm secure readings within established conventions has marginalized male prose writers such as De Quincey. As Mary Wollstonecraft observes, "moss-covered opinions assume the disproportioned form of prejudices, when they are indolently adopted."[2]

Thus, the fundamental error in assessing women and romanticism is not merely genre or merely periodization, but the habitual formulation of valuative principles that fail to account for women's writings. Literary history has not simply neglected texts that answer the culturally dictated interests of women: even when works by women writers engage the same issues and the same intellectual antecedents as their male contemporaries, the coincidence is overlooked, discredited, or systematically redefined so as to dictate its own exclusion. Nina Baym's article on "How Theories of American Fiction Exclude Women Authors" provides a useful model of the traditionally gendered operation of canon formation, which privileges a body of "literature that is essentially male" by relying on definitions of excellence or historical importance ("theories controlling our reading") that discount or exclude women writers.[3] To arrive at a more accurate sense of the era, readers of late eighteenth- and early nineteenth-century British texts need to reexamine traits identified with romanticism that critics traditionally have failed to identify in women writers or have defined so that women's texts fail to qualify.

In the present day, one major critical response to the historical hostility to women writers and readers, and the genres associated with them, has been to address the novel by separating it off as a women's realm. The dilemma of segregationism and separatism forms a troubling passage in the reinstatement of all minority cultures. In literary studies, the separatist practice of focusing on exclusively female lines of filiation recovers certain kinds of valuable information, but at the same time perpetuates the critical error of past generations which looked at texts in gender isolation, national isolation, and generic isolation, a segregationist practice that facilitated exclusionary notions such as "the five major Romantics" or "the great tradition." These gender-specific studies need to be situated alongside those which explore, for example, how women writers in the past attempted to appropriate and transform the highly visible male tradition which loomed before them – and vice versa.

Indeed, women of the Romantic era were actively interested in establishing their intellectual affiliations with literary precursors – male and female – not merely waiting for the pollinating breeze. Especially in the case of the novel, cross-generic affiliations were invoked to prevent it from being regarded as an abased form. "Why should an epic or a tragedy be supposed to hold such an exalted place in composition, while a novel is almost a nickname for a book?" demanded the novelist Mary Brunton in 1814. "A fiction containing a just representation of human beings and of their actions ... might be one of the greatest efforts of human genius ... Let it be all this, and Milton need not have been ashamed of the work!"[4] The Romantic era was especially eager to credit itself with generic breakthroughs – rebellion from established classifications – and Romantic critics championed the open genres. Just as De Quincey, in defining his "impassioned prose," declared poetry and nonfictional prose tread the same ground, Walter Scott, having left poetry for the novel, identified the shared project of Romantic poetry and fiction. Bestowing praise on Radcliffe, he appropriated the discourse of Romantic poetics in naming her

the first to introduce into her prose fictions a beautiful and fanciful tone of natural description and impressive narrative, which had hitherto been exclusively applied to poetry ... Mrs Radcliffe has a title to be considered as the first poetess of romantic fiction, that is, if actual rhythm shall not be deemed essential to poetry.

Putting into practice Wordsworth's assertion that poetry's distinction from prose was negligible, Scott identifies Radcliffe as one who, by breaking into the domain of natural description hitherto thought endemic to poetry, captured lofty achievements for the novel to become fiction's "first poetess."[5]

Radcliffe's novels themselves strove to legitimate the genre by transferring the inherited cachet of poetry to prose fiction, most conspicuously by popularizing the poetry-writing heroine and the use of chapter epigraphs drawn from the prestigious vernacular tradition of Milton, Shakespeare, and eighteenth-century British poets such as Thomson.[6] But her program of Miltonic referencing goes beyond mere quotation, and holds particular significance. First, it promoted an intellectual lineage for the novel at a time when the genre was increasingly, albeit anecdotally, associated with women writers (whose presence implicitly carried its own devaluation) and women readers (whose gullibility was a commonplace, but whose moral safety was unimpeachable with Milton). Second, by establishing a dialogue with Milton, Radcliffe's writings implicitly staked territory for women in the mainstream of male literature, a domain that had traditionally excluded them for lack of a classical education but which, it now appeared, could be annexed in the vernacular through Milton.

In the twentieth century, Harold Bloom is the critic who has most prominently postulated the response to Milton as the central Romantic experience. As many commentators have observed, however, Bloom's theory posits male rebellion from male texts as the central test of literary excellence, a model inadequate to describe women writers. Renovations of Bloom's psychoanalytic model of literary history include Sandra Gilbert and Susan Gubar's observation that women writers rebel by seeking female precursors; Annette Kolodny's discussion of how women actively decline to participate in male literary traditions; Elaine Showalter's emphasis on male reluctance to acknowledge women writers as predecessors; and Pamela Di Pesa's investigation of women's ambivalence toward the trope of the muse.[7]

Obviously, the study of relationships between texts of different eras has been one of the most intriguing and complex issues in literary history and criticism. Anxiety about influence can be no more than a corner of the panoramic discussion of the ways women navigated the traditional male landscape of literary convention, genre, and intertextual alliance: an alliance they could neither refuse nor join. In practice, it has only been a rather selective construct for explaining male textual referencing. One of Wordsworth's first extant poems is a fragment on Milton of fewer than a dozen lines written as early as 1788 in a copy of *Paradise Lost*. Tempting as it might be to seize this text as the pivotal initial response to his intellectual precursors, extending the same methodology compels us to consider that the earliest published work attributed to him is the 1787 "Sonnet on Seeing Miss Helen Maria Williams Weep at a Tale of Distress"; it goes without saying that critical history has privileged Wordsworth's rebellion from Milton over his allegiance to Williams.

Addressing such tendencies, Virginia Woolf's *A Room of One's Own* (1929) targeted Milton as epitomizing the tradition that excludes women, and many subsequent feminists have emphasized the defiant originality of those female texts that appear to reject or escape the intellectual iconography of the male colossi. In historical terms, however, it is useful to examine a different kind of challenge to male critical authority that existed in the earlier professional marketplace: the forgotten but equal defiance embodied in the appropriation of prestigious male texts by women. In trying to understand the Romantic era, we are engaging a culturally specific environment in which early women writers were motivated not by the anxiety to reject, but by the anxiety to affiliate: persecuted not by Milton's bogey but by the proscribed intellectual longings with which Satan tempted Eve. Women writers of the Romantic era, struggling to overturn their historical exclusion, seem less to have feared influence than sought to declare affinities. Alongside such formalist gestures as the revival of sonnet writing associated with Charlotte Smith and Anna Seward, Romantic women novelists sought to win prestige for prose fiction and for themselves as women writers by annexing the intellectual cachet of male writers such as Milton and Shakespeare. Incorporating textual referencing and formal echoes, however, did not necessarily presume ideological conformity, and the task of reclaiming the monumental works of the male past for feminist purposes by no means entailed unqualified approval. But it did constitute a specific stage of feminist endeavor not usually appreciated in the context of intellectual rebellion. The attempt by women writers to emphasize alliances with the male intellectual mainstream was a declaration of radical entitlement.

As British literature increasingly styled itself anticlassical in the late eighteenth century and revived a native tradition in place of the ancients, it indirectly promoted literary opportunities for the classically uninitiated. Nevertheless, the new critical values often held different connotations for

88

women and men (and for various social classes). Milton offers an excellent case study in this regard. His status as the emblem of British intellectual aspiration is testified to in such populist actions as the 1829 petition by Grub Street inhabitants to be renamed Milton Street. For unclassically educated women, allusion to Milton's works provided an accessible iconographic program. Traits that for men might constitute strict conformity to literary norms – such as unqualified quotation from Milton – might signal rebellion and intellectual assertion for women writers. Conversely, traits that constituted rebellion from tradition for male writers – simplicity, the personal, autobiography, the realm of childhood, all categories remasculinized by Romantic poets – constituted relative conformity to the intellectual docility prescribed for women. So while the familiar male Romantics were dismantling Miltonic convention in poetry, Radcliffe and kindred women were working to legitimate the novel by creating its Miltonic affiliations.

Many such gender implications complicate the notion of Romantic rebellion. For example, it is commonplace to regard the male Romantic poets in terms of their insistence on originality, but women writers were not in a position to declare independence from the literary tradition before they had been accepted by it. Women held an ambiguous relation to the fashionable repudiation of imitation promoted as early as Edward Young's *Conjectures on Original Composition* (1759) and William Duff's *An Essay on Original Genius* (1767). Coleridge and Wordsworth, for example, were notorious among their contemporaries for their insistence on originality even in ordinary conversation.[8] Women, however, could hardly relish denying intellectual indebtedness when they had been largely excluded from the education that would allow them voluntarily to repudiate those classical conformities casually disparaged by men who took such acquisitions for granted – just as it would have been thought sour grapes for former journeymen such as Samuel Richardson or working-class poets to proclaim rejection of the education they lacked. Yet all the same, both groups – women and working-class writers – were measured by the traditions they were excluded from, and faulted for the presumption of trying to acquire them.

Similarly, the Romantic rejection of overt classical referencing gave new life to vernacular traditions; but for women, posed another equivocal problem. Women, like working-class writers, benefited from the Romantic turn away from classical referencing. Yet few women with training seem to have clamored for the dispensations suggested by critics such as Duff and Young, who fashioned the vogue of praising inspired originality over classical imitation. Duff, for example, pronounced: "Poetic Genius is most remarkably displayed in the uncultivated state of society," and "The truth is, a Poet of original Genius has very little occasion for the weak aid of Literature: he is self-taught. "[9] While some working-class writers boasted of wood-notes wild, for aspiring professional women writers, such justifications resonated of the retrograde modesty topos enforced upon sixteenth- and seventeenth-century women writers.

From the same standpoint, the revived ethos of the Miltonic "fit audience ... though few" was unequally accessible by women. For women writers, commercial acceptance was equated with literary and social acceptance; already marginalized, they hardly welcomed declaring they wrote only for a few, and those hardly fit. Writing for women did not have select connotations and it was implausible for women to court an intellectual elite. Curiously, the commercial incentive provided one socially justifiable rationale for professional writing. Charlotte Smith vociferated the financial necessity of supporting her children. But while writing had been made available to women as one of the few genteel ways of earning money in need, a form of domestic production in the home, it actually became indelicate to write for other reasons. Barbauld instructed, "abandon each ambitious thought." Johnson's assertion, "To commence author is to claim praise," was countermanded, as Mary Poovey notes, by Hannah More's decree that a woman's use of "her talents ... as instruments for the acquisition of fame ... is subversive of her delicacy." Paradoxically, neither the audience of cognoscenti nor the desire for acclaim from a wide audience were allowable motives for women writers. Placed in this perspective, it was a defiant and radical declaration for Austen to assert, "I write only for fame, and without any view to pecuniary emolument."[10]

In these still early years of women's participation in the publishing community, while women writers were concerned less with declaring independence than with declaring affiliations with the dominant tradition, such assertions become even more significant amid the pressure to appear humble and apologize for deficiencies. Even as they were permitted to earn, women writers labored under the professional obligation to be domestic – it is well known how Charlotte Brontë hastened to assure the laureate Robert Southey that she had not been neglecting her household responsibilities in order to write, and even Godwin's 1798 *Memoirs* of Wollstonecraft bowed for once to conventional proprieties in claiming homebody talents for her. Radcliffe's early biographer Anne Katharine Elwood provided the same reassurance that Radcliffe "was minutely attentive to her domestic duties."[11] Novel writing was allowable within the prescribed realm of women's publishing: those who ventured further into the public eye did so at great risk to their personal reputations with scant chance for their intellectual validation.

Women writers who sought access to literary conventions collided with many gendered obstructions. The observation that women were denied access to forms requiring classical education is by no means new: in 1863 the writer Julia Kavanagh, more than a half-century before Virginia Woolf, regretfully imagined what would have been, "Had Anne [sic] Radcliffe been John Radcliffe, and received the vigorous and polished education which makes the man and the gentleman."[12] Of course, men without university education were similarly excluded, and among women, classical learning was no imprimatur of feminism. But there is no denying that even the most well-educated women lived in a world of circumscribed expectations, and cultural double standards constrained women writers in many ways. Although it is now commonly regretted that the novel of the sitting room has historically been deemed less important than the novel of war, scholars of romanticism still have failed to observe that the value system which admiringly lionized men for sexual transgressions ostracized women for the same; glorified opium hallucinations of male writers while attributing Radcliffe's creativity to eating raw pork; regarded women's reformist declarations as inconvenient or trifling and men's as revolutionary allegories; and still praise male exploration of the terrain of the mind, but fail to detect in Radcliffe's interest in perception and her visionary quality of writing anything more than a fondness for landscape.

Although the sexual double standard is the most obvious example, the Romantic era's critical emphasis on biographical theories of reading literature also gave rise to a wide collection of gender-based gothic apocrypha. An article by Hazlitt in the *Edinburgh Review* initiated or promoted the rumor that Radcliffe's husband (a newspaperman) was a diplomat and her descriptions came from their travels in Italy (which she never visited). This may have sparked the rumor that she was arrested as a spy in France – an espionage trope which attached itself to a number of seventeenth- and eighteenth-century women writers, giving a patriotic badge to transgressive behavior. In Radcliffe's case, in lieu of any documentable transgressions, her having been cast into a dungeon of "dripping walls and earthen floor" formerly occupied by Marie Antoinette was supposed the source of the imprisonment scenes of *The Italian*. In other legends, she derived inspiration from castles she visited, from mysterious disappearances and atrocities at the houses of neighbors, and by consuming raw pork in the evenings to induce fabulous dreams (Walter Scott was one who scoffed at the idea that she required "the mechanical aid to invention" suggested by one rumor that she insisted on staying overnight in the decaying gothic Haddon House). Explanations for her public silence during the last few decades of her life also literalized the gothic: some attributed it to insanity induced by nightmares or unnamed tragic incidents; others reported she had already died in an asylum from "mental alienation." In another piece of fabricated gothic biography she deterred a literary forger who mistook her for a ghost when she visited his house. Implicit in these popular anecdotes is the assumption that women's imaginative writing required a literal source – unlike the visionary inspiration that graced the reputations of contemporary male writers.[13]

The biographical double standard represented an intellectual double standard. Radcliffe's were among the earliest texts to generate the gothic vogue – early reviewers of her initial works were uncertain whether to attribute them to a man or a woman – but once the influential writer was revealed on the title page as "authoress," the gothic novel seems to have been quickly set aside as a female form.[14] The profusion and redundancy of Radcliffe's imitators contributed to draw her works into discredit, though the carloads of imitations of Thomson, Cowper, and Gray have never been regarded as anything but testimony of their significance.

Women could not annex many aspects of male romanticism without opprobrium, but following the usual course of gender alliance, the act of male appropriation elevated conventionally female literary traits. As noted earlier, when the male Romantics borrowed traits associated with women – private experience, simplicity, spontaneity instead of learnedness, wisdom in naivety, the interior mind – these traits were redefined as innovations. Male use of the gothic setting in poetry was praised as the sublime. Male appropriation of sensibility and intuitive perception (traditionally female realms) became feeling, the ethos of the male avant-garde, an intellectually inspired visionary insight. Sensibility was a modern quality not found among ancients, so its anticlassicism upheld Romantic critical principles, yet it had long been something women could exercise without special education.[15] Similarly, the Romantic rejection of classicism redirected attention to modern languages, a domain in which women were often well prepared. But though references to the works of Milton, Shakespeare, Thomson, Tasso, French romances, and other writers provided women with a way of connecting their writing to the respected literary tradition, this connection, like other alliances within the high cultural tradition, often proved morganatic, never quite conferring the ranks of high culture upon women, and their followers automatically disinherited.

Even in Radcliffe's case, where this program of referencing was not mere window dressing but a way of treating abstract literary questions of perception, and examining how texts precondition our view of literature – the same cultural endeavor as male writers – the name "Radcliffe school" came to stand for the formulaic ballast of early nineteenth-century Grub Street. Despite the scorn they have never quite shaken off, Radcliffe's novels were ambitiously communicating with the contemporary intellectual context, requiring a level of erudition far beyond the level of mass culture it came to symbolize for its male opponents.

Indeed, Radcliffe presents a successful case study of how women writers navigated a course between erudition and popular appeal to address the new inconsistently-educated mass audience. By emphasizing the vernacular tradition, women joined the general current toward a nativist past that extolled its medieval origins. When critics wanted to praise women writers like Baillie, Austen, and Radcliffe, it was customary to compare them to Shakespeare, whose unlettered genius, like theirs, was thought to spring from inspiration rather than learnedness. Nathan Drake named Radcliffe the "Shakspeare of Romance Writers,"[16] and other early reviewers and biographers, including Kavanagh, Barbauld, Talfourd, Scott, and Coleridge, repeated the claim.

In modern criticism, it is commonly remarked that the terror and supernatural of *Macbeth* and *Hamlet* appear in events and chapter epigraphs throughout Radcliffe's novels. Her theoretical essay "On the Supernatural in Poetry" credited these plays, along with Milton's poetry, as predecessors in exploring the mind's reaction to apparition. The Miltonic elements of Radcliffe, however, have drawn little notice beyond her Satanic villains, and critics remain unaccustomed to finding women writers and readers engaging Milton or other learned figures. Women's descriptive writings were complimented as "sublime" by contemporary reviewers; although current feminist critics have dwelt on the gendering of the sublime and the beautiful argued by Burke and Kant, it was apparently an aesthetic category women could unobstructedly scale. But the reputation of learnedness associated with Milton was not a quality conferred on women writers, and the ubiquity of Miltonic elements has yet to enter the critical range of vision.

Yet many women (and working-class) writers were determined to establish a firm relationship to Milton, whose writings more than any other represented a vernacular locus classicus. Milton provided a prestigious cultural source for quotations and allusions to enhance descriptions and validate perceptions, replacing Latin and Greek models they rarely knew directly. Above all, he provided what translations could not, a model of original vernacular achievement.

The transformative presence of Milton has been a hallmark of Romantic studies, though discussion has rarely strayed from *Paradise Lost*, with Satan, heroic transgression, and the transmuted epic its staple topics. The dialogue with *Paradise Lost* in works such as "The Rime of the Ancient Mariner," *The Prelude*, and the *Hyperion* poems confirms that the epic was often the test of achievement male writers posed themselves. Recent critics commenting on the gothic novel have likewise confined the study of Miltonic associations to *Paradise Lost*, in part because the preoccupation with *Frankenstein* and its Miltonic epigraph has dominated the field.[17] Yet the genre of epic was problematic for women. Lacking the classical background, women were less likely to attempt epic writing even if the conventional ancient materials of concubinage and military conquest had been more congenial.[18] Yet the classicisms of the Miltonic epic posed fewer perils than its theological subject and its proscriptive "she for God in him." Alongside the advantages of calling upon Milton, there was much to fear from the pitfalls of emulation, since his works represented the terrain where the classically unlettered female and working-class writers were most likely to be found in the emperor's new clothes.

Women, however, could with impunity become enthusiastic revivers of the nonepic Milton. With the rising interest in nature and nativism, the Milton of sublime landscape description and medieval fable assumed new preeminence, especially through *Comus*, "L'Allegro" and "Il Penseroso." The popularity of the minor poems, which enjoyed considerable vogue after 1750, was to a great extent due to their scenic detail and visual imagery, but they also engaged areas of prime Romantic speculation – the nature of perception, subjectivity, and the susceptibility of the imagination to literary convention. By virtue of their more modest generic status and humbler content, never aspiring above domestic theology, the minor poems were models women could communicate with unrestricted by education. Being Miltonic, they were no less authoritative, but there was no treading on unfamiliar terrain or risking proscribed theological realms. More important, women readers found in the minor poems female characters free of the usual Miltonic reprimand.

For women as well as men, there were many ways of appropriating and transforming tradition beyond the obvious program of Miltonic epigraphs in Radcliffe. As is often noticed but never explained, almost all of Radcliffe's many Miltonic mottos and quotations are taken from the shorter works (only one of the eleven in *Udolpho* and six in *The Italian* are from the epic Milton). Radcliffe embraced the fanciful gothic–medieval fabulist aspect of Milton that revivalists like Hurd, Reeve, and Warton emphasized.[19] But Milton's poem on the transgression of Eve is conspicuously absent from Radcliffe's program of references. It is this Milton, who espoused an ideologically conservative view of gender, who posed the great dividing line among women writers. The division is most conspicuous in the educational manuals of the age, the favorite genre of breadwinning women. Although it is dispiriting to discover that not all these women perceived the radical implications of their position as professional women writers, Milton's Eve became the litmus test of radical ideology: whether to endorse and idealize submissive docility, or resist the indoctrination of constricting models of female behavior. Wollstonecraft's *Vindication of the Rights of Woman* was, as usual, at the forefront in boldly denouncing Milton's infantilization of women in his picture of Eve – which her adversary Hannah More countered by idealizing Eve's marriageability (before her fall) in *Strictures on the Modern System of Female Education* (1799) and her didactic novel *Coelebs in Search of a Wife* (1809). In tracts such as James Fordyce's *Sermons to Young Women* (1766), the ponderous text the ridiculous Mr. Collins chooses for family reading in *Pride and Prejudice* (1813), clergymen had long been urging similar points of Edenic conjugality. The anonymous *Appeal to the Men of Great Britain in Behalf of Women* (1798), perhaps the most radical polemic of the age, sometimes attributed to Mary Hays, took the straightest route, and simply dismissed the hierarchy of Adam and Eve as a historically outmoded model. It was, however, a rare case when Mary Walker Hamilton tentatively suggested women might be entitled to Milton's arguments on divorce – her novel *Munster Village* (1778) includes an "*innocent, though oppressed*, wife" who absconds, after weeping through fourteen years of marriage, with the explanation, "Milton wrote *the doctrine and discipline of divorce*" justifying separation based on incompatibility (though later she relents). The prescription for marriage in Milton's pamphlet, like his vision of prelapsarian matrimony, was not without self-serving elements, and not without its perils for women.[20]

But there were many ways of engaging an oppositional dialogue with Milton rather than risking the overt denunciations dared by Wollstonecraft. One form of resistance was the renovation of the Miltonic legacy through a new emphasis. Even though women of the Romantic era such as Radcliffe and Wollstonecraft eschewed the Miltonic Eve, they proved that other portions of the Miltonic tradition could be transmuted to new uses. The lyrical Milton, usually regarded as his lighter side, provided an opportune medium for women to enter philosophical territory usually deemed beyond their realm. Women writers sought out Miltonic quotes to embellish scenic description, but also to legitimate socially and intellectually transgressive activities without risking infamy. Radcliffe's program of references to major poets of the English tradition gave the gothic novel a place in the intellectual dialogue of her contemporaries. Like the male Romantics, she referenced "L'Allegro" and "Il Penseroso" to fortify her exploration of the nature of perception, subjectivity, and cultural preconditioning; and in a new step, she posited *Comus* as the ancestor of the gothic novel's distressed female held captive, a genealogy she used to explore the fundamental relations of men and women and the cultural deterrents placed upon women who stray from home.

Barbara Lewalski's modern assessment that "the Lady in *Comus* is no one's favorite Miltonic character" is curiously inapplicable to the Romantic era, when Milton's unnamed Lady generated considerable interest and admiration, emerging among radical women as a preferable Miltonic alternative to Eve. Romantic women writers found in *Comus* a poem about the risks of unescorted women, but also a parable about the self-reliance and fortitude of women who venture outside the protection of men. Renewed interest in *Comus* as an exploration of sexual conduct has been similarly raised in recent years by critics such as Leah S. Marcus, whose examination of historical conditions suggests the masque responded to contemporary cases of sexual assault.[21]

The sense that the Circean archetype of enchantress and male captive needed remediation dates back to the medieval world. Susan Schibanoff has noted that Christine de Pisan's *Book of the City of Women* sought to revise the tradition of Circe (classically depicted as a wicked woman who led men astray) by emphasizing her learnedness.[22] Women writers of the late eighteenth and early nineteenth century were also eager to renovate the temptress legend. Milton's displacement of the blame onto the male tempter Comus, the child of Bacchus and Circe, provided a cultural authority for remodeling the traditional gendering of the Circe legend. In creating a male Circe who tempts women to their downfall, *Comus* depicts a situation which in reality precipitated far more dire consequences than the factitious Circean enchantress of male legend. The archetype of the corruptive female temptress pervades traditional depictions of the Fall which since the late twelfth century often portrayed the serpent with a woman's face. But the Lady of *Comus* revised the Miltonic indictment of Eve. In contrast to *Paradise Lost*, the new Eve of *Comus* – the unnamed Lady – is triumphant in her fortitude, firmly resisting temptation by drawing on resources independent of male protectors. Embedded in *Comus* is the gothic scenario of the innocent in distress, but its essential emphasis is on self-reliance rather than victimization. In this temptation, the woman resists from innate strength, rather than succumbing from innate weakness.

Elements of the gothic plot had existed long before Radcliffe or Milton – the heroine in distress was the staple of medieval and seventeenth-century French romance, and eighteenth-century Richardsonian romance. But Radcliffe sought a particular genealogy in her references to *Comus*, a context for discussing female action under threat of assault. Thus in *The Mysteries of Udolpho* Emily is visibly circumstanced like the Lady in *Comus*, held "prisoner" by the voluptuary Montoni, whose distant carousals in the castle of Udolpho are prefaced by quotes describing Comus advancing with his retinue. Schedoni in *The Italian* schemes against Ellena under a motto from *Comus*, "'under fair pretence of friendly ends.'" When Adeline in *The Romance of the Forest* is abducted from her solitary walk by the Marquis de Montalt, she finds herself secured in a room from which "all chance of escape was removed," but resplendent with tempting collations, silver cupids, an imposing bed, and a mural of Tasso's Circean temptress Armida: "the whole seemed the works of enchantment." Adeline asks "Is this a charm to lure me to destruction?" but unlike the immured Lady of *Comus*, it is in her power to do more than resist: she searches the room and resourcefully makes an escape.[23] Subsequent women novelists investigated less fortunate outcomes: in Wollstonecraft's *The Wrongs of Woman* (1798), the captive Maria yields to her delusive infatuation with Darnford under a quotation from *Comus*; the narrator of Mary Hays's *Victim of Prejudice* (1799) is sexually assaulted when she refuses her captor's blandishments and tries to creep by the Bacchanal.

Comus was a far more visible and visualized text for the Romantic audience than it is now, since it had been performed with some regularity throughout the eighteenth century in various stagings, which were widely available in print in early nineteenth-century drama anthologies.[24] Acting the role of the Lady was the highlight of Elizabeth Griffith's debut season on the Dublin stage. Clara Reeve and Joanna Baillie both approved of *Comus*, and Hester Thrale Piozzi described her adaptation of Samuel Johnson's fable "The Fountains" as "A Masque – in the Manner of Milton's *Comus*."[25]

It must always remain an issue in Milton studies whether Milton has been credited by feminists with a favorable reading he but slightly deserves. Yet it is apparent these modern readings are in good company: since at least the Romantic era women have appropriated Milton for their own purposes just as men have done. Coleridge, for example, credited himself as the first to call the moly passage of *Comus* an allegory of the Eucharist.[26] Indeed, Blake's illustrations of the poem (which show the semiclad Comus leading his followers, waving the wand he uses to immobilize the Lady), provide an illuminating example of contemporary male appropriation of the Miltonic tradition. Typical of Blake's personal iconography, there is some implied reproach in depicting the Lady as meekly shrinking from the revelry; yet this aspect of Blake's *Comus* is a testament to the gendering of literary readings, since it promoted a sexual ideology women could not realistically share. Keats's "Spirit here that reignest" (1818) epitomizes the male bon vivant use of *Comus*: women writers identified with the captive Lady, whereas Keats exclaims, "I join in the glee ... fresh from the banquet of Comus!"[27]

Women had little choice in this domain, and were far more likely to be blamed for wandering than commended for initiative. Eighteenth-century commentators on *Comus* such as Samuel Johnson and Thomas Warton debated the irresponsibility of the brothers in leaving the Lady unescorted, but her actions generally elicited neither reproach nor interest from male commentators. Echoes of the *Comus* dispute reverberate in Walter Scott's comments on Radcliffe's captive women; but in questioning the judgment of her female characters' lone explorations, he essentially blamed the victims for taking liberties: "Her heroines voluntarily expose themselves to situations, which in nature a lonely female would certainly have avoided. They are too apt to choose the midnight hour for investigating the mysteries of a deserted chamber."[28] Moreover, Scott, like Coleridge, and indeed, most contemporary male theorists of the gothic, failed to observe that most of the terrors in Radcliffe do not, in fact, concern the supernatural. Rather, they are the specifically female terrors of physical assault: terrors, as has been often observed, that women authors of sentimental and gothic novels do not explicitly chronicle, unlike novelists such as Samuel Richardson or Matthew "Monk" Lewis who permit scenes of sexual assault and counsel the restitution of Lucretia.

The implicit terrors of violence which threaten Radcliffe's captive female characters always remain unstated: the epigraph on the title page of *Udolpho* "Tells of a nameless deed." Emily in *Udolpho* considers Montoni's "presence a protection, though she knew not what she should fear"; she is "apprehensive of – she scarcely knew what." Taken to a remote house inhabited by ruffians, Ellena in *The Italian* is said to fear "she was brought hither" to be assassinated, but the lonely situation implies other terrors. Later she is hesitant of the supposedly paternal caresses of Schedoni when she realizes she has only his word for his kinship. A similar scenario lies unstated behind Schedoni's confession about her mother's remarriage: "'My passion would no longer be trifled with. I caused her to be carried from my house, and she was afterwards willing to retrieve her honour by the marriage vow.'" When Montoni withdraws his protection from Emily, it is soon apparent that it refers to her protection from sexual assault from his carousing friends. All of the novels depict women vulnerably assigned remote bedchambers with secret doorways that cannot be secured: they repose fully dressed, ready to flee.[29] *Comus* similarly leaves the threats to the Lady unstated but clear: "'O poor hapless Nightingale,' thought I," laments the Spirit, in tacit allusion to the assault against Philomela. Such fears are clear to female readers without delineation.

Women writers, like women travellers, tread uncertain ground, and the threat of sexual assault remained unstated in novels for reasons of their own virtue as well as that of their heroines. Romantic biographical theories of reading so explicitly equated texts with private life that any plot element might be inferred as personal experience. Women could not write novels about explicit transgressions and travel in good company as "Monk" Lewis did. It is worth noting, however, that the questionable endorsement of Donatien de Sade in favoring Lewis's *The Monk* over Radcliffe, was a preference shared with *Northanger Abbey*'s oafish John Thorpe.[30]

Even the conservative Anna Laetitia Barbauld voiced her qualms about Richardson's depiction of the heroine in distress: "That *Clarissa* is a highly moral work, has been always allowed; – but what is the moral?" Its indubitable merit, however, lay in its kinship with *Comus*: "In all ages, something saintly has been attached to the idea of unblemished chastity. Hence the dignity of the lady in *Comus*."[31] As read by Radcliffe, however, *Comus* was not merely a work about chastity at any cost, for its ending was triumphant. In contrast to the sexual assaults of *The Monk* or suicidal asthenia of *Clarissa* (after Pamela's parents instruct her, "resolve to lose your life sooner than your virtue," she declares, "May I ... *Lucretia* like, justify myself with my death"), *Comus* urges rational fortitude. The final chapter of *Udolpho* begins with a motto from the Spirit's closing affirmative song in *Comus*, and ends with "the prospect of rational happiness."[32]

In *Comus* the Lady's chief action is her ability to resist ("thou canst not touch the freedom of my mind"); she remains silent from the time Comus is routed midsentence ("Be wise, and taste —") through her release by the river goddess Sabrina. But Romantic women such as Radcliffe read the Lady in *Comus* as initiating new possibilities for women. Although Emily in *Udolpho* resolves she cannot be forced into marriage if she refuses to speak the words of the ceremony – just as in *Comus* the Lady's self-defence is passive – she finds herself making progressively more active choices. The Lady of *Comus* has only the power to refuse; a century and a half later, gothic heroines have the power to act. Radcliffe's heroines, on their own behalf and for the welfare of others, examine, initiate action, and explore – the very role Scott found unfathomable in reading about women who choose "investigating" situations they might have "avoided." Indeed, William Beckford's gothic parody, *Modern Novel Writing* (1796), assumed transgressing heroines would recite *Comus* – having fled from an assignation interrupted by her husband, "the virtuous and much injured" Amelia demurely consoles herself with a malapropic speech, "O where else / Shall I *deform* my *unattainted* feet."[33]

Contemporary uses of the *Comus* legend were not as simple as Barbauld wanted to believe. In 1798 Maria Edgeworth declared *Comus* too complex and unsuitable for children; but the more radical Charlotte Smith deemed it an appropriate vehicle for a children's version of Radcliffe's didactic gothic. In the final story of Smith's *Minor Morals*, three girls walking in a forest find themselves at nightfall ominously trailed by a mysterious figure, who first appears supernatural, then proposes to conduct them to a secluded house (alarms afterwards euphemized, once introductions prove him to be the son of a family friend, as "fears of making an improper acquaintance"); they muster courage by imagining "some friendly shepherd coming to protect us wandering virgins" amid the "'close dungeon of innumerable boughs,'" a favorite quote of Radcliffe also. The gothic apprehensions of the scene are intermingled with the Lady's fortifying sanction for adventures otherwise proscribed: "It is only fancying ourselves like the wandering lady in Comus, and we may indulge all sorts of romantic visions." The story's ending projects a future marriage with the new irregularly made acquaintance.[34] One might ask of Smith as well, but what is the moral? If Milton's text did not itself authorize roaming, it provided a vocabulary for women writers to indulge their own "romantic visions" in extending at least some male Romantic privileges to female characters.

In the telecommunications era it is difficult to recapture the eighteenth- and nineteenth-century experience of Milton's vivid imagery in the minor poems, which became staples of landscape description. Glimpses of castle towers through the treetops ("L'Allegro"), tournaments and enchanted forests ("Il Penseroso"), the dungeon of innumerous boughs (*Comus*), were gothic elements that lingered in the picturesque imagination and reappeared throughout the scenic vocabulary of poetry and prose. Early literary historians often cited as evidence of Milton's interest in romance "L'Allegro"'s "goblin," "tow'red cities" and "knights and barons," and "Il Penseroso"'s "tourneys" and "trophies," its reference to Chaucer's unfinished Squire's Tale, and above all, the "Forests and enchantments drear, / Where more is meant than meets the ear" (the latter becoming something of a motto – like Shakespeare's "how easily is a bush supposed a bear" – for the susceptibility of the imagination to superstition and to literary suggestion). When Radcliffe ties up loose ends by revealing the rational explanations behind mysterious events in *Udolpho*, she inserts her own storytelling into the romance lineage of Milton and Chaucer by quoting "Il Penseroso"'s lines, "Call up him, that left half told / The story of Cambuscan bold." Touring the English lake district she quotes *Comus* on how the "dire chimaeras and enchanted isles" of the old "sage poets" taught their intellectual offspring the "power to cheat the eye with blear illusion / And give it false presentments."[35]

The twin morning and evening poems enjoyed a revival from mid-century onward, and despite Wordsworth's mistaken assertion at the turn of the century that "L'Allegro" and "Il Penseroso" were little known, a considerable vogue for imitating the paired poems arose after 1750, at least in part due to the Wartons' critical attention. In 1756 Joseph Warton wrote in his *Essay on Pope* that the poems had become "now universally known," since Handel set them to music; Thomas Warton, editing the minor poems in 1785, named them "the two first descriptive poems in the English language." Hugh Blair, in his *Lectures on Rhetoric and Belles Lettres* (1783), said the twin poems supplied "the storehouse whence many succeeding Poets have enriched their descriptions." The two poems cued eighteenth-century descriptive poets such as Thomson, Cowper, Darwin, and the Wartons, as well as the "melancholy school" of Collins, Gray, and Young. Stuart Curran identifies twin poems in the works of Helen Maria Williams, Mary Robinson, Hannah Cowley, and Ann Yearsley.[36] "L'Allegro" and "Il Penseroso" were touchstones for the

Romantic exploration of the subjectivity of perception and the interaction of scenery and the imagination, and underlie Radcliffe's special interest in exploring the duress of distorted perception, and testing readerly susceptibility to the description of seemingly supernatural events.

Eighteenth-century critical analysis of the companion poems concentrated on debating the relationship between landscape description and mood. Hurd considered the poems therapeutic, causing favorable and deleting unfavorable emotions: in "Il Penseroso" Milton uses "the same kind of image to sooth melancholy which he had before given to excite mirth." Blair understood the poem as arousing the associative operations of the mind, presenting "expressive images" that "recal a number of similar ideas of the melancholy kind." Richard Richardson said Milton influenced mood through unified images, so "all the emotions the poet excites are of one character and complexion." Lewis Theobald argued that "more capable Readers" recognize in Milton's parallelism not simply that descriptive poetry induces moods, but that "the Images, in each Poem, which he raises to excite Mirth and Melancholy, are exactly the same, only shewn in different Attitudes," whereas inferior writers would use "contrary Images" to raise "contrary Passions." Johnson, the century's culminating and most influential commentator on Milton, viewed the twin poems not merely as illustrating or generating moods, but as diagnosing how the mind interacts with its setting: "The author's design is not, what Theobald has remarked, merely to shew how objects derived their colours from the mind, by representing the operation of the same things upon the gay and the melancholy temper, or upon the same man as he is differently disposed; but rather how, among the successive variety of appearances, every disposition of mind takes hold on those by which it may be gratified."[37]

Johnson clearly preferred the introspective "*pensive* man" to the "man of *chearfulness*," who "delights himself at night with the fanciful narratives of superstitious ignorance" and unreflectively "mingles a mere spectator" at the plays of Jonson and Shakespeare. "Il Penseroso"'s most famous Romantic successor, Keats's "Ode on Melancholy" (1820), reflects a continuing preference evident throughout the era, shared by Radcliffe. Scott traced *Udolpho*'s poem "To Melancholy" to Fletcher's *The Nice Valour*, the same source eighteenth-century critics cited for Milton's "Il Penseroso." Radcliffe's favorable characters invariably possess an inspired view of melancholy: Adeline wanders in the woods where "images insensibly soothed her sorrow, and inspired her with that soft and pleasing melancholy, so dear to the feeling mind"; Ellena experiences the "solemn kind of melancholy, which a view of stupendous objects inspires"; Emily's family enjoys the "melancholy and pleasing shade" of twilight, and Valancourt, foreshadowing Wordsworth at

Tintern Abbey, commends landscapes that "inspire that delicious melancholy" and "waken our best and purest feelings, disposing us to benevolence, pity, and friendship."[38]

The question Johnson posed of "L'Allegro" and "Il Penseroso," whether "objects derive their colours from the mind" or whether "every disposition of mind takes hold on those by which it may be gratified" adumbrated the Romantic inquiry into the subjectivity of perception. Milton's poems clearly coincided with the Romantic interest in the relationship of the mind and nature. But while the union of mood and scenery was everywhere evident in Milton's depictions, the precise nature of the interrelation had been left unexplained – motivating a central avenue of Romantic inquiry.

The companion poems appear as descriptive and pictorial landmarks throughout the era, ranging from Wordsworth's definition of the "Idyllium" in the "Preface" to *Poems* (1815) ("L'Allegro" and "Il Penseroso" treat "characters, manners and sentiments ... in conjunction with the appearances of Nature"), to De Quincey's description of the pleasures of opium in the 1821 *Confessions of an English Opium Eater* ("in his happiest state, the opium-eater cannot present himself in the character of *l'Allegro*: even then he speaks and thinks as becomes *Il Penseroso*"). Even in parody, one index of cultural saturation, the hero of Thomas Love Peacock's *Nightmare Abbey* (1818) cannot decide which of two women to choose, "the Allegra or the Penserosa." Descriptive references drawn from the twin poems appear in novels of manners such as Frances Burney's *Cecilia* (1782) and Maria Edgeworth's *Belinda* (1801), and unfailingly throughout the literature of landscape appreciation, where the picturesque castle turret "bosom'd" in the trees pops up in William Gilpin's *Observations on the River Wye* (1782), Richard Payne Knight's *The Landscape* (1794), and Humphrey Repton's "Red Book" for improving the grounds of Blaise Castle (1796). Blake's twelve illustrations of "L'Allegro" and "Il Penseroso" are indicative of contemporaneous readings in their concern with elements of the gothic and how the human imagination responds to nature under the influence of literary tradition. A towering monster dominates the fifth image of the "L'Allegro" series, "The Goblin"; the sixth image, "The Youthful Poets Dream," depicts Jonson and Shakespeare transmitting their wisdom to a sleeping poet writing in a book alongside a stream – a scene resembling the fifth image of Blake's "Il Penseroso," known as "Milton Sleeping on a Bank," as well as Radcliffe's earlier *Udolpho* poem, "To Melancholy" ("the wild romantic dream, / That meets the poet's musing eye / As, on the bank of shadowy stream, / He breathes to her the fervid sigh").[39]

Coleridge's *Lyrical Ballads* contribution, "The Nightingale: A Conversational Poem," borrows the gothic setting of Milton's twin poems to renounce the way literary preconceptions impose clichés about nature. He quotes "Il Penseroso" – "'Most musical, most melancholy' bird!" – to indict the poetic habit of unthinkingly repeating conventionalized images (as he had done two years earlier in "To the Nightingale") instead of contemplating nature directly: "Many a poet echoes the conceit ... When he had better far have stretched his limbs / Beside a brook in mossy forest-dell." Elsewhere in *Lyrical Ballads*, "Expostulation and Reply" and "The Tables Turned," which are quietly Wordsworth's own twin morning and evening poems, prescribe "wise passiveness" to optimize the perception of nature since we "cannot choose but see" anyway. Significantly enough, the initial illustration of the susceptibility of perception in *The Prelude* – the first test of the extent to which the mind is lord and master – is a gothic episode ([1850] XII.225–69). In boyhood, Wordsworth fled in ineffable terror from the gibbet near Penrith, amid a "visionary dreariness"; returning with loved ones as an adult, he finds the same landscape suffused with "a spirit of pleasure."

For Radcliffe, too, perception is a matter of reciprocity between the mind and nature. If she lacks direct access to the discourse of philosophical tradition, Radcliffe stands with Wordsworth and Coleridge in exploring the psychology of the mind and the impressionability and complex subjectivity of human experience, by chronicling the interplay of voluntary and involuntary response to natural phenomena – where more is meant than meets the ear.

Udolpho repeatedly introduces the difficulty of defining an impartial and immutable experience. Crossing the mountains inspires Emily with awe; suggests to her aunt the splendor of palaces ahead; reminds Montoni of Hannibal's passage over the Alps. When the family of the Count de Villefort arrive at Chateau-le-Blanc, individual perception of the setting is as subjective as Wordsworth's experience of Penrith: Blanche finds only delight, her stepmother only discontent, the fatuous romance-reading Mademoiselle Bearn only a setting of trapdoors and ghosts. Revisiting scenery produces different responses in the same person at different times. The Count himself had known the Chateau "at that age when the mind is particularly sensible to impressions," and "though he had passed a long intervening period amidst the vexations and tumults of public affairs, which too frequently corrode the heart ... the shades of Languedoc and the grandeur of its distant scenery had never been remembered by him with indifference." With the same voice found so often in Wordsworth, he meditates on his shifting perspective: "'though the grand features of the scenery admit of no change, they impress me with sensations very different from those I formerly experienced ... the landscape is not changed, but time has changed me.'"[40]

Nineteenth-century readers recognized Radcliffe's kinship to the discourse of perception in Romantic poetry. Julia Kavanagh wrote that the Count de

Villefort's impression of the Chateau ("the illusion, which gave spirit to the colouring of nature, is fading fast") reminded her of Wordsworth's "Immortality Ode" ("things which I have seen I now can see no more"). She called Radcliffe a poetic novelist, as had Scott, and identified her as the intellectual quarry for the metrical poets: "Vulgar minds," Kavanagh explained, "only took up the false and the horrible … but to fine poetical natures like Byron's, Wordsworth's, Mrs. Hemans's, and many of their generation" Radcliffe's works "were eminently suggestive." Thomas Noon Talfourd located Radcliffe's connections to Milton and Wordsworth – recommending that her readers assume "that 'wise passiveness,' in which the mind should listen to the soft murmur of her 'most musical, most melancholy' spells" – and found in her writings the primal aeolian impulses of childhood common to the Romantic poets: "Few there are, who, in childhood, have not experienced some strange visiting of serious thought, gently agitating the soul like the wind."[41]

Clearly "L'Allegro" and "Il Penseroso" inspired prose and metrical commentaries on the interaction of landscape and the mind. But whereas Johnson tried to polarize responses to the poem – does the mood in which we seek out nature determine the features we emphasize, or do settings inspire different reflections? – the Romantics explored how the action of the mind on scenery and scenery on the mind less predictably interfuse. As early as *A Sicilian Romance*, Radcliffe observes "We are operated upon by objects whose impressions are variable as they are indefinable." At the same time, every perception is freighted with preoccupations. *A Sicilian Romance* many times offers the reminder that "in other circumstances," characters would have contemplated the same scene "with rapture," or responded "with sensations of congenial tranquillity."[42]

Radcliffe's practice of tracing mysteries to their rational causes underscored how the susceptibility of perception under duress, characteristic of the gothic, illustrates the inescapable subjectivity of reading human behavior, landscape, or seemingly supernatural events. In *The Romance of the Forest*, Madame La Motte, her imagination "heated by the brooding of jealousy," finds that her discontent "taught her to misconstrue"; Adeline counsels La Motte not to "deceive yourself, by suffering the cloud of sorrow to tinge every object you look upon." And perhaps the main action of *Udolpho* lies in charting how accumulating strain makes it difficult for Emily to judge situations and resist superstitious doubts: "her mind, long harassed by distress, now yielded to imaginary terrors"; "the influence of superstition now gained on the weakness of her long-harassed mind"; she "thought she saw something glide along into the obscurer part of the room. Her spirits had been much affected by the surrounding scene, or it is probable this circumstance, whether real or

imaginary, would not have affected her in the degree it did." To the attentive
reader, however, no superstition or false presage goes without its warning:
"her imagination, ever awake to circumstance, suggested even more terrors,
than her reason could justify"; "Long-suffering had made her spirits peculiarly
sensible to terror, and liable to be affected by the illusions of superstition ... Yet
reason told her, that this was a wild conjecture." Radcliffe's novels are
concerned not with a simple depiction of gothic terrors, but in exploring the
mechanisms which awaken superstition. Thus she tests her readers' susceptibility to gothic and folk tradition by withholding the rational explanations for supernatural events. In *Udolpho* she inscribes the ghost story
Ludovico peruses just before he mysteriously vanishes from the haunted
chamber; when he is recovered, characters are ashamed at their conjectures of
supernatural intervention, a reminder turned toward her audience with
Ludovico's own testimony: "it was the story I had been reading that affected
my spirits."[43]
The very mutability of perception bespeaks the unreliability of the
imagination. In the gothic, terror depends on whether the mind is prepared to
receive incidents as rational or superstitious, and may well arise in one context
but not another. Wordsworth's flight from the gibbet near Penrith resembles
more than one scene of the terror of wandering travellers in Radcliffe's novels
as they encounter ominous sights at susceptible moments. When Emily and St.
Aubert begin to fear they have lost their way, "an object not less terrific struck
her, – a gibbet standing on a point of rock near the entrance of the pass ...
hieroglyphics that told a plain and dreadful story ... it threw a gloom over her
spirits, and made her anxious to hasten forward." Similarly, when Blanche
and the Count de Villefort anxiously search for shelter at dusk "their labour,
however, was not rewarded, nor their apprehensions soothed; for, on reaching
the object of their search, they discovered a monumental cross, which marked
the spot to have been polluted by murder"; the guide relates the story "as if
the sound of his own voice frightened him ... and the travellers, now alarmed,
quitted this scene of solitary horror." For criminally inclined characters such
as Schedoni and Montoni, the action of conscience spurs supernatural illusions
and guilty hallucinations (cued by *Macbeth* and *Comus*, "He that hides a dark
soul and foul thoughts ... Himself is his own dungeon"). Radcliffe and
contemporaries such as Byron and Coleridge were interested in exploring the
dark psychology of the mind – though Milton himself was to elucidate the
secular pairing of "L'Allegro" and "Il Penseroso" in a Christian context in
Paradise Lost: "The mind is its own place, and in itself / Can make a Heav'n
of Hell, a Hell of Heav'n," exemplified in Adam's consolatory "paradise
within thee" and Satan's self-torment "myself am Hell."[44]
In all of Radcliffe's novels, reactions to deserted and ruined buildings

illuminate characters' minds. Rome for Byron and Tintern Abbey for Wordsworth also triggered reflections based on the mind's engagement with its own and the historical past; Wordsworth selected the "gothic Church" to symbolize the relationship among his intellectual projects. Coleridge, who reviewed Radcliffe favorably and fancied himself something of an authority on the supernatural after the success of the "Ancient Mariner," closed the first volume of the *Biographia Literaria* (1817) describing his own model of the imagination as a scene from a gothic novel: "placed, and left alone, in one of our largest Gothic cathedrals in a gusty moonlight night of autumn ... often in palpable darkness not without a chilly sensation of terror," the literary tradition appears a set of leering gargoyles, "stonework images of great men ... whom I had been taught to venerate as almost super-human in magnitude of intellect, I found perched in little fret-work niches, as grotesque dwarfs." Volume Two of the *Biographia* reopens on the same subject; the description Coleridge gives of his *Lyrical Ballads* task to create supernatural characters and "procure for these shadows of imagination that willing suspension of disbelief for the moment which constitutes poetic faith" coincides with Radcliffe's own explanation in "On the Supernatural in Poetry": the "illusions of the imagination" depend not on awakening an actual belief in supernatural beings, but in effectively awakening the susceptibility of "those who have bowed the willing soul to the poet."[45]

As Nina Auerbach has remarked, even the most canonical of woman writers, Jane Austen, is rarely praised for what she does without citing what she fails to do. Radcliffe similarly has never been accorded entirely equal status, among her contemporaries or succeeding generations. The early twentieth century saw critics actively revive Radcliffe's name as an emblem of the folly of popular taste; as Terry Castle observes, "No English writer of such historic importance and diverse influence has been so often trivialized."[46]

In the present day we have our own ambiguous responses to Romantic women writers. Sonia Hofkosh sympathetically depicts rebellious women as forced to turn to "debilitating strategies of indirection and accommodation"; Margaret Homans describes them as "dislocated from the ability to feel that they are speaking their own language."[47] Yet indirection and defamiliarizing ordinary language and experience have always been among the chief strategies of literature. The act of demanding entitlement to male strategies is as important as refusing conformity. Strategic appropriation of the male tradition might be distrusted as ideologically problematic, but only if we define the subversive as having only one task, writing about things that do not interest men. The problem is that the "subversive" can mean anything: writing about women's traditional tasks can be subversive if we define it as writing about things that don't interest men, or it can be viewed as a retrogressive and docile reinforcement of women's place. Refusing to demand access to cultural traditions can be as problematic as borrowing them; as Wollstonecraft says of women who refuse "to spurn their chains" and demand entitlement: "Instead of asserting their birthright, they quietly lick the dust."[48]

Terry Lovell has emphasized the necessity of studying artistic forms associated with women, whatever their rank in the cultural hierarchy may be.[49] In this enterprise, we need to recognize that Radcliffe – the most famous novelist of the Romantic era in the years before *Waverley* – followed in the steps of radical tract writers like Mary Wollstonecraft, Catherine Macaulay, and Helen Maria Williams, by transforming a genre traditionally available to women. Beyond the radicalism of Miltonic appropriation, Radcliffe's novels made the feminist enterprise accessible to the uninitiated, showing women characters travelling, forming cross-class alliances, educating themselves, and securing their own finances – in effect, translating the radical agenda into a populist form. If the radical implications of Radcliffe have been today forgotten, it is only necessary to recollect the illuminating combination of slurs that a retrospective account gave of contemporary "calumnies about Mrs. Radcliffe, the blue-stocking, the sorceress, the Eumenide"; or a 1797 squib in the *Monthly Magazine* entitled "Terrorist System of Novel-Writing" which warned of what "the revolution" in novel-writing had precipitated "if not in our streets, and in our fields, at least in our circulating libraries, and in our closets": "Maximilian Robespierre, with his system of terror... taught our novelists ... to frighten and to instruct."[50]

Envious contemporaries wished to cast Radcliffe as a trifler, yet her works entailed an erudition and transmutation of conventions that defied common expectations for novels and for women writers. She attained a popular patronage that countered fit-though-few assumptions, and in her popularization of Miltonic elements, the novels of Radcliffe attempted to resolve one of the dilemmas of early industrial culture, the problem of reconciling the aspirations of the writer with the capacity of the audience. It is worth considering the "subversiveness" of the much-maligned circulating library in diffusing a body of literature common to women as classical education had done for men. For women especially, the desire to accommodate the prestige of the literary text and support the vocation of the writer had only one solution, the popular marketplace. Critical resentment concerning novels partly arose from confusion about the new audience and new market forces. Indeed, contemporary suspicion of Radcliffe's intellectual integrity reveals critics' bewilderment at the new bridging of trained readers and mass audience, which would later be more favorably regarded in writers such as Dickens, Brontë, and Balzac.[51] Although many familiar Romantic writers such as Wordsworth and Coleridge remained hostile to reconciliation with new market forces, Radcliffe was one of a number of prominent figures, including the most prolific writer of the era, William Cobbett, who attempted to come to terms with the new audiences brought into the cultural arena by technological advances in printing, circulating libraries, the growing accessibility of cheaper books, and the increasingly widespread, albeit shallower, literacy that was redefining the concept of the literary tradition.

NOTES

1 Ann Radcliffe (1764–1823), *The Castles of Athlin and Dunbayne* (London: Hookham, 1789); *A Sicilian Romance*, 2 vols. (London: Hookham, 1790); *The Romance of the Forest*, 3 vols. (London: Hookham and Carpenter, 1791); *The Mysteries of Udolpho*, 4 vols. (London: Robinson, 1794); *A Journey Made in the Summer of 1794, through Holland and the Western Frontier of Germany, with a Return Down the Rhine: to which are added Observations during a Tour to the Lakes of Lancashire, Westmoreland, and Cumberland* (London: Robinson, 1795); *The Italian*, 3 vols. (London: Cadell and Davies, 1797); and the posthumous "On the Supernatural in Poetry," *New Monthly Magazine* 16 (1826): 145–52, and *Gaston de Blondeville*, 4 vols. (London: Colburn, 1826). Citations from commonly available works will indicate volume and chapter numbers as well as, where appropriate, page references.

2 Wollstonecraft, *Vindication of the Rights of Woman* (1792) in *Works*, ed. Janet Todd and Marilyn Butler (New York: New York University Press, 1989), 5: 182. On Romantic epistemology, see Cafarelli, *Prose in the Age of Poets: Romanticism and Biographical Narrative* (Philadelphia: University of Pennsylvania Press, 1990), 119–20; E. Michael Thron, "Thomas De Quincey and the Fall of Literature," in *Thomas De Quincey: Bicentenary Studies*, ed. Robert Lance Snyder (Norman: University of Oklahoma Press, 1985), 9.

3 Nina Baym, "Melodramas of Beset Manhood: How Theories of American Fiction Exclude Women Authors," *American Quarterly* 33 (1981): 123–39.

4 Mary Brunton, letter of 15 August 1814, in *Emmeline ... to which is prefixed a Memoir of her Life* [by her husband Alexander Brunton], (London: Murray, 1819), lxxiv.

5 Scott, "Radcliffe," *Miscellaneous Prose Works*, 6 vols. (Edinburgh: Cadell, 1827), 3: 406–7; De Quincey, General Preface to *Selections Grave and Gay*, 14 vols. (Edinburgh: Hogg, 1853–60), 1: xviii. Compare Wordsworth's "there neither is, nor can be, any *essential* difference between the language of prose and metrical composition" (1802 Preface to *Lyrical Ballads*); Shelley's "The distinction between poets and prose writers is a vulgar error" (*A Defence of Poetry*, in *Shelley's Poetry and Prose*, 484); and Byron's "Good prose resolves itself into blank verse," in Thomas Medwin, *Conversations of Lord Byron* (1824), ed. Ernest J. Lovell (Princeton: Princeton University Press, 1966), 136.

6 J. M. S. Tompkins, *Ann Radcliffe and Her Influence on Later Writers* (New York: Arno, 1980), 27, believes Radcliffe set the fashion for epigraphs and interspersing poetry. "Poetic mottos admirably chosen," remarked Anna Seward in a 3 August 1794 letter, *Letters* (Edinburgh: Constable, 1811), 3: 390.

7 Harold Bloom, *The Anxiety of Influence* (London: Oxford University Press, 1973) and *A Map of Misreading* (London: Oxford University Press, 1975); Sandra M. Gilbert and

Susan Gubar, *The Madwoman in the Attic* (New Haven: Yale University Press, 1979), 46–49; Annette Kolodny, "A Map for Rereading: Gender and the Interpretation of Literary Texts," *New Literary History* 11 (1980): 451–67; Elaine Showalter, "Feminist Criticism in the Wilderness" (1981), in *Feminist Criticism* (New York: Pantheon, 1985), 265; Pamela Di Pesa, "The Imperious Muse: Some Observations of Women, Nature, and the Poetic Tradition," in *Feminist Criticism*, ed. C. L. Brown and K. Olsen (Metuchen, New Jersey: Scarecrow Press, 1978).

8 De Quincey says Coleridge "thought fit positively to deny he was indebted to Milton" ("Coleridge," *Literary Reminiscences*, 2 vols. [Boston: Ticknor, Reed, and Fields, 1851] 1: 158); Hazlitt, in "My First Acquaintance with Poets" (1823), said Wordsworth would not "own the obligation" to Bernardin de Saint-Pierre's *Paul et Virginie*; Leigh Hunt, *Lord Byron and Some of his Contemporaries* (London: Colburn, 1828), 1: 76, reports that when Byron took visitors to his library "he was anxious to show you that he possessed no Shakspeare and Milton; 'because,' he said, 'he had been accused of borrowing from them.'"

9 William Duff, *An Essay on Original Genius* (1767), ed. John L. Mahoney (Gainesville: Scholars' Facsimiles, 1964), 260–96; Edward Young, *Conjectures on Original Composition* (1759), ed. Edith J. Morley (London: Longmans, 1918), 15: "some are pupils of nature only, nor go farther to school."

10 Janet Todd, *The Sign of Angellica: Women, Writing, and Fiction, 1660–1800* (New York: Columbia University Press, 1989), 214, quotes Barbauld's "The Rights of Woman" (written c.1795, printed 1825) which repudiated Wollstonecraft's *Vindication of the Rights of Woman*; Austen, letter to Cassandra Austen, 14 January 1796, *Jane Austen's Letters to her Sister Cassandra and Others*, ed. R. W. Chapman, 2nd. revised edition (Oxford: Oxford University Press, 1979), 5. Mary Poovey, *The Proper Lady and the Woman Writer* (Chicago: University of Chicago Press, 1984), 35, quotes Johnson, *Rambler* 93 (1751), and Hannah More, *Strictures on the Modern System of Female Education*, 2 vols. (London: Cadell and Davies, 1799), *Works of Hannah More*, 8 vols. (London: Cadell and Davies, 1801), 8: 14.

11 Anne Katherine Elwood, *Memoirs of the Literary Ladies of England* (London: Colburn, 1843), 2: 167–68; Kazlitt Arvine, *Cyclopedia of Anecdotes of Literature and the Fine Arts* (Boston: Gould and Lincoln, 1852), 268–71, claimed Radcliffe's later silence was broken only on the subject of "puddings and gooseberry tarts"; on similar reassurances by earlier women writers, see Rebecca Gould Gibson, "'My Want of Skill': Apologias of British Women Poets, 1660–1800," in *Eighteenth-Century Women and the Arts*, ed. Frederick M. Keener and Susan E. Lorsch (New York: Greenwood Press, 1988), 79–86.

12 Julia Kavanagh, *English Women of Letters* (London: Hurst and Blackett, 1863), 2: 255. The *Journey*, 423, 434, contains Latin references, although the *Annual Biography and Obituary for the Year 1824* (London: Longman, Hurst, etc., 1824), 99, reported she "would desire to hear passages repeated from the Latin and Greek classics; requiring, at intervals, the most literal translations that could be given."

13 Hazlitt, "The Periodical Press," *Edinburgh Review* 38 (1823): 360; Scott, "Radcliffe," *Godey's Magazine and Lady's Book* 45 (1852): 225–27; Arvine, *Cyclopedia of Anecdotes*, 268–71; *Annual Biography*, 96–97; *New Monthly Magazine*, n.s. 9 (1823): 233; see also Maurice Lévy, *Le Roman "gothique" anglais, 1764–1824* (Toulouse: Publications de la Faculté, 1968), 223–35; E. B. Murray, *Ann Radcliffe* (New York: Twayne, 1972), 16;

Aline Grant, *Ann Radcliffe: A Biography* (Denver: Swallow, 1951), 143–44; Montague Summers, *The Gothic Quest* (1938; reprint, New York: Russell and Russell, 1964), 409; S. M. Ellis, "Ann Radcliffe and Her Literary Influence," *Contemporary Review* 123 (1923): 196; Thomas Noon Talfourd, "Memoirs of the Life and Writings of Mrs Radcliffe," in *Gaston de Blondeville*, 1: 95, 102–4; Kavanagh, *English Women of Letters*, 1: 250.

14 Clara Frances McIntyre, *Ann Radcliffe in Relation to her Time*, Yale Studies in English, vol. 62 (New Haven: Yale University Press, 1920), 96.

15 J. M. S. Tompkins, *The Popular Novel in England, 1770–1800* (1932; reprinted Lincoln: University of Nebraska Press, 1967), 92. Mary Jacobus, *Reading Women* (New York: Columbia University Press, 1986), 59–60, observes that the female intuitive talent for sensibility was increasingly being located in children and idiots as well.

16 Nathan Drake, "On Objects of Terror," in *Literary Hours* (1798), revised 4th edition (London: Longman, Hurst, etc., 1820), 1: 273.

17 On the Romantics and *Paradise Lost*, see Bloom, *The Anxiety of Influence*; Mario Praz, *The Romantic Agony*, revised edition (London: Oxford University Press, 1954), 59–63, and Joseph Anthony Wittreich, Jr., *Feminist Milton* (Ithaca: Cornell University Press, 1987). On *Paradise Lost* and the gothic novel see Gilbert and Gubar, *The Madwoman in the Attic*, 187–247, who see in the gothic an allegory for domestic confinement, and Kate Ferguson Ellis, *The Contested Castle: Gothic Novels and the Subversion of Domestic Ideology* (Urbana: University of Illinois Press, 1989), 35, who sees the gothic as justifying disobedience of child against parent.

18 Stuart Curran, "The 'I' Altered," in *Romanticism and Feminism*, ed. Anne K. Mellor (Bloomington: Indiana University Press, 1988), 189, 206, says ten women authored "poems of epic ambition."

19 Richard Hurd, *Letters on Chivalry and Romance* (1762); reprinted in *Works of Richard Hurd* (London: Cadell and Davies, 1811), 4: 239, 296; Thomas Warton, "Of the Origin of Romantic Fiction in Europe," in *The History of English Poetry, From the Close of the Eleventh to the Commencement of the Eighteenth Century* (London: Dodsley etc., 1774–81), 1 (unpaginated); and Clara Reeve, *The Progress of Romance* (1785; reprinted New York: Facsimile Text, 1930), 1: 53–54.

20 Only in the mid-nineteenth century did the concept of divorce initiated by women gain momentum. Lawrence Stone, *Road to Divorce: England, 1530–1987* (Oxford: Oxford University Press, 1990), 16–17, writes: "for women, divorce has always tended to involve serious financial loss ... advocates of radical change, such as John Milton, were always a tiny and unrepresentative minority who spoke only for themselves."

21 Barbara K. Lewalski, "Milton on Women – Yet Once More," *Milton Studies* 6 (1974): 15–17, approvingly argues that Milton allows the Lady freedom to make choices independent of guardians. Kathleen Wall, "A Mask Presented at Ludlow Castle: The Armor of Logos," in *Milton and the Idea of Woman*, ed. Julia M. Walker (Urbana: University of Illinois Press, 1988), 58, less enthusiastically observes that Milton gives the Lady nothing to say after she has been rescued. Richard Halpern, "Puritanism and Maenadism in *A Mask*" in *Rewriting the Renaissance*, ed. Margaret Ferguson, Maureen Quilligan and Nancy J. Vickers (Chicago: University of Chicago Press, 1986), 97, is willing to view *Comus* as exposing the decadence of masquing. Leah S. Marcus, "Justice for Margery Evans: A 'Local' Reading of *Comus*," in *Milton and the Idea of Woman*,

66–85, connects the 1634 debut of *Comus* with a rape case that gained visibility after the victim's petition reached the king in 1633, and suggests that the play posed the question of whether the Lady would be to blame for provoking the encounter.

22 Susan Schibanoff, "Taking the Gold Out of Egypt: The Art of Reading as a Woman," in *Gender and Reading*, ed. Elizabeth A. Flynn and Patrocinio P. Schweickart (Baltimore: Johns Hopkins University Press, 1986), 98.

23 This essay reproduces Radcliffe's quotations from Milton and other authors with her punctuation, capitalization, and orthography. *Italian*, 2 chapter 3; *Udolpho*, 2 chapter 7, 3 chapter 3; *Forest*, 2: 117–18 (chapter 10). There are ten direct quotations from *Comus* in Radcliffe's three major novels, six in her *Journey*.

24 *Comus*, presented 1634, was published anonymously as *A Mask Presented at Ludlow Castle*, 1637; the two-act version introduced by George Colman in 1772 competed in the last quarter of the century with the John Dalton version dating from 1738 which had bestowed the misnomer *Comus*; Thomas J. Dibdin's version was added in 1815. In 1737 it had been acted as *Sabrina, A Masque*; to provide for Milton's granddaughter, Johnson suggested the benefit performance of *Comus* in 1750, for which he wrote the "Prologue" spoken by Garrick. See *Milton 1732–1801: The Critical Heritage*, ed. John T. Shawcross (London: Routledge and Kegan Paul, 1972), 9–10, 169; R. D. Havens, *The Influence of Milton on English Poetry* (Cambridge: Harvard University Press, 1922), 432.

25 Dorothy Hughes Eshleman, *Elizabeth Griffith* (Philadelphia: privately printed, 1949), 3–4; Clara Reeve, *Plans of Education* (1792; reprint, New York: Garland Press, 1974), 60; Joanna Baillie, "Life" in *Dramatic and Poetic Works*, 2nd edition (London: Longman, 1853), viii; James Clifford, *Hester Lynch Piozzi*, 2nd edition (New York: Columbia University Press, 1987), 333.

26 Coleridge, in *The Statesman's Manual*, Appendix B (1816), and his 8 March 1826 letter to Edward Coleridge, says that it was "left to *me* to discover the meaning of, viz., that it is an allegory of the Gospel Dispensation or Redemption by Christ as represented in the Eucharist." *Collected Letters of Samuel Taylor Coleridge*, ed. Earl Leslie Griggs (Oxford: Clarendon Press, 1971), 4: 570; *The Romantics on Milton*, ed. Joseph Anthony Wittreich, Jr. (Cleveland: Press of Case Western Reserve University, 1970), 230, 269.

27 Between 1801 and 1820 Blake illustrated the major works of Milton, including different sets of eight illustrations to *Comus* for two patrons: the Joseph Thomas set, c.1801 (Huntington Library), and the Thomas Butts set, c.1815 (Boston Museum of Fine Arts). See Pamela Dunbar's analysis of Blake's *Comus* illustrations as a "parable" of strife between the sexes, *William Blake's Illustrations to the Poetry of Milton* (Oxford: Clarendon Press, 1980), 9–34; Martin Butlin, *The Paintings and Drawings of William Blake* (New Haven: Yale University Press, 1981), 1: 373–78. Joseph Wright of Derby's 1784 canvas *The Lady in Milton's "Comus"* depicted her isolated in a dark forest. For Keats's lines see *Poems*, ed. Stillinger, 295.

28 Scott, "Radcliffe"; in his *Life of Milton* (1779), Johnson allowed the admixture of supernatural characters, but criticized the Brothers' actions as unrealistic: "The action is not probable. A Masque, in those parts where supernatural intervention is admitted, must indeed be given up to all the freaks of imagination: but, so far as the action is merely human it ought to be reasonable, which can hardly be said of the conduct of the two brothers, who, when their sister sinks with fatigue in a pathless wilderness, wander both away in search of berries too far to find their way back, and leave a helpless Lady

to all the sadness and danger of solitude" (*Lives of the English Poets*, ed. George Birkbeck Hill [Oxford: Clarendon Press, 1905] 1: 167–69). Thomas Warton's edition, *Poems Upon Several Occasions* (London: Dodsley, 1785) replied: "Here is no desertion, or neglect of the lady ... they go to procure berries or some other fruit for her immediate relief, and, with great probability, lose their way ... It is certainly a fault, that the Brothers ... enter with so much tranquility, when their sister is lost, and at leisure pronounce philosophical panegyrics on the mysteries of virginity" (265). Henry J. Todd's edition, *The Poetical Works of John Milton* (London: Johnson, etc., 1801), explained: "It would now be dangerous for them to run about an unknown wilderness; and, if they should separate, in order to seek their Sister, they might lose each other." See *Milton 1732–1801: The Critical Heritage*, ed. Shawcross, 322.

29 *Udolpho*, 2: 62–63 (chapter 2); 2: 391 (chapter 9); *Italian*, 2: 243 (chapter 7); 3: 229 (chapter 6).

30 Donatien de Sade, prefatory essay "Idée sur les romans" to *Les Crimes de l'amour* (1800), in *Oeuvres complètes du Marquis de Sade*, ed. Gilbert Lely (Paris: Cercle du Livre Précieux, 1962–64), 10: 15; Todd, *The Sign of Angellica: Women, Writing, and Fiction* 229, observes that instead of the sexual assault and sadism of male writers like Richardson and Lewis, female writers dislocated their female characters to a frightening space.

31 Anna Laetitia Barbauld, "Richardson," in *The British Novelists; with an Essay; and Prefaces Biographical and Critical* (London: Rivington etc., 1810), 1: xxi, xxiv.

32 *Udolpho*, 4: 422, 426 (chapter 19).

33 William Beckford, *Modern Novel Writing, or the Elegant Enthusiast* (1796; reprinted New York: Garland, 1974), 1: 12.

34 Maria Edgeworth, *Practical Education* (1798; reprint, New York: Garland, 1974), 1: 374, said *Comus*, "L'Allegro," and "Il Penseroso" were poems too complex and full of "ancient and modern knowledge" for children. Charlotte Smith, "An Evening Ramble in the Forest," Dialogue VI in *Minor Morals* (London: Sampson, Low, 1798), 2: 132–34; see also *Conversations Introducing Poetry* (London: Johnson, 1804), 1: 105–6.

35 *Udolpho*, 4: 311 (chapter 14); *Journey*, 452–53.

36 Wordsworth's *Essay, Supplementary to the Preface* (1815) claimed the twin poems (written c.1631–34, printed 1645) "were little heard of till more than 150 years after their publication"; the 1800 Preface to *Lyrical Ballads* fretted that Milton was being driven back into neglect by degraded contemporary tastes. Joseph Warton, *An Essay on the Writings and Genius of Pope* (1756; reprint, New York: Garland, 1974), 1: 40; for Thomas Warton's edition of Milton's *Poems* (1785), see *Milton 1732–1801: The Critical Heritage*, ed. Shawcross, 319–20, 232–33; Hugh Blair, *Lectures on Rhetoric and Belles Lettres* (London: Strahan and Cadell, 1783), 2: 375. Handel's settings were printed in 1740. George Sherburn, *The Early Popularity of Milton's Minor Poems* (Chicago: University of Chicago Press, 1920), 78, 147, 171, claims Milton's lyrics were never neglected, but interest was considerably revived in the 1740s; Havens, *The Influence of Milton*, 441, dates the revival to 1742; Curran, "The 'I' Altered," 197.

37 Blair, *Lectures on Rhetoric*, 3: 376; Hurd, *Works*, 4: 293; Richard Richardson, *Mirror* (17 April 1779), see *Milton 1732–1801: The Critical Heritage*, ed. Shawcross, 286–87; Lewis Theobald, Preface to *The Works of Shakespeare* (1733–34), reprint, ed. Hugh G. Dick,

Augustan Reprint Society 20 (Los Angeles: Clark Library, 1949); Johnson, *Lives*, 1: 165–67.

38 *Forest*, 1: 188 (chapter 5); *Italian*, 1: 160–61 (chapter 6); *Udolpho*, 1: 6 (chapter 1); 1: 122 (chapter 4); Keats, "Ode on Melancholy" (1820); Scott, "Radcliffe." Thomas Warton's 1785 edition of Milton's *Poems* noted his debt to Fletcher's song of the melancholy man (see *Milton 1732–1801: The Critical Heritage*, ed. Shawcross, 27, 320), but by mid-century it was already common to gloss *The Nice Valour* (1615–17, printed 1646) as the source for *Il Penseroso*; see *Works of Beaumont and Fletcher*, ed. Lewis Theobald (London: Tonson and Draper, 1750), 10: 366.

39 "To Melancholy," *Udolpho*, 4: 409 (chapter 18). Blake's series of twelve watercolors, c.1815–16, for Thomas Butts (Pierpont Morgan Library) include short descriptions as well as verso titles; the fifth drawing of *Il Penseroso* is usually identified by the first line of Blake's description rather than its title, "Mysterious Dream." See Butlin, *The Paintings and Drawings of William Blake*, 1: 394–401; Dunbar, *William Blake's Illustrations to the Poetry of Milton*, 115–62; W. P. Trent and Chauncey Brewster Tinker, *L'Allegro and Il Penseroso: Milton and Blake* (New York: Limited Editions, 1954).

40 *Udolpho*, 2 chapter 1; 3: 338, 362–63 (chapter 10).

41 Kavanagh, *English Women of Letters*, 1: 330–31; Talfourd, "Memoirs of the Life and Writings of Mrs Radcliffe," in *Gaston de Blondeville*, 111, 121.

42 *Sicilian*, 1 chapter 2; 2 chapters 12, 14.

43 *Forest*, 1: 74 (chapter 2); 1: 198 (chapter 5); *Udolpho*, 2: 155 (chapter 4); 3: 40 (chapter 2); 4: 63 (chapter 4); 2: 173 (chapter 5); 2: 540 (chapter 11).

44 *Udolpho*, 1: 143–44 (chapter 5); 4: 232–33 (chapter 12); *Paradise Lost* I.254–5, XII.587, IV.75. On *Paradise Lost*, see Elizabeth MacAndrew, *The Gothic Tradition in Fiction* (New York: Columbia University Press, 1979), 38.

45 Wordsworth, 1814 Preface to *The Excursion*; reviews of *Udolpho* and *The Italian*, attributed to Coleridge, *Critical Review* 11 (1794): 361–72 and 23 (1798): 166–69; Radcliffe's "On the Supernatural" was printed in 1826, but probably written before 1800.

46 Nina Auerbach, *Romantic Imprisonment* (New York: Columbia University Press, 1985), 3; Terry Castle, "The Spectralization of the other in *The Mysteries of Udolpho*," in *The New 18th Century*, ed. Felicity Nussbaum and Laura Brown (New York: Methuen, 1987), 232.

47 Sonia Hofkosh, "The Writer's Ravishment: Women and the Romantic Author – The Example of Byron" in *Romanticism and Feminism*, ed. Mellor, 98; Margaret Homans, *Women Writers and Poetic Identity* (Princeton: Princeton University Press, 1980), 32.

48 Wollstonecraft, *Vindication*, 5: 121.

49 Terry Lovell, "Writing Like a Woman: A Question of Politics," in *The Politics of Theory*, ed. Francis Barker (Colchester: University of Essex, 1983), 15–26.

50 Arvine, *Cyclopedia of Anecdotes*, 268–71; *Monthly Magazine* 4 (1797): 102–4.

51 See Fredric Jameson, "Reification and Utopia in Mass Culture," *Social Text* 1 (1979): 134, 137–38, on the interdependency of high culture demands (the desire to broach a new "'horizon of expectations'") and mass cultural acceptance (the desire to see "the same thing over and over again").

CHAPTER FIVE

Wordsworth, Milton, and the inward light

NICOLA ZOE TROTT

IN M. H. ABRAMS'S INCISIVE explication, romanticism emerges from the crisis of the French Revolution as a more or less knowing and appropriate transition from external to internal modes of expression:

The recourse is from mass action to individual quietism, and from outer revolution to a revolutionary mode of imaginative perception which accomplishes nothing less than the "creation" of a new world.[1]

Abrams's might be styled the liberal school of literary history. Its more hostile successor, the new historicism, takes neither the recourse to the individual nor the perceptual "revolution" as given. Rather, it uses a variety of theoretical tools to disclose the suppressed evidence of a culture's material relations. Romanticism is defined as ideologically determined – positively, by its own idealizations, and negatively, by its sins of historical omission. Either way, "history," far from being unproblematically transcended or transposed, enters like a ghost to trouble the forms of culture.

Since ideology is necessarily absent to itself, the function of criticism is, in Jerome J. McGann's words, to "restore poetry to its historical determinations." This restoration is paradoxically the result of critical distance. In identifying a "romantic ideology," McGann's historicism casts an estranging eye, on both the ideology pe: se and the commentary that reflects it. His focus shifts between the supposed myopia of mimetic critics – Abrams, Hartman, Bloom – and the blindness of poems, as scrutinized by more insightful analysts. Wordsworth is placed at the centre of a romanticism whose "grand illusion" is an idealizing urge to shake "free of the ruins of history."[2] Following McGann, this newly exposed ideology has been seen to manifest itself variously in Wordsworth's "strategies of displacement and conceal-ment," his moments of "peripety" or acts of "suppression," and in a "nature" whose "denial" of history constitutes his "theory" of "Imagination."[3]

I wish to take up this theoretical debate from within the poetry of Wordsworth and its relation to the figure of Milton. I do so partly to suggest that there is in this relation an internal quarrel whose terms are, broadly speaking, replicated in the battle of the new historicists with formalism. Wordsworth's response to Milton arises out of dual, not to say rivalrous, contexts. In the mythic interpretations fostered by Abrams and Bloom, Wordsworth brings about the "earthing" of Milton by a humanist imagination, and romanticism is placed in secular competition with a Christian cosmology. In a historical frame, however, the poets are joint sufferers of failed revolutions, and their mutual dilemma shapes Wordsworth's representation of his problematic odyssey from "outer" to "inner" worlds. These contradictory settings are registered in Wordsworth's overt responses to Milton: one, of repudiation, defines the "main region" of his song by opposing Miltonic transcendentalism; the other, of identification, defines his historical situation by association with Milton – specifically, with Milton as political idealist. Two points may be made here: firstly, that Wordsworth is divided between realist and idealist impulses; secondly, that he exhibits an idealizing movement that is consciously implicated in history. There are, it seems, levels of historical determination of which the poetry is all too uneasily aware.

I want now to locate the conflict of response I have described rather more precisely, by turning to the period 1800–2. The most self-evident arena for Wordsworth's confrontation with his precursor is the 1800 "Prospectus" to *The Recluse*, whose density of Miltonic allusion has been amply documented. With a superb arrogance, the "Prospectus" summons the anthropomorphic machinery of *Paradise Lost*, then dismisses it in laying claim to the new epic "region" of "the soul of man."[4] Significantly, this poetic has the final purpose of reconciling the human soul with the world it inhabits. Wordsworth's allegiance to what *The Prelude* calls "the very world which is the world / Of all of us" (1805, X.725–26) is driven in part by a competitive relation to Miltonic supernaturalism. The "Prospectus" is contemporaneous with a less well known prose equivalent of its humanist opposition to Milton, Wordsworth's annotations to *Paradise Lost* itself.[5] One of the marginalia objects, in terms that suggest the politics of Wordsworthian poetics, to Milton's artifical and aristocratic imagery – his baroque Heaven with its "palace gate embellished with diamond and with gold," and its "golden stairs," only "occasionally let down." The rationale for this criticism is provided when Wordsworth asserts his own grounding in a common earth and nature:

It has been said of poets as their highest praise that they exhausted worlds and then imagined new, that existence saw them spurn her bounded reign &c. But how much … of the real excellence of Imagination consists in the capacity of exploring the world really existing

("Wordsworth's Marginalia," 170)[6]

As Hunt observes, this equation of the "real excellence of Imagination" with its "capacity of exploring the [real]" brings to mind another text of 1800, the Preface to *Lyrical Ballads*, and its controversial alliance between the language of poetry and "the real language of men."[7] Wordsworth's attack on Gray and Johnson is sufficiently notorious; but his related themes of language, poetic diction, and the poet are also articulated by contradistinction from Milton. In rejecting the classical division of poetry and prose, Wordsworth uses a quotation from *Paradise Lost* Book I to associate poetry with an anti-Miltonic and human reality:

Poetry sheds no tears "such as Angels weep," but natural and human tears; she can boast of no celestial Ichor that distinguishes her vital juices from those of prose; the same human blood circulates through the veins of them both.   (*Prose Works*, 1: 134)

In a parallel revision, added in 1802, the Preface answers the query "What is a Poet?" with the definition, "He is a man speaking to men" (*Prose Works*, 1: 138). The statement tacitly endorses what is for Milton a moment of fallen being – the moment, in *Paradise Lost* Book XI, when angelic substance takes on human form for the first time. The Wordsworthian poet's homocentricity recalls the archangel Michael's descent from Heaven to make his "solemn and sublime" appearance in a post-lapsarian world,

> Not in his shape celestial, but as man
> Clad to meet man   (XI.239–40).

Clearly, much more could be said of Wordsworth's realist antagonism to Milton; but I must leave it in outline, and move on to the opposing response, his idealist identification with Milton, and its relations to history. I shall do so by way of the "Ode: Intimations of Immortality from Recollections of Early Childhood."

The opening lines of the "Immortality Ode," written in March 1802, beatify the scenes of the past, and speak with haunting restraint of their bereavement in the present:

> There was a time when meadow, grove, and stream,
> The earth, and every common sight,
>   To me did seem
>   Apparell'd in celestial light,
> The glory and the freshness of a dream.

> It is not now as it has been of yore; –
> Turn wheresoe'er I may,
> By night or day,
> The things which I have seen I now can see no more.[8]

The loss is impalpable yet absolute; it is imaged as nothing less than a divorce of heaven from earth. The "celestial light," with its elusive "dream" of presence, makes a pained allusion to Milton's invocation to Light, in *Paradise Lost* Book III. Wordsworth's vanished aura at once acknowledges the blinded poet, and his state of grace. In his sightlessness, Milton had been "Presented with a Universal blanc / Of Nature's works," yet resolutely converted the "ever-during dark" of his physical deprivation into his spiritual glory:

> So much the rather thou Celestial Light
> Shine inward, and the mind through all her powers
> Irradiate, there plant eyes...
>   that I may see and tell
> Of things invisible to mortal sight.   (III.51–55)

Milton exhorts the light to "Shine inward." Wordsworth laments its disappearance from outward things, but his allusion is not merely disabling. As he later affirms, the infant is an "Eye among the blind" ("Immortality Ode," line 111). The child who perceives a "celestial light" in the world is the innocent challenger of the elderly Milton and his inner illuminations. Equally, the phrase suggests the Miltonic turn the "Immortality Ode" will take, on its completion in early 1804. It too will reach through darkness to an interior radiance. But the "master light" by which it sees derives from "shadowy recollections" – from a childhood that, in its "obstinate questionings / Of sense and outward things," avenges itself on a material reality (lines 156, 153, 145–46).

The larger movement of the "Immortality Ode," then, is from outer "glory" to inner "light." And it is here that matters of ideology come to the fore. The waning of the exterior force has provided a focus of interpretation, both for the poem itself, and for Wordsworth's poetic career as a whole. Harold Bloom, for instance, has written:

The outward form of the inward grace of Romantic imagination was the French Revolution, and the Revolution failed ... Milton, after the failure of his Revolution, turned inward like Oedipus, making of his blindness a judgment upon the light. Wordsworth's movement to the interior was more gradual, and ended in defeat, with the light of imagination dying into the light of another day, in which existing conceptions of the world seemed acceptable.[9]

The critical myth describes an ironic swerve: romanticism founds itself on ideals that the Revolution has failed to sustain, but this departure results in its conformist demise. Bloom's language recognizes Wordsworth's own expression of loss, and has him suffer again the poetic justice of seeing "celestial light" fade to "common day." While Milton retained his revolutionary "judgment" (in *Paradise Lost*), Wordsworth did not, and the "Immortality Ode" marks out his path towards a dingy status quo.

Bloom offers a classic explanation of the Romantic imagination as an internalizing of revolutionary influence. But the "Immortality Ode" has also been understood as an elegy for the Revolution itself. Hazlitt, when reviewing *The Excursion* in August 1814, uttered these memorial verses:

> "What though the radiance, which was once so bright,
> Be now for ever taken from our sight,
> Though nothing can bring back the hour
> Of glory in the grass, of splendour in the flower" :-

yet will we never cease, nor be prevented from returning on the wings of imagination to that bright dream of our youth; that glad dawn of the day-star of liberty; that spring-time of the world, in which the hopes and expectations of the human race seemed opening in the same gay career with our own.[10]

In a recent and materialist critique, Marjorie Levinson has argued for a post-revolutionary narrator, who "observes Nature's lack of personal meaning to him now that its public and ideological meaning has been discredited," and who responds by "transforming the 'golden hours' of the Revolution ... into a psychic and metaphysical postulate" (*Wordsworth's Great Period Poems*, 92). For McGann, on the other hand, the "Immortality Ode" "completes and perfects the tragic losses of Wordsworth's life and times." In raising its final thanks "for the activity of displacement itself, for the moments of loss," the work embodies a Romantic "transformation of fact into idea, and of experience into ideology" (*The Romantic Ideology*, 90).

These disparate acts of criticism have one thing in common: they single out the "Immortality Ode" as typifying the history of its age. And history dictates a poetics of loss, or a retreat to ideas. The "Immortality Ode" is riven between a "heavenly" imagination and its "earthly" medium, the one being destroyed by the other. In asserting an idealist origin as the antagonist of material culture, Wordsworth's "celestial light" ambivalently draws on the transcendental source of Milton's invocation.

In itself, this allusive moment is ideologically determined in the covert ways the new history is alert to detect. But a broader context suggests something less isolated, less removed from recognition. The "Immortality Ode" is not a solitary icon. On the contrary, within a dialogic model of literary history, it is surrounded both by other works, and by a longstanding debate between inner consciousness and outer action. The "Immortality Ode" is a powerful myth of withdrawal. Yet its allusion to a "celestial light" also connects it to a Wordsworth who habitually orients himself in relation to Milton, and to his own historical predicament. From the very beginning of the counter-revolution, and at successive stages thereafter, Wordsworth's changing poetic and political identity is marked by a dialectic between internal strength and outward influence. And the indwelling power of mind, to which he resorts when confronted by external force, is consistently figured as an "inward light." It is to this figure, and the uses it serves, that I shall direct my attention for the remainder of this essay.

Significantly, Wordsworth's first self-identification with Milton coincides with his first "movement to the interior" at a time of political duress. Furthermore, it occurs a full decade before the "Immortality Ode" is completed. Nicholas Roe finds the "earliest manifestation of [a] turn inward" among the additions Wordsworth made to *An Evening Walk* in the summer of 1794.[11] These additions waver uneasily between topography and political allegory.[12] Towards the end of the revised text, an apparently conventional apostrophe to a glow-worm – "Meek lover of the shade! in Quiet's breast, / With thine own proper light sufficed and bless'd" (1794, lines 668–69) – leads to a dual analogy:

> So Virtue, fallen on times to gloom consigned,
> Makes round her path the light she cannot find,
> And by her own internal lamp fulfills,
> And asks no other star what Virtue wills,
> Acknowledging, though round her Danger lurk,
> And Fear, no night in which she cannot work;
> In dangerous night so Milton worked alone,
> Cheared by a secret lustre all his own,
> That with the deepening darkness clearer shone.[13] (1794, lines 680–88)

Self-sufficiency is the chief virtue of the republican poet (and notably exacts an intransitive use of "fulfills," in line 682). Wordsworth's image of Milton is of the steadfast, yet blind and isolated, figure of *Paradise Lost* Book VII, "In darkness, and with dangers compast round, / And solitude" (VII.27–28). His personification of Virtue, however, derives from Milton's early masque, and its youthfully zealous assertion:

> Virtue could see to do what virtue would
> By her own radiant light, though Sun and Moon
> Were in the flat Sea sunk.   (*Comus*, lines 373–75)

The early Wordsworth echoes the early Milton, but from a position like that of the old and chastened poet. Virtue has "fallen on times to gloom consigned." At twenty-four, Wordsworth precociously associates himself with Milton as an ideal worker in a "dangerous night." The "gloom" of his own times is indeed considerable. There is the war with France; the Jacobin Terror; the arrests in May 1794 of friends of liberty by a repressive government at home, and the sense, later recorded in *The Prelude*, of being exiled in one's home-land.

Milton lost his sight writing propaganda for the republican Commonwealth. The blindness, which his enemies judged as a divine punishment, he strove to represent as the sign of his just reward. He had been compensated not just with poetry, but with insight into the otherwise "invisible" ways of God. In Wordsworth, too, the idea of a "celestial light" is inextricably bound up with his identity, both poetic and political. But the starkness of the counter-revolution, and the self-reliance it induces, have imposed dramatic revisions. As Roe observes, *An Evening Walk* contains a "misreading of *Paradise Lost* by which Wordsworth reduces the supernatural agency of Milton's creativity into an autonomous, 'internal lamp'" ("Wordsworth, Milton, and the Politics of Poetic Influence," 124). The couplets are also a stoic retrenchment of ones written in ecstatic confidence two years previously. Unlike Milton, Wordsworth experienced revolution in youth, not middle age, and as a foreign enthusiast, not as a native agent. From the Loire in 1792, he had prophesied the rising of the revolutionary phoenix out of the fire of its enemies, in the strains of Virgil's fourth *Eclogue* and the Apocalypse in *Paradise Lost*:

> Lo! from th' innocuous flames, a lovely birth!
> With it's own Virtues springs another earth[14]

By 1794, these powers have dwindled to the single "Virtue" of a "secret lustre," and the personality of Milton is invoked as the guarantor of a personal strength.

The "movement to the interior" is conspicuous, yet hardly synonymous with political abdication or apostasy. Wordsworth is an avowed republican in 1794. In a letter of 23 May, mentioning his work on *An Evening Walk*, he categorically places himself among "that odious class of men called democrats" (*Early Years*, 119). His intention, in this and the following letter, is to set out his beliefs to his Cambridge friend, William Mathews, in the hopes of co-founding a London miscellany. His plans for a politically educative journal, *The Philanthropist*, are thus exactly contemporaneous with his poetic representation of political troubles.

The "internal lamp" and republican letters are twin aspects of Wordsworth's response to the war and Terror. Under the brutally altered circumstances of 1794, Wordsworth at once internalizes the revolutionary impulse, and makes his first definition of a public role:

the people should be enlightened upon the subject of politics ... I know that the multitude walk in darkness. I would put into each man's hand a lantern to guide him and not have him to set out upon his journey depending for illumination on abortive flashes of lightning, or the coruscations of transitory meteors. (*Early Years*, 125)

The enlightened are to be a source of light for the multitude, in order that political agency may safely be devolved upon the individual. Wordsworth's letter to Mathews associates the wish to democratize knowledge with the "exertions in the cause of liberty" that Milton and others have made in prose (125).[15] As in the revised *Evening Walk*, there is a power that itself sheds light on things, and is associated by Wordsworth with Milton and his own sense of vocation. Journalism is ostensibly conceived as a modest "lantern" of guidance; its undercover mission is suggested by an exalted allusion to Isaiah's prophecy of the Messiah: "The people that walked in darkness, have seen a great light" (Isaiah 9.2).

It is the Miltonic prophet and light-bringer that lasts, not the rational reformer of society.[16] In 1798, the claim of biblical status recurs in less humble circumstances, when it characterizes the first of the Poet-Teachers who follow a Wordsworthian calling. The figure of the Pedlar is originally sketched in the Alfoxden Notebook, where,

> Transfigured by his feelings he appeared
> Even as a prophet – one whose purposes
> Were round him like a light[17]

The saint's halo and Christian transfiguration are here, remarkably, an effect of the feelings. But these emotions are taken as the sign of a "prophet" surrounded by his "purposes." The imaginary in itself casts "light," and the following lines greet, with a sense of immediate revelation, "The power miraculous by which the soul / Walks through the world that lives in future things."

The overcoming of post-revolutionary "gloom" could hardly be more ostentatious. In 1794, Wordsworth had already been thinking in terms of "a secret lustre all his own," and a work that would shed light on the world. This internalization points to his divergence from Miltonic supernaturalism; but the associated Miltonic ideal of the prophet is carried forward into the period, from 1798 to 1800, of Wordsworth's most concerted transumption of *Paradise Lost*. The draft describing the Pedlar, a mere six lines, derives its striking authority from Wordsworth's having acquired a prophetic purpose of his own. In early 1798, he and Coleridge devise the task of a redemptive epic, which is to be named "The Recluse," yet will reconcile the forces of "Nature, Man, and Society" (*Early Years*, 214). The moral "work" envisaged in the revised *Evening Walk*, the abortive wish of *The Philanthropist* to enlighten the multitude, are here given virtual shape.

On arriving in Grasmere at the end of 1799, Wordsworth takes the prophetic aura on himself. The "Prospectus" to *The Recluse* asks

> that my song may live, & be
> Even as a light hung up in heaven to chear
> The world in times to come.[18]

Magnificently raised aloft as the light of the world, Wordsworth's ambitious star is the reverse of self-solacing. But it is also remote in both space and time. This evasion of political immediacies itself has political motives. The longterm project of *The Recluse* is specifically determined by the French Revolution: it supposes that a natural, and hence gradualist and non-violent, revolution will follow the exultation and despair of the first. To this extent, it is an idealizing "denial" of history, but is not, in its conception, reactionary. In September 1799, Coleridge is entreating Wordsworth to address part of *The Recluse* "to those, who, in consequence of the complete failure of the French Revolution, have thrown up all hopes of the amelioration of mankind."[19] From its origins in the Alfoxden poetry, *The Recluse* is engaged with the happiness of humanity, but its hopes are based either in the future, or in the immediate circle of Wordsworthian insight. Hence the Pedlar is called prophet for bearing in himself an illumination that will one day be universally received.

Not only is *The Recluse* relentlessly prospective, its views of nature, man, and society demand a harmonizing of public and private spheres. When, in 1800, Wordsworth writes the first, nominally philosophic, book of his epic, he in effect attempts to domesticate an ideology. However, the deflection of the revolutionary impulse, which began in 1794 and was empowered by the idea of *The Recluse*, exists alongside a competing ideology of the poet's own making. *Home at Grasmere* celebrates the gift of mind, yet is troubled by its contrary desires of social communion and exclusive possession:

> Of ill advised ambition and of pride
> I would stand clear, yet unto me I feel
> That an internal brightness is vouchsafed
> That must not die, that must not pass away.
> Why does this inward lustre fondly seek
> And gladly blend with outward fellowship?
> Why shine they round me thus, whom thus I love?
> ...
> Strange question, yet it answers not itself.
> That humble Roof, embowered among the trees,
> That calm fire side – it is not even in them,
> Blessed as they are, to furnish a reply

That satisfies and ends in perfect rest.
Possessions have I, wholly, solely mine,
Something within, which yet is shared by none –
Not even the nearest to me and most dear –
Something which power and effort may impart.
I would impart it; I would spread it wide,
Immortal in the world which is to come.[20]

Wordsworth's assertion of his imaginative capacity, and questioning of its social role, instantly resuscitates the language in which he first learned to speak of his autonomous mental powers in relation to Milton. In *Home at Grasmere*, the "internal lamp" and "secret lustre" of the 1794 *Evening Walk* are brought back into the community. The "internal brightness" or "inward lustre" is domestically lent out; but this domesticity is neither its true home (which lies in the self), nor its highest office (which lies in the world to come). As in 1794, there is an inward power and outward effect; but the dialectic is now maintained in terms of a possessive origin and an eventual, universal function.

Home at Grasmere faltered as much because the genius of the place was rivalled by an egotistical sublime, as because Grasmere did not conform to the ideal. Yet *The Recluse* was supposed to tell "the world not of a private paradise regained, but of one available to all whose minds were 'wedded to this outward frame of things / In love'."[21] Insofar as this natural humanism failed to convince or to satisfy, it was superseded by an ideology of self-possession. Once again, however, history intervenes. And again, it does so in ways that parallel the case of Milton. In his essay, "Regaining the Radical Milton," Michael Wilding points out:

After the failure of the Good Old Cause and the re-establishment of the Stuart monarchy, Christ's Kingdom was no longer seen by most of the puritan sects as a military, political objective of this world, but as a moral objective of the spirit. At the end of *Paradise Lost* Michael offers Adam "A paradise within thee, happier far" [XII.587] – not a physical place but a set of moral precepts to prepare his soul for the Kingdom of Heaven.[22]

The outright collapse of the Puritan Revolution necessitated the internalizing of its ideals. Wordsworth too was made to recognize the inwardness of a happiness he once hoped would spread "To all the Vales of earth and all mankind" (*Home at Grasmere*, 52 [MS B, line 256]). Both poets shared a historically determined urge to idealize political failure – in McGann's terms, to transform experience into ideology. But the Romantic response was also shaped by very different conditions. Most obviously, the persistence of the French Republic meant that the Revolution was not over in the sense that the 1660 Restoration was, but in perverse continuum with itself.

Wordsworth's "movement to the interior," as distinct from Milton's, was thus an interrupted affair. Its discontinuousness was indicated by Wordsworth himself, who, when he came to summarize his shift of allegiance, assigned it to Napoleon's invasion of republican Switzerland in January 1798 (just prior to the formulation of *The Recluse*):

This just and necessary war, as we have been accustomed to hear it styled from the beginning of the contest in the year 1793, had, some time before the Treaty of Amiens, viz. after the subjugation of Switzerland, and not till then, begun to be regarded by the body of the people, as indeed both just and necessary ... a change or rather a revolution in circumstances had imposed new duties ... a deliberate and preparatory fortitude – a sedate and stern melancholy, which had no sunshine and was exhilarated only by the lightnings of indignation.   (*The Convention of Cintra, Prose Works* 1: 226–27)

There is in Wordsworth no single trajectory of dedication and withdrawal, but a further, grimly disciplined adaptation to a counter-revolutionary epoch. The prose claims to represent a national change of heart, and, significantly, insists on a "revolution" of 1798, eclipsing that of 1789. This revolution imposing "new duties" is precisely registered in Wordsworth's own poetic submission to "a new controul."[23]

The exigencies of the Napoleonic era begin to be felt in 1802, when the Treaty of Amiens provokes Wordsworth's first reassessment of the Revolution since 1792. During the phoney Peace, he becomes equally a defender and castigator of his nation, and directs a political rhetoric against Napoleonic invincibility and Whiggish appeasement alike.[24] In this context, the "Ode"- poet's loss of "celestial light" is not the privileged moment it is often taken for. Wordsworth has a new *casus belli*, and the concept of inner virtue he has inherited from Milton is turned outward on the world. The poet who repudiated the supernatural agencies of *Paradise Lost* now finds himself externalizing Miltonic ideals. Indeed, the unfamiliar form in which they are contained, the "narrow room" of the sonnet, is arrived at through Milton's specific example.[25] Wordsworth's tribute to his model, in a letter of November 1802, also implies a convergence of metrical and moral disciplines:

Milton's Sonnets ... I think manly and dignified compositions, distinguished by simplicity and unity of object and aim, and undisfigured by false or vicious ornaments ... an energetic and varied flow of sound crowding into narrow room more of the combined effect of rhyme and blank verse than can be done by any other kind of verse I know of.

(*Early Years*, 379)

In 1794, Wordsworth had identified with Milton as a republican at odds with his country. From 1802, the enemy is the foreign bogeyman, Bonaparte, and Milton becomes the embodiment of patriotic values now debased. Wordsworth turns in the sonnet to a form covering Milton's public life and rallying of national heroes, Cromwell, Vane, and Fairfax. Immediately after hearing his sister read Milton's sonnets on 21 May 1802, Wordsworth replied with one of his own, in which the anti-hero, Napoleon, is used to evoke an ideal leader:

> I griev'd for Buonaparte, with a vain
> And an unthinking grief! ...
> 'Tis not in battles that from youth we train
> The Governor who must be wise and good,
> And temper with the sternness of the brain
> Thoughts motherly, and meek as womanhood.
> Wisdom doth live with children round her knees

"I griev'd for Buonaparte" describes the indirect education of a ruler whose intellect is moderated by kinship. The emblem of the educated mind, Wisdom, is surrounded by the children usual in the iconography of Charity. Critics have objected to the sonnet as a domestication of power;[26] yet its effect is rather to put a homely check on the imperial ego, in the hope of forming a just as well as battle-hardened mind (the hint of steel being adroitly made by the process of "tempering").

Wordsworth's grief for Napoleon was occasioned by press reports of his first step towards the Emperorship, his election to Chief Consul for life.[27] In reply, the first Miltonic sonnet demands a feminizing of masculine *virtus* that harks back to the female Virtue of the 1794 *Evening Walk*. And this fusion of genders is now thought of as the special property of a Miltonic imagination. The figure of Milton, which has always served as a political ideal, now seems to embody an ideal "Union" of opposites – a union, moreover, that incorporates the "earthing" of the ideal which has been Wordsworth's ground of divorce from his precursor.

In February 1801, Lamb received from Wordsworth "a long letter of four sweating pages," peddling

a deal of stuff about a certain Union of Tenderness and Imagination, which in the sense he used Imagination was not the characteristic of Shakespeare, but which Milton possessed in a degree far exceeding other Poets   (*Early Years*, 316)

Lamb (who had rated the ballads of 1798 above those of 1800, and met the full panoply of Wordsworth's defensiveness) deliciously parries the judgmental and appropriative quality of the poet's self-definitions. But the synthesis of heart and mind also comes to define an ethic of public statesmanship. Alongside their condemnations of modern effeminacy, the sonnets on Milton and his times – "Great Men have been among us," "London, 1802" and "Written in London" – honour qualities of homeliness, meekness, and humility. Wordsworth exhorts an imaginary restoration of the English Commonwealth as a republican state of the mind, uniting the "male" and "female" virtues of public righteousness and "household laws." These acts of "Union" effectively close the divisions I identified earlier, between realist and idealist impulses in the response to Milton, and between private and public ambitions in *The Recluse*. In serving Wordsworth's political interests, the figure of Milton has an exemplary and unqualified status: the bases on which Wordsworth elsewhere represents his defining antagonisms and equivocations of temperament are assimilated and resolved.

It seems no accident that the oddly domestic nationalism of 1802 coincides with the time of Wordsworth's betrothal to Mary Hutchinson and journey to France to break with Annette Vallon. On his return to England in September 1802, his dismay at the degeneracy of London calls forth the sonnet in which Milton is invoked in denunciation of his modern inheritors, and where the equation of public with private virtue is overt:

> Milton! thou shouldst be living at this hour:
> England hath need of thee: she is a fen
> Of stagnant waters: altar, sword, and pen,
> Fireside, the heroic wealth of hall and bower,
> Have forfeited their ancient English dower
> Of inward happiness. ("London, 1802," lines 1–6)

Wordsworth's changed political attitudes make him identify Milton, not with the failure of the Republic, but with the heroic period of the Commonwealth; not with the blind poet of *Paradise Lost*, but the propagandist and Secretary for Foreign Tongues to Cromwell, who united in himself the trinity of religion, fighting, and writing ("altar, sword, and pen").

Wordsworth is keen to establish a glorious past, to which his country owes its foundation and fidelity. There is therefore a potent conflict between repudiation and reassurance, between the detection of venality and the litany of national insignia. Hence, perhaps, it is the symbols that pay the penalty: they, and not the people, are seen as having "forfeited" what has given them substance, the "dower / Of *inward* happiness" (my italics). The "dower," with its powerful ties to Milton and Coleridge (*Paradise Lost* V.215–19; "Dejection: an Ode," stanza 5), brings the wealth that England is wedded to by tradition; but it rests on an "inward happiness," without which the structures of culture are null and void. Wordsworth is deliberately passing off ideology as history: his sonnet delivers a rebuke to the materialism of his society by defining culture as a spiritual property from which it is disinherited.

The achievement of "Character of the Happy Warrior," written at the end of 1805, is that it reclaims the "happiness" lost in 1802.[28] Indeed, the Warrior is heir to the whole history of the inner light, and its militant application since the Treaty of Amiens. This resurgence is all the more extraordinary in context, for the poem closes the year in which Nelson dies winning the great naval victory of Trafalgar and, devastatingly, John Wordsworth, the poet's brother, is drowned with his ship. The poem is relatively neglected, but is interesting both as a counterpart to the "Elegiac Stanzas," and as a formal expression of the "new controul" in Wordsworth. It transposes private mourning into public deliberation in highly accomplished verse; and justifies the workings of imagination, so recently formulated in *The Prelude*, in connection with the most painful realities.

An earnestness of tone and elevation of style are immediately established, as "Character of the Happy Warrior" casts back to the heroic couplet, and to the opening phrase of the *Aeneid*, "Arma virumque cano":

> Who is the happy Warrior? Who is he
> Whom every Man in arms should wish to be?   (lines 1–2)

When, following the calamity of John's death, Wordsworth reaches for a definition of the hero, his questioning is anything but rhetorical. It receives the direct and unequivocal answer:

> – It is the generous Spirit, who, when brought
> Among the tasks of real life, hath wrought
> Upon the plan that pleased his childish thought:
> Whose high endeavours are an inward light
> That make the path before him always bright   (lines 3–7)

The ancient art of war has come to define a modern warrior of the spirit. The Happy Warrior conducts a moral warfare, and his character-type is nearer to a Christian than a military soldier.[29] As in all previous crises, Wordsworth has revived the terms of the 1794 *Evening Walk*, in which "Virtue ... / Makes round her path the light she cannot find." But the early couplets, with their self-dramatizing account of revolutionary failure, have been tempered by a neoclassical rectitude in meter and morals. "The Happy Warrior" assumes a self-reliance in order to stress the "generosity" with which it is spread or sacrificed to a larger sphere of influence.

In this "Spirit" the Warrior is purged of authorial doubt. Unlike the fragile and divided child of the "Ode," he makes "real life" conform to his imaginative "plan." He wins the victory over his Wordsworthian self, who would egotistically go looking to nature for confirmation. By being compelled to "Shine inward," as Milton had urged, the "light" is paradoxically restored to the external world. The Warrior's "powers [are] shed round him" (line 45), even as his "high endeavours are an inward light / That make the path before him always bright."[30]

The "inward light" now has multiple names and connotations. Not the least of these, for Wordsworth, is its affiliation with the politics and religion of the Puritan Revolution. As Wilding has commented, Milton's invocation to Light, in *Paradise Lost* Book III, provocatively asserts "the Puritan doctrine of the inner light, the belief that God's word is available directly to every man" ("Regaining the Radical Milton," 127). This doctrine was most fundamental to the Society of Friends, founded about 1650, and I want briefly to take up the Quaker connection.[31]

Wordsworth's sensitivity to the link would have been sharpened by Thomas Clarkson, who at the time of the "Character of the Happy Warrior" was writing *A Portraiture of Quakerism*, and who gave Wordsworth a copy on its publication in 1806.[32] In reviewing Clarkson's volumes, Francis Jeffrey mocked the sectarian eccentricity of Quaker dress, speech and culture, and confidently stated: "It is quite plain to us, that their founder George Fox was exceedingly insane."[33] Wordsworth, however, had several points of affinity with Quakerism (going back to his schooldays, when Ann Tyson took him to Friends' meetings at Colthouse): its doctrine of an inner light was close to Milton's own; it laid stress on the heart as opposed to the intellect; it appealed to the inner and spiritual as distinct from the outer and material life; and, in rejecting the Calvinist doctrines of election and reprobation, it affirmed human perfectibility in the form of growth.[34] Inspired largely by the opening verses of the Gospel according to John (where the Incarnate Word is "the light of men"), the Quakers asserted a connection between the Word of God and the divine principle in Christ and man. As Clarkson's *Portraiture* understood it:

if there be a communication between the Supreme Being and his creature Man, or if the Almighty has afforded to man an emanation of his own Spirit ... we may say with great consistency, that the Divinity resides in him, or that his body is the temple of the Holy Spirit.[35]

Like Milton's invocation to Light, this interpretation of scripture leaves Wordsworth free to humanize the godhead. And in this sense, the Warrior's "inward light" is indeed his resident divinity. However, "Character of the Happy Warrior" also flouts Quaker belief – the Friends, as Clarkson records, "believe it unlawful for Christians to engage in the profession of arms ... Hence there is no such character as that of a Quaker-soldier" (3: 25) – by ascribing the inner light to just such a "Character" or "Man in arms." Wordsworth writes in unambiguous support of the war against France, but also in stoic confrontation of the death of John. The poem evades the personal exposure of elegy. It fuses the "military character" instilled by the Napoleonic era with the intellectual characteristics of Wordsworth's merchant-seaman brother, dubbed "the Philosopher" by his messmates (Fenwick note, in *Poetical Works* 4: 419).

This new coalescence of public and private virtues again summons the language of Wordsworth's political idealism. The union of energies is achieved by a man

> Who, doom'd to go in company with Pain,
> And Fear, and Bloodshed, miserable train!
> Turns his necessity to glorious gain;
> In face of these doth exercise a power
> Which is our human-nature's highest dower;
> Controls them and subdues, transmutes, bereaves
> Of their bad influence, and their good receives ...   (lines 12–18)

Under Napoleonic conditions, imagination is annexed as the capacity to bring good out of evil.[36] The verse derives its sinewy authority partly from its determination to condense the formulations of the past. These lines conflate the joyful imagination of Coleridge's "Dejection Ode," with its rhyming equation of "power" and "dower"; the humane imagination of "Tintern Abbey," "of ample power / To chasten and subdue"; and the transforming mind of *The Prelude* (1805), whose action on "outward" things "So moulds them, and endues, abstracts, combines" (XIII.78–79).

But these definitions are operative within a newly-conceived imagination of moral imperatives. And its strongest lineage is in Milton. The speech of Raphael, in Book V of *Paradise Lost*, on the ascent of Creation to its God, is consistently associated by Wordsworth and Coleridge with the faculty of imagination (most famously, of course, in the epigraph to Chapter Thirteen of *Biographia Literaria*). In it, God's unfallen creatures are seen as "more refin'd, more spiritous, and pure, / As nearer to him plac't or nearer tending" (V.475–76). The romantically happy Warrior inherits this spiritualizing tendency, but is on the contrary

> More skilful in self-knowledge, even more pure,
> As tempted more; more able to endure,
> As more expos'd to suffering and distress;
> Thence, also, more alive to tenderness.   (lines 23–26)

Wordsworth's revision of *Paradise Lost* significantly constructs an alliance between moral progression and imaginative sympathy. And once again, there is the gendered dualism of sensitivity and strength, of an interior, feminine "Virtue" – in this case "tenderness" – and an exterior, masculine *virtus*.

If "I griev'd for Buonaparte" describes the path to just leadership, the Happy Warrior undergoes it.[37] But Wordsworth's much deeper grief of 1805 demands that ascendancy be achieved by a man who thrives on temptation and suffering. The "Character" (whose models are John Wordsworth–Milton–Beaupuy–Nelson[38]) is also an idealized self-portrait at a time of critical need. This admonishment of a possible heroism is at least partly coercive. A poet who has already "felt the weight of too much liberty" ("Nuns fret not," line 13) is seen to atone for his irresponsible freedom.

Here, too, Wordsworth's personal determinations are an uncanny echo of historical ones, his anti-libertarianism being both an internal requirement and a sign of the times. The movement of reaction is apparent in the triad of poems, the "Character of the Happy Warrior," "Elegiac Stanzas," and "Ode to Duty." In May–June 1806, the "Elegiac Stanzas" renounce "The consecration, and the Poet's dream" as a "light that never was, on sea or land." This searing clarity of judgment is delivered in the new voice of Wordsworth's tragic stoicism. Like the "celestial light" of the "Immortality Ode," the "light that never was" has a supernatural, and hence spurious, glamour. Wordsworth's corrective reply is found in the "Ode to Duty," which belongs largely to 1804, but in 1806 is completed with a stanza addressing the principle of moral enlightenment and discipline:

> Stern Daughter of the Voice of God!
> O Duty! if that name thou love
> Who art a Light to guide, a Rod
> To check the erring, and reprove.   (lines 1–4)

The poet who whimsically looked for guides in wandering clouds is brought back to the straight and narrow. It is of course in the name of Milton that Duty is invoked as a "Stern Daughter of the Voice of God." In *Paradise Lost*, the "Sole Daughter of his voice" had banned Adam and Eve from the fruit of the Tree of Knowledge. But Wordsworth's offspring is an inner mandate in a world where, as Eve remarks, "our Reason is our Law" (*Paradise Lost* IX.653–54).[39] The loss of revolutionary liberty, and its perversion into license, are judged to have enforced a code of rational obedience. If our "nature" were "happy," the power of "love" would be "an unerring light" ("Ode to Duty," lines 18–19). Things being what they are, however, the moral law is an austere and deliberate process. Wordsworth's "Light to guide" derives, not from God's prohibition before the Fall, but from the saving grace he ordains after it:

> And I will place within them as a guide
> My Umpire Conscience, whom if they will hear,
> Light after light well us'd they shall attain. ...
> (*Paradise Lost* III.194–96)

The "Ode to Duty" and "Character of the Happy Warrior" register changes brought on by the historically stressful years of 1802–6. Wordsworth's sense of self, which has long been tied to a revision of Milton, now admits of a tacit alignment. But there remains a line of distinction between Milton's God-given power and the more autonomous mind of the Romantic. Just prior to setting out the conscientious path to illumination, the God of *Paradise Lost* decrees his spiritual favourites with the words: "Some I have chosen of peculiar grace / Elect above the rest" (III.183–84). "Character of the Happy Warrior," for its part, characterizes the divinity of a man

> Whose powers shed round him in the common strife,
> Or mild concerns of ordinary life,
> A constant influence, a peculiar grace;
> But who, if he be called upon to face
> Some awful moment to which Heaven has join'd
> Great issues, good or bad for human-kind,
> Is happy as a Lover; and attired
> With sudden brightness like a Man inspired.   (lines 45–52)

In a pattern that goes back to *Home at Grasmere*, the diffused radiance of domestic life flares up in moments of heroic elation. Yet the Warrior as "Lover" retains a touching susceptibility to human feeling even in the press of action.

In the longer term, the inward light is absorbed by its moral function. A major revival occurs in Book IV of *The Excursion* (lines 1058–77), where it is used to describe a providential faculty of mind in the hope of recalling the Solitary from his despondency. Here, the moral imagination is restrictively defined as a way of coping with, rather than acting within, history. Tellingly, the passage is singled out by Lamb, in his review of *The Excursion*, as evidence of an "internal principle of lofty consciousness," whose effect is that of "an expanded and generous Quakerism."[40]

In the years 1802–6, the "internal principle" enables a quite different withdrawal, not into compliance, but into a national militancy. Yet the extraordinary nature of Wordsworth's relation to Milton rests in Milton's being a personally crucial, as well as publicly effective, figure. The most binding identification, perhaps, is that made in Wordsworth's letter of 1 May 1805, on the mourning for John:

When we look back upon this spring it seems like a dreary dream to us. But I trust in God that we shall yet "bear up and steer right onward."   (*Early Years*, 588)

Milton is appealed to, not as the symbol of a regenerate age, but as someone who has come through terrible adversity. The quotation is from Milton's courageously resilient sonnet, "To Mr. Cyriack Skinner Upon His Blindness":

> Cyriack, this three years' day these eyes, though clear
> To outward view of blemish or of spot,
> Bereft of light thir seeing have forgot;
> Nor to thir idle orbs doth sight appear
> Of Sun or Moon or Star throughout the year,

Or man or woman. Yet I argue not
Against heav'n's hand or will, nor bate a jot
Of heart or hope; but still bear up and steer
Right onward. What supports me, dost thou ask?
The conscience, Friend, to have lost them overplied
In liberty's defense, my noble task.   (lines 1–11)

Despite a will to transcend history, the Wordsworthian imagination is also chastened by and subdued to its development. I do not mean to argue, in the style of Alan Liu, for an "imaginatively 'dead'" and thus historically "redeemed" Wordsworth (*Wordsworth: The Sense of History*, 456). Rather, the figural repetitions by which the "inward light" is handed down in the period 1794–1806 reveal how often the historical and imaginative coincide, and how the latter comes to serve ideological uses that deny its elegiac or egotistical expression. The 1807 *Poems* exemplify a romanticism that is both idealizing of and responsive to history. "Character of the Happy Warrior," "Ode to Duty," and "Sonnets Dedicated to Liberty" resolve upon a chartered freedom. If, in putting on a martial harness, Wordsworth substituted the blindness of such insights for eyes that see into the life of things, he might have claimed, with Milton, "to have lost them overplied / In liberty's defense."

NOTES

1 M. H. Abrams, *Natural Supernaturalism: Tradition and Revolt in Romantic Literature* (New York: Norton, 1971), 338.

2 Jerome J. McGann, *The Romantic Ideology: A Critical Investigation* (Chicago: University of Chicago Press, 1983), 91–92.

3 James K. Chandler, *Wordsworth's Second Nature: A Study of the Poetry and Politics* (University of Chicago Press, 1984), xxi, 235; Marjorie Levinson, *Wordsworth's Great Period Poems: Four Essays* (Cambridge: Cambridge University Press, 1986), 42–45; Alan Liu, *Wordsworth: The Sense of History* (Stanford: Stanford University Press, 1989), 4–5.

4 "Prospectus," lines 28–29; "*Home at Grasmere*," Part First, Book First, of *The Recluse*, ed. Beth Darlington (Ithaca: Cornell University Press, 1977), 259.

5 Bishop C. Hunt, Jr., transcribes "Wordsworth's Marginalia on *Paradise Lost*" (*Bulletin of the New York Public Library* 73 [1969]: 167–83; hereafter cited as "Wordsworth's Marginalia"), and dates them 1798–1800. They appear in the second edition of 1674.

6 Wordsworth is killing two or three bards with one stone. His correction of Milton is achieved by a borrowing from Dr. Johnson in praise of Shakespeare, in the "Prologue Spoken at the Opening of the Theater in Drury Lane, 1747," lines 4–5 (*Samuel Johnson: Selected Poetry and Prose*, ed. Frank Brady and W. K. Wimsatt [Berkeley: University of California Press, 1977], 55).

7 "Wordsworth's Marginalia," 171; *Prose Works* 1: 150.

8 Lines 1–9; text quoted from *Poems, in Two Volumes, and Other Poems, 1800–1807*, ed. Jared Curtis (Ithaca: Cornell University Press, 1983).

9 Harold Bloom, *The Visionary Company: A Reading of English Romantic Poetry*, revised edition (Ithaca: Cornell University Press, 1971), 2.

10 *Complete Works*, ed. Howe, 19: 18.

11 Nicholas Roe, "Wordsworth, Milton, and the Politics of Poetic Influence," *The Yearbook of English Studies* 19 (1989): 125.

12 See *An Evening Walk*, ed. James Averill (Ithaca: Cornell University Press, 1984), 1794 text, lines 109–42, 111–32, 333–40, 358–409, 717–36 (hereafter cited as 1794).

13 For the glow-worm as an abiding image of the solitary yet cheerful poet, see *Prelude* (1805) VII.37–56 and "Scorn not the Sonnet" (1827).

14 *Descriptive Sketches*, ed. Eric Birdsall, assisted by Paul M. Zall (Ithaca: Cornell University Press, 1984), 782–83, alluding to *Paradise Lost* III.334–35.

15 The key prosifier in 1794 is of course Godwin, whose "rules of political justice" are invoked in the hope that they may avert violence even as they promote reform (*Early Years*, 124). A wariness of revolutionary action surfaces in the metaphor Wordsworth's letter borrows from Godwin's depiction of a state of anarchy: "Mind will frequently burst forth, but its appearance will be like the corruscations of the meteor, not like the mild illumination of the sun" (*An Enquiry Concerning Political Justice*, 2 vols. [London, 1793], 2: 735–36).

16 Among many similar analogies in Milton, compare this, from *The Reason of Church Government*: "The actions of just and pious men do not darken in their middle course; but *Solomon* tels us [Proverbs 4.18] they are as the shining light, that shineth more and more unto the perfet day" (*Complete Prose Works*, ed. Wolfe, 1: 795).

17 "*The Ruined Cottage*" and "*The Pedlar*," ed. James Butler (Ithaca: Cornell University Press, 1979), 123.

18 Prospectus, MS 1, lines 61–63; in *Home at Grasmere: Part First, Book First, of "The Recluse*," ed. Beth Darlington (Ithaca: Cornell University Press, 1977), 261.

19 Samuel Taylor Coleridge, *Collected Letters*, ed. E. L. Griggs, 6 vols. (Oxford: Clarendon Press, 1956–71), 1: 527.

20 MS B, lines 884–902, in *Home at Grasmere*, ed. Darlington, 94.

21 Jonathan Wordsworth, *The Borders of Vision* (Oxford: Clarendon Press, 1982), 148.

22 *The Radical Reader*, ed. Stephen Knight and Michael Wilding (Sydney: Wild & Woolley, 1977), 132.

23 "Elegiac Stanzas," line 34. For accounts of the change, see Carl Woodring, *Politics in English Romantic Poetry* (Cambridge: Harvard University Press, 1970), 128–31, and David Simpson, *Wordsworth's Historical Imagination: The Poetry of Displacement* (New York and London: Methuen, 1987), 40.

24 Liu describes the double-edged stance rhetorically, as the "motive of the form" of Wordsworth's Italianate sonnets (*Wordsworth: The Sense of History*, 434–35). They were published in the *Morning Post* during 1802–1803, and more fully in *Poems, in Two Volumes* (1807).

25 "Nuns fret not at their Convent's narrow room," 1.

26 See Robert C. Gordon, "Wordsworth and the Domestic Roots of Power," *Bulletin of Research in the Humanities* 81 (1978): 90–102.

27 The votes of the Tribunate on the question of Napoleon's life appointment were deposited on 14 May (24 Floréal). On 20 May, a state Legion of Honour, with the Chief Consul at its head, was formed for rewarding military and civil service.

28 Written by early January 1806, and sent to Beaumont on 11 February (*Middle Years*, 1: 6–7). I follow the text given in "*Poems, in Two Volumes," and Other Poems, 1800–1807*, ed. Curtis.

29 For the ancient tradition of the ideal man, see John Bowen Hamilton, "Restoration of 'The Happy Warrior,'" *Modern Language Quarterly* 16 (1955): 311–24, and Jane Worthington, *Wordsworth's Reading of Roman Prose* (New Haven: Yale University Press, 1946), 66. For Emerson's tracing of Wordsworth's "Character of the Happy Warrior" to Herbert's "Constancy," and a comparison with Vaughan's "Righteousness," see Theodore T. Stenberg, *Modern Language Notes* 40 (1925): 252–53. The closest literary model I have found is "An Epistle to the Lady Margaret, Countess of Cumberland," in Wordsworth's copy of *The Poetical Works of Samuel Daniel*, 2 vols. (1718), now at Dove Cottage; see also Sir Henry Wotton, *The Character of a Happy Life*.

30 The Warrior reverses the lamentation of Milton's Samson, that "inward light, alas, / Puts forth no visual beam" (*Samson Agonistes*, lines 162–63; and see lines 1687–91). See also Coleridge's fragment on Christ's "Inward Light," c.1806, beginning "His own fair countenance, his kingly forehead" (*Poems*, ed. J. B. Beer [London: Dent, 1974], 293).

31 George Fox's *Gospel-Truth Demonstrated, in a Collection of Doctrinal Books* (London, 1706) revolves around the theme "The Spirit of Man the Candle of the Lord" (17, 630), drawn from John, Matthew 5.16, Psalms 119.105 and Proverbs 20.27.

32 Thomas Clarkson, *A Portraiture of Quakerism*, 3 vols. (London, 1806); *Middle Years* 1: 60, 62, 253. With a house on Ullswater, Thomas Clarkson and his wife Catherine were the Wordsworths' close friends for most of the Dove Cottage years. Though not himself a Quaker, Clarkson had from 1785 been linked with the sect through his work as slave-trade abolitionist (a task Wordsworth saluted in the sonnet, "Clarkson! it was an obstinate Hill to climb").

33 Francis Jeffrey, *Contributions to the Edinburgh Review*, 4 vols. (London, 1844), 4: 250.

34 These tenets pertain to Quakerism as derived from Baptism, not to its Calvinist leanings under Robert Barclay. Milton's preference for an "inward oracle" is seen at *Paradise Lost* XII.511–26 and *Paradise Regained* I.460–44, IV.288–90. Clarkson illustrates the distinction between outward scripture and the inward of God's Spirit by quoting "Expostulation and Reply" (*Portraiture*, 2: 147–55).

35 *Portraiture*, 2: 122.

36 In 1809 Wordsworth described "Character of the Happy Warrior" to Coleridge as "relating to the social and civic duties, and chiefly interesting to the imagination through the understanding, and not to the understanding through the imagination" (*Middle Years* 1: 335). To Harriet Martineau, he said: "'You see, – it does not best fulfil the conditions of poetry; but it is' (solemnly) 'a chain of extremely valooable thoughts'" (*Harriet Martineau's Autobiography with Memorials by Maria Weston Chapman*, 3 vols. [London, 1877], 2: 237).

37 The Warrior's affiliation with the Governor of the 1802 sonnet is confirmed by their common ancestry in *Paradise Lost* Book V. The steps to power prescribed by the sonnet, and the surprising metaphor of the plant with which it concludes, are derived from the passage in Milton describing the ascending "degrees" of Creation (*Paradise Lost* V.479–82).

38 Nelson's "public life" was "stained with one great crime," the crushing of the 1799

Neapolitan rebellion (Fenwick note, *Poetical Works* 4: 419). Wordsworth's reservations about his tribute in the 1807 volume had been confirmed by Southey's *Life of Nelson* (1813); see Harry W. Rudman, "Wordsworth and Admiral Nelson," *College English* 15 (1953–54): 177–78.

39 Milton's phrase is borrowed for "Character of the Happy Warrior," line 27.

40 *Romantic Bards and British Reviewers*, ed. John O. Hayden (Lincoln: University of Nebraska Press, 1971), 57.

CHAPTER SIX

De-fencing the poet: the political dilemma of the poet and the people in Milton's *Second Defense* and Shelley's *Defence of Poetry*

MICHAEL CHAPPELL

THOUGH MUCH CRITICAL attention has been paid to Milton's influence on subsequent generations of poets, especially the Romantics, the prose is oftentimes slighted. Critics sensitive to the strength of Milton's poetry are frequently blind to the impact of his prose. One critic disparagingly calls Milton's political prose "part of a dreary tradition of backbiting and mud-slinging,"[1] and Milton himself set the tone for such critical disregard when he stated that the prose was the work of his "left hand," as if it were not to be considered in the same light as his poetry. For the most part, this attitude that the prose is dismissable relative to the poetry persists with Shelley criticism as well. It is significant, however, that both Milton and Shelley use prose to justify their existence as poets.

Though Milton's *Second Defense of the English People* is primarily a political treatise and Shelley's *Defence of Poetry* primarily a poetical manifesto, both essays take as a common theme the political role of the poet. Both examine the poet's relationship with society as a whole, with the "common people" who may or may not be their readers, but who nonetheless compose the society within which each poet lives and functions. While this relationship with the common people differs radically for Milton and Shelley, for Milton especially it is problematic: the fate of the Protectorate depends upon popular support, and though Milton wants to believe that this popular support will prove the bulwark of the Revolution, he doubts that the people will prove faithful to the ideals embodied by leaders like Cromwell and himself. Shelley's essay expresses a more democratic belief, both in the common people as able to appreciate change and beauty, and in the poet's ability to help them reach this appreciation.

My reading of these essays turns on two primary meanings of the word "defense." First, each poet is defending the society as a whole against the attacks of those who question the idea of liberty and the good of "the people." Each poet argues strongly for liberty as a key to a healthy society, but liberty to both means not only freedom from political oppression, but also freedom for the artist. Milton's and Shelley's defenses are self-vindicating arguments for the role of the poet within societies which have marginalized the poet and his usefulness. The word "defense" contains a second meaning that is central to my reading of these texts: a "defense" is also a "de-fencing," a removal of the fences that society has set up to limit the poet. Though both Milton and Shelley attempt to free themselves by "de-fencing" the poet, they meet with differing degrees of success.

By reading Milton's poetry independently of his revolutionary prose, critics have too often maintained a critical and interpretive fence around Milton as a poet. By de-emphasizing Milton's prose, critics have often overlooked that Milton "spent twenty years of his life in political pamphleteering and controversy, went blind in part as a result of his work for the republican administration, [and] had some of his writings burnt publicly by the hangman at the Restoration."[2] The critical approach to the poetry should be expanded to include the Milton embodied in the political prose. Such expansion would deepen our understanding of the poetry, especially if we keep in mind Christopher Hill's assertion that Milton "is the greatest English revolutionary who is also a poet, the greatest English poet who is also a revolutionary."[3]

Though the Second Defense is a defense of the English "people" for having beheaded the King, a good deal of Milton's argument turns on his defense of himself, especially of himself as a poet. Milton defends himself against a culture which accuses poets of juvenility and ineffectuality. Sir John Denham, in the "Epistle Dedicatory" to his Poems and Translations, says that Charles I advised him to stop writing poetry, for "when men are young, and have little else to do, they might vent the over-flowings of their Fancy that way" but that it serves no serious purpose once one is "thought fit for more serious Employments."[4] Charles's attitude is representative of seventeenth-century society's attitude toward poets. It trivializes poetry, and by extension, denigrates the poet. It makes poetry the play of a juvenile, not the work of an adult. A "man" would never write poetry because it is not serious or applicable to the "real world," the world of politics, power, and the social structure. Of course, Milton's epic poems are proof of the "serious employments" to which poetry can be put, just as his political prose is proof of the "serious employments" to which poets can be put. Nonetheless, Charles's attitude is a common one, and it is in part against this view that Milton (and later Shelley) reacts in writing his self-defense.

Underlying Milton's defense of himself, however, is his problematic relationship with "the people," for the Second Defense presents a Milton struggling with his own concepts of revolution and the society that that revolution is intended to further. On the one hand, he seems almost democratic in his defense of revolution as a good for the entire society. On the other hand, it becomes evident that revolution can only benefit a few "true believers." Just as Milton is marginalized as a poet by the masses he distrusts, he in turn marginalizes the masses – the uneducated, the laborers, the merchant classes, the people who need governance no matter whether it be by a king or a Cromwell – in his discourse.

In one of the key biographical sections of the *Second Defense*, Milton carves out his place in the Revolution and betrays his distrust of the common people:

I exchanged the toils of war, in which any stout trooper might outdo me, for those labors which I better understood, that with such wisdom as I owned I might add as much weight as possible to the counsels of my country and to this excellent cause, using not my lower but my higher and stronger powers. And so I concluded that if God wished those men to achieve such noble deeds, He also wished that there be other men by whom these deeds, once done, might be worthily praised and extolled, and that truth defended by arms be also defended by reason the only defence truly appropriate to man.[5]

Milton's complex relationship with the idea of the common man is here played out against his desire for the success of the Revolution. First, Milton links himself with the soldier, whose "toils of war" are matched equally by Milton's "labor" with the pen. Though he claims to be not as physically strong as the soldier – "any stout trooper might outdo me" – he legitimates himself by saying that with "wisdom" he can add as much "weight" as possible to the Revolution. The choice of the word "weight" links Milton to the working soldier, as if Milton's contribution were equally material. In this sense he comes close, at least in rhetoric, to democratic sympathy and almost seems to believe in the power of the people – the people as a whole, not just the leaders of the Revolution – to carry the Revolution to success. Furthermore, he equates the poet's role – that of praising and extolling the achievements of the great men of the Revolution – with those same achievers. It is equally important to lead, to fight, and to record the "noble deeds" of the Revolution. Momentarily at least, Milton appears to have obliterated the class differences that the Revolution was to fight against and to have replaced them with a single class struggling with a single purpose: fighting for the life and health of the Commonwealth.

However, Milton points out that his powers are "higher and stronger" than mere physical strength, and by doing so he effectively states that he is superior to the soldier, because he is not dependent on the un-reason of brute force. He chooses to defend truth by "reason," thus elevating himself over the common soldier (and, by extension, the majority of the populace). By stating that reason is "the only defence truly appropriate to man," Milton's self-defense all but obliterates the soldier's value. If the poet is superior to the soldier, then the poet's value to society is greater than that of the soldier, for where the soldier responds to violence with violence, the poet is the true defender of the Commonwealth because he symbolizes and enacts the only defense that is truly "appropriate" to humankind, the defense of reason.

Milton's relationship with the common people is obviously problematic. He knows that the Commonwealth depends on their support, yet he mistrusts that they will be willing or able to see its revolutionary program through to completion. Milton's further marginalization of the common people is evident when he writes that "nothing is more natural, nothing more just, nothing more useful or more advantageous to the human race than that the lesser obey the greater, not the lesser number the greater number, but the lesser virtue the greater virtue, the lesser wisdom the greater wisdom" (636). He knows that sacrifices must be made, and though the true believers – himself, Cromwell, and other enlightened Puritans – might be willing to sacrifice short-term temporal good for long-term liberty, he doubts the steadfastness of those who might be less-than-true believers. The multitude are prone to the baser appetites (lesser in virtue and wisdom) and thus more susceptible to the lure of a re-instituted monarchy.

Milton's marginalization of the masses is further exemplified in his writing of the *Defenses* in Latin. Though it is true that he wrote in Latin to reach an audience of educated men throughout Europe in an attempt to assure them that the English people were justified in replacing a monarchy with a republic, he also wrote in Latin because he mistrusted the very people he was supposed to defend. In the *Second Defense*, he regrets writing the divorce tracts in English because he met with "vernacular readers, who are usually ignorant of their own good, and laugh at the misfortunes of others" (610). Latin, therefore, protects Milton from the ignorance of the majority and limits his audience to the learned minority.

Perhaps Milton's problematic relationship with the English people is evidence that "Milton's age was facing for the first time in human history the problem of educating an electorate."[6] The electorate in this sense obviously does not refer to actual voters so much as the people – not simply leaders, but the entire populace – on whose muscle the Commonwealth depends for its success or failure. When Milton writes that "nothing can be more efficacious than education in moulding the minds of men to virtue (whence arises true and internal liberty), in governing the state effectively, and preserving it for the longest possible space of time" (625) he is addressing just this issue. The Commonwealth is dependent on the support of the majority of Englishmen if it is going to last, yet this same majority is not trusted by Milton. Though he believes that they need to be educated to know what liberty is and then to defend it, he seems unsure whether this mammoth and difficult task of educating the leviathan-like people can be done. From this standpoint, Milton seems in a poor position to defend the English people against the accusations of the supporters of monarchy: his personal mistrust of the people undercuts the larger political purpose of the *Second Defense*.

Perhaps Charles Geisst sums it up best when he states:

> While granting all men freedom of conscience, a tenet of Independency, [Milton] denied democratic reform on the basis of education. The natural right of conscience, or the ability of any man to attain justice, in no way specified a system of natural political rights. Rights such as these could only be achieved through the rule of merit by a particular class of virtuous men.[7]

Though Milton might grant people "freedom of conscience," he worries what would result if that conscience were not sufficiently educated to focus the majority of men on the idea of liberty. Of course, he must first convince the people that they truly want liberty and that liberty is not simply an excuse for replacing one ruler with another.

Milton, in spite of a desire to be integrated into the social structure as a poet, insists on keeping himself at least one remove from the community. He believes in a form of universal liberty, in education to set the English free, and in the need for the English people to fight unitedly for the Commonwealth. However, his own fears about the unstable nature of the masses, and his fears that the people will prove gullible to those who would restore the monarchy, undermine his belief in the longevity of the Commonwealth and in his own integration (acceptance) into society.

Milton's attempts to free the poet are linked to the need to *act* in the defense of the Commonwealth: "He alone is to be called great who either performs or teaches or worthily records great things" (601). Milton allows three activities by which a person can achieve greatness: performing a great deed (defeating Charles's armies, for example), teaching others the history of great deeds or how to perform them (Cromwell's leading the Commonwealth could be seen as a mode of teaching), or recording great deeds (as in writing the epic poem or defending the English people). To write is to act, for it records for successive generations the history of the culture. Not to write is to forget, and Milton does not want the people to forget the hard-fought-for freedoms that being liberated from monarchy has brought them. In this sense, then, the *Second Defense* is an epic work recording the history of the Commonwealth.

Milton's thought on this point, however, is very conflicted. First, he limits the common people to participating in the first of those acts, simply fighting for the Commonwealth. Yet, he admits that subsequent generations must be told about the acts of the present generation; the Revolution must be recorded and passed on at all class levels if it is to succeed. Though Milton has just argued for his acceptance by society, he is again marginalizing the majority of that society. The common people are good enough to die fighting the Royalists, but history will read of the acts of the leaders (Cromwell) through the words of the poet (Milton). It is a not-so-subtle political message that Milton is encoding here, and it differs little from the predominant monarchical stance: the common people are necessary as the political body, but they are less important than the political head, the leader(s) of the country.

In spite of Milton's obviously conflicted thought, his argument also attempts to "de-fence" the poet by linking him with the underlying social structure. Milton infuses the *Second Defense* with the idea that art and politics do not have to be separated, that the traditional mistrust or denigration of the poet serves the Commonwealth poorly. As David Loewenstein writes, in the *Second Defense* Milton

finds his literary powers put to a new test: the process of defending and shaping the revolutionary ideals of the state becomes an enterprise of heroic and often mythopoetic scope … The *Second Defense* concerns Milton's capacity to engage creatively and decisively in the new social order – to help shape the state and its revolutionary program, as well as to respond to its political realities, through the poetics of his polemical discourse.[8]

It is through Milton's linking of political with artistic tradition that he is able to point out to his educated countrymen (and his readers on the continent) the close relationship that exists between art and the underlying social structure. We might question, however, how "decisively" Milton is able to engage in the new social order. Writing the *Second Defense* is indeed a test of Milton's literary powers, for he is forced to argue in defense of a populace whose motivations he fears are subject to change at any moment.

Milton is more secure when he plays the role of poet rather than when he theorizes about the poet's usefulness. There are two aspects of Milton the poet in the *Second Defense* that deserve examination because they are linked both to defending the people and to "de-fencing" the poet: that of the prophet and that of the epic poet. Joseph Anthony Wittreich, Jr. tells us that prophecy is

literature as process, not literature as knowledge; it exists not for the truths it embodies but for those to which it provides access, and thus, once it has brought man to the final stage of consciousness, it ceases to be functional and then can be discarded. Prophecy, in short, mediates between man and God, between fallen reason and the visionary imagination, and, liberating the mind, enables it to become the mediator between earthly and heavenly things, between time and eternity.[9]

In the *Second Defense*, Milton both records and defends the past and prophesies the future in his hope for a secure Commonwealth. By doing so, he mediates between the "earthly" commons and the "heavenly" utopia the Republicans hope to create. He writes, "I perceived that men were following the true path to liberty and that from these beginnings, these first steps, they were making the most direct progress towards the liberation of all human life" (622). Prophecy ("literature as process") is meant to expand the understanding, and this is the goal of the *Second Defense*. It mediates between the believers, those who support the Commonwealth, and the doubters, those who support the monarchy (or at least fear its disablement). The problem is that the prophet is never simply one of the masses. The prophet stands out by virtue of his ability to be prophetic. Consequently, though Milton is pointing out one of the roles of the poet, he is again reinforcing his stance as removed from the common man. Rather than freeing the poet, Milton seems to be reinforcing (or at least accepting) the bulwark between himself and the society that considers the poet "juvenile."

Perhaps the most delphic of his statements is one that recalls his earlier-mentioned belief in the higher power of reason over the brute power of force:

Many men has war made great whom peace makes small. If, having done with war, you neglect the arts of peace, if warfare is your peace and liberty, war your only virtue, your supreme glory, you will find, believe me, that peace itself is your greatest enemy. Peace itself will be by far your hardest war, and what you thought liberty will prove to be your servitude. (680)

This serves as a prophetic statement to Cromwell and the leaders of the Revolution. In the fight for liberty, once the bloody battles of the field are done, the battle of the mind begins, and reason must be exercised to prevent war from breaking out again before peace (in this case embodied in the Commonwealth) can have a chance to succeed. Milton speaks to the leaders of the Commonwealth to look toward the good of the country as a whole. Peace and liberty must involve everyone (with the exception, perhaps, of the Catholics), not just a particular group or a few men. Physical battle destroys bodies only, not ideas; it is only through a prosperous, fair, and efficient peace that the battle for the hearts and minds of the citizens can be won, and this battle must be won if the Commonwealth is to succeed.

Parallel to his role as the prophet is Milton's role as epic poet. Throughout the *Second Defense* Milton refers to his blindness as a divine gift – "By this infirmity may I be perfected, by this completed. So in this darkness, may I be clothed in light" (590).[10] He notes that blindness connects him with the prophets and poets of ancient history. Terry Eagleton says that "the task of the revolutionary mythologer is to furnish the political process with a set of efficacious symbols, universalize its meanings by inscribing them within a global drama, unify its disparate forces by the power of the image, and summon the past into metaphorical compact with the present."[11] As "revolutionary mythologer" of the Commonwealth Milton has set himself up as the ultimate symbol of the political process – the blind prophet-poet, the latest in an antique line of such personages, who defends the English people in their "global drama" – and he attempts to unify the disparate forces of the Revolution within this image of himself. Thus, his mistrust of the common people notwithstanding, we can see him trying to embody their concerns and their relationship with the new rulers, to represent within himself the struggle that the Commonwealth must endure. But his relationship is still one of a superior (the epic poet) addressing the inconstant masses.

Milton's strongest statement relating his role as a poet to the needs of the Commonwealth and the English people comes near the end of the essay:

> I have borne witness, I might almost say I have erected a monument that will not soon pass away, to those deeds that were illustrious, that were glorious, that were almost beyond any praise, and if I have done nothing else, I have surely redeemed my pledge. Moreover, just as the epic poet, if he is scrupulous and disinclined to break the rules, undertakes to extol, not the whole life of the hero whom he proposes to celebrate in his verse, but usually one event of his life ... and passes over the rest, so let it suffice me too, as my duty or my excuse, to have celebrated at least one heroic achievement of my countrymen. (685)

Here Milton most emphatically justifies the poet. His dual role of bearing witness to the events of his society and of erecting a monument to those events and the people who performed them reiterates what he believes are the most significant roles of the poet. And yet we might detect a tone of despair – perhaps an indication of accepted marginalization – shadowing his self-inflationary confidence when he claims that if he has done nothing else he has at least redeemed his pledge to the people to defend them against the attacks of the monarchists.

Finally, the poem also functions as a gift to the people, for as Wittreich observes, "though he assumes ... an artistic superiority, he proceeds to draw his values from those he addresses and from the culture he celebrates."[12] Though he might believe in the intellectual superiority of a few, he knows that the support of the many is needed if the Commonwealth is to survive and if liberty and virtue are to reign among the English people. For we must not forget, though Milton might have been in Eagleton's words "the organic intellectual of the English revolution," he was still a creation of English society.[13] Perhaps this helps to explain his deep ambivalence toward the common man when he is trying to defend the Commonwealth and carve a place for himself in the revolutionary culture. On the one hand, it seems hypocritical to assume the strength of the laborer in his *Defenses*; on the other hand, however, he cannot escape (no matter how much his education encourages him) his dependence on the English working classes (that muscle on which the Commonwealth depends).

Shelley indirectly describes Milton's dilemma when he writes of the subjection of the poet in the Preface to *Prometheus Unbound*: "Poets, not otherwise than philosophers, painters, sculptors, and musicians, are, in one sense, the creators, and, in another, the creations, of their age. From this subjection the loftiest do not escape."[14] As the chief polemicist for the Revolution, Milton is one of the creators of his age. His defenses of the English people seek to justify the Revolution and the regicide to the world at large. Nonetheless, what he has helped to create also subjects him in time and history to the interpretations of his fellow citizens and to those of future generations. Liberty proves much more difficult to embody than it is to imagine. Freeing himself from the limits imposed on the poet by society also proves to be an impossible task. His sense of intellectual superiority proves too intransigent. The people will remain an untrustworthy mob until they have been "educated" to liberty. Until then, however inadvertently, Milton creates as many fences as he could have torn down, and considering that the monarchy was restored, perhaps his suspicions about the people's inability to assume responsibility were correct. In the end, perhaps it was impossible for Milton to "de-fence" the poet.

That Shelley is in the line of descent from Milton is unquestioned, and our concern here is less with poetic influence than with intellectual influence, the passing along of revolutionary ideology to a younger generation, and the liberation of the poet.[15] In this context, Shelley's *Defence of Poetry* can be read as a response to Milton's *Second Defense*. In it, Shelley responds to Milton's dictates on the nature of reason, the responsibilities of the poet, and the structure of society. In addition, it is in this essay that Shelley tries to "de-fence" himself, just as Milton had tried to do in his prose defense.

Shelley opens his essay by defining reason and imagination:

> Reason is the enumeration of quantities already known; imagination is the perception of the value of those quantities, both separately and as a whole. Reason respects the differences, and imagination the similitudes of things. Reason is to Imagination as the instrument to the agent, as the body to the spirit, as the shadow to the substance. (480)

This statement shows a major difference between Shelley and Milton. Shelley posits the importance of imagination and its role as something higher than reason, whereas Milton placed reason at the top of human traits. For Milton, imagination in the common man was a threat to the Commonwealth, for it might lead him away from the Commonwealth. For Shelley, imagination is the ultimate possession for any man, because it enables everyone to achieve freedom, whereas Milton's reason "respects the differences" in things. Thus, the man who uses Milton's reason will accept a social structure that places him within a hierarchy; he must accept that he is not an equal among equals.

Shelley's imagination, however, respects "the similitudes of things." Imagination enables us to see shared qualities. Shelley's imagination is a democratizing principle that can free all people.

We can therefore read Shelley's *Defence* not simply as an artistic manifesto, but as a document that espouses "a social and political aesthetic."[16] Though usually read as a manifesto of the imagination, in fact, in the *Defence* reason and imagination are irrevocably joined. Writing on the *Defence*, Paul Fry comments that "imagination must pave the way for the reason in every new venture of thought or else the mind will atrophy and fail to keep pace with the need for change in society. Moreover, reason has no useful function that is independent of, or different from, the function of the imagination."[17] Reason and imagination are thus inseparable. Imagination leads the way in conceiving the possibility of a new social order, but it relies on reason to help determine the particulars needed to bring about and implement this new order. Imagination originates the idea of liberty, but reason is put to use to determine (with imagination) what must be done to achieve liberty, what steps are involved in establishing liberty, how liberty is defined, and to whom it applies.

Reason also serves Shelley in another way: in league with the imagination, it is a tool that he uses in an attempt to free himself, to knock down the barriers that separate him from society at large. To accomplish this, Shelley places the poet in the center of human activity:

Poets ... are not only the authors of language and of music, of the dance and architecture and statuary and painting: they are the institutors of laws, and the founders of civil society and the inventors of the arts of life and the teachers, who draw into a certain propinquity with the beautiful and the true that partial apprehension of the agencies of the invisible world which is called religion. (482)

Poets can exist in any endeavor, as long as the imagination is in league with reason to create beauty or convey to others the beauty that the imagination can conceive. The poet can be a teacher (one of Milton's roles for the poet), but on the whole, Shelley's conception of the poet goes far beyond the role that Milton carves out for him. Milton's poet's primary role is to write about the great deeds performed by others. Shelley's poet achieves greatness by doing more than merely recording the history of a society. Shelley's poet is a metaphorical institutor of laws and a founder of "civil society." Poets are thus more integrally linked with the masses; they do not exist solely on the outskirts of society, for they function in all areas of the culture.

Furthermore, since all people have imaginations, they possess within themselves the primary quality of the poet. This is not to say that every man must be a poet. Scrivener says that Shelley shows "how imagination creates the 'liberty' by which society progresses ... Creativity is contagious and boundless, overflowing with a desire to propagate itself, so that creativity in one sphere tends to inspire the whole society."[18] Shelley's "imagination" inspires society to achieve and to create greater things. Milton's reason, on the other hand, convinces men to accept their roles within the socio-political structure as necessary to the continuation of the Commonwealth. Milton would have men seek liberty, but he would be less likely to have them liberated in Shelleyan terms. Since the imagination is Shelley's motive force, and since it exists in practitioners of all modes of creative labors, it aligns him with the *demos* as he further attempts to free the poet from the rigid dictates of a repressive (or unsympathetic) society.

As with Milton, Shelley's poet also functions as a prophet:

> Poets, according to the circumstances of the age and nation in which they appeared, were called in the earlier epochs of the world legislators or prophets: a poet essentially comprises and unites both these characters. For he not only beholds intensely the present as it is, and discovers those laws according to which present things ought to be ordered, but he beholds the future in the present, and his thoughts are the germs of the flower and the fruit of latest time.
> (482–83)

People inspired with the spirit of the poet – no matter what their function in the social construct – are subject to being prophets, for they (like the poet) perceive intensely the present, and from the present the seeds of the future are planted and incubated. Note, however, that the imagination continues to be joined with reason: "laws" and making things "ordered" is a function of reason following the lead of imagination. This section of the *Defence* reads as if it were a gloss to Milton's prophecy to Cromwell. Milton's "thoughts" contain the "germs of the flower" of liberty within Cromwell's Commonwealth, and they might grow to fruition if properly nurtured. If the Commonwealth fails, however, then the plant will die or the seeds of revolution lie dormant (perhaps awaiting a Shelley to discover them?).

Shelley's continuing attempt to "de-fence" himself takes its most direct form in the section of the *Defence* where he addresses poetry's function. In this section Shelley justifies his "profession" and himself as a fully involved member of society. He says that poetry contains pleasure, wisdom, refined sentiments, and moral teaching (486) and that it "awakens and enlarges the mind itself by rendering it the receptacle of a thousand unapprehended combinations of thought" (487). To enlarge the mind is to democratize it, to open it to the variety and wonders of the world that surround each person. Shelley states that

> A man, to be greatly good, must imagine intensely and comprehensively; he must put himself in the place of another and of many others; the pains and pleasures of his species must become his own ... Poetry strengthens that faculty which is the organ of the moral nature of man, in the same manner as exercise strengthens a limb.
> (487–88)

Shelley here speaks of the ability to empathize with one's fellow human beings, and in this sense he is Milton's moral superior. Milton was unable fully to empathize with the common man. Milton could intellectually conceive of the common man, but he could never really let himself feel what it was like to be below himself. Milton is too intransigently intellectual to let his imagination take him "downward." Rather, he looks perpetually "upward." Shelley says that the imagination can convey feeling into an intensely realized moment and leave one with the belief of having experienced that moment. Thus, the democratizing of society will only occur when many people learn to put themselves "in the place of another" and make the pains of the society their own. Once those pains have been felt, and an emotional bond established, the possibility for successful revolution exists.

The political life of societies, however, is cyclical, and they are therefore subject to losing their democratic structure and susceptible to tyranny and despotism. Shelley reminds us that societies fall "from the extinction of the poetical principle" and that "lust, fear, avarice, cruelty and fraud" characterize societies that are found incapable "of *creating* in form, language, or institution" (496). Shelley fears this loss of creativity (imagination), perhaps because he sees an England from which he is estranged and which he is afraid is in danger of losing its creative heritage. Revolution is needed to keep creativity alive, and if people become more and more distanced from one another, the possibility of maintaining creative and political liberty diminishes every day. When Shelley argues for a more democratic structure and for the increased imaginative involvement of the people, he is arguing against the Miltonic class structure which would keep the people in order. For Shelley, societies depend on a constant influx of imagination to avoid stagnation. A stagnant society – one in which people are intellectually removed from their leaders and from one another – soon dies.

Just as societies evolve and grow, so does great poetry. It exists for the good of all who can experience it, and the more who experience it, the better off will be the world of human thought and practice:

All high poetry is infinite; it is as the first acorn, which contained all oaks potentially. Veil after veil may be undrawn, and the inmost naked beauty of the meaning never exposed. A great Poem is a fountain for ever overflowing with the waters of wisdom and delight; and after one person and one age has exhausted all its divine effluence which their peculiar relations enable them to share, another and yet another succeeds, and new relations are ever developed, the source of an unforeseen and an unconceived delight. (500)

The great poet's great poem destroys the boundaries that separate people. Paul Fry sums up Shelley's belief when he says: "True poetry by its very existence symbolizes the moral and political condition to which humanity can aspire."[19]

The great poem is the ultimate liberator. It obliterates ignorance and obtuseness and infuses the reader with a historical and moral ethos (as well as simply providing pleasure). It records the acts and accomplishments of the people and educates others in the achievements of a culture. Poetry can effect emotional and imaginative change in the people, and Shelley sees this as important to the continued existence of a society.

At the conclusion of the *Defence* Shelley writes that his age is populated by "such philosophers and poets as surpass beyond comparison any who have appeared since the last national struggle for civil and religious liberty" (508). He is referring, of course, to the English Revolution, and just as that age produced its Milton, so he sees great poets in his own age. What is significant here, however, is the emphasis on political struggle. As a poet-prophet, Shelley sees his own age in turmoil and struggling for rights, for the establishment of a civil culture that should consider the good of all, not simply the ruling or monied few, and he believes that poetry is "the most unfailing herald, companion, and follower of the awakening of a great people" (508). True to the people and to the role of the poet to the very end, Shelley here again posits the poet as one of the people. The poet simultaneously *leads* (by virtue of his strong imagination), is a *companion* (because he refuses to place the people below himself), and *follows* (since the culture needs someone to record its history). From this tripartite structure of the poet, Shelley confidently states that "Poets are the unacknowledged legislators of the World."

There is a final irony, however, in the differing roles the poet plays in the political structure for Milton and Shelley. Milton was a part of his society and argued from the perspective of one who was involved in the day-to-day operations of the Commonwealth. Shelley argues from the position of the outsider, cast off from his own country, sensitively aware of his loss, and unable except in writing to initiate change. It is Shelley, however, who is the more secure of the two. Milton's government existed on a shaky foundation, and his *Defenses* of the Commonwealth are both evidence of this instability and attempts to shore up a Commonwealth under attack. Shelley, on the other hand, is an outcast, but he seems more secure in his arguments for the good of society as a whole. Because he is an outcast, he is unacknowledged. Milton is acknowledged, for his *Defenses* spoke for the Commonwealth. Shelley sees what the result was for Milton of being acknowledged: afflicted with blindness brought on by overwork, nearly executed as a regicide, and ignored in his later years. Though Shelley wants the poet to receive his due in the realm of ideas and with regard to his impact on society, he might very well feel that it is better to be unacknowledged, alone with his teeming imagination and his pen. Fry seems to have reached this conclusion as well at the end of his study of Shelley's *Defence*:

On the one hand, the unifying tendency of his work sets at defiance the isolation of the individual; it is indeed "collectivist," both spiritually and socially. On the other hand, his awareness that we receive and make use of knowledge piecemeal until we lose ourselves in its veils returns the individual to his isolation, with no objective basis for coherence or for a definite place in any "history" that could be fully or systematically grasped.[20]

Sometimes the desire to "de-fence" oneself simply leaves one more vulnerable. Shelley (as well as his fellow Romantics) might have been disengaged from his society as he argued for change, but he spared himself the frustrations and dangers that Milton faced. For Shelley and for Milton, fences came to mean different things, while functioning similarly. For Shelley – living outside the dominant culture – fences were barriers behind which he could launch attacks on a repressive bourgeois society. For Milton – living on the inside of the ruling culture, but removed from the majority of the populace – fences isolated and protected him from the threat that the populace posed.

NOTES

1 Bruce Boehrer, "Elementary Structures of Kingship: Milton, Regicide, and the Family," *Milton Studies* 23 (1987): 109.
2 Michael Wilding, *Dragons Teeth: Literature in the English Revolution* (Oxford: Oxford University Press, 1987), 3.
3 *Milton and the English Revolution* (New York: Viking, 1978), 4.
4 Sir John Denham, *Poems and Translations with the Sophy* (London: Herringman, 1671), unpaginated.
5 *The Complete Prose*, 4: 1: 553. All quotations from the *Second Defense* are from volume 4, part 1 of Wolfe's *The Complete Prose*. Hereafter all citations to the *Defense* are noted by page number in the text.
6 Hill, *Milton and the English Revolution*, 168.
7 *The Political Thought of John Milton* (London: Macmillan, 1984), 40.
8 "Milton and the Poetics of Defense," in *Politics, Poetics, and Hermeneutics in Milton's Prose*, ed. David Loewenstein and James Grantham Turner (Cambridge: Cambridge University Press, 1990), 171.
9 Joseph Anthony Wittreich, Jr., "'A Poet Amongst Poets': Milton and the Tradition of Prophecy," in *Milton and the Line of Vision*, ed. Joseph Anthony Wittreich, Jr. (Madison: University of Wisconsin Press, 1975), 110.
10 Compare this with Wilding's comment: "In stressing his blindness, he is reasserting his radical beliefs; in asserting that his blindness has been compensated for by 'a far surpassing inner light', he is claiming that God has rewarded him for the radical political commitment, that God approves of revolutionary activity" (*Dragons Teeth: Literature in the English Revolution*, 241).
11 "The god that failed" in *Re-Membering Milton: Essays on the Texts and Traditions*, ed. Mary Nyquist and Margaret W. Ferguson (New York: Methuen, 1987), 342.
12 Joseph Anthony Wittreich, Jr., "'The Crown of Eloquence': The Figure of the Orator in Milton's Prose Works," in *Achievements of the Left Hand: Essays on the Prose of John*

Milton, ed. Michael Lieb and John T. Shawcross (Amherst: University of Massachusetts Press, 1974), 47.

13 *Re-Membering Milton*, ed. Nyquist and Ferguson, 346.

14 *Shelley's Poetry and Prose*, 135. Hereafter all Shelley citations are noted by page number in the text.

15 I cite Curran and Wittreich as representative of the prevailing attitude toward Milton/Shelley influence. In "The Siege of Hateful Contraries: Shelley, Mary Shelley, Byron, and *Paradise Lost*," Stuart Curran says that "*A Defence of Poetry* is an enduring testament to the healthy, vital, and continual influence of Milton on the future course of English poetry" (*Milton and the Line of Vision*, 229). Wittreich sums it up well when he says in the Introduction to *The Romantics on Milton: Formal Essays and Critical Asides* (Cleveland: The Press of Case Western Reserve University, 1970) that as "the hero of political radicalism during the Romantic era, Milton – more than any other poet – taught the Romantics what it meant to be a revolutionary artist and how it was that a poet could fuse the parts of his poem into a massive unity. It is this lesson that they sought to embody in their criticism and to transmit to subsequent generations" (21).

16 Michael Henry Scrivener, *Radical Shelley: The Philosophical Anarchism and Utopian Thought of Percy Bysshe Shelley* (Princeton: Princeton University Press, 1982), 247.

17 *The Reach of Criticism: Method and Perception in Literary Theory* (New Haven: Yale University Press, 1983), 130.

18 *Radical Shelley*, 251.

19 *The Reach of Criticism*, 147.

20 *The Reach of Criticism*, 159.

CHAPTER SEVEN

Keats's marginalia in *Paradise Lost*

BETH LAU

▆▆▆▆

KEATS'S NOTES IN HIS two-volume 1807 edition of *Paradise Lost* were the first examples of the poet's marginal annotations to be published and therefore have long been available to scholars and critics.[1] The extensive underscorings and marginal lines in these volumes have never been published, however, or even described and analyzed as Caroline Spurgeon and R. S. White have done with the markings in Keats's copies of Shakespeare.[2] Keats's markings in *Paradise Lost* valuably supplement and deepen our understanding of the brief and sometimes cryptic remarks made in the marginal notations. In addition, the markings reveal interests in or reactions to Milton's poem that are not expressed in the notes. Certainly a fuller record of Keats's response to *Paradise Lost* emerges from studying all the marginalia than from examining only the nineteen previously published notes.

The present essay points out and provides examples of some of the dominant patterns in Keats's markings. These include an emphasis on descriptive passages and a relative indifference to direct speech; an interest in setting and sensory details; an interest in female decorum and solitude; a tension between the appeal of disciplined ambition and the pull of luxury and ease; a general fascination with contrasts; and a sensitivity to the pathos of separation from loved ones and familiar surroundings. The last section of the essay explores implications of the most striking of these patterns: Keats's neglect of speeches and dialogue in *Paradise Lost*. This neglect of speeches calls into question Keats's dramatic sense and may help to explain why the poet failed to fulfill his playwriting ambitions.[3]

In Keats's copy of *Paradise Lost*, passages describing setting are marked; epic similes are marked; and third-person accounts of characters' appearances and actions are marked. When a character begins to speak, however, the marking commonly ceases, except for occasional brief passages notable for arresting phrases or imagery but seldom for central concepts or character traits. Thus in Book I, the description of Satan before he addresses his assembled host is heavily marked, but the address itself – lines 622–62 – is left clean. Marking resumes, however, as soon as the speech has ended; Keats underscores lines 663–66, describing the response of the fallen angels to Satan's inspiring words. In the important council of Hell scene in Book II, the introductions of Belial and Beelzebub are underscored (II.109–13, 302–9), as are the accounts of audience response to Mammon's and Satan's speeches (II.285–90, 476–77, 488–93), but very little in the speeches themselves is noted. Later in Book II, there is another example of this recurring pattern. In the passage in which Satan encounters Chaos, Keats underscores "and him thus the Anarch old / With faultering speech and visage incomposed / Answer'd" (II.988–90), but what Chaos actually says is passed over. Only lines 87–88 and 259 are underscored in the conversation between God and Christ in Book III, though as soon as Christ has finished speaking Keats underscores "His words here ended, but his meek aspect / Silent yet spake" (III.266–67). In Book IV, several lines (15–18, 27–31) leading up to Satan's first soliloquy are marked, and the three lines immediately following the soliloquy are marked (114–16), but among the eighty-one lines that make up the speech itself, only 73 and 96–97 are distinguished by Keats's pen strokes.

Numerous examples of this tendency could be cited. Little of the conversations between God and Raphael, Raphael and Adam, Satan and his army, Christ and God, or God and Adam is marked in books V–VIII (though Keats does mark passages where Raphael as narrator recounts to Adam the War in Heaven and creation of Heaven and Earth). Likewise in the climactic Book IX, few passages in the key conversations – between Adam and Eve at the beginning of the book, between Eve and Satan, or between Adam and Eve after her and then his fall – are marked, though intervening descriptive passages frequently are. For example, the serpent's movements and appearance as he leads Eve to the tree of knowledge are heavily marked (IX.631–43, 664–78), but the ensuing temptation speech is completely untouched by Keats's pen. The descriptions of Adam's anxious expectation of Eve's return and of her appearance with a bough of fruit in her hand are marked with a marginal line (IX.838–54), though the speech in which Eve announces her transgression is not. Following her speech, Keats underscores "But in her cheek distemper flushing glow'd" (IX.887), as well as the lines describing Adam's reaction:

> Astonied [he] stood and blank, while horror chill
> Ran through his veins, and all his joints relax'd;
> From his slack hand the garland wreath'd for Eve
> Down dropt, and all the faded roses shed.   (IX.890–93)

The moving passages that follow, however, in which Adam reflects on his situation and decides to share Eve's fate, are not marked at all. Similarly, in Book X Keats leaves unmarked the despairing soliloquy in which Adam wonders why he was created and longs for death (X.720–844), but he does underscore the description of Adam after this speech: "On the ground / Outstretch'd he lay, on the cold ground; and oft / Cursed his creation" (X.850–52).

Keats clearly seems more interested in what characters convey through their appearances, gestures, and posture than through their words. He is particularly struck by facial expressions. Some of the passages already quoted describe the countenances of Chaos, Christ, and Eve. The lines on Satan, "but his face / Deep scars of thunder had intrench'd" (I.600–601), are not only underscored but also quoted in the first of Keats's notes (*The Romantics on Milton*, 553). Similarly, "round he throws his baleful eyes" (I.56) is underscored and quoted in a note on page 3, volume 1 of Keats's *Paradise Lost* (*The Romantics on Milton*, 553). Several passages describing Satan's face distorted with passion after his first soliloquy in Book IV are marked (IV.114–16, 126–27, 570–71); the second passage – "on the Assyrian mount / Saw him disfigured" – is distinguished by both underscoring and triple marginal lines and is also quoted in one of Keats's notes (*The Romantics on Milton*, 559). In Book VIII, Keats does not mark Adam's enraptured celebration of Eve's beauty, but he does note Raphael's worried reaction: "To whom the Angel with contracted brow" (VIII.560). Raphael's explanation of what exactly displeases him about Adam's feeling for Eve, however, is unmarked.

Among Keats's notes in *Paradise Lost*, the one most closely related to the pattern under discussion is that in which Keats praises Milton's "*stationing or statu[a]ry.*" Milton, writes Keats, "is not content with simple description, he must station – Thus here, we not only see how the Birds '*with clang despised the ground*' – but we see them '*under a cloud in prospect*' So we see Adam '*Fair indeed and tall – under a plantane* and so we see Satan '*disfigured – on the Assyrian Mount*'" (*The Romantics on Milton*, 559). As Nancy Goslee explains, the term "stationing" derives from theories of the visual arts and refers to a static composition of one or more figures "caught in a suspended, significant moment" or positioned within a particular setting.[4] Keats seems to have experienced *Paradise Lost* largely as a series of pictures or tableaux – or, in the language of our own day, as a series of still shots, whether medium-range views of complete figures or close-ups of revealing facial expressions.

Long-shots too appealed to Keats. A number of marked passages describe characters surveying a panorama from some lofty vantage point. Thus in Book III Satan, from the foot of the stairs leading up to Heaven, gazes on the earth " As when a Scout ... / Obtains the brow of some high climbing hill, /

Which to his eye discovers unaware / The goodly prospect of some foreign land" (III.543–48). A marginal line flags a passage in Book V in which Raphael looks down on the earth from the gate of Heaven (V.247–69), and later in the same book Raphael describes Satan on his rebel throne, "High on a hill, far blazing, as a mount / Raised on a mount" (V.757–58); Keats underscores the lines. The poet who wrote of "stout Cortez when with eagle eyes / He star'd at the Pacific" from the top of "a peak in Darien" ("On First Looking into Chapman's Homer") obviously was fond of panoramic views. In reading *Paradise Lost*, moreover, Keats like Cortez seems to have "star'd" eagerly at pictorial compositions of scenes, figures, or countenances.

A number of marked – often heavily marked – passages from Satan's speeches provide the chief exception to the pattern of disregarding dialogue that generally prevails in Keats's marginalia. Satan is the one character whose words Keats seems to value for their expression of emotion and psychology – especially violent, tortured emotions and psychic conflict. In Book I, the lines "Fallen Cherub, to be weak is miserable, / Doing or suffering" are underscored and marked with triple marginal lines (I.157–58). Keats also underscores exclamations like "Me miserable! which way shall I fly" and "O indignity!" (IV.73; IX.154). Several passages are marked in which Satan initially responds to Adam and Eve with admiration and affection, but then forces his feelings back to their wonted channel of hatred and revenge (IV.366–75; IX.472–76). One phrase that particularly struck Keats was Satan's reference to "the hateful siege / Of contraries" (IX.121–22). These lines are underscored and marked with triple strokes in the margin. The phrase is also quoted in a letter of 21 September 1818, in which Keats describes the "continual fever" that results from immersing himself in *Hyperion*'s "abstract images" in order to forget his dying brother's presence (*Letters*, ed. Rollins, 1: 369). It is clear that Keats, like many of his contemporaries, was struck by Satan's intense, tormented, and divided personality.[5] Nonetheless, given the amount of space devoted to Satan's speeches in *Paradise Lost*, the number of lines Keats marks are still minimal and do not alter the overall conclusion that descriptive passages are more heavily marked than dialogue or soliloquy.

As mentioned previously, descriptions of settings are frequently highlighted in Keats's copy of *Paradise Lost*. In these passages, Keats departs from the visual emphasis of most of the marked lines describing characters and responds to various sensory impressions. Among the patterns one notices in the markings is a recurring interest in mild, balmy, and sweet-smelling air. Thus Keats marks references to "the soft delicious air," "the buxom air, embalm'd / With odours," and the "pure, now purer air" of Paradise, where "gentle gales / Fanning their odoriferous wings, dispense / Native perfumes" (II.400,

842–43; IV.153–54, 156–58). Keats also marks the famous simile describing the pleasure of a city dweller who

> Forth issuing on a summer's morn, to breathe
> Among the pleasant villages and farms
> Adjoin'd, from each thing met conceives delight;
> The smell of grain, or tedded grass, or kine,
> Or dairy, each rural sight, each rural sound.　　　(IX.447–51)[6]

Keats does not note only pleasant odors, however. He also underscores "Asmodeus with the fishy fume" (IV.168) and the passage in which Death "snuff'd the smell / Of mortal change on Earth" (X.272–73; 279–81 are also marked). The lines just quoted have been linked to *Hyperion* I.167–68, in which the old sun god "still snuff'd the incense, teeming up / From man" (*Poems*, ed. Allott, 406n). One also recalls that the retreat of the fallen Titans in *Hyperion* is characterized by close, stagnant air: "No stir of air was there" (I.7). One of the characteristics Keats seems to have picked up from his study of *Paradise Lost* was an attention to odors and atmosphere.

Leigh Hunt reported that "Keats ... observed to me, that Milton, in various parts of his writings, has shown himself a bit of an epicure, and loves to talk of good eating."[7] Hunt does not mention what particular passages from Milton Keats cited, but a number of lines describing eating, appetite, and taste are marked in Keats's *Paradise Lost*. The account of the meal Eve prepares for Adam and Raphael, which has been linked to the food Porphyro prepares for Madeline in *The Eve of St. Agnes* and the half-eaten meal the speaker discovers in *The Fall of Hyperion*, is heavily underscored (V.303–7, 326–27, 341–51, 367–70, 391–95).[8] Keats also marks passages describing the angels' eating habits and digestive systems (V.434–45, 627–39), as well as one in which Adam tells Raphael that the latter's discourse is sweeter "Than fruits of palm-tree pleasantest to thirst / And hunger both, from labour, at the hour / Of sweet repast" (VIII.212–14). The role of appetite in the temptation scene likewise is noted. Keats underscores a passage in which the serpent tells Eve that, as he approached the tree of knowledge,

> 　　　　　　　　a savoury odour blown,
> Grateful to appetite, more pleased my sense
> Than smell of sweetest fennel, or the teats
> Of ewe or goat dropping with milk at even,
> Unsuck'd of lamb or kid, that tend their play.　　　(IX.579–83)

Keats also underscores the lines on Eve: "Greedily she ingorged without restraint, / And knew not eating death" (IX.791–92). Just as he notes both sweet and rank odors, however, Keats also marks foul as well as pleasant eating experiences in *Paradise Lost* (Eve's eating of the fruit from the tree of knowledge could of course be considered both pleasant and unpleasant). Several lines are underscored describing the disgust of the devils in Hell when they eat fruit that turns to ashes in their mouths: "which the offended taste / With spattering noise rejected" and "With hatefullest disrelish writhed their jaws" (X.566–67, 569).

Keats's markings also reflect a sensitivity to sound imagery, both somber or sublime and sweet and melodious. In the first category, Keats marks passages describing thunder (I.175–78; II.476–77), the echoing of Satan's voice in Hell (I.313–15), organ music (I.706–9), "The sound of blustering winds" in "hollow rocks" (II.285–90), the sound of trumpets (II.516–18; VI.59–60), "The voice of God" after the fall (X.97–99), and "The brazen throat of war" (XI.713). In addition, the single word "noise" is underscored in II.957. Among the soothing and celestial sounds Keats marks, one finds references to the fallen angels singing (II.546–52, 554), to angels in heaven playing musical instruments and singing (III.365–68; V.546–48, 655–57; VII.594–600), to music of the spheres (V.625–27), and to nightingales (III.38–40; IV.771–73; VIII.518–19).

Keats's poetry has long been remarked for its rich, arresting imagery that draws upon all of the senses, even the "lower" ones of taste and smell. The marginalia in *Paradise Lost* make clear that Keats found and relished a congenial range of sensory details in Milton's verse. Indeed, Milton may have been one of the masters who helped teach Keats how to "load every rift" of his poems with the "ore" of luxuriant, powerful sense impressions (*Letters*, ed. Rollins, 2: 323).

Paradise Lost contains a number of sensuous passages describing the emotional and physical relationship between Adam and Eve, but Keats does not reveal much interest in these sections. Victor Lams concludes, after studying Keats's poems and letters, that "Keats's response to Eve was intense – and it was intensely physical."[9] One would be unlikely to reach the same conclusion, however, from a study of Keats's markings in Milton's poem. Keats does underscore "And sweet reluctant, amorous delay," as well as an account of Adam and Eve embracing in Book IV (311, 492–502). There is also a marginal line beside the passage, "A pomp of winning graces waited still, / And from about her shot darts of desire" (VIII.61–62). In Book VIII, however, which contains Adam's account of the creation of Eve, his great love for her, and Raphael's discourse on love and description of the angels' lovemaking, Keats's markings are rare and restrained. The only line underscored in Adam's narrative of the birth of Eve is "Yet innocence and virgin modesty" (VIII.501). Keats also underscores the description of the bower where Adam leads Eve on their first night together, but the emphasis here is on stars, birds, and breezes, rather than on human interaction

(VIII.509–20). The only lines marked in Adam's rapturous praise of his wife are "Those thousand decencies that daily flow, / From all her words and action" (VIII.601–2). Keats marks two passages in Book IX celebrating Eve's beauty (IX.386–96, 424–35), but he also underscores the lines "but more soft, and feminine, / Her graceful innocence" (IX.457–58). Keats's markings suggest an emphasis on feminine modesty and purity, rather than on the physical beauty of Eve or the pleasures of conjugal love.

Some of the darker aspects of relations between men and women are noted. Keats marks the line in Book IX, "Not terrible, though terror be in love" (490), as well as a passage in Book IV in which Eve is compared to Pandora who "insnared / Mankind with her fair looks, to be avenged / On him who had stole Jove's authentic fire" (IV.717–19). In the marked passage describing Adam's forlorn awakening after his lascivious lovemaking with Eve, Adam is compared to Samson, rising "from the harlot-lap / Of Philistean Dalilah … Shorn of his strength" (IX.1059–62). In marking these passages, Keats may reveal his fear of women as beautiful deceivers – les belles dames sans merci – who destroy the men who succumb to their charms.

One rather curious pattern in Keats's markings is an interest in references to solitude, especially in relation to female figures. In the midst of a largely unmarked section of text in Book IX, one finds the underscored phrase "Sole Eve" (IX.227). Similarly, a reference to Eve "Thus early, thus alone" is underscored (IX.457). In Sin's narrative of her life, "Pensive here I sat / Alone" (II.777–78) is singled out for attention. Keats also underscores "Alone as they" referring to Adam and Eve, as well as Adam's statement that "solitude sometimes is best society, / And short retirement urges sweet return" (IV.340; IX.249–50). There are a number of imposing solitary goddesses in Keats's poetry, such as "mother Cybele! alone – alone" in *Endymion* (II.640), as well as Melancholy, Moneta, and Autumn in later poems. Keats's interest in solitary female figures may reflect the appeal for him of chaste women who keep themselves apart from men. On the other hand, isolated female figures may reflect Keats's fear of powerful women who betray and abandon men, withdrawing to their own self-sufficient solitude. Perhaps, however, Keats also sympathized with Eve and Adam in their solitude, perceiving in them a loneliness and separation from others that was intensely pathetic to him – as I shall discuss further below.

Solitude was not always threatening to Keats, however, nor was it always associated for him with women. In a letter to George and Georgiana Keats, written in October 1818 when he was composing his Miltonic *Hyperion*, Keats says, "I hope I shall never marry" and claims that his "Solitude is sublime" because "No sooner am I alone than shapes of epic greatness are stationed around me" (*Letters*, ed. Rollins, 1: 403). Brian Wilkie comments that this letter reveals Keats's association of ascetic solitude with the epic tradition in literature.[10] Perhaps Keats was struck by references to solitude in *Paradise Lost* as he was rising to the challenge of composing his own austere epic poem *Hyperion* – a challenge he felt required a stoic sacrifice of all common diversions and social pleasures.

Keats's assumption that the writing of epic poetry required heroic resistance to the siren call of pleasure is clearly expressed in the first note on the half-title page of *Paradise Lost*. Milton, Keats writes,

had an exquisite passion for what is properly in the sense of ease and pleasure poetical Luxury – and with that it appears to me he would fain have been content if he could so doing have preserved his self respect and feel of duty perform'd – but ... he devoted himself rather to the Ardours than the pleasures of Song, solacing himself at intervals with cups of old wine – and those are with some exceptions the finest parts of the Poem With some exceptions – for the spirit of mounting and adventure can never be unfruitful or unrewarded – had he not broken through the clouds which envellope so deliciously the Elysian fields of Verse and committed himself to the Extreme we never should have seen Satan as described

> " But his face
> " Deep Scars of thunder had entrench'd &c. "

> (*The Romantics on Milton*, 553)

Wilkie remarks that "Keats's exaggerated version of Milton's moral struggle between luxury and duty is clearly a projection of his own conflicts" (*Romantic Poets and Epic Tradition*, 162). In fact, Keats's account of Milton's self-division may not be exaggerated. Several critics have discussed the centrality in Milton's work of the temptation motif, in which a character is presented with difficult choices between disciplined obedience and sensory gratification or other pleasures of this world.[11] Nonetheless, Keats's characterization of Milton's divided allegiance to both "the Ardours" and "the pleasures of Song" has obvious relevance to the Romantic poet's own experience. From the beginning of his literary career Keats vacillated between the attractions of "the realm ... Of Flora, and old Pan" and a world characterized by "the agonies, the strife / Of human hearts," as he expressed the conflict in *Sleep and Poetry* (101–2, 124–25), or between "a Life of Sensations" and a life of "Thoughts," as he wrote in his 22 November 1817 letter to Bailey (*Letters*, ed. Rollins, 1: 185). In a 24 April 1818 letter to Taylor, Keats writes of his choice of life in terms that sound very similar to those in the note on Milton. After telling Taylor that he plans to devote himself to the acquisition of knowledge, Keats concludes, "I have been hovering for some time between an exquisite sense of the luxurious and a love for Philosophy – were I calculated for the former I should be glad – but as I am not I shall turn all my soul to the latter" (*Letters*, ed. Rollins, 1: 271). Keats perceived a similar conflict between "poetical Luxury" and mental application in *Paradise Lost* and was impressed by the apparent triumph of superego over libido in Milton's psyche.[12]

Many of Keats's markings in *Paradise Lost* flag passages that describe ambition, discipline, determination, and the overcoming of obstacles. In the opening invocation, the lines "That with no middle flight intends to soar / Above the Aonian mount" and "That to the height of this great argument" are marked (I.14–15, 24). Later in Book I, a number of Satan's inspirational words to the fallen angels are scored, such as:

> the unconquerable will,
> And study of revenge, immortal hate,
> And courage never to submit or yield,
> And what is else not to be overcome;
> That glory never shall his wrath or might
> Extort from me.   (I.106–11)

Keats also underscores the lines in which Satan scornfully asks his comrades if they wish "To slumber here, as in the vales of Heaven?" and summons them to "Awake, arise, or be for ever fallen" (I.321, 330). "Proud imaginations" is underscored in Book II (10), as is Moloch's argument that reentry into heaven should be easy since "descent and fall / To us is adverse," that is "if the sleepy drench / Of that forgetful lake benumb not still" (II.76–77, 73–74). The phrase "upright wing" in the same passage is underscored (II.72). Marked passages describing characters looking down from a great height, mentioned previously, also may have appealed to Keats for the sense of achievement or "spirit of mounting" they conveyed.

The pull of luxury and ease in *Paradise Lost* seems to have attracted Keats's attention too. The various marked passages describing the sensory delights of Eden fall into this category, since they depict a world similar to the one Keats characterizes in his own poetry as the immature and self-indulgent "realm ... of Flora, and old Pan." Keats also underscores several references to "Lethe, the river of oblivion," including one in which the damned long desperately to drink from "The tempting stream, with one small drop to lose / In sweet forgetfulness all pain and woe" (II.583, 607–8). Here the desire to slumber, forget, and escape is stronger than the desire to struggle and aspire. Moreover, Keats drafted the "Sonnet to Sleep," with its luxurious invocation to darkness and oblivion, in the flyleaf of the second volume of *Paradise Lost*. Was this an act of rebellion against Milton's Puritan sense of duty, along the lines of Keats's later declaration that "Life to [Milton] would be death to me" (*Letters*, ed. Rollins, 2: 212)?

Finally, several marked passages express fears or doubts about soaring ambition. In the invocation to Book VII, Keats underscores Milton's initial reference to soaring "Above the flight of Pegasean wing" but then also marks

Milton's desire to descend "Lest from this flying steed unrein'd ... Dismounted, on the Aleian field I fall, / Erroneous" and his assertion that "Standing on Earth, not rapt above the pole, / More safe I sing with mortal voice" (VII.4, 17–20, 23–24). In the opening of Book IX, Milton's fear that "an age too late, or cold / Climate, or years, [may] damp my intended wing" is marked by Keats (IX.44–45), as is a passage in Book XII on the tower of Babel, "where thin air / Above the clouds will pine [man's] entrails gross, / And famish him of breath, if not of bread!" (XII.76–78). These passages are similar to many in Keats's poems that express either a fear of failure in a presumptuously ambitious attempt (e.g., *Sleep and Poetry* 301–12, "On Seeing the Elgin Marbles"), or an anxiety about the inappropriateness of otherworldly soaring for mortal men (e.g., *Endymion* IV.646–55, "God of the meridian," "There is a joy in footing slow across a silent plain" 29–40, and, one could argue, "La Belle Dame sans Merci" and most of the odes).

Several of Keats's notes praise Milton's skill in weaving together contrasting elements. Most directly, Keats's second note declares, "There is a greatness which the Paradise Lost possesses over every other Poem – the *Magnitude of Contrast* and that is softened by the contrast being ungrotesque to a degree – Heaven moves on like music throughout – Hell is also peopled with angels it also move[s] on like music not grating and ha[r]sh but like a grand accompaniment in the Base to Heaven –" (*The Romantics on Milton*, 553). Another note celebrates "The light and shade – the sort of black brightness ... the sorrow, the pain, the sad – sweet Melody" in Book I.535–65 (*The Romantics on Milton*, 555). In addition, a note at the beginning of Book III looks forward to the shift from Satan and Hell to "the Great God" and Heaven, saying "we are getting ripe for diversity" (*The Romantics on Milton*, 558). As Bernice Slote points out, the *Paradise Lost* notes express "Keats's central poetic conception ... the constant use of contrasts and oppositions."[13] Keats's appreciation for the harmony of opposites in *Paradise Lost* is further expressed in the poem "Welcome joy, and welcome sorrow," which has for a motto "Under the flag / Of each his faction, they to battle bring / Their embryo atoms," a slight misquotation from Book II.899–901. Keats's poem yokes together a variety of images associated with pleasure and pain, life and death, for, as the speaker declares, "I do love you both together!" (line 4).

The markings in *Paradise Lost* frequently single out passages notable for their contrasting elements. Many of these have already been mentioned: the descriptions of odors both sweet and noisome, the gentle and tremendous sounds, the delicious and disgusting tastes. Keats also marks a number of passages that sharply contrast Hell to Eden or Heaven. For example, in Book I Keats underscores Satan's remark, "Farewell happy fields, / Where joy for ever dwells: Hail horrors, hail / Infernal world, and thou profoundest Hell"

(I.249–51). In Book VI, Raphael describes Satan's army being driven to the "bounds / And crystal wall of Heaven; which, opening wide, / Rowl'd inward, and a spacious gap disclosed / Into the wastful deep" (VI.859–62). Double marginal lines mark this passage, which dramatically juxtaposes the two regions, celestial and infernal. Similarly, in Book VIII Raphael reports passing by the gates of Hell and hearing within "Noise, other than the sound of dance or song, / Torment, and loud lament, and furious rage. / Glad we return'd up to the coasts of light / Ere Sabbath evening" (VIII.243–46). In this passage, which Keats underscores, sound and light imagery establish the contrast between the suffering of Satan's host and the bliss of the obedient angels. To the fallen angels, of course, the contrast between their present and former conditions is not a source of delight, and we recall that Keats heavily marked Satan's agonized reference to "the hateful siege / Of contraries" (IX.121–22) and quoted the same lines to describe the experience of composing *Hyperion* while his brother was dying (*Letters*, ed. Rollins, 1: 369). The juxtaposition of joy and sorrow or life and death was not always fascinating to Keats. In *Paradise Lost*, he found examples of both the rich and the unbearable effects of stark oppositions. Keats's sympathy for Satan and the other fallen angels is further reflected in one of his longest notes, written in volume 1, pages 44–45 of *Paradise Lost*. "Milton," writes Keats,

is godlike in the sublime pathetic. In Demons, fallen Angels, and Monsters the delicacies of passion living in and from their immortality, is of the most softening and dissolving nature. It is carried to the utmost here – Others more mild [II.546] – nothing can express the sensation one feels at "*Their song was partial* &c. [II.552]... There are numerous other instances in Milton – where Satan's progeny is called his "*daughter dear*" [II.817], and where this same Sin, a female, and with a feminine instinct for the showy and martial is in pain lest death should sully his bright arms "*nor vainly hope to be invulnerable in those bright arms*" [II.811–12]. Another instance is "*pensive I sat* alone [II.777–78] We need not mention "*Tears such as Angels weep*" [I.620].   (*The Romantics on Milton*, 557)

The last line quoted is among the most heavily marked in Keats's copy of *Paradise Lost*; it and the line above it are underscored and have three lines in the margin beside them.

What Keats seems to find pathetic in the passages he cites is immortal or supernatural characters betraying human emotions. The same response appears to inform Keats's marking of other passages that describe the fallen angels' initiation into pain and suffering. The lines "to starve in ice / Their soft etherial warmth" (II.600–601) are underscored. In the battle-in-Heaven scene, Keats marks the passage in which "Satan first knew pain" (VI.325–31), as well as that in which Moloch "Down cloven to the waist, with shatter'd arms / And uncouth pain fled bellowing" (VI.361–62). He also underscores in the same book a line describing the condition of Satan's defeated army:

"Exhausted, spiritless, afflicted, fallen" (VI.852). In addition, in Book X Keats underscores a reference to Sin and Death as Satan's "children dear" (X.330). The appeal here, as in the reference to Sin as Satan's "daughter dear" cited in Keats's note, seems to be the pathos of family feeling existing among monstrous creatures like Satan, Sin, and Death.

Keats was not moved solely by the feelings of supernatural creatures in *Paradise Lost*, however. One of the most striking of the marked passages in Keats's copy of the poem is Eve's lament in Book XI at the prospect of leaving Paradise. This passage, along with some of Satan's soliloquies, provides the major exception to Keats's habit of ignoring speeches in the poem. Here, for the first and only time, Keats marks the lines leading up to a speech and then continues marking the entire spoken passage. The introductory lines (XI.265–67) are underscored and marked with a marginal stroke, and the speech itself (XI.268–85) has double lines running along its margin. Keats also refers to this passage in a 21 April 1819 letter to his brother and sister-in-law, in which he associates Eve's horror at the prospect of leaving her home with the experience of leaving this world in death (*Letters*, ed. Rollins, 2:101). In her speech Eve dwells especially on the pain of forsaking the flowers she has tended. Similarly, when Keats was ill he wrote to James Rice, "How astonishingly does the chance of leaving the world impress a sense of its natural beauties on us. Like poor Falstaff, though I do not babble, I think of green fields. I muse with the greatest affection on every flower I have known from my infancy" (*Letters*, ed. Rollins, 2: 260). Other passages in *Paradise Lost* that describe the pain of exile are marked by Keats. Book XII has the fewest markings of all the books in the poem, but Keats does underscore the lines on Abraham: "He leaves his Gods, his friends, and native soil, / Ur of Chaldea, passing now the ford / To Haran; after him a cumberous train / Of herds and flocks, and numerous servitude" (XII.129–32). Also underscored is Michael's grim statement to Adam, "see the guards, / By me encamp'd on yonder hill, expect / Their motion; at whose front a flaming sword, / In signal of remove, waves fiercely round" (XII.590–93), and the final twenty-two lines of Book XII, describing Adam and Eve's expulsion from Paradise, are all underscored. The depiction of exile or separation from familiar surroundings appears to have been particularly poignant for Keats. Given his sensitivity to this issue, Keats's horror at the prospect of journeying to Italy for his health becomes understandable (see *Letters*, ed. Rollins, 2: 315), and his death in a foreign land seems especially tragic.

Leon Waldoff argues that Keats suffered from separation anxiety, probably as a result of experiencing a number of deaths in his family and especially of "losing his mother twice: first, shortly after his father's death, when she made a hasty, ill-considered second marriage and, upon its failure, left Keats (then nearly eleven) and the other children with her mother while she went to live elsewhere ... second, when she returned sick with consumption and died."[14] Certainly a fear of banishment or exile could be considered one form of separation anxiety. Keats also marks passages in *Paradise Lost*, however, that fit Waldoff's theory more closely, in that they depict the yearning of one person for another who is absent. Thus Keats draws a marginal line alongside a passage in which Adam gazes after Eve when she departs alone for her morning labor: "Her long with ardent look his eye pursued / Delighted, but desiring more her stay" (IX.397–98). These lines are similar to a passage from *Cymbeline* that, according to Charles Cowden Clarke, brought tears into Keats's eyes. Clarke identifies the passage as "the departure of Posthumus, and Imogen saying she would have watched him –

> 'Till the diminution
> Of space had pointed him sharp as my needle;
> Nay follow'd him till he had melted from
> *The smallness of a gnat to air*; and then
> Have turn'd mine eye and wept.'[15]

Both passages recall Keats's statement in his 30 September 1820 letter to Brown, "The thought of leaving Miss Brawne is beyond every thing horrible ... I eternally see her figure eternally vanishing" (*Letters*, ed. Rollins, 2: 345). In all three examples, one person sadly and helplessly watches a beloved figure dwindle and disappear into the distance. The lines that Keats in a note singles out as "specimens of a very extraordinary beauty in the Paradise Lost" (Wittreich, 559) also describe experiences of separation. Keats cites "which cost Ceres all that pain" and "Nor could the Muse defend / Her son" (IV.271; VII.37–38), passages which are also marked in the text of the poem. Both the Ceres and Proserpine and the Orpheus and Calliope myths alluded to in these lines concern a mother's loss of her child. Keats clearly regarded loss of or separation from a loved one as among the most moving experiences described in *Paradise Lost* and other literary works.

The above discussion outlines some of the most notable patterns in Keats's *Paradise Lost* marginalia, with selected examples to illustrate each point. Other examples in most cases could be offered, and many more patterns or individual passages of significance could be pointed out and interpreted. Such comprehensive analysis must await the publication of a complete transcription of the marginalia.

Before closing the present essay, however, I should like to comment further on what is probably the most curious pattern in Keats's markings: the poet's tendency to concentrate on descriptive passages and ignore speeches. This tendency would seem to have significant implications both for Keats's impression of *Paradise Lost* and for his own poetry – especially his dramatic and narrative works.

Keats's neglect of speeches in his study of *Paradise Lost* implies first of all a selective reading of Milton's work. Much of the poem is composed of dialogue and soliloquy, and it is largely in these sections that major themes, plot elements, and character traits are developed. Keats told Reynolds that he thought Milton's "Philosophy, human and divine, may be tolerably understood by one not much advanced in years" (*Letters*, ed. Rollins 1: 281). Apparently he regarded Milton's theology and depiction of both human and immortal nature as fairly simplistic and beneath serious consideration or emulation. In the same letter to Reynolds, Milton is considered inferior to Wordsworth because Milton "did not think into the human heart, as Wordsworth has done" (*Letters*, ed. Rollins 1: 282). This statement implies that Keats preferred Wordsworth's concern with humanity and human psychology to Milton's treatment of supernatural beings and cosmological issues.

Keats's comments on Milton in the letter to Reynolds might lead one to assume that the passages Keats slighted in *Paradise Lost* were those devoted to theological doctrine. Such an assumption, however, is not borne out by an analysis of Keats's markings. It is true that few explicitly doctrinal passages receive attention, but in the examples cited above of speeches ignored and descriptive passages marked, the speeches conveying characters' feelings and thoughts are no more theological than the accounts of the same characters' posture and facial expressions. Neither does Keats mark sections of *Paradise Lost* devoted to Adam and Eve more heavily than those concerned with immortal characters, as one would expect if Keats's focus in Milton's poem was on human rather than superhuman material. The determining factor in what Keats marked and what he failed to mark in *Paradise Lost* would seem to have more to do with stylistic matters or narrative technique than with content.

Considered in the light of aesthetic issues, Keats's characterization of Wordsworth as a more humane or psychologically sophisticated poet than Milton appears unfair or even ludicrous. Milton is far more successful in depicting distinct, complex, believable characters than is Wordsworth, who as Keats declared was "an Egotist" skilled in expressing his own moods and sensations but unconvincing in his portrayals of characters other than himself (*Letters*, ed. Rollins, 1: 223). As Hazlitt says in his review of *The Excursion*, "the dialogues introduced in the [poem] are soliloquies of the same character, taking different views of the subject. The recluse, the pastor, and the pedlar, are three persons in one poet ... there is no dramatic distinction of character."[16]

Keats himself aspired to the Shakespearean ideals of negative capability and the chameleon poet (see *Letters*, ed. Rollins 1 : 193, 387) and declared that his "greatest ambition" was "the writing of a few fine Plays" (*Letters*, ed. Rollins 2 : 234). It therefore seems odd that Keats paid so little attention to one of the chief dramatic elements of Milton's poem: the way in which characters reveal themselves and interact with others through speech. Ultimately, Keats's lack of interest in speech and character development must call into question his own dramatic sense and ability to realize his playwriting ambitions.

Bernice Slote, who made an extended study of Keats's dramatic ability and relationship to the theater, claims that Keats had more of a dramatist's temperament than any of the other major Romantic writers. His sympathetic imagination, or ability to lose his own identity in the contemplation of other beings, and his delight in contrasts, Slote argues, are essential components of the dramatic impulse. To illustrate Keats's empathic nature, Slote refers to many memorable examples of the poet's identification with life around him: Charles Cowden Clarke's account of Keats's imitation of a bear; Joseph Severn's report of Keats's absorption in nature while walking on Hampstead Heath; Keats's comment that "if a Sparrow come before my Window I take part in its existence and pick about the Gravel"; and his assertion, according to Woodhouse, that "he can conceive of a billiard Ball that it may have a sense of delight from its own roundness, smoothness volubility. & the rapidity of its motion."[17] What Slote does not remark, however, is that nearly all of the extant examples of Keats's ability to project himself into other natures involve animals, natural scenery, or even objects, rather than people. In the same way Keats's poetry is rich with vivid imagery and sensory details, but contains few if any memorable characters. Moreover, the fascination with contrast for which Keats is deservedly celebrated usually manifests itself in the poetry through imagery – juxtapositions of images of cold and warmth, youth and age, and feasting and fasting in *The Eve of St. Agnes*, for example, or of life and death in "To Autumn" – rather than through conflicting characters as is usual in the drama. Complex patterns of contrasting and parallel characters are also among the major structural principles of *Paradise Lost*, but such patterns are likely to go unnoticed by readers who ignore dialogue and soliloquy.

Apart from the *Paradise Lost* marginalia, one of the best ways of ascertaining Keats's response to Milton is to examine the poetry Keats wrote that is most clearly indebted to Milton's work. Keats's most Miltonic poem, as has long been recognized, is *Hyperion*, which features a debate among the fallen Titans clearly modeled on the council of Hell scenes in Books I and II of *Paradise Lost*. In this poem, Keats does create distinct characters who express individual points of view through direct speech. Although Keats did not mark the speeches of the fallen angels in his copy of Milton's poem, one might argue, the fact that he followed Milton's formula of debate and dialogue among a set of disparate personalities suggests that he was impressed and influenced by these passages and the dramatic technique they employ. Nonetheless, Keats's assembly of fallen Titans differs from Milton's council in Hell in significant respects. In R. D. Havens's words, "The meeting of the Titans is not pre-arranged, no one calls it or presides over it, no plans are discussed and no action is decided on ... It is hard to see wherein Keats could have made his assembly any less like Milton's if he had tried." Throughout *Hyperion*, Havens continues, "Nothing really happens ... Much noble description, many lofty speeches, Keats has certainly given us, but *Hyperion* is supposed to be a *narrative* poem. In reality it is nothing of the kind; it is distinctly static and sculpturesque, with a tone, style, and manner admirably adapted to depicting the colossal deities of an elder world, but to Keats at least hampering and cumbersome when it came to making them move."[18] Paul Sherwin also points out that "There is ... no movement or action on a grand scale in *Hyperion*, only static moments of reflection or passion ... The epic poet traditionally soars, but the gravity of Books I and II of *Hyperion* precludes the possibility of flight." Sherwin concludes: "An epic less Miltonic in spirit would be difficult to imagine" and "Behind Keats's methodical ponderousness is a temperament resolutely at odds with Milton's."[19] Keats's focus in his reading of *Paradise Lost* on static, sculpturesque images and descriptive passages to the neglect of dialogue, character development, and action would appear to have con-tributed to flaws in his own epic, dramatic, and narrative works.

A number of qualifications, however, need to be made at this point. First, there is evidence that Keats's approach to Milton was typical of his age. Balachandra Rajan writes: "What was valuable to Milton's readers [in the nineteenth century] was the style itself and not the doctrines it organized, the elaborate harmonies and the recondite allusiveness, the deep insight into unchanging human emotions. For the nineteenth century Milton's achieve-ment was primarily one of music and feeling."[20] William Hazlitt declared: "The genius of Milton was essentially *undramatic*" and celebrated the musical and visual elements of Milton's verse. "He makes words tell as pictures," Hazlitt remarks in his *Lectures on the English Poets*, which Keats attended. In the same lecture, Hazlitt describes the central characters of *Paradise Lost* in terms that recall Keats's note on Milton's gift for "stationing or statu[a]ry." "The persons of Adam and Eve, of Satan, &c. are always accompanied, in our imagination, with the grandeur of the naked figure; they convey to us the ideas of sculpture" (*Complete Works*, ed. Howe, 5: 230, 59, 60). In addition, the proliferation of paintings and illustrations from Milton's poetry in the late eighteenth and early nineteenth centuries by such artists as J. H. Fuseli, James Barry, William Blake, Samuel Palmer, and John Martin attests to the fact that many people of the time responded to the pictorial quality of Milton's work.[21]

In focusing on static scenes rather than dialogue or action in *Paradise Lost*, Keats may simply have been following contemporary interests and tastes.

Milton was not the only popular literary source of subjects for painters in the late eighteenth and early nineteenth centuries. Shakespeare's plays also were frequently illustrated, most notably by the artists who participated in the Boydell Shakespeare Gallery, initiated in 1786. Timothy Webb cites the proliferation of Shakespeare paintings as evidence of a prevailing "tyranny of the eye" in approaches to drama during the Romantic period.[22] The large size of Drury Lane and Covent Garden theaters, Webb explains, encouraged or coincided with an emphasis on spectacle, scenery, and stage effects at the expense of the spoken word in theatrical productions. In order to reach their audiences in these vast theatres, the actors were required to boom out their lines and employ conspicuous, exaggerated gestures. A number of Romantic writers, including Walter Scott, Samuel Taylor Coleridge, Leigh Hunt, Charles Lamb, and William Hazlitt complained about the way in which, in Scott's words, "Show and machinery have ... usurped the place of tragic poetry; and the author is compelled to address himself to the eyes, not to the understanding or feelings of the spectators."[23]

Keats also seems to disparage the conditions of the theater of his day when he writes in his *Champion* essay on Edmund Kean that Kean "acted *Luke* in *Riches*, as far as the stage will admit, to perfection" (Hampstead Keats, 5: 228). Nonetheless, it is likely that Keats was influenced by, or to some extent participated in, the theatrical values of the period. Another remark by Hazlitt is particularly telling in relation to Keats and the drama. In a review of Kean as Richard III, first published in the 15 February 1814 *Morning Chronicle* and reprinted in Hazlitt's 1818 *A View of the English Stage*, Hazlitt writes that "Mr. Kean's acting ... presents a perpetual succession of striking pictures. He bids fair to supply us with the best Shakespear Gallery we have had!" (*Complete Works*, ed. Howe, 5: 184). As Webb notes, Hazlitt's comment must refer to "Kean's capacity for pointing his performance and for achieving the memorable posture" ("The Romantic Poet and the Stage," 37). As Keats's *Champion* essay makes clear, Kean was a favorite actor and indeed an important cultural hero for the young poet; "one of my Ambitions," he told Benjamin Bailey, "is to make as great a revolution in modern dramatic writing as Kean has done in acting" (*Letters*, ed. Rollins, 2: 139). Kean's flair for "present[ing] a perpetual succession of striking pictures" on stage, and the overall visual emphasis of early nineteenth-century theater, might well have affected Keats's understanding of what drama signifies. If our own age regards conflict, action, and dialogue as the essence of drama, Keats and others of his time perhaps considered arresting visual compositions, music, and isolated passages of poetic language more important.

One final qualification must be made to the argument that Keats's *Paradise Lost* marginalia reveal deficiencies in the poet's appreciation of Milton and understanding of dramatic principles. If Keats – as well as most of the other major Romantic writers – was unsuccessful in genres requiring character development, there is no doubting his achievement in lyric poetry. When Keats applies to his lyric poems the characteristics he found most fascinating in Milton, moreover, the results are very effective indeed. The dense and vivid imagery, often charged with contrary implications, the rich tableaux, and the memorable figures, faces, and settings in Keats's odes, *The Eve of St. Agnes*, *The Fall of Hyperion*, and other great works can all be linked to patterns and emphases in the *Paradise Lost* marginalia. In addition, in poems like "Bright star, would I were stedfast as thou art," "Ode to a Nightingale," and "Ode on a Grecian Urn," the speaker engages a central symbol in a debate that is charged with dramatic tension, climax, and resolution. Recent critical interpretations of Romantic poems as dialogic works highlight dramatic elements in lyric poetry, and some critics have argued that Romantic plays need to be understood on their own terms as explorations of individual psychology, or "mental theatre" in Byron's words, rather than as failed attempts at traditional drama.[24] Perhaps in a number of ways our concept of Romantic drama needs to be broadened and redefined, to include genres and characteristics not previously considered in that category.

In conclusion, the focus on static, descriptive passages and neglect of dialogue and action in Keats's *Paradise Lost* marginalia may help to explain some of the shortcomings in Keats's narrative poems. At the same time, the marginalia may enhance our understanding of the ways in which Milton and other epic or dramatic works were regarded in Keats's day. A study of Keats's markings in *Paradise Lost* points to some of the techniques and preoccupations that were incorporated so successfully into Keats's best lyric poems. If his study of Milton assisted the development of Keats's own gifts for arresting visual compositions, for sensory description and the juxtaposition of contrasting qualities in poetry, as well as his handling of the themes of loss, separation, and consolation, we should have to call Keats one of Milton's most apt pupils.

NOTES

1 Eleven of the nineteen notes initially appeared in the form of a letter by James Freeman Clarke to the editor of the American periodical *The Dial* for April 1843. Clarke's transcription derived from a copy of *Paradise Lost* George Keats possessed, into which he apparently had reproduced his brother's annotations (see *The Poetical Works and Other Writings of John Keats*, ed. Harry Buxton Forman, revised by Maurice Buxton Forman [Hampstead Edition], 8 vols. [New York: Charles Scribner's Sons, 1938–39],

5: 291. This work hereafter is referred to as Hampstead Keats.) Richard Monckton Milnes reprinted the *Dial* notes in his 1848 *Life, Letters, and Literary Remains of John Keats* (2 vols. [London: Edward Moxon, 1848], 274–81), and in an 1872 *Athenaeum* article, Sir Charles Dilke provided the marginal comments not printed by Clarke and Milnes (An Admirer of Keats, "Unpublished Notes on Milton, by John Keats; and Original Version of the Sonnet 'To Sleep,'" *The Athenaeum*, 26 October 1872, 529–30. In a note written on a flyleaf of volume 1 of Keats's copy of *Paradise Lost*, Sir Charles Dilke identifies himself as the author of this article.) Beginning in 1883, Harry Buxton Forman published all of Keats's notes on *Paradise Lost* in his editions of Keats's poetry and prose (*The Poetical Works and Other Writings of John Keats*, ed. Harry Buxton Forman, 4 vols. [London: Reeves & Turner, 1883, 1889]; *The Complete Works of John Keats*, ed. Harry Buxton Forman, 4 vols. [Glasgow: Gowans & Gray, 1900–1901]), and for many years the Hampstead Keats edition has been the standard source for Keats's annotations in Milton and several other works. John Barnard reprinted the *Paradise Lost* notes from Hampstead Keats as an appendix to his Penguin edition of Keats's poetry (*The Complete Poems*, ed. John Barnard, 2nd edition [Harmondsworth: Penguin, 1977] Appendix 4, 517–26), and Joseph Anthony Wittreich, Jr., in *The Romantics on Milton*, also drew upon the Hampstead Keats text of the notes, though he altered some of the punctuation based on his own consultation of the original volumes (*The Romantics on Milton: Formal Essays and Critical Asides* [Cleveland: The Press of Case Western Reserve University, 1970], 553–60).

Although Wittreich's is the most accurate of the published editions of the Milton notes, my own examination of Keats's marginalia in *Paradise Lost* revealed a number of minor errors or omissions in Wittreich's transcription. In the present essay, quotations from Keats's notes are taken from my own transcription, but the appropriate page number in Wittreich is cited in the text for the aid of readers who wish to consult an available edition of the notes. (Elizabeth Cook's transcription of the *Paradise Lost* annotations, published in her 1990 Oxford University Press edition of Keats's poetry and selected prose, came to my attention too late to be incorporated in the present essay. Cook's is the most accurate transcription of the notes now in print.)

Permission to reproduce Keats's marginalia in his copy of *Paradise Lost* has been granted by Christina M. Gee, Curator of Keats House, and by the London Borough of Camden. I wish to thank Christina Gee and her assistant, Roberta Davis, for their cooperation and kind assistance with this project during a very pleasant month I spent working at Keats House. The research and writing of this essay were funded in part by a California State University, Long Beach, Scholarly and Creative Activities Award.

Quotations from *Paradise Lost* are taken from Keats's two-volume, duodecimo edition, printed in Edinburgh for W. and J. Deas in 1807.

2 Caroline F. E. Spurgeon, *Keats's Shakespeare: A Descriptive Study Based on New Material*, 2nd edition (London: Oxford University Press, 1929) and R. S. White, *Keats as a Reader of Shakespeare* (Norman: University of Oklahoma Press, 1987). Miriam Allott (*The Poems of John Keats*, ed. Allott, 3rd impression with corrections [London: Longman, 1975]) and Helen Vendler (*The Odes of John Keats* [Cambridge: Harvard University Press, 1983]) cite marked passages in Keats's copy of *Paradise Lost* as sources for some of Keats's poems. Neither Allott nor Vendler provides anything approaching a complete record of Keats's markings, however.

3 I am at work on a complete edition of Keats's *Paradise Lost* marginalia. In the introduction to that edition, I discuss in some detail the question of when Keats acquired and annotated his copy of Milton's poem. There is not space to reproduce my argument here, but I can briefly summarize my conclusions. The bulk of evidence indicates that the notes and markings were written in the early months of 1818. Some of the marginalia, however, are associated with later periods: fall of 1818, spring of 1819, and late summer of 1819. Keats probably read through the entire poem, marking as he went, in the winter and early spring of 1818 and then returned to particular sections of the work as his interests or preoccupations shifted.

4 Nancy M. Goslee, "'Under a Cloud in Prospect': Keats, Milton, and Stationing," *Philological Quarterly* 53 (1974): 205–6, 213–14.

5 Alan Richardson discusses the appeal Satan's "tormented, restless self-consciousness" had for the Romantics: *A Mental Theatre: Poetic Drama and Consciousness in the Romantic Age* (University Park: Pennsylvania State University Press, 1988), 8; see also 15–16 and passim.

6 Keats does not mark the well-known opening line of this simile – "As one who long in populous city pent" (IX.445) – which is considered a source for his 1816 sonnet, "To one who has been long in city pent." Perhaps the line was so familiar to Keats that he did not consider it worth singling out for special attention.

7 *The Autobiography of Leigh Hunt*, 3 vols. (London, 1850) 2: 208–9, quoted in *The Romantics on Milton*, 548.

8 Ernest de Selincourt (*The Poems of John Keats*, ed. de Selincourt, 5th edition [London: Methuen, 1926], 470–71) and R. K. Gordon ("Keats and Milton," *Modern Language Review* 42 [1947]: 445) compare the food preparations in *Paradise Lost* to those in *The Eve of St. Agnes*; de Selincourt, *The Poems of John Keats* (520), Gordon, "Keats and Milton" (445), Stuart Sperry (*Keats the Poet* [Princeton: Princeton University Press, 1973], 317–18), Allott, *The Poems of John Keats* (659n), and Barnard, *The Complete Poems* (678) compare Eve's meal to the one in *The Fall of Hyperion*. Gordon, "Keats and Milton" (445), also draws parallels between the *Paradise Lost* passage and "To Autumn." W. B. C. Watkins points out that in all of his poetry Milton "is preoccupied with eating – literal and figurative." Watkins also finds similarities between Milton's descriptions of sumptuous food and Keats's in *The Eve of St. Agnes* (*An Anatomy of Milton's Verse* [Baton Rouge: Louisiana State University Press, 1955], 16–17, 21–22).

9 Victor J. Lams, Jr., "Ruth, Milton, and Keats's 'Ode to a Nightingale,'" *Modern Language Quarterly* 34 (1973): 427.

10 Brian Wilkie, *Romantic Poets and Epic Tradition* (Madison: University of Wisconsin Press, 1965), 145–47.

11 See, for example, James Holly Hanford, "The Temptation Motive in Milton," *Studies in Philology* 15 (1918): 176–94; Watkins, *An Anatomy of Milton's Verse*, 87–146; Leslie Brisman, *Milton's Poetry of Choice and Its Romantic Heirs* (Ithaca: Cornell University Press, 1973), esp. ix–54.

12 Greg Kucich argues that Keats and other Romantic writers found in Spenser's poetry evidence of a mental conflict between the competing claims of "duty and indulgence" or "aesthetic luxury and intellectual responsibility." The Romantics' focus on Spenser's divided consciousness, Kucich claims, helped them to identify and come to terms with their own inner conflicts between imagination and reality, truth and beauty (*Keats,*

Shelley, and Romantic Spenserianism [University Park: Pennsylvania State University Press, 1991], 108). Perhaps Keats's interpretation of Milton's self-division follows a pattern similar to the one Kucich traces in the Romantics' response to Spenser.

13 Bernice Slote, *Keats and the Dramatic Principle* (Lincoln: University of Nebraska Press, 1958), 32.

14 Leon Waldoff, *Keats and the Silent Work of Imagination* (Urbana: University of Illinois Press, 1985), 27. See also 28–30 and 86–91, where Waldoff discusses patterns of "separation, abandonment, and betrayal" (90) in Keats's poems and letters.

15 Charles and Mary Cowden Clarke, *Recollections of Writers* (1878; reprint, Fontwell, Sussex: Centaur Press, 1969), 126.

16 *Complete Works*, ed. Howe, 4: 113.

17 Slote, *Keats and the Dramatic Principle*, 16–17; *The Keats Circle*, ed. Hyder E. Rollins, 2nd edition, 2 vols. (Cambridge: Harvard University Press, 1965) 1: 59.

18 R. D. Havens, *The Influence of Milton on English Poetry* (Cambridge: Harvard University Press, 1922), 206, 208–9.

19 Paul Sherwin, "Dying into Life: Keats's Struggle with Milton in *Hyperion*," *PMLA* 93 (1978): 387.

20 Balachandra Rajan, *Paradise Lost and the Seventeenth Century Reader* (1947; reprint, London: Chatto & Windus, 1962), 13. Wittreich generally disagrees with Rajan's characterization of nineteenth-century attitudes as typical of the Romantics, but he admits that Keats and Hunt tend to conform to the outlook Rajan describes (19).

21 See Marcia R. Pointon, *Milton and English Art* (Manchester: Manchester University Press, 1970), chapters 3 and 4, and Ronald Paulson, *Book and Painting: Shakespeare, Milton, and the Bible* (Knoxville: University of Tennessee Press, 1982).

22 Timothy Webb, "The Romantic Poet and the Stage: A Short, Sad History," in *The Romantic Theater: An International Symposium*, ed. Richard Allen Cave (Totowa: Barnes and Noble, 1986), 36.

23 "Essay on the Drama" (1819); quoted in Webb, "The Romantic Poet and the Stage," 34.

24 Critics who argue for a new understanding of Romantic plays as psychological drama include Richard M. Fletcher, *English Romantic Drama, 1795–1843: A Critical History* (New York: Exposition Press, 1966), esp. 49, 52–55; Webb, "The Romantic Poet and the Stage," 11–12; and Richardson, *A Mental Theatre*, chapter 1 and passim. Richardson offers a compelling and sophisticated reassessment of Romantic drama but does not include Keats in his analysis. Richardson's neglect of Keats may indicate that the poet was less concerned than other Romantic writers with inner, mental theater and more influenced by the visual emphasis of the contemporary stage. Some examples of dialogic readings of Romantic poems are cited by Richardson (191n.3).

CHAPTER EIGHT

What the mower does to the meadow: action and reflection in Wordsworth and Marvell

FREDERICK BURWICK

IN HIS INTRODUCTION to *The Romantics on Milton*, Joseph Anthony Wittreich, Jr. makes a strong and still-enduring case that the Romantics turned to Milton as their political mentor, that they shared with Milton republican sentiments and republican actions.[1] More recently, new historicists such as Jerome J. McGann and Marjorie Levinson have judged Wordsworth and his fellow Romantics as having escaped rather than embraced politics.[2] This essay follows the latter view by arguing that Wordsworth's relation to politics is at best ambiguous. I argue here that Wordsworth's political dis-ease becomes more clear when he is compared with another politically active poet-patriot of Milton's era, Andrew Marvell.

In "Great men have been among us," Wordsworth gives tribute to Marvell as poet-patriot.[3] The tribute has special significance to Wordsworth, who confesses in *The Prelude* his own inability in the midst of the French Revolution to take up "A service at this time for cause so great" (X.135).[4] In his "Reply to Mathetes," Wordsworth places Marvell within the "circle of glorious Patriots."[5] The problem Wordsworth addresses in his "Reply" is how one should respond to the age-old question, "Should one lead the active or the contemplative life?" Wordsworth's answer, "Yes, Always," affirms a dialectic of action and passion, engagement and reflection, much in the manner that he admired in Marvell's lyric. While it would seem that Wordsworth could make this dialectic work well enough in his nature poetry, and that it only failed him when he tried to turn it to political poetry, his difficulty may well stem from his very act of prescinding the poetry of political consciousness and treating it as if it were an essentially different kind of poetry. For Marvell, as I will try to show in a brief examination of the Mower Poems, there is no such difference.

Among those sonnets composed by Wordsworth at the time of his trip to

France in 1802, "Great men have been among us" must be considered together with "It is a beauteous evening," the sonnet addressed to his daughter Caroline. The purpose of the trip, after all, was to arrange a settlement with Caroline's mother, Annette Vallon. Inevitably in re-visiting France, Wordsworth again had to consider his experience of the Revolution. The sonnets of 1802, however, keep the personal utterly separate from the political. The poetic record of 1792, as we have it in the *Descriptive Sketches*, does not reveal what we need to know about France. When his residence in France is recollected in *The Prelude* (1805), Wordsworth already sees himself torn between zealous commitment and guilty estrangement: on the one hand, he refused merely to grieve, "but thought / Of opposition and of remedies" (X.128–29) and how, "in the teeth / Of desperate opposition from without," he might "Have cleared a passage for just government" (X.183–85); on the other hand, he despairs that his powers of eloquence, meager enough even in English, were "all unfit for tumult or intrigue" (X.133). Thus he returns to England convinced of his political ineptitude, "well assured / That I both was and must be of small worth, / No better than an alien in the Land." He sees himself, then, as "A Poet only to myself, to Men / Useless" (X.191–93, 199–200).

There are poets not useless to men, and to such poets he turns his thoughts in 1802. They are the poets of the English Revolution under Cromwell. With the Treaty of Amiens (25 March 1802), the official declaration of peace under Napoleon, an Englishman, for the first time since 1793, could again travel in France. But Wordsworth was not happy with the accord. The English, no less than the French, continued to betray the cause of freedom. When England endured its Revolution, it had the moral leadership lacking in the present political context, both at home and abroad:

> Milton! thou shouldst be living at this hour:
> England hath need of thee: she is a fen
> Of stagnant waters　　　　　　　("London, 1802," lines 1–3)

The confession of irresponsibility, "We are selfish men," is much like the confession in "The world is too much with us" that "We have given our hearts away." There Wordsworth sought a possible resolution by resorting to the mythic imagination of the pagan past. In the sonnet to Milton, the moral resolution depends upon the resurrection of Milton, "raise us up, return to us again." In the same temper, he calls upon those "who called Milton friend":

> Great men have been among us; hands that penned
> And tongues that uttered wisdom – better none:
> The later Sydney, Marvel, Harrington,

Young Vane, and others who called Milton friend.
These moralists could act and comprehend:
They knew how genuine glory was put on;
Taught us how rightfully a nation shone
In splendour: what strength was, that would not bend
But in magnanimous meekness. France, 'tis strange,
Hath brought forth no such souls as we had then.
Perpetual emptiness! unceasing change!
No single volume paramount, no code,
No master spirit, no determined road;
But equally a want of books and men.[6]

While the English had ample justification in pointing to the parliamentary reform that had been achieved as a result of the Cromwellian revolt and the Glorious Revolution that toppled James II, it was apparently easy to let that pride in the historical past lapse into a supercilious sense of superiority over the French in their struggle for political freedom. The sonnet to the "Great men" acknowledges none of the "stagnant waters" of the "London, 1802" sonnet. Rather, it assumes that the wisdom which these moralists taught has been learned. Wordsworth seems less than apologetic in his volto from octave to sestet: "'tis strange," he says. Not England, but France alone is caught up in the immorality and ignorance of the age.

Even in voicing the superiority of the English over the French, Wordsworth does not assume a political responsibility. Milton, or Sidney, or Marvell, or Harrington, or Vane are put forward as arbitrators, mediators, legislators. This is, of course, the crux in his "Reply to Mathetes." For Coleridge's *The Friend*, Dr. Alexander Blair and John Wilson prepared a paper, signed "Mathetes." "Mathetes" blames the downward spiral of moral degeneration on the false optimism of youth which, always thinking it can build a better world and correct the mistakes of the present, actually undermines the virtues of the past and contributes to a further deterioration. Wordsworth's "Reply" was forwarded in two parts. In the first (14 December 1809), he corrects the adulation of the past (the very sort of nostalgia which he seems to have assumed in "Great men have been among us"). In the second (4 January 1810), he distinguishes between cultural history and the maturation of mind, and he then asks whether any of the old ethical saws still hold relevance as "solemn Mandates."[7]

From the time of Elizabeth, he argues, we can "call up to mind the Heroes, the Warriors, the Statesmen, the Poets, the Divines, and the Moral Philosophers" who wrought the great cultural advances of her reign. Or we can remember those from the time of Cromwell, "if we be more attracted by the moral purity and greatness, and that sanctity of civil and religious duty, with which the Tyranny of Charles the first was struggled against." But even in giving praise to "that circle of glorious Patriots," Wordsworth answers Blair and Wilson by pointing to the meanness and weakness of the past. "Mathetes" had indulged two commonplace errors: the first "lies in forgetting, in the excellence of what remains, the large overbalance of worthlessness that has been swept away"; the second results from a simplistic division of history into present and past, ignoring the brevity and ephemerality of the present (by which we seldom mean more than the last thirty years) as opposed to the vast and collective immensity of the past.[8] In his second installment, Wordsworth dismisses the historical argument and counters the presumption of moral degeneration in terms of the formative processes of mind. We recognize here familiar Wordsworthian oppositions: the "law and impulse" by which nature tutors Lucy; the "beauty and fear" which fosters the poet in "Fair-seed time" (The Prelude, I.305–6). Knowledge and feeling, duty and inclination, reason and nature are not alternative choices. Because "there is a startling and a hesitation," the mind must sustain both the active and contemplative.[9]

Like most of his contemporaries, Wordsworth read Marvell in Captain Edward Thompson's edition (1776). Since Thompson exalted Marvell as a stalwart champion of virtue and freedom and lamented "this degenerate age, when virtue does not even nominally exist amongst us," Wordsworth must have recognized the similar argument in the query of "Mathetes."[10] Other direct references to Marvell are few but telling. Wordsworth thought of Marvell, for example, when he was attempting to fulfill his promise to Rev. Wrangham to write a poem on the model of Juvenal's Eighth Satire. In his imitation, Wordsworth casts Frederick, Duke of York, in the role of Juvenal's misguided nobleman who has confused aristocracy with virtue.[11] Replacing Rome with Yorkshire challenges Wordsworth's ingenuity in providing parallel figures, but he has no difficulty in matching Juvenal's appeal to Cicero as spokesman of moral integrity in Rome. Cicero's Yorkshire counterpart was born in Holderness and served as Member of Parliament for Hull: "what follows about Cicero," Wordsworth notes, "might be parallelized by some lines about Andrew Marvel."[12]

When Sir Walter Scott was annotating "Absalom and Achitophel" for his edition of The Works of John Dryden,[13] Wordsworth advised him that the Duke of Monmouth was also "mentioned in Andrew Marvels Poems ... which I think you might peep into with advantage for your work" (7 November 1805).[14] On this occasion Wordsworth claimed, "somewhat disingenuously" according to Elizabeth Donno, that he had not looked at the poems "these many years."[15] Of course he was to return to Marvell again in his "Reply to Mathetes" in 1809. And in 1814, he urged Dr. Robert Anderson to make room for Marvell in a revised and expanded version of A Complete

Edition of the Poets of Great Britain (1792–95).[16] That Wordsworth fails to comment explicitly on the pastoral or rural poetry should not surprise us, for Marvell's reputation in his own day and throughout the eighteenth century, we should remember, rested primarily on his satire and his polemical prose.[17] Nor would it have been easy for Wordsworth to reconcile the two aspects of Marvell's literary career. In his own efforts, Wordsworth had presumed radical differences separating the personal from the political modes of poetic expression.

For Marvell, however, the private merged with the public. The poems of the country are, in fact, poems of the state. The four Mower Poems are concerned with intrusive forces which disrupt natural order and harmony, but also with the incapacity of factions to perceive the total order. Like Wordsworth, Marvell delights in interchanges of "within" and "without." This by no means implicates the error which Donald Friedman justly charged against "nineteenth-century critics who saw him as an unabashed pantheist, a worshipper of nature who had somehow hit upon the Wordsworthian mode of apprehension in the middle of the seventeenth century."[18]

Marvell's rustic is not the heroic shepherd, "Ennobled" and "spiritual almost," of *The Prelude* (VIII.411, 417). Nor has Marvell simply indulged the pastoral tradition. His rustic is not a shepherd, but a mower: not one who protects the flocks, but one who fells the fields. Marvell knows, and uses, his mower's kinship with the Grim Reaper. There is not a single thread of pantheism in the easy transposition of landscape and mindscape which provides the refrain in "The Mower's Song":

> For Juliana comes, and She,
> What I do to the Grass, does to my Thoughts and Me.   (lines 23–24)

In the five stanzas of "The Mower's Song," Marvell traces the incremental changes in perception wrought by Juliana's mowing of the mower's mind.

The first stanza describes the mind as mirror which not only reflects "all these Medows fresh and gay" (2) but also sees "in the greenness of the Grass / ... its Hopes as in a Glass" (3–4). This happy equation of self and nature, of course, is disrupted by Juliana's mind-mowing, but it is the mower himself who has absorbed this image of Juliana and put the scythe in her hand. The "Glass" both reflects and projects: the "greenness of the Grass" (3) mirrors the mower's "hopes" (4) because he intends to make hay with his scythe. The ripening "greenness" will be destroyed. In the second stanza, the mower mourns, not because he has felled the grass, but because he has not. He pines "with Sorrow" (7) while the grass "Grew more luxuriant still and fine" (8). As perceived by Juliana, the grass blossoms into a symbol of fecundity with "a

Flower on either side" (10). In the third stanza, the mower accuses the meadow of betraying him. According to his perception of the natural order, the "fellowship" of mower and meadow is consummated in his act of mowing. What is unnatural, then, is passion. The intrusion of Juliana and "gawdy May-games" (15) disrupts the mower's world. Instead of the grass, the mower "lay trodden under feet" (16). In the fourth stanza, he claims his revenge. The mower becomes the Grim Reaper, "And Flow'rs, and Grass, and I and all, / Will in one common Ruine fall" (21–22). In the final stanza, the mirror is turned around. Just as the "greenness of the Grass" has reflected his hopes, the mower's own decaying body will become a companion to that greenness as the grass, in turn, becomes the "heraldry" adorning the mower's tomb.

The four Mower Poems describe a process of degeneration culminating in the devastation of "The Mower's Song." The first of the four songs, "The Mower against Gardens," is a diatribe against "Luxurious Man" (1) for engendering a garden of artifice. A useful analog to this text, as previous critics have pointed out, is the dialogue between Polixenes and Perdita in *The Winter's Tale* – their debate on nature and artifice is laden with double meaning, for Polixenes is proposing, and Perdita is rejecting, an illicit bond with the Prince as mistress rather than as bride.[19] From the very opening lines we can recognize that Marvell's mower registers his complaint with similarly salacious insinuations:

> Luxurious Man, to bring his Vice in use,
> Did after him the World seduce:
> And from the fields the Flow'rs and Plants allure,
> Where Nature was most plain and pure.   (lines 1–4)

Adorned in showy dress, with painted cheeks and "strange perfumes" (11), the flowers are gathered from distant lands, bred, and displayed to please a "sov'raign" (20). His garden becomes a "*Seraglio*" (27); his ornamental fruit trees stand as eunuchs. Emphasizing the artificial splendor wealth has purchased, the mower points to the forgotten beauty of the "sweet Fields" (32) "Where willing Nature does to all dispence / A wild and fragrant Innocence" (33–34). Were they not charged with mocking irony, the concluding lines might be read as Wordsworthian pantheism. The rich man may have his polished statues, says the mower, but "The *Gods* themselves with us do dwell" (40).

Wordsworth, too, mockingly describes the garden as nature tamed and confined – a condition which he finds uncomfortably familiar. Returning to Hawkshead on his first summer vacation from Cambridge, he seeks out the garden sanctuary and engages in an imaginary dialogue with

> that unruly child of mountain birth,
> The froward brook, which, soon as he was boxed
> Within our garden, found himself at once
> As if by trick insidious and unkind,
> Stripped of his voice, and left to dimple down
> Without an effort and without a will
> A channel paved by the hand of man.
> I looked at him and smiled, and smiled again,
> And in the press of twenty thousand thoughts,
> 'Ha,' quoth I, 'pretty prisoner, are you there!'
> – And now, reviewing soberly that hour,
> I marvel that a fancy did not flash
> Upon me, and a strong desire, straitway,
> At sight of such an emblem that shewed forth
> So aptly my late course of even days
> And all their smooth enthralment, to pen down
> A satire on myself.   (*The Prelude*, IV.39–55)

As in Marvell's "The Garden," Wordsworth recognizes that the garden may offer peaceful sanctuary, but it is achieved only with a loss of freedom. The mind will ultimately rebel, "Annihilating all that's made / To a green Thought in a green Shade" ("The Garden," 47–48). The boy who ravages the bough in Wordsworth's "Nutting" replicates the rebellion in the garden of Eden. Man cannot linger long, Marvell writes, in "that happy Garden-state" ("The Garden," 57).

Although "The Mower against Gardens" argues clearly enough how the tensions between natural and artificial are, in fact, the same as between virtue and vice, it must be remembered that Marvell is not the mower. The laborer of the fields is accusing "Luxurious Man" for a self-indulgent want of productivity and for neglecting the vitality in nature. But the mower's understanding of the providence and order of nature is both limited and faulted. Marvell makes this more evident in the next poem, "Damon the Mower."[20] In "The Mower against Gardens," the mower saw what was inside the garden as perverted, what was outside as innocent and pure. In "Damon the Mower," however, what is inside the mower's mind is corrupted. As a tormented Petrarchan lover, he perceives nature in terms of disrupting passion: "hot desires" are confounded with "hot day[s]" (26). He accuses Juliana for scorning his overtures—which are sufficiently blatant:

> To Thee the harmless Snake I bring,
> Disarmed of its teeth and sting.
> To Thee *Chameleons* changing-hue,
> And Oak leaves tipt with hony due.
> Yet Thou ungrateful hast not sought
> Nor what they are, nor who them brought.   (lines 35–40)

178

Proffering his toothless, stingless snake to woo the "fair Shepheardess" (33), Damon apparently wants to show that the serpent of primal sin in the Edenic garden is actually a harmless creature in the scheme of nature. Similarly, his gift of "*Chameleons*" suggests that changing colors, perhaps even changing loyalties, is equally natural. The oak-leaf, because of the tale of Charles II and the "Royal Oak" at the Battle of Worcester, was the special symbol of the Restoration, and the mower presents his "Oak leaves" dripping with promised fecundity.[21]

The shepherdess, no matter what she might think of the mower's gifts, is not apt to be especially impressed with the mower's boast. Utterly lacking in diplomacy, the mower stresses how mowers and shepherds are opposing factions. Mowers, after all, vanquish meadows where sheep might graze. Damon claims his superiority to the shepherd: "This Sithe of mine discovers wide / More ground then all his Sheep do hide" (51–52). He insists on his intimacy with nature, but he cannot accept Juliana's place in nature unless she acquiesces to his dominion. Having failed to win her favor, he resorts again to confounding inside and outside: "Sighing I whet my Sythe and Woes" (72). Thus he becomes the victim of his own confusion. "The edged Stele by careless chance / Did into his own Ankle glance" (77–78). Even in nursing his wounded ankle with natural cures ("Shepherd's-purse" and "Clowns-all-heal" [83]) – plant names which ironically recall his boast – he continues to blame "*Julianas* Eyes" (86) for his wounded feelings. For the latter wound, the ultimate natural cure is death: "For Death thou art a Mower too" (88). The mower has set himself at odds with the pastoral world of the shepherds and has accepted a dread alliance.

Each stanza of "The Mower to the Glo-worms" provides a conceit on the light of the "glo-worms": in the first, glow worms are lamps by which the nightingale studies its nocturnal songs; in the second, they are mere "Country Comets" (5) portending no fall of a prince, presaging for the mower nothing more dire than "the Grasses fall" (8); in the third, they become the guiding lights for stray mowers who have pursued the "foolish Fires" (12); in the last stanza, the mower confesses that he has gone too far astray to be rescued by the glow worm's guidance. He has pursued the false light of his desire for Juliana, and "She my Mind hath so displac'd / That I shall never find my home" (15–16).

Wordsworth shares with Marvell the easy inside/outside movement. In the boat-stealing episode of *The Prelude* (I.372–426), for example, "mountain-echoes" (390) move with the boat as it is rowed out onto the lake, the optical illusion of the mountain rising chastises the deed, and dark images continue to haunt the brain at night. In "Nutting" or "The Boy of Winander," Wordsworth attends to a dialogue with nature. But where Wordsworth uses the subjective–objective dialectic to explore a reciprocity between the mind and nature, Marvell uses the relation of subject and object to provoke a metaphysical paradox. The primary paradox of the Mower Poems is that sexual passion is seen as an intrusion into the natural order.[22] By exaggerating the promiscuity and profligacy of the garden, and insisting upon the innocence and purity of nature, the mower, in his first poem, reveals his own distorted perception. The mower's confused inversions of "within" and "without" renders his whole world topsy-turvy. In "Damon the Mower," the mower boasts to the shepherdess his superiority as mower, then clumsily fells himself, "By his own Sythe, the Mower mown" (80). In "The Mower to the Glo-Worms," he is lost because Juliana has "displac'd" (15) his mind. In "The Mower's Song," the mower reproaches the grass for standing "While I lay trodden under feet" (16). He claims that the act of mowing is a harmonious part of the natural order, yet, when the situation is reversed, he finds being mown most unnatural and cruel. What he does to the grass is just and natural, not what she "does to my Thoughts and me."

Marvell, it should be noted, has kept himself separate from the confused perceiver in this poem. Damon's self-centered way of looking on nature is as faulty as Peter Bell's. Marvell is not rejecting the idea of natural order and harmony, but only Damon's perverted way of seeing it. Elsewhere, as in *Upon Appleton House*, Marvell further develops the idea of natural order, and carefully places the mower within the scheme of things. The personal values embodied in the Mower Poems correspond directly with the political values expressed in the satires and the poems of state. Although Marvell is not always consistent in his political opinions, he shares none of Wordsworth's fears and inadequacies at taking on public and political responsibility. The reason, as I have argued, is that the private poems involve the same methods and assumptions as the public ones. Marvell demonstrates in the Cromwell Poems, just as he does in the Mower Poems, the self-deceptions of the factional mind. The moral of the "fall" is thematic in both sets of poems. In both, he examines the processes of opposition through distorted perception. The mower's pride in his mowing is not unlike the rationale for revolutionary violence, and the definition of natural order requires a larger range of perception than is given to the individual caught up in immediate concerns, be they public or private.[23]

Although Wordsworth and his contemporaries followed Thompson in praising Marvell as "a brave and powerful fighter against intolerance, both political and ecclesiastical," the reception of Marvell shifted during the later nineteenth century. Marvell began to be compared to Wordsworth as "a poet of nature and simplicity."[24] It is an irony in the historical reception of Marvell that twentieth-century critics have found themselves compelled to argue what Wordsworth himself knew all too well – that he was very different from

Marvell. In explaining why "the Nature which Marvell knew was plainly different from that which Wordsworth … knew," M. C. Bradbrook and M. G. Lloyd Thomas emphasize the rise of natural science that commenced during the later seventeenth century:

Politics are for Marvell part of the natural order of the world: from the rational and most conscious organizations of corporate man to the return of the seasons and the procession of the heavens there is a continuum. The correlation of man's life with the natural order of day and night, the order of the spheres, the rhythm of the year, means that the terms are poetically interchangeable.[25]

For Wordsworth, by contrast, the turn to nature meant a turn away from political activity. It required an elaborate poetic argument to reclaim the possibility of "Love of Nature Leading to Love of Man" (*The Prelude*, Book VIII). Even then, the argument falters in confrontation with the vicissitudes of the French Revolution (*The Prelude*, Books IX–X). For Marvell the reciprocity between mind and nature was a given; for Wordsworth it had to be nourished and educated in solitude. The "ministry" of nature operates only when the boy is isolated from his comrades and alone with the tutelary "spirits." Even in his concluding celebration of the moon, as "The perfect image of a mighty mind, / Of one that feeds upon infinity" (*The Prelude*, XIII.69–70), Wordsworth stands apart from the companions with whom he had ascended Mount Snowdon.

When J. Crofts, writing at the same time as Bradbrook and Thomas, tries to sort out the "un-Wordsworthian" characteristics of Marvell's descriptions of nature, he too blames the advent of the new science for having "invalidated" the traditional belief in divine immanence and the essential unity of man and nature. Crofts claims that Marvell's scenes of nature seem Wordsworthian "only when he is in an idle mood":

The moment his feelings are seriously engaged he has the impulse, as he says, to

> … create[], transcending these,
> Far other Worlds, and other Seas;
> Annihilating all that's made
> To a green Thought in a green Shade. ("The Garden," stanza vi)

The landscape may remain clear only so long as it is meaningless. If it is to mean something it must lose definition and disappear in a blur of Platonic fancies. Nothing could be more un-Wordsworthian.[26]

Crofts is wrong, I think, in separating the passive from the active moments in Marvell's poetry and designating the latter as "un-Wordsworthian." In defining what Wordsworth shares with Marvell, the dynamics of active and passive response are far more important than a mere description of landscape. To be sure, once we observe how that interchange operates, we cannot overlook vast religious and ideological differences.

To be fair to Crofts, Bradbrook, and Thomas, we must acknowledge the difficulties under which they were laboring in 1940. Marvell's pastoral poetry had long been celebrated for its Romantic character. When John Greenleaf Whittier, in 1848, chose Marvell as a champion of individual freedom in his essay for the *National Era*, an abolitionist weekly, he made a case for the balance of the active and contemplative life that has much in common with Wordsworth's "Reply to Mathetes."[27] Marvell's sensitivity to nature as a mirror of the mind is sustained in Wordsworth, Whittier wrote, and his "proud manliness and self-respect" is preserved in Thomas Moore. Describing a boat ride down the river, "floating along its dreamy shores where the dropping ferns, azaleas and witch-hazels mirror themselves in the water," Whittier quotes Marvell:

> Where all things gaze themselves, and doubt
> If they be in it or without.   (lines 637–38)

The lines are from the eightieth stanza of *Upon Appleton House*, but the situation is fraught with Wordsworthian perplexity of introspection and recollection.[28] Whittier might well have cited Wordsworth's simile of

> one who hangs down-bending from the side
> Of a slow-moving boat ...
> ...
> and cannot part
> The shadow from the substance, rocks and sky,
> Mountains and clouds, from that which is indeed
> The region, and the things which there abide
> In their true dwelling.   (*The Prelude*, IV.247–48, 254–58)

American critics of the later nineteenth century seem to have been more inclined than their British contemporaries to romanticize Marvell. In any case, it was not until Herbert Grierson and T. S. Eliot began to emphasize the "metaphysical wit" of Marvell that a new appraisal of his accomplishments was forged.[29] But in trimming away the residue of romanticism in the reception of Marvell, it tended to be forgotten that Wordsworth, although he failed in his own endeavor to combine the private and public poet, gave tribute to Marvell precisely because he was both.

Marvell may err in presuming his own moral authority, but Wordsworth raises no objections against Marvell's moral stance. Marvell takes his place within the "circle of glorious Patriots" because of his moral vigor. Long before Wordsworth, Marvell developed a poetic out of the interaction of subject and object. It differed from Wordsworth's dialectic, but it enabled Marvell to do what Wordsworth could not: assert personal values in a political arena.

NOTES

1 *The Romantics on Milton: Formal Essays and Critical Asides* (Cleveland: The Press of Case Western Reserve University, 1970).
2 See, for example, Jerome J. McGann, *The Romantic Ideology: A Critical Investigation* (University of Chicago Press, 1983) and Marjorie Levinson, *Wordsworth's Great Period Poems: Four Essays* (Cambridge University Press, 1986).
3 *Poetical Works*, 3: 116.
4 Quotations from *The Prelude* are from the 1805 edition.
5 *Prose Works*, 2: 9.
6 *Poetical Works*, 3: 116; Algernon Sidney, *Discourses concerning Government* (posthumous, 1698) and *Love* (posthumous, 1884); James Harrington, *The Commonwealth of Oceana* (1656), *The Prerogative of Popular Government* (1657–58), *The Art of Law-Giving* (1659), and *Aphorisms Political* (1659); Sir Henry Vane, Puritan statesman; the reference to "others who called Milton friend" replaces the specific praise in the MS draft for "Cyriac Skinner, Milton's friend."
7 *Prose Works*, 2: 9, 54n.
8 *Prose Works*, 2: 9.
9 *Prose Works*, 2: 15.
10 Andrew Marvell, *Works, Poetical, Controversial and Political etc with a new Life by Capt. Edward Thompson*, 3 vols. (London, 1776), 1: lvi.
11 U. V. Tuckerman, "Wordsworth's Plan for his Imitation of Juvenal," *Modern Language Notes*, 45 (1930): 209–15.
12 *Early Years*, 176.
13 *The Works of John Dryden, Illustrated with Notes, Historical, Critical, and Explanatory, with a Life of the Author*, ed. Sir Walter Scott, 18 vols. (Edinburgh: James Ballantyne, 1808).
14 *Early Years*, 642. A deed such as "Amnon's murther" ("Absalom and Achitophel," line 39) is not mentioned by Marvell; Wordsworth may have had in mind "Upon the cutting of Sir John of Coventry's Nose," Margoliouth, *Marvell*, 1: 456–58; Marvell, as Member of Parliament for Hull, frequently met with the town's High Steward, the Duke of Monmouth, see 2: 642ff. John Dixon Hunt, *Andrew Marvell: His Life and Writings* (Ithaca: Cornell University Press, 1978), 183, notes that Marvell's meetings with Monmouth were cordial: "Whether he would have supported Shaftesbury's armed promotion of Monmouth as Protestant successor to Charles II, and what he would have thought of Titus Oates, we may surmise, but cannot know. For by then Marvell was dead."
15 Elizabeth Story Donno, *Andrew Marvell: The Critical Heritage* (London: Routledge and Kegan Paul, 1978), 124.
16 *Middle Years*, 154.
17 Donno, in *Andrew Marvell: The Critical Heritage*, 9–11, 129–40, documents the change in critical reception in selections from William Lisle Bowles, Charles Lamb, William Hazlitt, and Leigh Hunt.

18 Donald Friedman, *Marvell's Pastoral Art* (Berkeley: University of California Press, 1970), 124.

19 Alexander Grosart (*The Complete Works of Andrew Marvell*, 4 vols. (1875; reprint, New York: AMS, 1966), 1: 66; Grosart cites *The Winter's Tale* (IV.iv) in his note to the poem; for critical discussion of the parallel see Frank Kermode, *English Pastoral Poetry* (London: Harrap, 1952), 248 and Friedman, *Marvell's Pastoral Art*, 122.

20 Not all critics agree in reading the four Mower Poems, first published in the posthumous folio of 1681, as a narrative sequence; Rosalie L. Colie, "*My Ecchoing Song.*" *Andrew Marvell's Poetry of Criticism* (Princeton: Princeton University Press, 1970), 30–39, declares that "the person of the Mower ... cannot be identical in the four poems." See, however, Joan Webber, *The Eloquent "I"* (Madison: University of Wisconsin Press, 1968); Ann E. Berthoff, *The Resolved Soul: A Study of Marvell's Major Poems* (Princeton: Princeton University Press, 1970), 132–42; John Klause, *The Unfortunate Fall: Theodicy and the Moral Imagination of Andrew Marvell* (Hamden, Connecticut: Archon Books, 1983), 62–63.

21 W. Carew Hazlitt, *Faiths and Folklore of the British Isles. A Descriptive and Historical Dictionary* (1905; reprint, New York: Benjamin Blom, 1965), 2: 456.

22 A. J. Smith, "Marvell's Metaphysical Wit," and John Carey, "Reversals Transposed: An Aspect of Marvell's Imagination," in *Approaches to Marvell: The York Tercentenary Lectures*, ed. C. A. Patrides (London: Routledge and Kegan Paul, 1978), 56–86, 136–54.

23 H. Kelliher, *Andrew Marvell: Poet and Politician* (London: The British Library, 1978); R. I. V. Hodge, *Foreshortened Time: Andrew Marvell and Seventeenth Century Revolutions* (Cambridge: D. S. Brewer, 1978).

24 M. C. Bradbrook and M. G. Lloyd Thomas, *Andrew Marvell* (Cambridge: Cambridge University Press, 1940), 1.

25 Bradbrook and Thomas, *Andrew Marvell*, 55.

26 J. Crofts, *Wordsworth and the Seventeenth Century* (The Warton Lecture, 1940; reprint, Folcroft Library Editions, 1974), 17–18.

27 John Greenleaf Whittier, "Andrew Marvell," in *National Era* (18 May 1848).

28 *The Letters of John Greenleaf Whittier*, ed. John B. Pickard, 3 vols. (Cambridge: Belknap Press of Harvard University Press, 1975); Letter to Charles Sumner (26 March 1848), 2: 101; Letter to Celia Thaxter (8 August 1867), 3: 159–60; Letter to John Boyle O'Reilley (22 May 1879), 3: 408.

29 T. S. Eliot, "Andrew Marvell," in *Selected Essays, 1917–1932* (New York: Harcourt, Brace; London: Faber & Faber, 1932); Herbert J. C. Grierson, *Metaphysical Lyrics and Poems of the Seventeenth Century* (Oxford: Clarendon Press, 1921).

CHAPTER NINE

Kidnapping the poets: the Romantics and Henry Vaughan

JOHN T. SHAWCROSS

THE FATE OF THE POETRY OF Henry Vaughan has been unhappy: unhappy because what he wrote is often not read while what a critic thinks he should have written is; unhappy because most critical reviews of his work have dealt with only some of the poems of his collection *Silex Scintillans* (1650, 1655), although generalizations are drawn therefrom for all the work; and unhappy because these two approaches have frequently led to misreadings of the poems.[1] Balance and revision have been appearing as a result of a series of articles and an edition of the "secular" poems by E. L. Marilla (1942–58), and through studies by such people as James D. Simmonds and Jonathan F. S. Post.[2] Largely due to the hermetic activities and writings of his twin brother Thomas and his own *Hermetical Physick: or, The right way to preserve, and to restore Health. By That famous and faithfull Chymist, Henry Nollius. Englished by Henry Vaughan, Gent.* (London, 1655), Vaughan and his "sacred" poetry have also been viewed as exhibiting hermetic philosophy, although more recent commentators have minimized that subtention and have read the poems with fewer preconceptions.[3] Yet an attitude that the treatment of "Nature" in his work places Vaughan in the company of William Wordsworth (and other poets of the British Romantic period) persists. The problem is, however, not only an inadequate reading of Vaughan but a questionable understanding of romanticism, which grew first out of comparisons with the poetry of the eighteenth century and then from a rejection of the so-called "Romantic agony."

The poems of Henry Vaughan were available only in original editions in some of the major libraries of the British Isles until a few examples appeared in Henry Headley's *Select Beauties of Ancient English Poetry* (1787). None appeared in George Ellis's first edition of *Specimens of the Early English Poets* in 1790, a few in the 1801 and 1802 editions and then with asterisks in the 1811 edition. In 1819 a few items (all from *Silex Scintillans*) were included by Thomas Campbell in *Specimens of the British Poets with Biographical and Critical Notices and an Essay on English Poetry* (seven volumes); in 1822 by John Bullar in *Selections from the British Poets, Commencing with Spenser and Including the latest Writers*; in 1827 by John Johnstone in *Specimens of the Lyrical, Descriptive, and Narrative Poets of Sacred and Serious Poetry from Chaucer to the Present Day*, republished with some revision in 1828; and in 1827 by James Montgomery in *The Christian Poet, or Selections from Verse on Sacred Subjects*, reprinted in 1827 and 1828. The most popular collections of poetry and critical lives of poets at the end of the eighteenth century did not include Vaughan: those from Samuel Johnson (1779 and many later editions), John Bell (1779 and many later editions), Robert Anderson (1792–95), and even Alexander Chalmers's *The Works of the English Poets, from Chaucer to Cowper* in 1810 ignored him.[4] It was not until 1847 when H. F. Lyte published *The Sacred Poems and Private Ejaculations of Henry Vaughan with a Memoir* that the poems were again available, and Alexander B. Grosart's important collection in four volumes, *The Works in Verse and Prose Complete of Henry Vaughan, Silurist, for the first time collected and edited* was privately printed in 1871. An account of Vaughan's life was added to Anthony Wood's *Athenæ Oxonienses* in 1721 (2: 926–27), and this reappeared in Philip Bliss's amplified edition in 1813 (2: 62). Jane Campbell points out that Thomas Campbell lifted a line from "The Rainbow" (which was included in his selection) for a poem of his own, and Bernard Barton transposed lines 25–28 of "The Night" as a motto for his *Poetic Vigils* (1824) (*The Retrospective Review* [*1820–1828*], 50). Barton had written to Charles Lamb about a motto and the title of the collection (although Lamb's reply does not mention Vaughan at all), and he sent copies of his book to both Lamb and Wordsworth.[5] But significantly, there is an anonymous review of *Olor Iscanus* in the *Retrospective Review* 3, Part 2 (1823): Article VIII, 336–54, the only discussion of Vaughan during the Romantic period. The reviewer promised to look in a later issue at *Silex Scintillans*, but failed to do so. The published review employs much quotation, discusses a quotation from Vaughan's "Preface" concerned with poetasters, and speaks of Vaughan's "conversion" of 1650 (or thereabouts).

The upshot of these bibliographical data is that Wordsworth (and other Romantic poets) would have found it difficult to come by Vaughan's poetry, certainly to come by sufficient items for a strong attitude toward him as author. It is difficult to understand how Wordsworth (1770–1850) could know of it in relation to the poetry published by 1798, 1800, 1802. How he or John Keats or Percy Bysshe Shelley or Lord Byron might have been influenced by Vaughan's poetry prior to the early eighteen-twenties (when the last three in fact died in 1821, 1822, and 1824, respectively) boggles the imagination. Jane Campbell asserts, "despite theories concerning the supposed indebtedness of Wordsworth to Vaughan there is no proof that either Lamb or Wordsworth ever read Vaughan's work, and no reference to him in Coleridge" (*The Retrospective Review* [*1820–1828*], 50). Yet there are those few printed poems and there is the *Retrospective Review*.

This reviewer praises Vaughan's rhythm and what appear to him to be experiments with rhyme (343, 346), the versification being adapted to the subject matter. There is also "both feeling and imagination." But as Jane Campbell points out, "The reviewer reflects the prejudices of his age when he censures Vaughan for his use of 'frigid and bombastic conceits'" (50). This comment points toward the legacy of Johnsonianism and the period following the first quarter of the century, "metaphysical" to some meaning harshness and obscurity.[6] Marilla saw later critics in the century reflecting "evangelical fervor" rather than aesthetic appreciation, and Simmonds remarks that nineteenth-century readers responded to Vaughan's treatment of nature in terms of Wordsworth's poetry. The prime example was "The Retreate," seen as precursing, even directly influencing, "Ode: Intimations of Immortality from Recollections of Early Childhood," written during 1802–6 and published in 1807. Here the equation lay in the Platonic concept of the soul's preexistence and in an idealized image of childhood. The belief in Wordsworth's reading and use of Vaughan was directly stated by Richard C. Trench, when he spoke of Wordsworth's alleged annotated copy of *Silex Scintillans*.[7]

What occurred in the later nineteenth century and has continued into most of the twentieth is a "kidnapping" of Vaughan, an image presented by Merritt Y. Hughes when he wrote of "Kidnapping Donne."[8] Hughes observed the way in which modern critics had made Donne a contemporary through a "critical self-consciousness" which has led to reading his poetry out of context. The recent approach of new historicism should deal with such kidnapping although it has not, just as Hans Jauss's theories of reception should lead to revised readings of authors like Donne, Vaughan, and Marvell. Perhaps, though, the most misleading critical stance is that built upon the reading of a poem or two rather than upon the corpus of work, a corpus which, of course, may alter over time or may exhibit variations within time. The kidnapping of Donne rested largely upon the reading of some of the songs and sonnets with, for example, the verse letters and the epicedes and obsequies (including the Anniversary poems) being quite ignored – or rather, in truth, probably simply unread by the critic. The kidnapping of Vaughan as a proto-Romantic has resulted from the same unscholarly emphasis on a few anthologized pieces which strike the would-be critic as having similarities to a few anthologized pieces of, say, Wordsworth. Indeed, Vaughan scholarship has often suffered by such ignorance: the poems of *Poems* (1646), almost unnoted and thus dismissed by Bennett ("Vaughan never appears to be interested in his subject," *Four Metaphysical Poets*, 72) and Hutchinson (there is "little enough in it to employ his time," *Henry Vaughan*, 50), must immediately call into question the pronouncements of Vaughan's achievement or its lack, the generalizations of his subjects (*Olor Iscanus* is also usually unnoticed), and the invidious comparisons declaimed.[9]

Trench's contention that Wordsworth owned an annotated edition of Vaughan (reported also by Grosart and repeated by Empson, among others), based on a claim by an unknown correspondent of having purchased such a copy at the sale of Wordsworth's library, was refuted by Helen N. McMaster in 1935.[10] Dr. John Brown of Edinburgh, in *Horæ Subsecivæ*, II (1861), seems to have been the first to compare the two poets, and it became thereafter a commonplace to talk of Wordsworth's indebtedness to Vaughan. Grosart (1.xx) linked Vaughan with Shelley in the picturesque and fanciful and with Wordsworth in the pantheistic and pious. For W. J. Courthope, Vaughan was the "lineal progenitor of Wordsworth"; for Hutchinson, only a few unforgettable lines and a rare vein of thought kept Vaughan's poems worthy to be read.[11] It is to Hutchinson we owe the outrageously inept comment that a poem of Vaughan's cannot sustain "the magic of the opening lines." That is, the poem he read was not the poem he thought should have been written on the basis of his reading of the opening lines, and so it was condemned. It has not dawned on generations of critics to read what *Vaughan* wrote in order to judge his work.[12]

L. R. Merrill pursued the topic in 1922, working through "The Retreate" and the "Immortality Ode," where stress was placed on the substance of the world, the development of the child into adulthood, and the gradual absorption of spirit against the material in life.[13] While the conclusions differ, the vision of childhood and the beauties in nature link the two. One evaluation Merrill derives from this coupling is that Vaughan's poem does not offer the philosophic profundity that Wordsworth's does. But since Vaughan's ideas appear in other of his works – "Regeneration," "The Water-fall," "Distraction" – and these emerge in Wordsworth's "Song at the Feast of Brougham Castle" (1807) and "The world is too much with us" (1806–7), Merrill concludes that there is ample evidence of Wordsworth's familiarity with the work of Vaughan. Two years later Muriel Morris added further parallels: "Misery," "The Constellation," "Anguish" alongside "Ode to Duty" (1805–7) and "The Rainbow" (that is, "My heart leaps up," 1802–7).[14] Edmund Blunden's *On the Poems of Henry Vaughan: Characteristics and Intimations*, reviewed in *The Dial* by T. S. Eliot, examined parallels with Wordsworth and Herbert, Eliot's demurrals arising from his contention that Vaughan was neither a great mystic nor a very great poet. Again it is "The

Retreate" and the "Immortality Ode" which are the focus, and again it is the prejudice of the reviewer against the Romantic nature of poetry that creates his opinions. The "Ode" is superb verbiage, "The Retreate" a simple and sincere statement of feeling (but this feeling is secular and thus it is removed from the realm of Herbert's religious sentiments). Herbert's poetry is clear, definite, mature, and sustained; Vaughan's is vague, adolescent, fitful, and regressive – what Eliot sees as "pantheistic confusion." For Empson in 1929, accepting the parallels but iterating distaste for the Romantic, Wordsworth's "dream-like or hypnotic intensity is never far out of sight in Vaughan's work (hence, like the Romantics, and unlike Herbert, the ruck of his work is merely bad); when it can be combined with the self-respect of conceits he is very impressive" ("An Early Romantic," 496).[15] George Williamson found the source of Vaughan's mysticism and conception of nature in Christianity and hermeticism, and he points out a predilection for evening and night, for "twilight regions whose Nature speaks to him in pantheistic terms that anticipate Wordsworth, and where he may become reminiscent of childhood."[16] These are the chords that are continuously struck by some critics after 1950.[17]

Even so otherwise perceptive a critic as Ruth Wallerstein read Vaughan with clouded eyes.[18] To her his "constructive gift seems so largely the by-product of general vision" (155):

After his essentially unfruitful time in London, and after a period of personal tension including the shock of his brother's death, Vaughan found his vein of poetry when he learned, deliberately or unconsciously or both, from the Bible or elsewhere, the power to put into words that spontaneous and integrated impression of a landscape, that flashing insight into nature, which was for him the substance on which he nourished his religious insight. (313)

For Pettet Vaughan anticipated the Romantic treatment of nature but was not a poet of nature: "The Water-fall" and its sequence were "chosen for their symbolic value, not – as Wordsworth's are – as 'beauteous forms', chosen for their aesthetic and emotional value in the life of the poet. That is to say, they are determined by the preconceived complex of ideas which they are to represent, not by Vaughan's personal experience of a place" (Of Paradise and Light, 17–18). Yet for Durr Vaughan is not a meditative poet but one whose theme of regeneration is revealed through poignancy, feeling. For Wallerstein, Pettet, Durr, and others, the turning point for Vaughan as poet was his brother's death and his "conversion." Despite Bourdette's assertion that "The earlier view of Vaughan as a pre-Romantic influencing Wordsworth has been generally discredited" ("Recent Studies in Henry Vaughan," 303) the relating of the two goes on even in the work of Vaughan's best recent critic, who perhaps wanted to avoid its brash dismissal, deserved though brashness is. Post, in Henry Vaughan: The Unfolding Vision, remarks about "The Water-fall":

If Vaughan seems at his most Wordsworthian here, it is because both poets, however much they might disagree over origins, were deeply committed to retrieving from nature intimations of immortality ... But the celebration of nature here becomes ultimately for Vaughan (as for Wordsworth) a celebration of the inspired mind, both in its immediate perceptions and in its growth. (153)

An earlier statement provides a better avenue into a reading of Vaughan through its casting aside of both Wordsworth and Eliot as conduit:

To a modern reader what is immediately apparent in the responses to these two "opening" poems [of *Olor Iscanus*, "To the River *Isca*" and "The Charnel-house"] is a difference between a vision of poetry influenced largely by the presence of Wordsworth and a later corrective determined essentially by the tastes of Eliot. Though the gap is considerable, the two views do share at least one thing in common: the part of *Olor* that least conforms to the critic's particular standard is inevitably judged a poetic failure. (28)

The solution to a defensible reading of Vaughan's poetry is clearly to read *Vaughan's* poetry, not Wordsworth's, not Eliot's, and not what a latterday critic thinks it should be.

I hope a reading of the only two Vaughan poems specifically cited as Wordsworthian – "The Retreate" and "The Water-fall" – can demonstrate an avenue into reading his work cogently, remembering, of course, that the "secular" poems particularly may offer other and additional critical conclusions. Other poems will be glanced at to refute a so-called "Romantic" reading of Vaughan. Remarks on Wordsworth's "Immortality Ode" and "The world is too much with us" – two often cited poems – may suffice to point us toward a more meaningful understanding of the Romantic than some readers seem to favor, which in turn will be seen to divorce Vaughan from that label.

"The Retreate" appears in Part I of *Silex Scintillans* as the twenty-first poem, after "The Call," "Thou that know'st for whom I mourne," and "Vanity of Spirit," and before "Come, come, what doe I here?" and "Midnight." Each poem has a different and contrastive metrical form, "The Retreate" having a simple pattern of sixteen tetrameter couplets, with a paragraph break. The simple and straightforward metrical form is appropriate to the poem's theme of what the poetic voice's "Angell-infancy" was before he came to his "second race," that maturity into the evil world surrounding him and of which he has become a part.[19] The poem ends with a wish to "return" by the time death descends ("when this dust falls to the urn") to "that state" he enjoyed before. This is "The Retreate" which is wished, one not *to* infancy but *from* the world, as Hughes insisted.[20] This variation on the common *contemptus mundi* theme sees the pre-"world" condition as one where there was "white, Celestiall thought," where his "first love," with "his bright-face," would gild a "*Cloud*, or *flowre*," "weaker glories" that showed forth "Some shadows of eternity." Presently he "taught [his] tongue to wound / [His] Conscience with a sinfull sound," and he found "the black art to dispence / A sev'rall sinne to ev'ry sence." One might think of Donne's *Holy Sonnet* 175:

> I am a little world made cunningly
> Of Elements, and an Angelike spright,
> But black sinne hath betraid to endlesse night
> My worlds both parts   *(Complete Poetry*, ed. Shawcross, 347)

He wishes to return to "that plaine, / Where first [he] left [his] glorious traine," so that, again filled with enlightened spirit, like Moses, he can see "That shady City of Palme trees." The plain is the valley of Jericho, the city of the plains, promised to Abraham and his progeny by God (Deuteronomy 34.1–4), but it metaphorizes the plains of Heaven and the City of God, appropriate images for the final metaphor of his hoped-for return to his original dust. The funerary urn in which "this dust" will be implies that the dust is ashes, ashes which have resulted from the great conflagration ending the world (2 Peter 3.10) and leading to the Last Judgment. Should he then again be in the state in which he came into life (the "Angell-infancy" or the "Angelike spright"), Judgment would place him in that City. The return is one of a renunciation of sinfulness within; the retreat, a reversal of the motion imagery depicting humankind's life as a race (a common simile): his "second race." He "had not walkt above / A mile, or two," "looking back (at that short space)," when he longs "to travell back / And tread again that ancient track" (that is, the track of the first race), when he left the "glorious traine" (that is, the moving "line" of people proceeding into life on a path of glory); but he stands still at this point in time ("my soul with too much stay / Is drunk"), he "staggers in the way." Others "forward motion love"; he "by backward steps would move" and so "retreat."

The poem is broken into two verse paragraphs at line 20. Significantly this is the focal point of the poem, the golden section, becoming the point toward which the poem moves before resolution.[21] The first paragraph sets out what the far past has been and what it has been replaced with; the second paragraph pleads for return. Line 20 indicates the possibility of such return for "through all this fleshly dresse" is felt "Bright *shootes* of everlastingnesse." Though he has outwardly reflected the evil and sin of this world, inwardly his soul shoots out like a star or comet bright radiances of its eternal being. The line is one of numerous appropriations by Vaughan from Owen Felltham's *Resolves*.[22] These "shootes" are the means to dispel the darkness of the world, the black art that has dispensed his sins; they are the humanly image of the "white, Celestiall thought" and the "bright-face" which gilds nature. As Seelig writes, "The Retreate," like "Regeneration," "is neither simply auto-biography nor convention: it is a recapitulation of the history of mankind in the experience of the poet" (*The Shadow of Eternity*, 75). "It shows the persona" wanting to move "from bondage and darkness" to a former freedom and light. The imagery and the thought of the poem reprise the title of the collection and its frontispiece: "Silex Scintillans," the "flashing flint," is represented in the craggy heart (fashioned as faces) that is being struck by thunderbolts from heaven, set on fire on its dark left side, and dropping tears (or blood). It recalls the lines of the Passover psalm, No. 114, on the Mosaic exodus through the Red Sea: "Tremble, thou earth, at the presence of the Lord, at the presence of the God of Jacob; which turned the rock into a standing water, the flint into a fountain of waters."

The poems that surround "The Retreate" relate and direct one's reading of it, just as each poem in Herbert's *The Temple* comments upon its neighbors. "The Call" addresses the poet's heart and head, "dead / Some twenty years," to awaken and score his sins on the glass of time; their "heavy State" can then be weighed and rated against his tears of repentance: "That done, we shalbe safe, and good." The untitled "Thou that know'st for whom I mourne" (perhaps Vaughan's brother William, who died in 1648) records the sharp awareness of mortality, the need to reject the "vanity [which] is man" (13) seen in the "shreds" of one's "Twenty" years.[23] Death has been placed outside man by God so "That heaven within him might abide, / And close eternitie" (29–32). And the poet begs God to "make my soule white as his [William's] owne, / My faith as pure, and steddy" (61–62). The next poem picks up the vanity of the previous poem, which should be dispelled through the "glorious Ring" of God, but the poet has only "Weake beames, and fires flash'd to [his] sight, / Like a young East, or Moone-shine night" (19–20). "That little light [he] had was gone," and since under vails he cannot approach God with his "*Ecclips'd Eye*," he will "*disapparell*" to see God.[24] To see God directly was to die: yet "to buy / But one half glaunce, [he would] most gladly dye."[25]

The imagery and content of these immediately preceding poems chart the imagery and content of "The Retreate," and the awakening awareness of the reality of humankind's mortality indicates the impetus for this poem. Immediately following is another on his brother's death: "Come, come, what doe I here? / Since he is gone / Each day is grown a dozen year, and each houre, one." The poet's wish to "be with him" and to "sleep / To wake in thee [God]" leads to the next poem, "Midnight," when "(Whilst deep sleep others catches)," his "Eyes" will "survey / Each busie Ray" of "Thy heav'ns," which "Are a firie-liquid light, / Which mingling aye / Streames, and flames thus to the sight." The poem ends with a verbalization of the frontispiece:

And thou shalt see
Kindled by thee
Both liquors burne, and streame.
O what bright quicknes,
Active brightnes,
And celestiall flowes
Will follow after
On that water,
Which thy spirit blowes!   (lines 24–32)

Appended is a quotation of the words of John the Baptist from Matthew 3.11: "I indeed baptize you with water unto repentance, but he that commeth after me, is mightier than I, whose shooes I am not worthy to beare, he shall baptize you with the holy Ghost, and with fire." These words are an appropriate comment on these preceding poems with the mourned one becoming for the poet a type of John the Baptist leading him to Christ. The next poems (there are eight) will move into related concerns, employing much of this previous imagery, until, at the end of "Buriall," another biblical verse appears: Romans 8.23, "And not only they, but our selves also, which have the first fruits of the spirit, even wee our selves grone within our selves, waiting for the adoption, to wit, the redemption of our body."

The alleged effusiveness of the Romantic, the revelling in nature as manifestation of God rather than revelation of divine being, the varied, dynamic, and individualistic qualities superficially associated with romanticism by some critics are not part of Vaughan's poetic work. There is devotional belief and God is seen as revealed in the Book of Nature, but much of the imagery is not unlike that in the work of other poets of the period – Herbert, Crashaw, Quarles – and is ultimately biblical. The poetry does not have the seeming spontaneity and linear quality that superficial criticism of the Romantics found in the past. The points of tangency for the casual reader seem to be only, first, the significance of childhood (the child of Herbert's "The Collar" or "Longing" and such poems as his "Affliction [1]," "Mortification," and "Pilgrimage" might be compared more profitably with "The Retreate"), and, second, the imagery of nature (though Vaughan's usage undergoes change, similar images appear in such poems as Herbert's "Peace," "Artillerie," and "The Flower"). The concern of "The Retreate" is the mortality of humankind and the readiness of each person for the end of life and Judgment; hope of such readiness lies in the revelation of God within seen in parallel with the revelation of God in things of nature. There is nothing pantheistic about Vaughan's use of nature, here or elsewhere.

"The Water-fall" illustrates the same point. This poem from Part II of *Silex Scintillans* has two metrically contrasting parts. First, two lines of pentameter, two lines of dimeter, two lines of pentameter, four lines of dimeter, and two lines of pentameter describe the waterfall, the varied line lengths suggesting free-flowing and at times constricted water, some horizontal movement as the water streams and some vertical movement as it falls. These impressions about the water are also in the words: "deep murmurs," "staid Lingering," "a longer course"; "flowing fall," "All must descend / Not to an end." This section hieroglyphically shows both a waterfall and, particularly in view of the reference to "times silent stealth" in the first line, an hour glass. (The water is also "transparent" and "clear as glass.") While the first part of the poem describes the waterfall in visual terms, it also metaphorizes the stream of life passing smoothly and continuingly, roughly and precipitously through time. There is no ecstatic viewing of the waterfall; it is used as a metaphor to state an observation about human existence. People are "quickned" (made "alive," "active") by the "deep and rocky grave" which commonly attends "All" who "must descend": such trial will cause them to "Rise to a longer course more bright and brave."

Second, twenty-eight lines of tetrameter address the stream, the bank, and the waterfall as the "pensive eye" of the poet observes them. The imaging of their properties leads to the thought that one should not fear shade or night (death) since, like the water, one's soul came "from a sea of light," for each drop presumes an endless store to continue running thither as it had before. Replenishment comes by way of precipitation through God's order of things: thus one should not doubt that he will restore the frail flesh that has been taken. Apostrophes to the "useful Element" (water), as in baptism and the fountain of life of the Lamb, proclaim its "mystical" message. Further observation of the "incessant fall" of the water, which then moves in circles in the pool that is formed beneath, with "restagnation" at its banks, so that a specific ring of water is no longer viewed as moving turbulently, leads to another metaphor: the poet's "soul seeks" that "Channel," not the one "with Cataracts and Creeks." The second part, like the first, presents observation of nature which metaphorically provides entry into a concept of life, or of hoped-for life. The stream and waterfall offer "sublime truths, and wholesome themes." It is not a pantheistic or ecstatic communion with nature that is presented in the poem: it is an observation and poetic use of that observation to express a thought. Behind some of the poem's language seem to be hermetic properties: the soul coming from a sea of light, the fountains of life, the sublime truths and mystical, deep streams, the Spirit of God moving upon the face of the waters in the Creation (Genesis 1.2) and thus hatching the world "with his quickning love." But the use of this nature imagery is so very different from that in Wordsworth, and despite the apostrophes (which have, perhaps, made this poem most Wordsworthian for some people), Vaughan is not manifesting God in nature but indicating God's revelation which provides lessons for the poet and the reader. If "Romantic" stresses individualism, this poem is not "Romantic"; if "Romantic" implies an escape from the harsh realities, this poem is not "Romantic" but devotional.

Wordsworth's sonnet "The world is too much with us" is clearly an apostrophe to nature and his revelling in nature: the lament is that humankind has forgotten nature and its beauty because of our everyday concerns with existing. Even a return to mythic explanations of nature, as long as they focus one upon the things of nature, is more desirable. The Pagan appreciated nature more than the contemporary follower of the Great God, whose work is ignored and disharmonious with those who have given their hearts away. The play is between feeling and crassness. We do not find these attitudes in Vaughan's work.

The "Immortality Ode" poses human loss as one grows up, the past as a better world: it becomes a more feeling and personal statement for the author and the reader of the medieval concept of "sic transit gloria mundi." Wordsworth writes: "But yet I know, where'er I go, / That there hath past away a glory from the earth." Nature itself, though it be the same, is not the same to the experienced poet, now looking with older eyes: "The things which I have seen I now can see no more." Clearly there will be an emphasis on infancy, when heaven lay about us; life seen in the metaphor of moving westward alters the light and its source and godhead, man becoming less nature's priest thereby. But something may remain in the embers of older age, something no "noisy years" "Can utterly abolish or destroy!"

> Though nothing can bring back the hour
> Of splendour in the grass, of glory in the flower;
> We will grieve not, rather find
> Strength in what remains behind.   (lines 178–81)

For Wordsworth there is the desire to return *to* childhood, which of necessity has been relinquished, but since that is impossible, he praises "the faith that looks through death" and the "years that bring the philosophic mind." In the final verse paragraph (significantly the eleventh, a mystic number signifying resurrection or regeneration of spirit) he presents a more metrically ordered statement of the sensitive heart that in its tenderness, joys, and fears can love even the meanest things of nature; that this latter time of life, like a new-born day, "Is lovely yet." The line, a dimeter, bifurcates the verse paragraph and makes, thus, the thought emphatic: though nature may be seen with experienced eyes, it "Is lovely yet."

There is much one should say about this wonderful poem, and much has been. There is an ecstatic statement of the magnificence of nature, but the effusiveness that has sometimes been cast on the Romantic poet implies qualities that are not here: mere feeling, lack of thought and art, a gushy tumbling out of images. There is a spontaneity, an excitement felt as the reader becomes involved in the expression, but the poem is not "spontaneous" and "linear" (meaning something like "written line after line in some kind of organic, unplanned way"). The well-planned verse paragraphs, with their contrastive forms and interrelationships, and the building of images and thoughts, belie such prejudiced epitomes. The birds and lambs and tabor of stanza 3 recur in stanza 10, not now to bring a thought of grief but to proclaim "the primal sympathy / Which having been must ever be." There is a revelling in nature, and nature is a manifestation of God, and communion with nature leads to understanding. But the harsh realities of the world are only resolved by faith and love, never escaped from. Wordsworth believed, as he wrote in "Ode to Duty":

> Serene will be our days and bright,
> And happy will our nature be,
> When love is an unerring light,
> And joy its own security. (lines 17–20)

In some ways Friedrich Nietzsche has enunciated the difference between a poet like Vaughan and the Romantic (that is, if one accepts Nietzsche's epitome of the Romantic). While remarking the "harmony which is contemplated with such longing by modern man," he wrote, "in fact this oneness of man with nature ... is by no means a simple condition ... [O]nly a Romantic age could believe this."[26] Such oneness is not part of Vaughan's thought. Nature offers metaphors for man's life but is not one with it:

> I will not fear what man,
> With all his plots and power can;
> Bags that wax old may plundered be,
> But none can sequester or let
> A state that with the Sun doth set
> And comes next morning fresh as he.
>
> Poor birds this doctrine sing,
> And herbs which on dry hills do spring
> Or in the howling wilderness
> Do know thy dewy morning-hours,
> And watch all night for mists or showers,
> Then drink and praise thy bounteousness.[27]

Further, Nietzsche talks of "two kinds of sufferers: first, those who suffer from the *over-fullness of life* – they want a Dionysian art and likewise a tragic view of life, a tragic insight – and then those who suffer from the *impoverishment of life* and seek rest, stillness, calm seas, redemption from themselves through art and knowledge, or intoxication, convulsions, anaesthesia, and madness. All romanticism in art and insight corresponds to the dual needs of the latter type."[28] Vaughan is not such a sufferer: he is one who appreciates a commonplace *ars moriendi*, one who recognizes the sinfulness of humankind and its manifestation in himself which may cause salvation to bypass him. He accepts the things of nature as the work and thus revelation of the godhead, and humankind as the "Secretarie of [His] praise" (as Herbert wrote in "Providence," a poem that encompasses the *fauna* and *flora* of life in relationship with man). Vaughan's "The Bird" iterates this point:

> And now as fresh and chearful as the light
> Thy little heart in early hymns doth sing
> Unto that *Providence*, whose unseen arm
> Curb'd them, and cloath'd thee well and warm.
>   All things that be, praise him; and had
>   Their lesson taught them, when first made.
>   ...
> Brightness and mirth, and love and faith, all flye,
> Till the Day-spring breaks forth again from high.   (lines 7–12, 31–32)

We do not hear the ecstasy of Wordsworth observing a rainbow in "My heart leaps up," an enthusiasm in nature that occurred when he was a child, now that he is middle-aged, and hoped for when old. Should such joy in seeing a rainbow not continue, he would rather die: he hopes, instead, that every day of life will be united in continued "natural piety" (reverence, affection). For Vaughan "The Rain-bow" is paramountly the sign of the Covenant between God and humankind:

> When I behold thee, though my light be dim,
> Distant and low, I can in thine see him,
> Who looks upon thee from his glorious throne
> And mindes the Covenant 'twixt *All* and *One*.
> O foul, deceitful men! my God doth keep
> His promise still, but we break ours and sleep...
> For though some think, thou shin'st but to restrain
> Bold storms, and simply dost attend on rain,
> Yet I know well, and so our sins require,
> Thou dost but Court cold rain, till *Rain* turns *Fire*.
>
>   (lines 15–20, 39–42)[29]

It is not a manifestation of God in nature; it is not really treated as a part of nature; it is not an element of nature with which the poet feels harmony. Wordsworth's line "Or let me die!" expresses the meaninglessness of life were he no longer affected enthusiastically by the sight of a rainbow. Vaughan's line in "Anguish" occurs as the second line in aborted stanza 4, representing such anguish that he cannot go on. His anguish comes from a conceived inability to be a true "secretary of God's praise":

> O! 'tis an easie thing
>   To write and sing;
> But to write true, unfeigned verse
> Is very hard! O god, disperse
> These weights, and give my spirit leave
> To act as well as to conceive!
>
> O my God, hear my cry;
>   Or let me dye! –   (lines 13–20)

The major difference, it seems to me, between a seventeenth-century poet like Vaughan and a Romantic poet like Wordsworth is the attitude toward God that has been stated here a few times. The earlier seventeenth century, still a part of the Renaissance, saw God revealing truth in nature; it was through observation of nature, which was created by God, that humankind could come to understanding, learn God's lessons, receive spiritual guidance. The point was, they believed in God and still in the centrality of man (and earth) in God's scheme. With the advent of the "New Philosophy" of astronomical discoveries, the displacement of the earth and man as focus of all creation, the revision of theories concerning the blood (William Harvey's *Exercitatio Anatomica de Motu Cordis et Sanguinis in Animalibus* was first expounded in 1616 and published in 1628), the complexities of science and mathematics explored by Francis Bacon, René Descartes, and Isaac Newton, among others, God's being in nature became less viable as instruction, less certain. On the one hand, Thomas Burnet in *The Sacred Theory of the Earth* (1684–90) called mountains excrescences caused by disruptive action, not things of beauty planned by God; and on the other, Isaac Newton in *Principia*, Book III (1687), rationalized: "This most beautiful system of the sun, planets, and comets, could only proceed from the counsel and dominion of an intelligent and powerful Being ... This Being governs all things, not as the soul of the world, but as Lord over all."[30] The crisis of religion in the late seventeenth century lay in the revelation or the manifestation of God: a continuing guide or a mere presence, a Calvinistic/Arminian God or a Deistic one. That former understanding of God and of his revelation had fairly disappeared by the time of the Romantics. The transitional period, in Alexander Pope's words, concluded, "What can we reason, but from what we know?"; "Heaven from all creatures hides the book of fate"; "All are but parts of one stupendous whole, / Whose body Nature is, and God the soul."[31]

While it is fruitful to investigate the reading of such seventeenth-century authors as John Donne and John Milton by the Romantics, and to recognize their influence in compositional matters, imagery, quotation and allusion, the realm of philosophic ideas should be trod cautiously. Many, even through the twentieth century, misread Donne by kidnapping him and by reading so little of his work, and when we consider Coleridge's comments on Donne's sermons, we should acknowledge that they tell us more about Coleridge and the way he thought than about what Donne believed. Milton, needless to say, is constantly debated as to meaning and personal attitudes in his epic, overwhelming though the influence has always been from John Dryden on. When we come to Vaughan or Traherne, the cautions are compounded, not only because of the inaccessibility of their poetry, but also because of their difference of attitude toward and belief in God and his workings. Though they both are observant of nature and see nature from the hand of God, neither reflects the Romantic earmarks usually advanced rightly or wrongly. But further, Vaughan and Traherne will be distanced from each other when we read more of Vaughan's work and read it without preconceptions of what it should be.

NOTES

1 See such influential studies as Joan Bennett, *Four Metaphysical Poets* (1934; reprint, Cambridge: Cambridge University Press, 1953); Edmund Blunden, *On the Poems of Henry Vaughan: Characteristics and Intimations* (London: R. Cobden-Sanderson, 1927; reprint, New York: Russell & Russell, 1969); T. S. Eliot, "The Silurist," *The Dial* 83 (September 1927): 259–63; F. E. Hutchinson, *Henry Vaughan: A Life and Interpretation* (Oxford: Oxford University Press, 1947); J. B. Leishman, *The Metaphysical Poets: Donne, Herbert, Vaughan, Traherne* (Oxford: Oxford University Press, 1934); E. C. Pettet, *Of Paradise and Light: A Study of Vaughan's Silex Scintillans* (Cambridge: Cambridge University Press, 1960); Helen C. White, *The Metaphysical Poets* (1936; reprint, New York: Macmillan, 1962).

2 See, among others, E. L. Marilla, "Henry Vaughan and the Civil War," *Journal of English and Germanic Philology* 41 (1942): 514–26; "The Significance of Henry Vaughan's Literary Reputation," *Modern Language Quarterly* 5 (1944): 155–62; "'The Publisher to the Reader' of *Olor Iscanus*," *Review of English Studies* 24 (1948): 36–41; "The Secular and Religious Poetry of Henry Vaughan," *Modern Language Quarterly* 9 (1948): 394–411; and *The Secular Poems of Henry Vaughan* (Uppsala: Lundequistska Bokhandeln, 1958); and Simmonds, *The Masques of God: Form and Theme in the Poetry of Henry Vaughan* (Pittsburgh: University of Pittsburgh Press, 1972), and Post, *Henry Vaughan: The Unfolding Vision* (Princeton: Princeton University Press, 1982). Other studies that should be consulted are John T. Shawcross, "Vaughan's 'Amoret' Poems: A Jonsonian Sequence," in *Classic and Cavalier: Essays on Jonson and the Sons of Ben*, ed. Claude J. Summers and Ted-Larry Pebworth (Pittsburgh: University of Pittsburgh Press, 1982), 193–214, and the series of essays in a special issue of the *George Herbert Journal* 7 (1983), ed. Jonathan F. S. Post.

3 The most influential work for this contention is Elizabeth Holmes's *Henry Vaughan and the Hermetic Philosophy* (Oxford: Oxford University Press, 1932), but see also Edward

Chauncey Baldwin, "Wordsworth and Hermes Trismegistus," *PMLA* 33 (1918): 235–43; Thomas O. Calhoun, *Henry Vaughan: The Achievement of Silex Scintillans* (Newark: University of Delaware Press, 1981); Wilson O. Clough, "Henry Vaughan and the Hermetic Philosophy," *PMLA* 48 (1933): 1108–30; Patrick Grant, *The Transformation of Sin: Studies in Donne, Herbert, Vaughan, and Traherne* (Amherst: University of Massachusetts Press, 1974); two studies by A. C. Judson, "Cornelius Agrippa and Henry Vaughan," *Modern Language Notes* 41 (1926): 178–81, and "The Source of Henry Vaughan's Ideas Concerning God in Nature," *Studies in Philology* 24 (1927): 592–606; L. C. Martin, "Henry Vaughan and 'Hermes Trismegistus'," *Review of English Studies* 18 (1942): 301–7; various articles by A. W. Rudrum, including "Henry Vaughan's 'The Book': A Hermetic Poem," *Journal of the Australasian Universities Language and Literature Association* 16 (1961): 161–66; "Vaughan's 'The Night': Some Hermetic Notes," *Modern Language Review* 64 (1969): 11–19; and "The Influence of Alchemy in the Poems of Henry Vaughan," *Philological Quarterly* 49 (1970): 469–80; Arthur J. M. Smith, "Some Relations Between Henry Vaughan and Thomas Vaughan," *Papers of the Michigan Academy* 18 (1933): 551–61; Bain Tate Stewart, "Hermetic Symbolism in Henry Vaughan's 'The Night'," *Philological Quarterly* 29 (1950): 417–22; R. H. Walters, "Henry Vaughan and the Alchemists," *Review of English Studies* 23 (1947): 107–22; and Ralph M. Wardle, "Thomas Vaughan's Influence Upon the Poetry of Henry Vaughan," *PMLA* 51 (1936): 936–52.

See also "Recent Studies in Henry Vaughan" by Robert E. Bourdette, Jr., in *English Literary Renaissance* 4 (1974): 299–310; "Hermeticism, Mysticism, Meditation" is given extensive treatment on pp. 301–2. Judicious reexaminations will be found in Ross Garner, *Henry Vaughan: Experience and the Tradition* (Chicago: University of Chicago Press, 1959); R. A. Durr, *On the Mystical Poetry of Henry Vaughan* (Cambridge: Harvard University Press, 1962); Simmonds, *The Masques of God*; and Sharon Cadman Seelig, *The Shadow of Eternity: Belief and Structure in Herbert, Vaughan, and Traherne* (Lexington: University Press of Kentucky, 1981).

4 Compare Appendix 1, "Collections and Anthologies of Seventeenth-Century Poetry," in Jane Campbell, *The Retrospective Review (1820–1828) and the Revival of Seventeenth-Century Poetry* (Waterloo, Canada: Waterloo Lutheran University, 1972), which gives a listing of such publications between 1765 and 1832. Campbell writes that "Vaughan had been virtually unknown in the eighteenth century" and that he was "a poet who was still comparatively obscure in the 1820's" (49). J. Sturrock notes that a letter from Wordsworth to Anderson, dated 17 December 1814, gives a list of proposed additions to Anderson's voluminous anthology, but does not include Vaughan, clearly pointing to Wordsworth's ignorance of Vaughan's work at that time; see "Wordsworth and Vaughan," *Notes & Queries* 24 (1977): 322–23.

5 See *The Letters of Charles Lamb to which are added those of his sister Mary Lamb* (London: J. M. Dent & Sons, & Methuen & Co., 1935), ed. E. V. Lucas; 2: 418–19, no. 506 to Barton, dated 25 February 1824.

6 These matters underlie Joseph E. Duncan's *The Revival of Metaphysical Poetry* (Minneapolis: University of Minnesota Press, 1959); note particularly the influence of Samuel Taylor Coleridge and Robert Browning in fostering changes in attitude and awareness. See also John T. Shawcross, "Opulence and Iron Pokers: Coleridge and Donne," *John Donne Journal* 4 (1985): 201–24.

7　*A Household Book of English Poetry* (London: Macmillan, 1870), 411. Such a copy would have been of the original 1655 edition since it contains both parts and parallels have been alleged with poems from both parts. The reviewer in the *Retrospective Review* would have had at his disposal this edition, and the *Olor Iscanus* copy would have been from 1651 or its reissue (not a reprint or new edition) of 1679.

8　See the *University of California Publications in English* 4 (1934): 61–89.

9　A common comparison is between George Herbert, a "strong" poet, and Vaughan, a "weak" one: see Post, *Henry Vaughan*, 81 and note 17, where he cites Bennett, *Four Metaphysical Poets*, 89; E. C. Pettet, *Of Paradise and Light: A Study of Vaughan's "Silex Scintillans"* (Cambridge: Cambridge University Press, 1960), 70; Durr, *On the Mystical Poetry of Henry Vaughan*, 10; and Barbara K. Lewalski, *Protestant Poetics and the Seventeenth-Century Religious Lyric* (Princeton: Princeton University Press, 1979), 317. For William Empson, "Vaughan is a continual and close imitator of Herbert, both as to images...actual conceits, subjects and forms of poems as a whole" ("An Early Romantic," *The Cambridge Review* 31 [May 1929]: 495). Needless to say had any of these people read *Poems*, they would have recognized Ben Jonson as an important influence, as well as Donne, with no Herbert in sight. The same can be said of *Olor Iscanus* except for some possible emergence of Herbert in a few poems. The composite collection *Thalia Rediviva* (1678) is likewise omitted from consideration in these epitomes and evaluations of Vaughan as poet. In fairness, however, it should be remembered that some of the studies are directed only to the 1655 collection. For a balanced view from one who has read all the poetry perceptively, see Post, *Henry Vaughan*. That Vaughan was influenced by Herbert in *Silex Scintillans* and that some of the poems are specifically intertextual with works from *The Temple* (one thinks of each poet's "Man," for instance) will be manifest to any reader of these two authors. Herbert's title page (1633) is, *The Temple. Sacred Poems and Private Ejaculations*, and Vaughan's (1650) is, *Silex Scintillans or Sacred Poems and Priuate Eiaculations*. Between the two is Richard Crashaw's *Steps to the Temple. Sacred Poems, With other Delights of the Muses* (1646), which has not been accorded critical company with Vaughan. See also Bourdette, "Recent Studies in Henry Vaughan," 301, under "Herbert."

10　"Vaughan and Wordsworth," *Review of English Studies* 11 (1935): 313–25.

11　Henry Vaughan, *Works in Verse and Prose*, ed. A. B. Grosart, 4 vols. ([Blackburn]: privately printed, for Fuller's Worthies' Library, 1871), 1: xx; Courthope, *A History of English Poetry* (London: Macmillan, 1903), 3: 235; F. E. Hutchinson, "The Sacred Poets," in *Cambridge History of English Literature* (Cambridge: Cambridge University Press, 1911), 7: 43–44.

12　For criticism that looks at *Vaughan's* poems, see, among others, Claude J. Summers and Ted-Larry Pebworth, "Vaughan's Temple in Nature and the Context of 'Regeneration'," *Journal of English and Germanic Philology* 74 (1975): 351–60, and Leland H. Chambers, "Vaughan's 'The World': The Limits of Extrinsic Criticism," *Studies in English Literature* 8 (1968): 137–50. Bourdette's summary of the state of criticism is particularly apt: "The judgment of Vaughan as a poet of 'single stanzas, lines, or even half lines' has been modified in the past quarter century by the many studies which have used Vaughan's sources to demonstrate the unity and intention of the individual poems." However, this has led to an overshadowing of "Vaughan's ability to assimilate and reshape his sources" and "to a detailed criticism of only a fraction of Vaughan's work from a *corpus* numbering over two hundred poems" ("Recent Studies in Henry Vaughan," 305).

13 "Vaughan's Influence Upon Wordsworth's Poetry," *Modern Language Notes* 37 (1922): 91–96.

14 "A Note on Wordsworth and Vaughan," *Modern Language Notes* 39 (1924): 287–88. The point of similarity in "Anguish" and "My heart leaps up" is the line "Or let me die!"

15 Empson also remarks that "his most effective passages are not metaphysical at all; it is often an apprehension of Nature, not an intellectual activity, which is at the focus of his consciousness" ("An Early Romantic," 495).

16 *The Donne Tradition* (Cambridge: Harvard University Press, 1930), 123, 132–33. In "The Theme of Pre-existence and Infancy in 'The Retreate'," *Philological Quarterly* 20 (1941): 484–500, Merritt Y. Hughes reviewed the puerile tradition of the child eternally clad in swaddling clothes. The themes of the tradition are regeneration, the mystic union between God and the soul, and the realization of the presence of the living God in the soul and in nature.

17 For other Romantics related by recent critics to Vaughan, see William Harrold, "Blake's 'Tyger' and Vaughan's 'Cock-Crowing'," *Notes & Queries* 212 (1967): 20–21; and Leah S. Marcus, "Vaughan, Wordsworth, Coleridge, and the 'Encomium Asini'," *ELH* 42 (1975): 224–41. Harrold, finding echoes and the spirit of Vaughan's poem in Blake's, concludes that Blake knew Vaughan's work. "Tyger" was published in *Songs of Experience* (1794); Blake would have had to have acquired and read *Silex Scintillans*, Part 2 (1655), which I think unlikely.

18 Ruth Wallerstein, *Studies in Seventeenth-Century Poetic* (Madison: University of Wisconsin Press, 1950).

19 Vaughan's poems are quoted from *The Complete Poetry of Henry Vaughan*, ed. Ernest Sirluck. The gloss for "second race" in Mario Di Cesare's edition of *George Herbert and the Seventeenth-Century Religious Poets* (New York: Norton, 1978), 148, is "refers to the preexistence of the soul," a reading that has no bearing on the poem, it seems to me, preexistence not entering into it at all, but particularly one that has not paid attention to the phrase in context: "Before I understood *this* place / Appointed for my second race" (emphasis added).

20 Ernest Sirluck compares "from those follies a resolv'd Retreat," from Vaughan's "Retirement" (*The Complete Poetry of Henry Vaughan*, 33).

21 The artistic compositional principle of focal interest (the golden section) is based upon a ratio of .618 to .382; classical and Renaissance authors employed the principle to focus significance and to contrast the greater with the lesser. For this poem that focal position is line 19.776. Compare Vaughan's use of this principle in "To *Amoret*, of the difference 'twixt him, and other Lovers, and what true Love is" from *Poems*, 1646; see Shawcross, "Vaughan's 'Amoret' Poems," 206 and 213, n. 15.

22 See *Resolves; Divine, Moral, and Political*, 10th edition (London, 1677), The First Century, no. 64 ("Of the Soul"), 98: "The *conscience*, the *Character* of a *God* stampt in it [the soul], and the apprehension of *Eternity*, do all prove it a *shoot of everlastingnesse*." Compare "The Retreate" with Felltham's *Resolves* entitled "Of the Worship of Admiration" (I, no. 14, 22); as well as "That Spiritual Things are better, and Temporal worse, than they seem" (II, no. 66, 299). See also Jean Robertson, "The Use Made of

Owen Felltham's *Resolves*: A Study in Plagiarism," *Modern Language Review* 39 (1944): 108–9, and Richard F. Kennedy, "Henry Vaughan's Borrowings from Owen Felltham," *George Herbert Journal* 7 (1983/84): 109–19.

23 The references to twenty years in these two poems are to youth; upon reaching majority at twenty-one one has moved into a second race. Compare Felltham's "*Man is twenty years* increasing, and his life is *fourscore*," I, no. 97 ("That 'tis best increasing by a little at once"), 151; and "Is it [the soul] not childish in *Infancy*, luxurious and unbounded in *Youth*, vigorous and discerning in the *strength of Manhood*, froward and doting in the *declining age* of his *life?*" I, no. 64 ("Of the Soul"), 98.

24 Compare this quotation from Felltham with Vaughan's "Vanity of Spirit" and "The Retreate": "the *Soul* is *eclipsed* and *imprisoned* so, as it cannot appear in the *vigor* it would shew, if the *Bodies* composition were perfect; and open. A *perfect Soul*, in an *imperfect Body*, is like a *bright Taper* in a *dark Lanthorn*: the fault is not in the *light*, but in the *case* which *curtains* it with so dull an *outside*, as will not let the *shine* be transparent" (I, no. 95, "Of the Causes that make Men different," 147).

25 The concept underlies Moses' hiding his face from the Lord (Exodus 3.6), who appears in a burning bush, and the Lord's later words to him, "Thou canst not see my face: for there shall no man see me, and live" (Exodus 33.20). Cognate is the Greek myth of Semele, who was destroyed by the fire of Zeus' thunderbolts when she asked him to appear in his true shape.

26 *The Birth of Tragedy* in *The Philosophy of Nietzsche*, trans. Clifton P. Fadiman (New York: Modern Library, n. d.), Section 3, 963.

27 "Providence," lines 19–30. Line 21 refers to Luke 12.33–34 ("provide yourselves bags which wax not old, a treasure in the heaven that faileth not, where no thief approacheth, neither moth corrupteth. For where your treasure is, there will your heart be also"). Compare Matthew 6.19–21 cited above.

28 Friedrich Nietzsche, *The Gay Science*, trans. Walter Kaufmann (New York: Random House, 1974), Book 5, Section 370, 328.

29 The final line, of course, contrasts the covenant with Noah, the sign of the rainbow ending the punishment of humankind by flood, and the promised conflagration ending the mortal world (2 Peter 3.10); "The Fire Next Time" (James Baldwin's title) will be "penal flames" (line 38). The play of fire and water imagery in the final verse paragraph of Milton's *Paradise Lost* might also be recalled, as well as Adam and Eve's leaving Paradise with Providence their guide.

30 *Sir Isaac Newton's Mathematical Principles of Natural Philosophy and His System of the World*, trans. Andrew Motte; revised by Florian Cajori (Berkeley and Los Angeles: University of California Press, 1934), 2: 544.

31 *Essay on Man*, Epistle 1.18, 77, 267–68.

CHAPTER TEN

"Against the stream upwards": Coleridge's recovery of John Donne

ANTHONY JOHN HARDING

IT HAS BECOME COMMONPLACE for scholars tracing the history of John Donne's reputation to give Samuel Taylor Coleridge much of the credit for initiating the nineteenth-century revival of interest in Donne's work. Late eighteenth-century critics such as Joseph Warton saw Donne as inventive but grotesque, even as not much more than a literary curiosity. "Are there ten lines of poetry in all his works?" asked Warton, and gave the all-too-blunt answer: "No."[1] More judiciously, Samuel Johnson considered the much-vaunted "wit" of the metaphysicals, including Donne, to be dearly bought, their thoughts "often new, but seldom natural," so that the reader of metaphysical poetry, "though he sometimes admires, is seldom pleased."[2] When Coleridge studied and profusely annotated Lamb's copy of Donne's poems, lectured on him in the 1818–19 lecture series, and proselytized for Donne during his years at Highgate, he was helping to set in motion the rise in Donne's reputation that resulted in the Grierson edition of 1912 and the Gardner edition of 1965, as well as the praise heaped on Donne by critics such as Leavis and poets such as Yeats. This reading of the story has at least won widespread assent.[3]

What has not been widely examined is just how anomalous is the emergence of Samuel Taylor Coleridge as one of Donne's earliest champions, how it runs counter to most of our assumptions about romanticism, and, in particular, how far it challenges one influential recent interpretation of the relations between the Romantics and the seventeenth century. According to this view, principally associated with the name of Joseph Anthony Wittreich, Jr., although also present in the work of other critics as various as John Beer, Stuart Curran, Jacqueline Di Salvo, and David Erdman, British romanticism was – predominantly and in its definitive or most significant works – radical, utopian, prophetic, visionary, tending to republicanism in politics and dissenting protestantism in religion. Romanticism, so interpreted, was also "Protestant" in the sense that it drew largely on the heritage of Protestant and Puritan writing of the seventeenth century, primarily of course the poetry of Milton and the prose of Bunyan, but also on the records of Dissent and the tradition of apocalyptic writing that existed within the dissenting churches down to the late eighteenth century. Thus, Wittreich argues in his introduction to *The Romantics on Milton* that whereas Shakespeare was too protean, too much of a chameleon, to become the Romantics' model of what a poet should be, Milton was "ideal man" and "ideal poet," "the literary hero of the Romantic period."[4] Wittreich's *Angel of Apocalypse: Blake's Idea of Milton* (Madison: University of Wisconsin Press, 1975) confirmed this placement of Milton at the head of the Romantic pantheon, and it was further consolidated in a volume of essays by several critics aiming to establish a "Line of Vision" rivalling or displacing the "Line of Wit," *Milton and the Line of Vision*. Wittreich's remark in his own essay in that volume may be taken as summarizing the reason for Milton's preeminence as the type of the prophetic poet, exponent of a genre which has the Book of Revelation as its first Christian source and most perfect exemplar:

By virtue of his uniting all aspects of the genre in his own writings, Milton restored the art of prophecy to its original perfection and thus should be regarded as the father of a poetic tradition resurrected by the English Romantics and used by later poets, British and American, both in the nineteenth century and now.[5]

In almost every respect, the qualities that Coleridge admired in Donne are contrary to those that go to make up this picture of British romanticism and what it derived from the seventeenth century. Donne's Satyre III, the poem on which Coleridge expended more comment and praise than any other single poem, is very far from being utopian, visionary, or singlemindedly Protestant. It accepts, indeed, the impossibility of achieving certainty, acknowledges the necessity for hard thought and patient enquiry, and counsels the avoidance of extremes. Coleridge praised Donne's lyrics for their toughness of mind, the compression and paradoxical nature of their thought, and the close weave of their versification, their ruggedness (the same quality that Johnson noted, though disparagingly) – not for visionary intensity or prophetic power. And when Coleridge came to write extensive marginalia on Donne's Sermons, he more than once commended Donne for his emphasis on the place that the Church, its teachings and liturgy, must hold in the life of a believer, and his ability to see how the measures taken to consolidate the separation from Rome had damaged the Church of England – clearly not the view of a thorough-going Protestant. What we commonly (and carelessly) think of as "Romantic taste" – whether we mean by that Blakean vision, Wordsworthian plainness

(the "real language of men"), or Shelleyan loftiness and grace, "the breath
and finer spirit of all knowledge" – is hardly to be found in Donne's poetry,
and his Sermons are much more the work of a thoughtful, earnestly-inquiring
though gifted churchman than that of an inspired prophet. John T. Shawcross
has argued that Donne needs to be rescued from too close an association with
romanticism, arguing "The false specter of Romantic effusion has blighted
poetic criticism for a long time."[6] Perhaps we might start by noticing how
little the revaluation of Donne by a "Romantic" has to do with current
perceptions of romanticism.

As Coleridge's early enthusiasm for Donne was shared with his close friend
Charles Lamb, it has been suggested that it might owe something to the Elian
taste for the eccentric, arcane, and antiquarian; that it is a product, in other
words, of that minor kind of romanticism which delighted in poring over
musty folios and deciphering forgotten metaphysical disputes.[7] (Carlyle
claimed to have detected this trait in the young Browning.) I do not think that
this view can stand scrutiny in the light of the evidence. Whether or not
Lamb's partiality for Donne was, as it has been called, "indiscriminate,"
Coleridge's was judicious and sympathetic, very much the expression of an
active mind weighing the merits and faults of the writer it engages with.
Indeed, the fact that Coleridge so often tried to "improve" Donne's
versification, not only altering the erratic punctuation of the 1669 edition of
Donne's poems (which he annotated) but also changing the order of the words
and adding or deleting the occasional "but," "the," or "and" to make the
verse run better, shows that Coleridge felt himself to be dealing with an alien
poetic dialect. Yet even before acquiring the 1669 edition, when he knew
Donne's poetry only from the selections in Anderson's *British Poets* (1792–95),
he recognized and admired the vigor of Donne's expression, and praised the
way in which Donne's verse, though knotty and challenging to the intellect of
the reader, embodied perfectly the movement of the thought and carried the
reader along with it.

When in 1796 Coleridge envisaged writing a series of satires, presumably,
in that turbulent and disputatious period, addressing the social and political
issues that he had tackled in his weekly newspaper *The Watchman*, Donne was
the example he had in mind.[8] The famous epigram on Donne, beginning
"With Donne, whose muse on dromedary trots, / Wreathe iron pokers into
true-love knots," may have been written in its first version as early as 1798,
and it sums up as well as exemplifies the characteristics Coleridge associated
with Donne in the 1790s and early 1800s: irregularity of meter, outlandish
images, compression of thought to the point of becoming enigmatic, and use
of the "conceit."[9] Shawcross, exploring the connection of this epigram with
a pair of poems about suicide (a connection established by a manuscript now

at the University of Kentucky), and with "Human Life: On the Denial of Immortality," suggests that Coleridge may also have associated Donne's poetry with peculiarity of thought and a predilection for paradoxical reflections on questions such as "what is life and how do we reconcile death to being" ("Opulence," 215). These things are characteristic of only part of Donne's output, as Shawcross warns, and Coleridge may have passed on to later readers an idea of Donne that was too "metaphysical" and ignored much of the play of irony and strategic adoption of stances not his own that we have more recently learned to see in Donne's work. Yet the more important truth is that in Donne, Coleridge found a writer who was no Romantic optimist, and whose poetry included not only political and social satire but also a sense of self-loathing, and horror of sensuality, equal to his own. A poet who could compare the soul imprisoned in the body to an anchorite "Bedded and bath'd in all his Ordures" – a line from Donne's *The Second Anniversarie* which Coleridge copied into a notebook in 1803 – would have struck a chord with the Coleridge of "The Pains of Sleep" and the darker passages of the *Notebooks*.[10]

Donne's poetry eschewed easy assertion and raised difficulty to a high art. His theology also accepted doubt and skepticism as inevitable conditions of faith. A full rendering of Romantic taste must take into account Coleridge's admiration for Donne not merely as a rule-proving exception but as an event that reveals something subversive of romanticism in one leading representative of Romantic taste: the acceptance of difficulty and ambiguity, the recovery, perhaps to some extent the reconstruction, of a seventeenth-century progenitor of what we have come to know as Romantic irony.

The Donne that Coleridge read was not, of course, "our" Donne, the Donne we are familiar with from the editions of Grierson, Gardner, and Shawcross. The texts Coleridge had access to were the selections in Anderson's *British Poets* and Chalmers's *The Works of the English Poets* (1810), and what Coleridge himself called the "grievously misprinted" seventh edition of 1669 (see *Marginalia* 2:216). We should remind ourselves, that is, that Coleridge did not read

> If our two loves be one, or, thou and I
> Love so alike, that none doe slacken, none can die.

but

> If our two loves be one, both thou and I
> Love just alike in all, none of these loves can die.[11]

Again, he read not

> Loves mysteries in soules doe grow,
> But yet the body is his booke.
> And if some lover, such as wee,
> Have heard this dialogue of one,

Let him still marke us, he shall see
Small change, when we'are to bodies gone.

(Complete Poetry, ed. Shawcross, 132)

but

Loves mysteries in Souls do grow,
But yet the body is the book,
And if some lover such as we,
Have heard this dialogue of one,
Let him still mark us, he shall see
Small change when we are to bodies grown.   *(1669,* 43)

Not being able to take his text for granted in the way that some New Critics mistakenly did, Coleridge "edited" as he went, emending punctuation here and there, changing word-order, and supplying conjectural readings. Coleridge was in other words Donne's "fellow-laborer," in a very real sense. A surprisingly large number of Coleridge's emendations correspond to those of Donne's twentieth-century editors, but the more interesting point to be made is that for Coleridge the process of reading Donne was, even more than usual, an intensely active one, involving simultaneous response to the meter, the sense, and the tone, with a constant questioning of the obviously corrupt texts in front of him. Reading Donne was an act of recovery, of rescuing meaning from the thick fog of textual indeterminacies, and therefore inevitably an act of reconstruction.

The best known of Coleridge's comments on Donne's meter actually occurs in a margin note of (probably) 1818 or 1819 on the works of Beaumont and Fletcher:

Since Dryden the metre of our Poets leads to the Sense: in our elder and more genuine Poets the Sense, including the Passion, leads to the metre. – < Read even Donne's Satires as he meant them to be read and as the sense & passion demand, and you will find < in > the lines a manly harmony. >   *(Marginalia* 1: 377)

The phrase "our elder and more genuine Poets" has behind it all the urgency of the nineteenth century's felt need for a strong native tradition, for some sufficiently "manly" and English precursors. But as Coleridge perceptively remarked in a note written in the front endpapers of Lamb's copy of 1669, borrowed in 1811 (and not returned for many years!) the very toughness and difficulty of Donne's meter is quite closely related to the question of textual corruption:

not one in a 1000 of his Readers have any notion how his Lines are to be read – to the many 5 out of 6 appear anti-metrical. – How greatly this aided the Compositor's negligence or ignorance, & prevented the Corrector's remedy, any man may ascertain by examining the earliest Editions of Blank Verse Plays, Massinger, Beaumont & Fletcher, &c – Now Donne's Rhy~~mesthm~~ ~~wer~~as as inexplicable to the many as Blank Verse, spite of his Rhymes – Ergo, as Blank Verse, misprinted.   *(Marginalia* 2: 216–17)

Far from making excuses for the difficulty of Donne's meter, then, Coleridge pointed to the union of rhythm and thought as the distinguishing characteristic of Donne's work, in "Poems where the Author *thinks* & expects the Reader to do so" but also in the "Songs" where a greater degree of smoothness in the rhythm was to be preferred (*Marginalia* 2: 221). Coleridge, who himself experimented with a more purely accentual meter in "Christabel," hailed Donne's accentual verse – his "manly ... & yet strict metre" – across what he saw as the wasteland of essentially unEnglish accentual-syllabic poetry of the later seventeenth and early eighteenth centuries, even while also believing that he was almost alone in knowing how to read Donne ("not one in a 1000 of his Readers have any notion how his Lines are to be read"). "To read Dryden, Pope &c," Coleridge writes, "you need only count syllables; but to read Donne you must measure *Time*, & discover the *Time* of Each word by the Sense & Passion" (*Marginalia* 2: 216). This may be read as Coleridge's answer to Johnson's rather puzzling statement that the metaphysical poets wrote "such verses as stood the trial of the finger better than of the ear; for the modulation was so imperfect, that they were only found to be verses by counting the syllables" ("Life of Cowley," 347). Johnson's ear, accustomed to hearing meters formed on accentual-syllabic principles, simply could not hear the rhythms of Donne's verse; Coleridge by contrast found Donne's meter correct and even "strict," because harmonious with the "Sense & Passion." This is why Coleridge's reading of Donne seems an example of poetry "bringing the whole soul of man into activity." Coleridge also had the advantage of realizing that as Donne's meter had perplexed his readers for a century and more, his poems were inevitably misprinted in successive editions as editors and compositors struggled to "correct" the versification.

Coleridge's comment on "The Triple Fool" exactly illustrates his sense of distance from Donne, his sense that Donne's verse was what I have called an alien dialect, along with his grasp of the peculiar strengths of Donne's verse. Reading the lines

> Some man his art or voice to show,
> Doth Set and sing my pain,
> And, by delighting many, frees again
> Grief, which Verse did restain [*sic*]   (*1669*, 11)

Coleridge comments:

–∪|–∪∪|–. a good instance, how D. read his own verses. We should write, The Grief, Verse did restrain. But D. roughly emphasized the two main words, Grief & Verse, and therefore made each the first Syllable of a Trochee: – ∪, or Dactyl.   (*Marginalia* 2: 221)

The observation about the emphasis on "Grief" is just, but so too is the scansion of the rest of the line; for, instead of reading the line as "*Grief*, which

¦ *Verse* did ¦ *restrain*" (trochee, trochee, iamb) – which is what would be suggested by accentual-syllabic theory – Coleridge notices that the heavy accents on "Grief" and "Verse" override the demands of regularized trimeter, pulling the first syllable of "restrain" into a dactyl with "Verse did," and leaving the last syllable on its own, filling up the space of one metrical foot.

It is in his annotation of the Satyres, however, especially Satyres III and V, that Coleridge shows most his willingness to cooperate with Donne and give full weight to the complexity of his thought as a determinant of meter. The lines from Satyre V, printed in 1669 as "The iron Age was, when justice was sold, now / Injustice is sold dearer far, allow," still a textual crux, prompted him to make one of his strategic rearrangements, reading "In th'Iron Age was Justice sold; (but) now ..." Despite recognizing the strangeness of the line, however, Coleridge could see how its meter *might* be defended: "But rather throw a very strong emphasis on 'Justice,' & you will find the line read" (*Marginalia* 2: 229). Meter follows thought: it is not that justice was sold, but that where *justice* was once sold, *injustice* is sold dearer far.

Of the lines:

> If Law be in the Judges heart, and he
> Have no heart to resist letter, or fee,
> Where wilt thou appeal? power of the Courts below,
> Flow from the first main head, and these can throw
> Thee, if they suck thee in, to misery,
> To fetters, halters. But if the injury
> Steel thee to dare complain, Alas, thou go'st
> Against the stream upwards, when thou art most
> Heavy and most faint; and in these labours they,
> 'Gainst whom thou should'st complain, will in thy way
> Become great seas   (*1669*, 137)

Coleridge remarks that "one feels oneself yielding to the Stream after vain efforts" (*Marginalia* 2: 229).

"Satyrs," as Coleridge notes à propos of Satyre V, "were supposed to come all rough from the woods, with a rustic accent" (*Marginalia* 2: 230). But Coleridge clearly revelled in the twists and turns of Donne's rhythms, finding the roughness of the versification more an addition to the thrill of following the poet's thought than a detraction from it. When in Satyre III Donne breaks a word at the end of a line, both to complete a rhyme and to maintain the meter – "So doth, so is Religion; and this blind- / ness too much light breeds" (1669, 127) – Coleridge is exhilarated: "a fine instance of free, vehement, verse-disguising Verse. Read it as it ought to be read; and no Ear will be offended" (*Marginalia* 2: 227). Here and in most of Coleridge's marginalia on

Donne we see not so much a response to "the psychological process ... that vitalized the external form" (Granqvist, *The Reputation of John Donne*, 79) as a delight in the reconciliation of idea with image, of intellect with feeling, and of all these with "strict metre." Coleridge does not discuss what he might imagine to have been the state of Donne's mind or feelings; his response is to the words themselves as embodying in meter, sense, and syntax a model of how to think about the problem at hand, rather than an expression of a given state of mind or "psychological process."

Perhaps enough evidence has now been presented to show that Coleridge's interest in Donne was far more than that of a Romantic antiquarian; rather, Coleridge seems to have felt himself to be rediscovering a true voice of English poetry, perhaps "all rough from the woods" but none the worse for that. This eagerness for a national tradition undoubtedly had an element of chauvinism in it. In his notes for a lecture series delivered in 1818, Coleridge characterizes the poets of the English Renaissance (he is thinking principally of Spenser) as having "a common root":

the arts and philosophy of the South superinduced ~~the~~ on the deeper sensibility, the wilder imagination, ~~and more robust morals~~ in one word, the greater Inwardness of the North, – and combined into one complex Whole, ~~by the~~ fixed and concreted ~~and~~ by the vital air of ~~reli~~ a common Faith.[12]

Such comments demonstrate how in the immediate postwar period it became expedient to envision a distinctive national tradition protected against the skepticism of the French Enlightenment by its innately "northern" or Germanic strengths: sensibility, imagination, inwardness, religion, and, clearly in Coleridge's mind even though he deleted the phrase, "more robust morals." Cut off from most European influences by the conflict, the country experienced two decades of relative cultural isolation, and after Waterloo, the validation of a homegrown and therefore (by contrast with France especially) a *northern* and Germanic tradition became part of the cultural agenda, at least for those who welcomed the defeat of Napoleon. (The three lecture series Coleridge delivered in 1818 and 1819 are punctuated with disparaging references to all things French.) Coleridge's championing of Donne and his comparison of Donne's intellectual "opulence" with that of Shakespeare (*Marginalia* 2: 219) similarly reflects the turning-in of itself that characterized English culture during the Napoleonic War. The unclassical irregularities of Donne's verse could be defended as part of a rough-hewn, native English tradition, rather as Shakespeare's neglect of Aristotelian principles had been; this is of a piece with De Quincey's praise of the "masculine vigor" of Donne's verse.[13]

Yet the role of authentic, robust Englishman seems in other ways an unlikely one for John Donne: he is far too complex, the elements too mixed in him, not unequivocally Protestant, not quite an aristocrat nor yet a commoner, part sensualist and part intellectual. The intellectual qualities which Coleridge thought he perceived in Donne's peculiarly tough-grained verse, and which he sees as compelling the reader to think "with" the poet, are inseparable from another quality which one would not expect a Romantic, as traditionally conceived, to admire. The writer of *Biathanatos* (which Coleridge read in 1811–12 if not earlier[14]) could contemplate and find justifications for the darkest choice a human being can face as an individual. Even the better-known poems, such as the Satyres, show a poet who can fearlessly explore doubt, and his avoidance of premature commitment, his close examination of rival theologies, suggests a mind fundamentally at odds with the kind of deictic stance and intuitive thinking that supposedly characterize romanticism. For the obscurity of which Donne was said to be guilty, in poems such as Satyre III, was not – according to Coleridge – an obscurity attributable to wilfulness, carelessness, or fascination with his own wit; it was rather the obscurity which inevitably accompanies the searching examination of difficult questions. This is somewhat different from the "constant scrutiny of personal emotions" and "introspective intensity" which Barbara K. Lewalski finds characteristic of Protestant writing of the sixteenth and seventeenth centuries.[15] Where Johnson associated the term "metaphysical" with unnecessary violence of mind, and love of far-sought figures and knotty reasoning, Coleridge found "metaphysical Poetry" according to *his* definition to be clear and precise, not because it described a psychological state but because it tackled the intellectual problem of describing complex things, whether an emotion, a geometrical principle, or an article of religious faith. What Johnson regarded as settled questions were for Coleridge once more open to inquiry. Shawcross suggests that, in attempting to rehabilitate Donne by claiming a "serious" function for the conceit, Coleridge may have missed much of the irony, elusiveness, and ventriloquistic quality that modern readers see in Donne, and overemphasized the "metaphysical" aspect of his work, implying that Donne's poetic genius was mainly revealed in the particular kind of figure we call the conceit ("Opulence," 206, 219). In effect, this is to say that Coleridge may have devoted too much time to answering Johnson, rather than developing a new and fuller appreciation of Donne's powers and the variety of his poetic personae. While irony and the elusiveness of authorial presence are important to us, however, it must have seemed more urgent to Coleridge in the 1810s to establish the existence of a vigorous English tradition in which not irony nor yet vatic affirmation but a bedrock of logic and philosophical insight (derived, it may be, from introspective thought, from "inwardness") gave strength to the verse.

Coleridge cannot present this tradition as if it had flourished without interruption for two centuries, of course. An important part of the reform of literary taste and critical principles he wishes to bring about in *Biographia Literaria* is the rehabilitation of the poetry of the early seventeenth century, which he wishes to represent as more inquiring and introspective, while he represents Dryden and his successors as a false path, now to be abandoned. The rehabilitation of Donne's style plays a significant part in this enterprise. It may not be very surprising for a supposed Romantic to allege that the metaphysical poets from Donne to Cowley "sacrificed the passion, and passionate flow of poetry, to the subtleties of intellect, and to the starts of wit." What *is* surprising is that – in the same passage in *Biographia* – Coleridge ascribes to them "the most fantastic out-of-the-way thoughts, but in the most pure and genuine mother English." Still more unexpectedly, perhaps, it is the poets *since* Cowley who are accused of sacrificing "passionate flow" to "the glare and glitter of a perpetual, yet broken and heterogeneous imagery, or rather to an amphibious something, made up, half of image, and half of abstract meaning."[16] The charges of "broken and heterogeneous imagery" and of "amphibiousness" in the combination of abstract and concrete sound more like Johnson's criticism of the metaphysicals themselves than what we are accustomed to hearing about Dryden and Pope. This is Coleridge's version of Eliot's "dissociation of sensibility," however. After Cowley, according to this view, imagery became "broken" because, however much an image may be appreciated by the reader, it is experienced separately from the "abstract meaning" to which it is attached, whereas in Donne's work, an image does not merely illustrate but incorporates the "abstract" meaning.

Coleridge's unfavorable comparison of the half-abstract, half-imagist language of poetry after Cowley to the "pure and genuine mother English" of the metaphysicals makes more sense in the context of a passage he quotes from Donne's "Progress of the Soul." Disputing Wordsworth's emphasis (in the 1800 "Preface" to *Lyrical Ballads*) on observation, and pointing to "the excitement produced by the very act of poetic composition," Coleridge continues:

The *rules* of the IMAGINATION are themselves the very powers of growth and production ... We find no difficulty in admitting as excellent, and the legitimate language of poetic fervor self-impassioned, DONNE's apostrophe to the Sun in the second stanza of his "Progress of the Soul."

> Thee, eye of heaven! this great soul envies not:
> By thy male force is all, we have, begot.
> In the first East thou now beginn'st to shine,
> Suck'st early balm and island spices there;

And wilt anon in thy loose-rein'd career
At Tagus, Po, Seine, Thames and Danow dine,
And see at night this western world of mine:
Yet hast thou not more nations seen, than she,
Who before thee one day began to be,
And, thy frail light being quenched, shall long, long outlive thee!

(*Biographia* 2: 83–84)

The power of poetic invention that can describe the headlong daily course of the sun in such intense yet plain terms, with no more than a nod in the direction of the traditional image of Phoebus' chariot ("loose-rein'd"), yet then dismiss this sun as but a "frail" thing compared to the everlasting symbol of that first-created light, *lux perpetua*, cannot be confined either to mere "point and drapery" or to the expression of transient feeling or psychological states. It is here that Coleridge's comparison of Donne to Shakespeare makes most sense. The passage (and Coleridge's praise of it as "the legitimate language of poetic fervor self-impassioned") shows a delight in, not "wit" in the sense of intellectual dexterity, but the grand image that dramatizes the mind's sense of its own grandeur. This is one form of wit Coleridge admired, because it is an ironic recognition of the absurd failure of the visible world to match the grandeur of the mind's sense of its own powers, "the Godlike within us" (*Lectures 1808–1819* 2: 173).

The generosity of Donne's power of poetic invention nevertheless baffled Coleridge at times, when he thought it applied to unworthy objects. Attempting to distinguish the particular qualities of Donne's kind of wit – and to distinguish it from Butler's, Pope's, Congreve's, and Sheridan's – Coleridge found it characterized by "Wonder-exciting vigour, intenseness and peculiarity of thought, using at will the almost boundless stores of a capacious memory, and exercised on subjects, where we have no right to expect it" (*Marginalia* 2: 17). The phrase "exercised on subjects, where we have no right to expect it" betrays the bafflement of a later poet feeling himself weaker than Donne in sheer poetic invention and unable to understand why Donne would waste his capacities on apparently trivial subjects – "dissolving orient pearls, worth a kingdom! in a health to a Whore!" as Coleridge puts it – or "squandering golden Hecatombs on a Fetisch, <on> the first stick or straw met with at rising" (*Marginalia* 2: 218–20).

Coleridge cannot quite embrace the idea that a display of wit might be worthwhile in and of itself, quite apart from any serious idea underlying the play of intellect. He argues that, even at his most fanciful, Donne never writes without "a substrate of profound, tho' mislocated, Thinking" (*Marginalia* 2: 220), and he is ready to point to the presence of a "practical" – that is, a worthwhile and useful – truth in the lines from "The Good Morrow,"

"What ever dies, is not mixt equally: / If our two loves be one, both thou and I / Love just alike in all, none of these loves can die": "Too good for mere wit. It contains a deep practical truth – this Triplet" (*Marginalia* 2: 218). Coleridge's puritanical distrust of the expenditure of great intellectual powers on sticks and straws, of brilliance that aims at "mere" wit, does not prevent him interpreting the far-fetched imagery, where he can, as revealing profound moral truth almost in spite of itself. In other words, Coleridge sought even in the apparently fanciful parts of Donne's poetry a "substrate of profound, tho' mislocated Thinking." A remark in one of the 1818 lectures – "A seriousness in Humor – Spain & England" – suggests that Coleridge saw nothing wrong with the sort of humor that conceals serious thought. (Mere "wit," meanwhile, he associated with France, and therefore with superficiality.) Word-play and all kinds of verbal complexity should be welcomed, then, if a philosophical truth can be detected lurking under the complex surface. The poet who pored over Berkeley's essay on tar-water (*Siris*) and found food for his philosophical speculations in Boehme the mystic and other recondite sources, would not have been slow to believe that the laws of logic could appear as well in arcane or trivial matters as in more formal philosophic writing. Even such lowly forms of word-play as the pun could display the same sensitivity to precise meanings and derivations of words that is necessary to truly philosophical thought, as John A. Hodgson has pointed out ("Coleridge, Puns, and 'Donne's First Poem,'" 186). In its weirdest quirks and caprices, the wit of a poet richly learned in eccentric knowledge might come to grasp the laws of mind much sooner than more conscientious but pedantic reasoners.

We could remember here Hazlitt's observation about Coleridge's preference for composing while "walking over uneven ground, or breaking through the straggling branches of a copse-wood," while Wordsworth liked to write "walking up and down a straight gravel-walk, or in some spot where the continuity of his verse met with no collateral interruption."[17] To Coleridge, thought *should* be difficult: an "easy" thought was ipso facto suspect. Even to "stand inquiring right" (Satyre III, line 78) was preferable, in Coleridge's eyes, to sailing bravely down a wrong course with all flags flying, and in Donne, Coleridge recognized a fellow "inquiring spirit."

It was on this quality, transferred to the realm of the theological and ecclesiastical, that Coleridge's admiration for Donne's prose was largely based. Donne's lack of sectarianism (in an age that suffered grievously from this disease), his willingness to criticize the Reformation and even, as Coleridge put it, to "say better things for the Papists than they could say for themselves" (*Marginalia* 2: 220), did not betray him into woolliness or banality after he took holy orders: nor did he subside into being a mere good church-party man. Rather, he retained all his "depth of intellect ... nervousness of style ... variety of illustration [and] power of argument" in the service of an Anglicanism that was far from complacent.[18]

Perhaps it can be argued that in Coleridge's marginalia on Donne's prose we are faced with a compromised and compromising "late Coleridge," his critical faculties fatally dulled by the effort to formulate a tenable Christian position from within the Church of England. Most of the marginalia on Donne's *LXXX Sermons* do date from a "late" period in Coleridge's life, 1831–32, although those in Copy A are probably from much earlier, 1809–10. It was in 1830, too, that Coleridge made the remark "Why is not Donne's volume of sermons reprinted at Oxford?" which prompted Alford to begin work on the first modern edition of the sermons (see *Marginalia* 2: 244). But there is no very dramatic discontinuity between the 1811 marginalia on the poems and the 1831–1832 marginalia on the Sermons. Evidence concerning Coleridge's opinion of Donne's theology before 1810 is scanty. The only comment on Donne in any of the three copies of Anderson's *British Poets* known to have been annotated by Coleridge is a note on a poem called "On the Blessed Virgin Mary" expressing surprise that Donne would assert full belief in the Immaculate Conception of the Virgin Mary herself – as distinct from the Immaculate Conception of Jesus (*Marginalia* 1: 43–44). But the poem in question is of doubtful authorship, and no longer considered to be Donne's. Nevertheless the note suggests that even before 1810 Coleridge was prepared to accept in Donne, with no more than a mild expression of surprise, such "Roman" traits as devotion to the idea of the complete purity of the Virgin. Nor was the later Coleridge in any way complacent about the shortcomings of the Church of England, a church he described as "chilled and starved ... by Preachers & Reasoners, Stoic or Epicurean," with "Prudence, Paleyianism, substituted for Morality" (*Marginalia* 2: 291). Donne seems to have exemplified for Coleridge the need to recognize that no human being, and no human institution, is completely free from ignorance and error. It is worth pointing out that one of the passages Coleridge singled out for praise in the *LXXX Sermons* was this:

And therefore let no Church, no man, think that he hath done enough, or knowes enough ...

The wisest must know more, though you be *domus Israel*, the house of Israel already; and then, *Etsi crucifixistis*, though you have crucified the Lord Jesus, you may know it, *sciant omnes*, let all know it. S. *Paul* saies once, *If they had known it, they would not have crucified the Lord of life*; but he never saies, if they have crucified the Lord of life, they are excluded from knowledge. I meane no more, but that the mercy of God in manifesting and applying himself to us, is above all our sins. No man knowes enough; what measure of tentations soever he have now, he may have tentations, through which, this knowledge, and this grace, will not carry him; and therefore he must proceed from grace to grace. So no man hath sinned so deeply, but that God offers himself to him yet; *Sciant omnes*, the wisest man hath ever something to learn, he must not presume; the sinfullest man hath God ever ready to teach him, he must not despaire.[19]

Despite distrusting what he saw as the "patristic leaven" in Donne – his wish, shared with other divines of the period, "to bring back the stream of the Reformation ... to the channel & within the banks, formed in the first six centuries of the Church," and his "alienation from the great patriarchs of ... Protestantism, Luther, Calvin, Zuinglius, &c" (*Marginalia* 2: 260, 304) – Coleridge saw Donne's avoidance of the more extreme kinds of Protestantism as a positive quality. To him, Donne was a Catholic in the true sense. In a notebook passage assigned by Coburn to May 1812, Coleridge suggests that the "spleen" Donne refers to at the beginning of Satyre III results from the fact that "tho' fully awake to the Corruptions of the Romish Court & Church, [Donne] was yet evidently hostile to the *measures* of the Reformation, & seems (at a certain period of his Life at least) to have considered the Reformers as having unnecessarily made a wide Schism or Rent in the unity of the Catholic Church, & weakened Faith & *Religiosity* by their constant Disputes" (*Notebooks* 3, entry 4152). The 1812 date of this entry, if correct, also indicates that there was a certain consistency in Coleridge's assessment of Donne's doctrinal position, at least from about 1810 onward. Coleridge himself was certainly enough of a Protestant to insist that "A Christian Preacher ought to preach *Christ* alone" (*Marginalia* 2: 291). Yet he had no patience with the notion that the existence of Scripture made the Church redundant. In particular he found admirable Donne's view that neither "the light and notification of God, which we have in nature," nor the "clearer light, which we have in the Law and Prophets," nor even the light "clearer then that in the Gospell," suffices for Christian faith: in addition to all these, the Church is needed, to give "a nearer light then the written Gospell," and to "[make] this generall Christ particular to every Christian" (*Sermons* 8: 306–8). Coleridge comments: "The Papacy elevated the Church to the virtual exclusion or suppression of the Scriptures; the modern Church of ~~Languages~~ England, since Chillingworth, have so raised up the Scriptures as to annul the Church" (*Marginalia* 2: 290). (Why did Coleridge first write "Church of Languages" in error for "Church of England"? Did he perhaps associate this Church with questions of translation, interpretation, hermeneutics?) Coleridge recognized that warnings against the danger of ignoring the Church's teaching were that much more convincing from one who had advised, in Satyre III, "That thou mayst rightly obey power, her bounds know; / Those past her nature, and name are chang'd; to be, / Then humble to her is Idolatry" (*1669*, 128).[20]

This brings us back to what I would argue is the common thread running through all Coleridge's comments on Donne: the sense of "relativeness" (to use the term Coleridge uses of the divines he admires [*Marginalia* 2: 322]); the sense that no text, no statement of position, no formulation of belief can do without interpretation, and that strong intellects are revealed not in unquestioning adherence to predetermined positions but in a constant dialogue with alternatives. Whether Coleridge was swimming altogether against the stream in his response to John Donne must remain a moot point. There are so many cross-currents and eddies in the Romantic movement that it would be difficult to think of any development in nineteenth-century literary taste that did not show affinity with some aspect of romanticism.

Donne's reckless "squandering" of poetic brilliance on trivial topics might be expected to shock the (in this respect) more puritanical Coleridge, whose annoyance at Wordsworth's wasting his time on trivia when *The Recluse* should have been his sole study is well known. Similarly, the nationalistic desire to construct a native English poetic tradition must have played a part in Coleridge's championing of Donne as an inheritor of Shakespeare's fecundity of invention and "manliness." In several ways, however, Coleridge's reading of Donne's poetry and prose does run counter to our expectations of romanticism, at least as those expectations have been formed by recent theories of the movement. The attention Coleridge paid to Donne's versification and the meticulousness of his observations on Donne's meter testify to a much more lively interest in prosody than one might expect from a Romantic. Moreover, as I have tried to show, Coleridge admired in Donne's poetry not the expression of something "fully and firmly believed," nor the Romantic "effusion" of feeling, but the subtle exploration of genuine intellectual problems – witness the comments on Satyres III and V, in particular, and the admiration Coleridge evidently felt for *The Second Anniversarie* and *Biathanatos*. Lastly, Coleridge's comments on the *LXXX Sermons* show that Donne's freedom from reforming zeal, and his critical view of the Reformers as having "weakened Faith ... by their constant Disputes," attracted Coleridge despite the later writer's distrust of Rome and of those patristic writers on whom Donne drew so heavily. Coleridge's Anglicanism, which built on his reading of Donne along with other seventeenth-century divines such as Waterland, Stillingfleet, and Taylor, may itself be against the stream of romanticism. However we wish to judge it, though, Coleridge's response to Donne is a dramatic example of the way in which a writer of one age constructs from the records of a complex past the image of the predecessor that writer needs.

NOTES

1 Quoted in A. J. Smith, "Donne's Reputation," in *John Donne: Essays in Celebration*, ed. A. J. Smith (London: Methuen, 1972), 7.
2 "Life of Cowley," in *Selected Poetry and Prose*, ed. Frank Brady and W. K. Wimsatt (Berkeley and Los Angeles: University of California Press, 1977), 347–48. Hereafter cited in text.
3 Raoul Granqvist, *The Reputation of John Donne 1779–1873*, Studia Anglistica Upsaliensia 24 (Uppsala: University of Uppsala, 1975), 93: "The weight of Coleridge as a literary person, coupled with his noted respect for Donne, was a decisive factor in the restoration of Donne's reputation." Hereafter cited in text as *The Reputation of John Donne*. See also A. J. Smith, "Donne's Reputation," 1–27. John T. Shawcross, while agreeing that references to Donne's poetry by eighteenth-century commentators were often negative, cites many previously neglected allusions to Donne in works that Coleridge could have read, arguing that "While Donne certainly does not have the visibility of Milton or Cowley, he is known as a poet, prose writer, and sermonist" ("Opulence and Iron Pokers: Coleridge and Donne," *John Donne Journal* 4 [1985]: 203.) Hereafter cited in text as "Opulence."
4 *The Romantics on Milton: Formal Essays and Critical Asides* (Cleveland: The Press of Case Western Reserve University, 1970), 12, 13.
5 "'A Poet Amongst Poets': Milton and the Tradition of Prophecy," in *Milton and the Line of Vision*, ed. Joseph Anthony Wittreich, Jr. (Madison: University of Wisconsin Press, 1975), 101.
6 John T. Shawcross, "Poetry, Personal and Impersonal: The Case of Donne," in *The Eagle and the Dove: Reassessing John Donne*, ed. Claude J. Summers and Ted-Larry Pebworth (Columbia: University of Missouri Press, 1986), 57.
7 On Lamb's importance as a sharer in Coleridge's enthusiasm see Granqvist, *The Reputation of John Donne*, 74–76.
8 *The Notebooks of Samuel Taylor Coleridge*, ed. Kathleen Coburn, (New York: Pantheon Books/Princeton: Princeton University Press, 1957–) 1, entry 171. Hereafter cited as *Notebooks* plus volume and entry number.
9 Samuel Taylor Coleridge, *Marginalia*, ed. George Whalley, 3 vols so far, *Collected Coleridge*, vol. 12 (Princeton: Princeton University Press, 1980–) 2: 16 and n. Hereafter cited in text as *Marginalia*. Mary Lynn Johnson, in "How Rare is a 'Unique Annotated Copy' of Coleridge's *Sibylline Leaves*?" *Bulletin of the New York Public Library* 78 (1975): 451–81, presented some evidence that the lines may date from even earlier than 1798, since Coleridge says that they were part of a poem to Tom Poole of which some other lines appear in a letter to Thelwall of 31 December 1796; but the *Marginalia* editors reject this admittedly doubtful evidence. The word "Cripple-god," in the third line of the epigram in the *Sibylline Leaves* version Johnson prints (476), unfortunately appears in the *Marginalia* notes as "Cripple." See also John T. Shawcross, "Opulence," 210–20. Shawcross (213) prints another version, previously unpublished, of the first two lines of the epigram, different from those in margin notes to *Sibylline Leaves* and Chalmers's *English Poets*. This version occurs in a postscript to two poems on suicide, in a holograph MS now in the University of Kentucky Library. Evidence presented by Shawcross suggests this version of the epigram is earlier than the other two.

10 *Notebooks* 1, entry 1787. The quotation is taken from Robert Anderson, *The Works of the British Poets*, 14 vols. (London and Edinburgh, 1792–95), 4: 79.

11 Shawcross, *The Complete Poetry of John Donne*, 89; John Donne, *Poems*, &c. *With Elegies on the Authors Death* (London, 1669) [Wing D1871], 3. Hereafter cited in text as "*Complete Poetry*, ed. Shawcross" and "*1669*" respectively. See also Shawcross's textual notes, which give the 1669 readings.

12 *Lectures 1808–1819 On Literature*, ed. R. A. Foakes, 2 vols., *Collected Coleridge*, vol. 5 (Princeton: Princeton University Press, 1987), 2:111. Hereafter cited in text as *Lectures 1808–1819*.

13 Granqvist, *The Reputation of John Donne*, 85. Coleridge's tendency to associate Donne with Shakespeare is further illustrated by the reference to the flea on Bardolph's nose in "On Donne's first Poem" (his tribute to "The Flea," the poem that stands first in the 1669 edition), printed, in part, in *Complete Poetical Works*, ed. E. H. Coleridge, 2 vols. (Oxford: Clarendon Press, 1912), 2: 980–81. See John A. Hodgson, "Coleridge, Puns, and 'Donne's First Poem': The Limbo of Rhetoric and the Conceptions of Wit," *John Donne Journal* 4 (1985): 190–95 (hereafter cited in text) for a discussion of the poem's full text as well as the Shakespeare connection.

14 See *Notebooks* 3, entries 3242n and 4050n. Shawcross thinks Coleridge may have read *Biathanatos* earlier than 1811; he also judges that Coleridge read it "incorrectly as a defense of suicide" (see "Opulence," 218). Camille Wells Slights's suggestion that *Biathanatos* does not actually *work* as satire, because Donne himself remained ambivalent about the lawfulness of suicide, is perhaps relevant here: see *The Casuistical Tradition* (Princeton: Princeton University Press, 1981), 142.

15 Barbara K. Lewalski, *Protestant Poetics and the Seventeenth-Century Religious Lyric* (Princeton: Princeton University Press, 1979), 20.

16 Samuel Taylor Coleridge, *Biographia Literaria*, ed. James Engell and Walter Jackson Bate, 2 vols., *Collected Coleridge*, vol. 7 (Princeton: Princeton University Press, 1983), 1: 23–24. Hereafter cited in text as *Biographia*.

17 William Hazlitt, "My First Acquaintance with Poets," in *Complete Works*, ed. Howe, 17: 119.

18 The phrases quoted here are from a report of Coleridge's conversation in [R. E. A. Willmott], *Conversations at Cambridge* (London: John W. Parker, 1836), 15.

19 John Donne, *Sermons*, ed. George R. Potter and Evelyn M. Simpson, 10 vols. (Berkeley and Los Angeles: University of California Press, 1953–62) 4: 349–350. Hereafter cited in text. For Coleridge's comments see *Marginalia* 2: 330.

20 See the useful comments on Satyre III as an exploration of the "duty to search for truth in spite of the deceptions and difficulties of the fallen world" in Slights, *The Casuistical Tradition*, 164–67.

CHAPTER ELEVEN

Coleridge, Keats, Lamb, and seventeenth-century drinking songs

ANYA TAYLOR

CAVALIER LYRICS ON THE topoi of wine, women, and song have long delighted readers with their nostalgic view of the English countryside, their metrical perfection, and their skilled and playful participation in an ancient *carpe diem* tradition inherited from Catullus and Anacreon. The Cavalier celebration of simple pleasures will seem at first very far from the consciousnesses of Romantic poets who sought to incorporate into their poems serious reflection on the political, religious, economic, social, and psychological upheavals of their time. Remarkably, however, the *carpe diem* tradition endured in certain aspects of the lives, thought, and poetry of Coleridge and Keats, and of several other Romantic poets, who shared a love of the convivial pleasures of drinking, and wrote a surprising number of songs and narrative poems on the subject in the manner of their seventeenth-century predecessors.

Not only is this *carpe diem* element usually ignored in examinations of Romantic poetry, but so also are the profound resemblances between Coleridge and Keats in their handling of these topoi of abandon. Though readers have often focused on Keats's famous criticisms of Coleridge as a poet of systematic knowledge, "irritabl[y] reaching after fact & reason," Keats in fact absorbs from Coleridge's poetry and criticism a powerful radiance of supernatural and human mystery, and shares with him, either by inherent nature or by immediate influence, a love of pleasure, physical movement, sensuous joy, and vivacious appetite, both hungering for physical delights often unrealized, gleeful in revelry, and recording with delight the "fine isolated verisimilitude."[1]

If appetite for drink came naturally to Coleridge and Keats, their drinking poems are modelled in some ways on those simple, sensuous, and passionate seventeenth-century lyrics that affirmed the continuity of the *carpe diem* theme through a thousand years of European literature. For Lamb, Coleridge, and Keats, Robert Herrick and Abraham Cowley suggested that *carpe diem* could be a way of thinking even for poets in an ostensibly Christian culture, not exclusive, that is, to the sometimes shocking pagans of classical antiquity. Lamb, Coleridge, and Keats (and Byron, too), in other words, looked back through eighteenth-century revellers like John Gay and Robert Burns to the "mother tongue" of these earlier English hedonists to justify their search for pleasure and to find the forms to express it in their own language. But the quality of pleasure shifts subtly between the seventeenth and the nineteenth centuries. Singing about it becomes less easy, more troubled by religious, social, and political changes. Coleridge and Keats can never seem entirely carefree, in the manner of Herrick or Cowley.

Religious changes are the most difficult to assess, particularly the expectation or non-expectation of immortality. The fear of death, and the urgency it generates, have been essential to the *carpe diem* tradition since the beginning, as the skull lurks in the easeful verdure of the earthly paradise, and as the clause "for tomorrow we die" inevitably follows "Let us eat and drink." But while this *memento mori* may have increased the seventeenth-century pleasure-seeker's sense of urgency, such fear was enclosed in a larger faith that a Christian heaven awaits the revellers. Herrick may hurry his mistress in "A Meditation for his Mistresse," by reminding her that she will die, but both these lovers, the ardent and the reluctant, will meet again after death.[2]

The mocking inscription *Et in Arcadio Ego* is more difficult to laugh off in a post-Enlightenment era, its menace only briefly forgotten in wine, women, and song. Among the Romantics, some are more terrified than others of the ominous mortality surrounding the warmly lit scene of pleasure. Coleridge had few times in his life when he doubted the goodness of God and his promise of future life, when "So lonely 'twas, that God Himself / Scarce seemed there to be." Even in his revolutionary youth he declared his love of Jesus and his belief in original sin. Keats, on the other hand, investigated Christian consolations during the early months of 1819 when he struggled in vain to believe in a future reward. He died without "this last cheap comfort – which every rogue and fool have," eased perhaps in the last weeks by Joseph Severn's reading from a different aspect of seventeenth-century tradition, Jeremy Taylor's *Holy Living and Dying*; or perhaps the easing was just the process of dying.[3] Keats's quest for pleasure is ringed round with "The weariness, the fever and the fret," his "heart high-sorrowful and cloyed." Coleridge, with thirty-seven years of life more than Keats had – time in which to solve the problems posed by his inner torment – generated out of his personal dissatisfaction ingenious proofs for immortality. He reinvented a Christian afterlife out of the very nature of the suffering human being, for God would not have created the human being with a yearning for a better world if he did not plan to satisfy it.[4]

Such desperate measures respond to the erosion of Christian certainties between the seventeenth and the nineteenth centuries. Herrick, Cowley, and Rochester sang like grasshoppers in the bosom of Abraham. Romantic writers, troubled by the witty skeptics of the intervening century, and by an obligation to argue with them even if they disagreed, sometimes found the earthly paradise windswept and solitary, and its amusements hectic and imaginary. Individual Romantics assuaged the solitude in different ways: some, like Coleridge, by reinventing Christianity; some, like Keats, by accepting a pagan universe with all the luxuriance and anguish of that heroic choice.

While the seventeenth-century *carpe diem* singers can be content surrounded by a larger hope for future joys, Romantic *carpe diem* singers are shadowed not only by skepticism, and the need constantly to reinvent belief if there is to be any, but also by a keen recognition of the sufferings of others – the poor, the oppressed, the dislocated, the mad – brought on by the revolutionary interest in social reform. One of the most acute social problems of their time was the increased use of gin and other distilled liquors, and the resulting increase in public drunkenness, sickness, and addiction visible especially in the lower classes. Moreover, prominent doctors like Thomas Trotter and Benjamin Rush were arguing that recurrent drunkenness was a disease, if only a disease of the mind. These changes are technological, and then social, and then psychological, and they distinctly alter the quality of pleasure: the Romantic imitation of the Cavalier drinking song has a reckless tone; the long poem on Bacchus modelled on Milton's *Comus* explores the ambivalences of pleasure and its aftermath in a fragmented self. Pleasure is entangled with guilt and pain.

Of possible pleasures Coleridge and Keats most consistently chose drink. Both appreciated tavern life and tavern songs and thought of themselves as participating in an old English tradition. Both Coleridge and Keats knew and imitated some of the drinking songs of the seventeenth-century Cavalier poets; they knew Milton's *Comus* and Dryden's "Alexander's Feast." Both occasionally introduced Bacchus or Dionysus as a figure in thoughts and poems. In doing so, they expanded the meanings of Dionysianism, Coleridge in lectures on drama and plans for an extended poem on Bacchus, Keats in *Endymion* and "Ode to a Nightingale." Both of them recognized that Bacchus was not just a drinking god, but, as Coleridge said in a lecture on the origins of drama given 5 February 1808, "among the most aweful & mysterious Deities," a figure for the "organic energies of the Universe, that work by passion and Joy without apparent distinct consciousness," "something innate, and divine, a felicity above and beyond Prudence," a figure defiant of rational certainty, personal distinctness, and the trammels of self-control.[5]

These two generous, uncalculating, unselfish chameleons, these sensualists, luxuriants, sensation-lovers, and enthusiasts, both insulted by the egotism and prudence of Wordsworth, enjoyed drink as one source of rapture, though both knew the sorrows and pains of its excessive use. Where love and lust often failed them, drink was accessible: wine, brandy, and spirits for Coleridge; claret for Keats. Coleridge, who learned at nine to drink with a sottish uncle, and was "almost continually intoxicated" during his second and disastrous year at Jesus College before enlisting in the dragoons, spent his most joyously inebriated times with Charles Lamb at their favorite tavern (Lamb later called it "heaven"). In 1794 Coleridge exults to Southey, "Every night since my arrival I have spent at an Ale-house by courtesy called 'a Coffee House' – the Salutation & Cat, in Newgate Street – we have a comfortable Room to ourselves & drink Porter and Punch round a good fire." Coleridge's letters twinkle with enjoyment of "the intoxicating bowl," "sweet intoxication," "rich and precious wines," and "drinkings and discussings," interspersed with apologies for drunken behavior, vows to abstain, moderate, or gradually abandon fermented or spirituous liquors, and criticisms of other drunks worse off than himself, such as William Collins, George Burnet, or the Prince of Wales. Mixing opium, spirits, brandy, and beer, he knows fairly early that his ecstatic appetite has tipped over into "my intemperance," and he worries more about his drinking than about his opium-taking. Coleridge's drinking was a source of worry and disapproval to the abstemious Wordsworths and to busy and efficient Southey. His intemperance surely influenced, by heredity and by observed behavior, the later sottishness of his son Hartley. It was the immediate cause of the 1810 quarrel with Wordsworth, when Wordsworth told Basil Montagu, a reformed drunkard turned proselytizing teetotaler, that Coleridge was "a rotten drunkard," "rotting out his entrails with intemperance," and that he was "*in the habit* of running into debt at little pot-houses for gin."[6] In London in 1810 Lamb gleefully describes him to William and Dorothy as "Bacchus ever sleek and young. He is going to turn sober, but his Clock has not struck yet, meantime he pours down goblet after goblet, the 2nd to see where the 1st is gone, the 3d to see no harm happens to the second, a fourth to say there's another coming, and a 5th to say he's not sure he's the last."[7]

Ironically, Keats's quest for pleasure in claret seems more consistently joyful than Coleridge's, erupting in several drinking songs in the *carpe diem* mode, and only briefly a source of anguish, if we accept Benjamin Haydon's report that after Tom's death Keats was scarcely sober for six weeks. To his brother and sister-in-law, 19 February 1819, suggesting that they start a vineyard in the new world, Keats writes one of the clearest explanations ever written of the pleasure of drinking to a point just short of intoxication:

> now I like Claret whenever I can have Claret I must drink it. – 't is the only palate affair that I am at all sensual in … For really 't is so fine – it fills the mouth one's mouth with a gushing freshness – then goes down cool and feverless – then you do not feel it quarelling with your liver – no it is rather a Peace maker and lies as quiet as it did in the grape – then it is as fragrant as the Queen Bee; and the more ethereal Part of it mounts into the brain, not assaulting the cerebral apartments like a bully in a bad house looking for his trul and hurrying from door to door bouncing against the waistcoat; but rather walks like Aladin about his own enchanted palace so gently that you do not feel his step – Other wines of a heavy and spirituous nature transform a Man to a Silenus; this makes him a Hermes – and gives a Woman the soul and imortality of Ariadne for whom Bacchus always kept a good cellar of claret – and even of that he could never persuade her to take above two cups – I said this same Claret is the only palate-passion I have I forgot game"[8]

Elements of magical enchantment, transformations, Platonic exaltations, and Greek myths of Silenus and Bacchus mingle with vivid realities of London low life to capture the synaesthetic motion from sense to soul that appears in *Endymion* Book IV, "Ode to Melancholy," and stanza two of the "Ode to a Nightingale."

In his *Autobiography* (1853) Haydon tells the story of Keats sprinkling his palate and throat with cayenne pepper to intensify the fierce joy of claret, a *dérégulation des sens* that anticipates Rimbaud, participates in the Renaissance Dionysian interest in the figure of Marsyas carrying his own flayed skin, and corroborates Christopher Ricks's interpretation of Keats as a delighter in the intensity of sense.[9] Charles Cowden Clarke tries to rebut Haydon, saying he never saw Keats purchase a bottle of claret, but Clarke's absence from Keats's gregarious years from 1817 on disqualifies his argument, though it is still possible, as Lionel Trilling believes, that Haydon's story is "apocryphal."[10] About Keats's drunkenness in the period after Tom's death the biographers differ, with Bate minimizing the amount consumed, and Ward believing that Keats was dissipated to the point of danger. The specter of his mother, addicted to brandy after her second marriage, may have haunted as well as spurred him.[11]

Despite their age difference, and Coleridge's appearance of middle-aged rotundity when they met on Hampstead Heath and talked of nightingales and consciousness, both Coleridge and Keats had a personal, and then poetic and philosophical, interest in drinking. The tavern life that gave them pleasure was then, as it is now, a community of men, enjoying exuberant discussions, being free and sometimes wild in warm places reminiscent of the Tabard Inn, the Mermaid Tavern, and other gathering spots for poets and enthusiasts throughout the history of English literature. In its most positive form, it is the poetry of men in groups, of witty fellowship, of songs composed to amuse others, in conditions of communal ease rather than solitary struggle. The occurrences of such forms in the poetry and letters of Coleridge and Keats – even if they were singing in the dark – help to recall the Falstaffian natures of these vivacious and sociable men.

In appreciating tavern life and tavern songs, Coleridge and Keats both participated in an old English tradition. They knew and appreciated their seventeenth-century predecessors in revelry: *Comus*'s presence in the under-consciousness of Romantic poets needs hardly be documented. In a letter to William Sotheby, Coleridge describes *Comus* as a platonizing Christian allegory, and an allusion to *Comus* passes so quickly in a letter from Woodhouse to Keats as to suggest the everpresent absorption of Milton's language in their daily talk.[12] Coleridge and Keats both knew Dryden's bacchanalian "Alexander's Feast." Both recommended what Coleridge called the "genuine mother English" of the older poets to the moderns, Cowley being a favorite. Lamb recommends Cowley to Coleridge as "delicious"; Coleridge dubs him a poet of the Fancy; Hazlitt finds him "quaint, far-fetched, and mechanical," except in his *Anacreontiques*, which he believes are "the perfection of that sort of gay, unpremeditated lyrical effusion. They breathe the very spirit of love and wine."[13]

The poetry of Herrick, like that of John Donne, experienced a revival at the turn of the century. After the very large and widely disseminated issue of Herrick's *Hesperides* in 1648, he is mentioned by William Winstanley in *Lives of the Most Famous English Poets* (London, 1687), by Granger in *Biographical History of England* (1769–74), and by Ellis in *Specimens of the Early English Poets* (1790), though he does not appear in the fourteen-volume anthology compiled by Robert Anderson in 1792–95, *The Works of the British Poets*. However, at the beginning of the nineteenth century, as George Walton Scott reveals, his reputation revived: "Nathan Drake in *Literary Hours or Sketches Critical, Narrative, and Poetical* in 3 vols 1804, Vol. III, took a positive though restricted view of *Hesperides* in three appreciative articles... Barron Field in 1809 recorded that Herrick's poems were still surviving by oral tradition at Dean Prior. At the turn of the century, then, *Hesperides* was beginning to be read again and selections started to appear. In 1810 the *Quarterly Review* said Herrick had been unjustly neglected. This year also saw the appearance of the first volume to be devoted to his poetry since the appearance of his original work – *Select Poems from the Hesperides*, edited by J. Nott, Bristol, which included 284 poems." While Coleridge never mentions Herrick directly, it is hard to imagine – especially given Lamb's love of Herrick – that he would be ignorant of this revival of interest in an older British poet. Lamb's 1818 volume, which included the Herrick-inspired "A Farewell to Tobacco," was dedicated to Coleridge and memories of their nights drinking at the Salutation and Cat. Keats's library contained a copy of the Bristol edition of Herrick's *Select Poems*.[14]

Lamb's love of Herrick shows in the homage he pays to Herrick's "His Fare-well to Sack" in his brilliantly accomplished "A Farewell to Tobacco." This poem was written in 1805, that is, five years before the 1810 Bristol edition of Herrick's *Select Poems*, and therefore, presumably, derived from Lamb's reading of earlier collections, either the selections noted above or the 1648 edition itself. Lamb addresses Tobacco:

> Sooty retainer to the vine
> Bacchus' black servant, negro fine,

and

> Brother of Bacchus, later born,
> The old world was sure forlorn
> Wanting thee, that aidest more
> The god's victories than before
> All his panthers, and the brawls
> Of his piping Bacchanals.

Tobacco was Bacchus's "true Indian conquest"; this great plant now "weaves / A finer thyrsus of thy leaves."[15] It is likely that Lamb derives the theme and technique from analogous lines in Herrick's "His Farewell to Sack":

> O thou the drink of Gods, and Angels! Wine
> That scatter'st Spirit and Lust
> …
> 'Tis thou, alone, who with thy Mistick Fan,
> Work'st more then Wisdome, Art, or Nature can,
> To rouze the sacred madness; and awake
> The frost-bound-blood, and spirits; and to make
> Them frantick with thy raptures.[16]

Both Herrick and Lamb bid farewell for their healths' sakes. Herrick "enforc'd, must say / To all thy witching beauties, Goe, Away," and both look back to forbidden pleasures that they will stealthily resume. Lamb's poem allows for the play of his often metaphysical wit in concert with Herrick's, as if the two poets were drinking companions spanning a century and more. As if instructed by Lamb's "Farewell to Tobacco," Coleridge believes that if Lamb would leave off tobacco he would not turn so magnetically to gin.[17]

Coleridge shares with Lamb as well as Keats a general interest in Bacchus, recalling once again the pleasures they took in each other's conversation. As in his letter describing Coleridge as Bacchus ever sleek and young, Lamb is drawn by his own love of drink to Bacchus figures and bacchanalian feasts even in his art criticism. In Titian's *Bacchus and Ariadne*, in the National Gallery in London, he sees Bacchus as "precipitous, with his reeling satyr rout about him, re-peopling and re-illuming suddenly the waste places, drunk with a new fury beyond the grape ... born in fire." He describes *Belshazzar's Feast* and Veronese's *Marriage at Cana* with pleasure in the revelry, the crowds, and the wine-pots. He closely analyzes Hogarth's *Gin Lane*. Coleridge also turns eloquent before a painting by the school of Rubens called "Triumph of Silenus":

> But Oh! what a wonderful picture is that Triumph of Silenus! It is the very revelry of hell. Every evil passion is there that could in any way be forced into juxtaposition with joyance. Mark the lust, and, hard by, the hate. Every part is pregnant with libidinous nature without one spark of the grace of Heaven. The animal is triumphing – not over, but – in the absence, in the non-existence, of the spiritual part of man."[18]

The drinking poem as a literary sub-genre in the seventeenth century comprises a complex array of poems by Herrick, Cowley, Rochester, Wycherley, and Dryden. Herrick's drinking songs are "When He Would Have His Verses Read," "His Fare-well to Sack," "The Welcome to Sack," "A Lyrick to Mirth," "A Bacchanalian Verse," "A Hymne to Bacchus," "An Ode to Sir Clipsebie Crew," "The apparition of his mistress calling him to Elysium," and "To live merrily, and to trust to Good Verses." Cowley's poem "Drinking," from the volume, *Anacreontiques*, surely qualifies him for Lamb's adjective, "delicious," for it depicts and recreates in sound a fluidity coursing through nature:

> The thirsty *Earth* soaks up the *Rain*,
> And drinks, and gapes for drink again.
> The *Plants* suck in the *Earth*, and are
> With constant drinking fresh and fair.
> The *Sea* it self, which one would think
> Should have but little need of *Drink*,
> Drinks ten thousand *Rivers* up,
> So fill'd that they or'eflow the *Cup*.[19]

The jaunty tetrameter couplets complete the circle of evaporation, precipitation, and general insobriety, and conclude with a plea to include human beings in nature's round of drunkenness.

Typical of the genre is Herrick's cheer, the Healths going round to Homer, Virgil, Ovid, Catullus, Propertius, and Tibullus, the ecstatic poet heating up with the contents of larger and larger vessels. Composing in an ancient song tradition, Herrick calls in "A Lyrick to Mirth" for merriment amid mutability:

> Drink, and dance, and pipe, and play;
> Kiss our *Dollies* night and day;
> Crown'd with clusters of the Vine;
> Let us sit, and quaffe our wine
> Call on *Bacchus*; chaunt his praise;
> Shake the *Thyrse*, and bite the *Bayes*;
> Rouze *Anacreon* from the dead;
> And return him drunk to bed;
> Sing o're *Horace*; for ere long
> Death will come and mar the song:
> Then shall *Wilson* and *Gotiere*
> Never sing, or play more here.[20]

Like similar songs by Horace, Catullus, and Anacreon, these poems circle around congenial themes. They cherish simple physical things, fleeting joy in the shadow of death, and the community of poets dead and alive, reunited in the great tavern in the sky. At the same time their praise of wine leads to less simple ideas, such as the cultivation of sacred madness, poetic creativity, the permanence of the art work (which here means verses or songs), and the eventual immortality, through verses, of the poet whose drinking is now inspiring his song. Frequent suggestions that drink is magical, that brews and potions release incantations, link the poems with Platonic and neoplatonic themes of enthusiasm and musical ecstasy. Lines like Herrick's "blood and spirit are roused, O Divinest Soule!" suggest a Platonic ladder of love rising from flesh to soul, but not rejecting the flesh. Herrick shows particular interest in Bacchus, in his familiar paraphernalia of thyrsus, bays, and fan, referring to his legend in at least five poems. Cowley's "Drinking" celebrates a unity of man and nature in the universal thirst of the liquid globe; liquids, spirits, and flames are frequent images. These delights are tempered by awareness of mortality, illness, and passing time, emphasized in the same years by Robert Burton in chapters on drink in diet in *Anatomy of Melancholy*, a book beloved by both Coleridge and Keats. Indeed, the terrors of death have been a part of the tradition of drinking songs since earliest times.

This Cavalier tradition, sustained in a variety of forms throughout the eighteenth century, culminates in the drinking songs of Robert Burns, who in "Scotch Drink," "John Barleycorn," and "Tam O'Shanter" continues the tradition of tavern pleasure, of drinking outside in the long summer evenings, and of exultation in particular drinks like whisky, sack, ale, or claret. Charles Lamb, in "Old Familiar Faces" – "I have been laughing, I have been carousing, / Drinking late, sitting late, with my bosom cronies" – brings the tavern tradition into the center of romanticism (though his own problems with excessive drinking, especially of gin, vividly described in his "Confessions of a Drunkard," came to discredit him along with his rowdy friends in the opinion of mid-nineteenth-century commentators like Carlyle). Tom Moore's *Anacreontiques* and Byron's songs like "Fill the Goblet Again" and "To Thomas Moore" also hark directly back, through Robert Burns, to Herrick, Cowley, and Rochester.

Balancing between the simple immediacy of experience and an intricate tradition of *furor poeticus*, which conflates the vinously inspired verse with the immortality of the intoxicated singer, the drinking song takes the short form of an anacreontic, or the long forms of the ode or narrative, sometimes modelled on Milton's *Comus*. Coleridge and Keats both use the short song form rather than the long witty form that Lamb adapts. Their serious efforts to analyze the power of Bacchus, on the other hand, call for narrative verse.

Coleridge's drinking songs have not been set in the contexts of his own bacchanalian nature or of his admiration for the seventeenth-century drinking song: indeed, they have not been noticed at all. Two of Coleridge's verses on drinking were published in the *Morning Post* in 1801; two occur in letters and were known in his own time only by drinking companions who were the lucky beneficiaries of his high spirits at frolicsome feasts when he would aim forks at wine glasses. The first, "Song to be sung by the Lovers of all the Noble Liquors comprised under the Name of Ale," begins

> Ye drinkers of Stingo and Nappy so free
> Are the Gods on Olympus so happy as we?

and ends

> Why, then we and the Gods are equally blest,
> And Olympus an Ale-house as good as the best!

Here, as in Herrick's mythology of drinking, ale-drinking is itself a divine activity, and it turns the drinkers in their intoxication, power, and joy, into Olympian beings. Drinking rouses an energy that is "innate and divine, a felicity above and beyond prudence"; such "passion and joy" unites Romantic poets to seventeenth-century poets and both to the Greek gods themselves. The second drinking song to appear in the 1801 *Morning Post* a week later, called "Drinking versus Thinking," rejects philosophy and embraces mirth and merriment:

> Away, each pale, self-brooding spark
> That goes truth-hunting in the dark,
>   Away from our carousing!
> To Pallas we resign such fowls –
> Grave birds of wisdom! ye're but owls,
>   And all your trade but *mousing*!
>
> My merry men all, here's punch and wine,
> And spicy bishop, drink divine!

> Let's live while we are able.
> While Mirth and Sense sit, hand in glove,
> This Don Philosophy we'll shove
> Dead drunk beneath the table![21]

Coleridge's charm and metrical skill hardly suggest a poet irritably reaching after philosophical certainty; he rejects his own reputation as a philosophical poet, revealing the schism in his impulses toward drinking and thinking. A third poem, also describing the divine bliss achieved through drink, was dashed off soon after Lamb's depiction to Wordsworth of Coleridge as a Young Bacchus, downing glass after glass when he was supposed to be mourning his broken friendship with Wordsworth. On 30 April 1811, Coleridge wrote the composer John Whitaker that, inspired by "your wine and the Pipe" the previous night, he had written three songs that could be set to music – one imitated from Schiller praising Iacchus and Cupid and calling for refills:

> Hah! – we mount! On their pinions they waft up my Soul!
> O give me the Nectar!
> O fill me the Bowl!
> Give, give [h]im the Nectar!
> Pour out for the Poet!
> Hebe! pour free!
> Moisten his eyes with celestial Dew,
> That STYX the detested no more he may view,
> But like one of us Gods may conceit him to be!
> Thanks, Hebe! I quaff it! Io PAEAN, I cry!
> The wine of the Immortals
> Forbids me to die.

Similarly playing with themes of inspiration, immortality, and the defiance of death, the last drinking song riotously warns the lower classes against all excesses that might weaken them in the face of the cholera epidemic then sweeping across Europe:

> Cry, Avaunt, New Potato!
> And don't get drunk, like old Cato!
> Ah beware of Dys Pipsy,
> And there*fore* don't get tipsy!
> For tho' Gin and Whisky
> May make you feel frisky,
> They're but Crimps for Dys Pipsy.[22]

The poem rattles on and ends with a fanfare of "Hurras."

Keats is far more energetic in his production of drinking songs. Not only do his drinking poems reveal his admiration of "the older poets" (as he calls them by contrast with the modern poets like Wordsworth) but they also anticipate the combination of later themes and attitudes toward gusto under the gun. Some of the most accomplished are "Fill for me the brimming bowl" written in August 1814, but not published until 1905; "Hence burgundy, claret, and port," written 31 January 1818, drawing on Sabrina's rejection of Comus and anticipating the "Away! Away!" of the "Ode to a Nightingale"; "Lines on the Mermaid Tavern," written in February 1818, indicating his wish to join the Sons of Ben. Comic rhymes as in Herrick's "A Hymne to Bacchus" –

> I sing thy praise Iacchus
> Who with thy Thyrse dost thwack us –

emerge in a short exercise written in 1816:

> I am as brisk As a bottle of Whisk-
> Ey and as nimble
> As a milliner's thimble.

The joviality of men in groups plays off the old topos:

> Give me wine, women, and snuff,
> Until I cry out "hold, enough!"[23]

Other poems from this experimental period seem likewise to borrow themes from Herrick's countryside poems and poems about diminutive magic and fairies under mushrooms, for example Keats's "Ye Devon Maid," and "Over the hill and over the dale." Like the drinking songs, these also urge pleasure, warmth, simplicity, country dance, and provincial song. Clearly in the *carpe diem* mode popularized in the seventeenth century, Keats's warm-up exercises help to generate his later tragic hedonism, but also cast a new light on Bacchus's appearance in his major poems. Coleridge's merriment is, on the other hand, sometimes severed from the guilt that usually follows, troubling the unity of his nature, leading to dualism and sometimes to derision of the flesh.

Coleridge's knowledge of Bacchus or Dionysus as "among the most aweful & mysterious Deities" participates in his lifelong study of the springs of creativity.[24] He is interested in how passion and joy are energies in the universe and in human beings; in how these energies rise up without having been planned in a rational way before they appear; and in how they release in human activity a power that seems to be innate to human beings, but also seems to come from elsewhere, to be divine in itself or at least a divinely given blessing or spontaneous gift.

Coleridge's sources for his interest in Bacchus and his profound under-standing of Bacchus's power are probably mixed, but one of the sources is

English literature of the sixteenth and seventeenth centuries, with its tradition of allegorical readings. Coleridge draws from Spenser and many other sources for understanding the complexity of Dionysian felicity. In a letter to Hugh Rose, 23 May 1818, he cites "The Shepheardes Calender," October, lines 109–15, to support his use of "the true Dionysiac sense [of] the word, wine ... for 'the passion void of care,' the gladsome ebullience of which is impossible for him whose every Tomorrow is haunted by the Ghost of Yesterday." Such wine lifts the muse, makes the rhyme rage, and, banishing the distracting and oppressive worries of time past and future, releases the sort of ebullient force that Coleridge described in "Kubla Khan" in a freedom made possible, he later claims, by a few grains of opium.

Coleridge seems to associate such an allegorical reading of wine with Milton also, for he shows how the method works in an analysis of the Haemony plant in *Comus*, where the plant becomes "blood-wine" and then a symbol of death on the cross. In a notebook entry of 1806 he planned to write a poem using the multiple levels of Platonic reading, "to describe Sotting allegorically, losing the way to the temple of Bacchus, come to the Cave of the Gnome, &c &c."[25] Coleridge accuses Dryden of ignoring these many levels of meaning in "Alexander's Feast." He argues that Dryden takes a narrow view of Bacchus as a mere drinking god and forgets that Alexander, a legendary drunkard, and Bacchus both conquered India.[26] But Coleridge overlooks Dryden's intricate intertwining of pleasure and pain in a refrain:

> *Bacchus* Blessings are a Treasure;
> Drinking is the Soldiers Pleasure;
> Rich the Treasure, Sweet the Pleasure;
> Sweet is Pleasure after Pain

and in the "fallen, fallen, fallen, fallen" stanza four that ends:

> Revolveing in his alter'd Soul
> The various Turns of Chance below;
> And, now and then, a Sigh he stole;
> And Tears began to flow.

Alexander's rapture in stanza four – "The Master saw the Madness rise; / His glowing Cheeks, his ardent Eyes" (lines 69–70) – has hitherto unrecognized resemblances to the meter and content of "Kubla Khan" – "And all should cry, Beware! Beware! / His flashing eyes, his floating hair" (49–50).

In addition, the Janus-faced rapture and disintegration of Dryden's pleasure/pain refrains, saturated with the rhapsodic tradition of Renaissance platonism enunciated by Pico della Mirandola and others, may have contributed to Coleridge's plan for a long poem on Dionysus, sketched in the *Notebooks* in February 1808 at about the same time as his lecture on the origins of drama. John Beer was the first person to discover this plan as well as to track Coleridge's many references to Bacchus, who is often conflated, Coleridge believes, with other double-sided figures such as Orpheus, Adam, or Moses. The plan for the poem goes as follows:

Man in the savage state as a water-drinker or rather Man before the Fall possessed of the Heavenly Bacchus as (see Boehmen's Sophia or celestial Bride) his fall – forsaken by the *Διονυσος* the savage state – and dreadful consequences of the interspersed vacancies left in his mind by the absence of Dionysus – the Bastard Bacchus comes to his Relief or rather the Gemini, the one *Οινος* permitted by the Dionysus – the other a *Gnome* – this pursued, in the mixt effects of the god – Mem. Accursed thing of the Aztecs...
     A most delightful Poem may be made of it.[27]

This plan seems to associate the prelapsarian bliss with Dionysus in his full rapture, ebullience, freedom, and felicity. With the Fall Dionysus loses his role as unifying force in man and nature and sinks into a mere drinking god split between artificial excitement and inevitable disappointment, embodied in the Gnome. The Fall is thus a diminishment of the human experience of bliss. After the Fall bliss is attained only momentarily as a release from "interspersed vacancies." It is then punished with remorse and pain in a circle of self-generated alterations of consciousness. This strange amalgamation of themes also found in "The Rime of The Ancient Mariner," "Kubla Khan," and "The Pains of Sleep," resounds with a history of European rhapsody from Plato's *Ion* and *Phaedrus*, to the neoplatonic hymns, to Pico and Ficino, to Spenser and Milton, up to the Romantic mythologist Thomas Taylor, and even, astonishingly, to Immanuel Kant, whose *Anthropology* of 1797 describes with approval the *raptus*, the *furor poeticus*, the genius, and the witty wine-drinking social man.[28] Coleridge's proposed narrative about Dionysus is an outgrowth of a long allegorical method of reading, rooted in Spenser, Dryden, Milton, and their philosophical sources.

Of these feeding streams one of the most powerful is *Paradise Lost* IX.1008–13. At the moment of Adam's willed transgression nature also falls, beginning the process of decay that we now deem "natural." Grapes immediately start to ferment, as man, too, starts both to desire and to die. Coleridge recreates a similar moment in his projected poem when water-drinking turns to wine-drinking, with its concomitant thirsts, yearnings, desires, obsessions, corruptions, and self-loss.

This moment Milton describes as a transformation, alluding to Circe in describing Eve, and calling the realization of guilt and knowledge an intoxication:

> As with new Wine intoxicated both,
> They swim in mirth, and fancy that they feel
> Divinity within them breeding wings
> Wherewith to scorn the Earth: but that false Fruit
> Far other operation first display'd,
> Carnal desire inflaming

Milton chooses to call the effect of the two transgressions intoxication because the eaters are artificially and falsely lifted above their natures and filled with delusory images of their own powers; at the same time, they poison themselves, cloud their perceptions, and prepare a plunge into disillusion. The new wine, from the now suddenly decaying fruit, is poised at the moment before vinegar sets in, and by a parallel with their own new mortality, putrescence. Once Adam and Eve satisfy their hunger and thirst, they break out of the artful pastoral stasis, begin the process of tragic descent, and enter the human world. As the drunken exaltation dissipates, the disordered consciousness breeds lust, recrimination, and cruelty, and in nature, climactic change, floods, famine, pestilence and decay, in its many gradations.

In his commentary on *Paradise Lost* Alastair Fowler extends the allusions further, with Adam's dropped garland recalling "Statius' *Thebeid*, vii, 149 and following, when Bacchus, frightened by the impending destruction of Thebes, drops his thyrsus, and unimpaired grapes fall from his head." Adam is already cast as Bacchus in a premonitory description in Book IV line 279 in a list of other unsuspecting frail strangers in mythological gardens who will be snatched by Death, ripped to pieces, or transformed from their original shapes.[29] Though Milton does not emphasize the less noble elements of the Bacchus legend – his riotous, irrational, cruel, and transfiguring nature – these elements inevitably surround the mention of Bacchus, and by contagion darken the figure of Adam.

Keats is also inspired by this multi-layered reading of the powers of Bacchus, whether he learns it from Coleridge directly or from the ferment of Dionysian thinking going on in the first decade of the nineteenth century. What is more, Keats writes the poems he plans. In the "Ode on Melancholy," in *Endymion* Book IV, and in "Ode to a Nightingale," Keats reads Milton's Dionysian moment in a largely positive way, that is, as heroic choice.

The Miltonic moment poised between stasis and decay is captured by Keats in the "Ode on Melancholy":

> She dwells with Beauty – Beauty that must die;
>   And Joy, whose hand is ever at his lips
> Bidding adieu; and aching Pleasure nigh,
>   Turning to poison while the bee-mouth sips;
> Ay, in the very temple of Delight

> Veil'd Melancholy has her sovran shrine,
>   Though seen of none save him whose strenuous tongue
> Can burst Joy's grape against his palate fine.   (lines 21–28)[30]

This contorted and dissonant sentence holds the moment when time, decay, and loss begin at the very heart of pleasure, a moment which Milton describes as a sudden universal decay. For Keats, who perhaps, unlike Milton, makes the best of a bad thing in a godless universe, only the brave can see the fierce destruction required by joy, as the delicious grape bursts on the palate and as aching pleasure turns to poison. Such a splicing of ecstasy and disillusion can be compared to the moment when intoxication slips into irrational drunkenness, when the perfect grape, at Adam's choice, starts to ferment.

Because of the fragility of this moment and the suddenness of its transformation, images of enchantment sometimes accompany images of intoxication. Enchantment fixes forms and also dissolves them, as liquids change forms by evaporating, precipitating, distilling, and dissipating (to use the imagery of Cowley's "Drinking"), or as persons do by imbibing, dissipating, altering their consciousness, raging, stumbling, frolicking, or bursting into song. Magic is associated with the power of wine to transform behavior and personality, represented already in *The Odyssey* by Circe's drinks that changed swinish men into pigs, and with the magical shape-shifting of Dionysus himself, capable of being whatever he imagined or wished and of changing others, like Pentheus, as well. Such an ancient concatenation of magic, drink, and song or charm passes through *Comus* to *Endymion*.[31]

Milton's *Comus* is an important source for Romantic narratives about the temptations of uncalculated pleasure. Lamb believes that Milton was in his courtier phase when he wrote *Comus*, suggesting that Lamb takes Comus' arguments at face value. Keats, rejecting Milton's Puritanism and superstition, may also have read Comus's speech, lines 706–55, as persuasive; he may well have used Comus's vocabulary of luxuriance in "To Autumn," for example, and incorporated Comus's arguments for enjoying and spending the fleeting joys of a brief life, without acknowledging the predatory nature of these arguments as they regard other people. Comus's lineage from both Circe and Bacchus is vinous, magical, and hedonistic; his power to lead and transform into animals his herd of followers contributes to Keats's *Endymion* IV where Bacchus's herd flows like a river of wine, sweeping sorrow before it.[32] The Indian Maid recounts Bacchus's invasion of her melancholy solitude:

> And as I sat, over the light blue hills
> There came a noise of revellers: the rills
> Into the wide stream came of purple hue –
>   'Twas Bacchus and his crew!

> ...
> Like to a moving vintage down they came,
> Crown'd with green leaves, and faces all on flame;
> All madly dancing through the pleasant valley,
>   To scare thee, Melancholy!   (lines 193–96, 200–3)

Like the Lady in *Comus* the Indian Maid follows the Damsels, Sileni, and Satyrs "tipsily quaffing" (217) into the "forests drear / Alone, without a peer" (270–1). Bewitched, she loses "in grieving all my maiden prime" (278). But where a strict virtue triumphs in *Comus*, in *Endymion* sorrow returns after momentary rapture "in a Dionysian analogy to Christ's dispersal of the dark deities in the Nativity Ode," as Stephen Steinholt has argued.[33]

Endymion IV.188–290 is *The Conquest of India in Hexameters* that Coleridge planned but never wrote. The triumph of Bacchus draws on Comus's herd in rout, on his inexorable power sweeping sober consciousness before him, and on the figure of the isolated young woman resisting the invasion of lust, fertility, and oblivion. The sorrow of the Indian Maid in the midst of surrounding revels recalls Sabrina's "Hence with thy Brew'd Enchantments!" and Herrick's reluctant "Away!" in "His Fare-well to Sack." It also anticipates the "Away! Away! ... Not charioted by Bacchus and his pards" of the "Ode to a Nightingale." As Sabrina rejected Comus's fertile and luxurious charms, as Herrick promised Sack that "what's done by me / Hereafter, shall smell of the Lamp, not thee" (though he does not keep his promise, returning instead a more "fierce idolator"), so Keats, too, comes to reject this powerful force of vitality, exuberance, joy, and inspired creativity in favor of sober hard work, but not without struggle. Coleridge summarizes the problem: "Genius too has it's intoxication, which however divine, leaves it's headaches and it's nauseas."[34]

In the perspective of the well-known tradition of seventeenth-century drinking poems, themselves distilled from earlier poems and criticisms, and given intellectual dignity by Coleridge's lectures, by Thomas Taylor's translations of Dionysian Mysteries, and by Lamb's imitation of Herrick, a new way of looking at stanza two of the "Ode to a Nightingale" arises. Few critics have seen stanza two as more than a frivolous option on the way to the troubled, morbid, tantalizing, and treacherous choice of Poesy. But, given Keats's many exultant praises of wine and Bacchus, however riotous, stanza two emerges as the only one in the Ode not to include any mention of death, as the only one to cherish pleasure, warmth, light, human community, and a free, happy culture; it emerges as well as the only life-affirming and joyful stanza in an ode otherwise shadowed by tragic realization of illness, suffering, death, and deceit. From such clarity of vision, from such consciousness of death and generations passing, from such solitude and abandonment, wine has always solaced mortals and inspired their songs. The solace is temporary, but that is at least something. When the poet banishes Bacchus and his pards he enters a world that is more teasing, more illusory, and more sorrowful than anything the beaded bubbles offer.

Thomas Taylor's 1790 recognition that Dionysus thrives at the heart of both desire and death expresses a complex history of the god that Coleridge and Keats knew and felt: "Dionysius [sic] ... is the guardian of life because of generation, but of death because wine produces an enthusiastic energy: and we become more enthusiastic at the period of dissolution."[35] Coleridge and Keats expressed the enthusiastic energy in their drinking songs modelled on seventeenth-century forms, and explored the dissolution in the moment of joy in long poems completed or merely dreamed.

NOTES

1 *Letters*, 1: 193–94. For Coleridge on pleasure, see *Biographia Literaria*, ed. James Engell and W. Jackson Bate, 2 vols., *Collected Coleridge*, vol. 7 (Princeton: Princeton University Press, 1983), 1: 23; 2: 12–13. Hereafter cited as *Biographia*.

2 Isaiah 22.13; *The Poetical Works*, 87–88.

3 For Keats's interest in arguments for a Christian immortality following the death of his brother Tom, see Robert M. Ryan, *Keats: The Religious Sense* (Princeton: Princeton University Press, 1976), 178–211. For his unconsoled death, see 212–17. Ryan notes areas where Keats and Coleridge might have coincided in their views, 185–86, 202–3.

4 Coleridge, *Biographia*, 1: 243–44.

5 Samuel Taylor Coleridge, *Lectures 1808–1819 On Literature*, ed. R. A. Foakes, 2 vols., *Collected Coleridge* vol. 5 (Princeton: Princeton University Press, 1987), 1: 44–45; see also 1: 517–18.

6 Samuel Taylor Coleridge, *Collected Letters*, ed. E. L. Griggs, 6 vols. (Oxford: Clarendon Press, 1956–71), 1: 99, 107, 110; 2: 1059, 1116; 3: 29; 1: 215, 322; 2: 1066, 711, 884, 930, 933–34, 940; 3: 125, 318–20. For Wordsworth's references see Coleridge, *Collected Letters*, 3: 296 and 298n. For a full discussion of Coleridge's drinking see Anya Taylor, "Coleridge and Alcohol," *Texas Studies in Literature and Language*, 33 (1991): 355–72.

7 Charles and Mary Lamb, *The Letters*, ed. Edwin W. Marrs, Jr., 3 vols. (Ithaca: Cornell University Press, 1975), 3: 62.

8 Keats, *Letters*, 2: 64. For Haydon's view see Walter Jackson Bate, *John Keats* (Cambridge: Belknap Press of Harvard University Press, 1963), 463.

9 Bate, *John Keats*, 274, 463; Edgar Wind, *Pagan Mysteries in the Renaissance* (New York: Norton, 1958), 172–85; Christopher Ricks, *Keats and Embarrassment* (Oxford: Clarendon Press, 1974), 202.

10 *The Keats Circle*, ed. Hyder E. Rollins, 2 vols. (Cambridge: Harvard University Press, 1965), 2: 319–21, but see 1: lxxii–lxxiv for Clarke's absence; Lionel Trilling, "The Poet as Hero: Keats in his Letters," *The Opposing Self* (New York and London: Harcourt Brace, 1978), 14. Trilling writes (15) that "ingestion supplies the imagery of our largest and most intense experiences: we speak of the wine of life and the cup of life; we speak

also of its dregs and lees, and sorrow is also something to be drunk from a cup ... But with Keats the ingestive imagery is pervasive and extreme. He is possibly unique among poets in the extensiveness of his reference to eating and drinking and to its pleasurable or distasteful sensations."

11 Bate, *John Keats*, 464; Aileen Ward, *John Keats: The Making of a Poet* (New York: Viking, 1963), 252–55.

12 Coleridge, *Collected Letters*, 2: 866; *The Keats Circle*, 1: 49; for the general importance of Milton, see Joseph Anthony Wittreich, Jr., *The Romantics on Milton* (Cleveland: The Press of Case Western Reserve University, 1970).

13 Lamb, *The Letters*, 1: 88; Coleridge, *Biographia*, 1: 23, 84; William Hazlitt, *Lectures on the English Poets* (1824) in *Collected Works*, ed. P. P. Howe, 5: 372.

14 Herrick's developing reputation is discussed in George Walton Scott, *Robert Herrick 1591–1674* (London: Sidgwick & Jackson, 1974), 156–59; and by J. Max Patrick, in *"Trust to Good Verses": Herrick Tercentenary Essays*, ed. Roger B. Rollin and J. Max Patrick (Pittsburgh: University of Pittsburgh Press, 1978), 228–29, 240–41, and 248–49. See *The Keats Circle*, 1: 253–260, for Brown's list of Keats's books.

15 *The Works of Charles and Mary Lamb*, 5: 32–33.

16 *Poetical Works*, 45–46.

17 Coleridge, *Collected Letters*, 3: 340.

18 Lamb, "On the Productions of Modern Art" and "On the Genius and Character of Hogarth," *The Complete Works and Letters of Charles Lamb* (New York: The Modern Library, 1935), 202–6, 311–13.

19 In *Seventeenth-Century Verse and Prose*, ed. Helen C. White, Ruth C. Wallerstein, and Ricardo Quintana (Toronto: Macmillan, 1969), 1: 455.

20 *Poetical Works*, 39.

21 *Complete Poetical Works*, ed. E. H. Coleridge, 2 vols. (Oxford: Clarendon Press, 1912), 2: 978–79.

22 Coleridge, *Collected Letters*, 3: 321–22, 6: 917.

23 *The Poems of John Keats*, 46, 47.

24 From Coleridge's notes for a lecture on the origin of drama, in *Lectures 1808–1819*, 1: 44. While Coleridge's lectures on Greek drama are indebted to August Wilhelm von Schlegel's 1808 lectures, this lecture on the origins of drama, which exists only in scanty notes, antedates the publication of Schlegel's lectures.

25 Coleridge, *Collected Letters*, 4: 862; 2: 866; R. D. Bedford, "Right Spelling: Milton's *A Masque* and *Il Penseroso*," *ELH* 52 (1985): 815–32; *The Notebooks of Samuel Taylor Coleridge*, ed. Kathleen Coburn (New York: Pantheon Books/Princeton: Princeton University Press, 1957–), 1, entry 1646, and 2, entry 2842.

26 *The Poems of John Dryden*, ed. James Kingsley (Oxford: Clarendon Press, 1958), 3: 1428–33. For Coleridge's analysis of "Alexander's Feast," see *Lectures 1808–1819*, 1: 44–45. For his plans (in 1803) to write hexameters on the conquest of India by Bacchus, see *Notebooks*, 1, entries 803 and 1646, and nn.

27 *Notebooks*, 3, entry 3263; see Coburn's note for further explanation and John Beer, *Coleridge the Visionary* (New York: Collier Books, 1959), 63, 68, 73, 103, 204, 272, 274, 275, 282.

28 "A Dissertation on the Eleusinian and Bacchic Mysteries" (London, 1790 or 1791), *Thomas Taylor the Platonist: Selected Writings*, ed. Kathleen Raine and George Mills

Harper (Princeton: Princeton University Press, 1969), 343–426. Immanuel Kant, *Anthropology from a Pragmatic Point of View* (1797), trans. Mary J. Gregor (The Hague: Martinus Nijhoff, 1974), 43–48.

29 John Milton, *Paradise Lost*, ed. Alastair Fowler (New York: Longman, 1971), 490, 211.

30 *The Poems of John Keats*, 375.

31 For magical elements in *Comus* see Angus Fletcher, *The Transcendental Masque: An Essay on Milton's Comus* (Ithaca and London: Cornell University Press, 1971), 40–86; Joan Larsen Klein, "The Demonic Bacchus in Spenser and Milton," *Milton Studies* 21 (1985): 93–118; Richard Halpern, "Puritanism and Maenadism in *A Mask*," in *Rewriting the Renaissance: The Discourses of Sexual Difference in Early Modern Europe*, ed. Margaret W. Ferguson, Maureen Quilligan, and Nancy J. Vickers (Chicago and London: Chicago University Press, 1986), 88–105; Jacqueline Di Salvo, "Fear of Flying: Milton on the Boundaries Between Witchcraft and Inspiration," *English Literary Renaissance* 18 (1988): 114–37. For magic in Keats, see Anya Taylor, *Magic and English Romanticism* (Athens: University of Georgia Press, 1979), 240–50.

32 For Comus's connection to a Bacchanalian tradition see *A Variorum Commentary on the Poems of John Milton*, ed. A. S. P. Woodhouse and Douglas Bush (New York: Columbia University Press, 1972), 2, part 3: 768–69; 774–75, 863–66.

33 Stephen T. Steinholt, *Keats's Endymion: A Critical Edition* (Troy, New York: The Whitson Publishing Co., 1987), 24 and 240, note on lines 182–272.

34 Coleridge, *Collected Letters*, 2: 1162.

35 *Thomas Taylor the Platonist*, 409. Tilottama Rajan, *Dark Interpreter: The Discourse of Romanticism* (Ithaca and London: Cornell University Press, 1980), 143–203, sees Dionysus in Keats as a Nietzschean and fatal, rather than a joyful, power.

CHAPTER TWELVE

Marvell through Keats and Stevens: the early modern meditation poem

LISA LOW

A GREAT DEAL HAS BEEN WRITTEN – by Joseph Anthony Wittreich, Jr., among others – about Milton, but little about Marvell, as a predecessor to the Romantics.[1] There are obvious reasons for the disparity, the most important of which is that the Romantics knew Marvell less as a poet than as a patriot.[2] As Frederick Burwick points out in his essay "What the mower does to the meadow: action and reflection in Wordsworth and Marvell," elsewhere in this volume, "in his own day and throughout the eighteenth century" Marvell's reputation rested "primarily on his satire and his polemical prose." Still, the claim has often been made that, like his contemporaries Vaughan and Traherne, Marvell seems sometimes uncannily to have anticipated the Romantics, especially in his love of nature and in his studies of consciousness.[3] If it is clear that Marvell did not influence the Romantics as significantly as Milton, is it possible nonetheless to consider Marvell as a precursor to them?

There are two schools of thought regarding the relationship between the metaphysical and the Romantic lyric. In the nineteenth century it was commonly claimed that the second-generation metaphysicals anticipated the Romantics, especially in their keen sensitivity to nature.[4] Such claims have been supported in the twentieth century by maverick critics William Empson, Christopher Hill, and Paul de Man. Hill, for example, has argued that the second-generation metaphysicals anticipated Romantic political themes of "Adamic pleasure" taken in nature,[5] and Paul de Man, taking an apparently contrary approach which finds its starting-point in Empson's *Some Versions of Pastoral*, has commented that Marvell is no less alienated from nature than Keats.[6] But the claim that the metaphysicals were proto-Romantic enjoyed perhaps its most controversial hour when William Empson suggested in *Seven Types of Ambiguity* (1930) that "the later metaphysical poets were approaching" Romantic technique in the "fortunate confusion" of their conceits.[7] Empson's claims were attacked by New Critics such as Ruth Wallerstein, Rosemond Tuve, and Joseph Summers, each of whom responded roundly and, for the most part, victoriously[8] that to claim that Marvell was a modern was to misinterpret him, and to do seventeenth-century poetry an injustice: it was to apply Romantic standards to the seventeenth century, something which could not – or in any case – *should not* be done.[9] Seventeenth-century poetry, these critics claimed, was Christian in a traditional sense, more Augustinian than Hegelian, built upon allegory and abstraction rather than devoted to present time, present space, or present philosophies.[10] But to demand of the seventeenth-century poets a medieval rather than a modern sensibility may be, through what John Carey calls "misplaced erudition,"[11] to ignore – in a way that new historicism no longer tolerates – the political and social realities of that troubled century, a century in which the English government reorganized itself around the ravages of the Civil War, and one in which, as Basil Willey observes, at least as early as Bacon, a new scientific view of nature emerged.

Willey writes that beginning with Bacon the seventeenth century sought "to give a philosophical account of matters which had formerly been explained unscientifically" and further that this has been "the main intellectual concern of the last three hundred years."[12] Christopher Hill confirms a similar principle of historical continuity when he speaks of the seventeenth and nineteenth centuries as participating together in a revolution (including a revolution in consciousness) not to be considered as a punctual event but as taking place over multiple centuries.[13] More recently, the renaming of the Renaissance as the "Early Modern" period indicates the contemporary theorists' perception that the Renaissance is best interpreted more as the beginnings of the modern world than as a resurrection of the classical past. Leah S. Marcus, for example, in an essay defining the "Early Modern," tells us that "we are moving away from interpreting" the Renaissance as "the reawakening of an earlier era"; rather, "we are coming to view the period more in terms of ... those features of the age that appear to us precursors of our own twentieth century, the modern, the postmodern."[14]

The seventeenth century's break with the past was set in motion at least as early as Bacon, in science; and in lyric poetry, as early as the young John Donne who wrote, casting aside formalities, "For Godsake hold your tongue, and let me love," and who, even in his later religious poetry, broke through old artifices to declare him*self* and his world directly.[15] If such poems as Donne's "Goodfriday, 1613. Riding Westward" retain many medieval characteristics of high religiousness, icon, and allegory, and especially of a direct connection supposed between the religious self and the God toward which it aspires, they also look forward to a Wordsworth-like declaration of a strongly realized self in meditation situated at a particular moment and in a particular time.

It is the argument of this essay (and in many ways of this book) that metaphysical poetry should not be read exclusively, as it typically has been, as coming before the watershed that produces romanticism. Rather, as Christopher Hill has suggested, metaphysical poetry already demonstrates the conflict between the old and the new worlds, between faith in the grounds of one's society and faith only in oneself and the nature the self observes. More specifically, this essay argues that Andrew Marvell's "The Garden" can be read as the *locus classicus* for the early modern turn away from faith in God to what John Middleton Murry calls a human-centered but spiritualized view of nature and the self.[16]

Andrew Marvell stands before the "fall" into the Enlightenment, at the very tail end of a Renaissance which had introduced, but had not yet fully felt, the impact of the breach between science and theology. For poets in the Romantic period, coming some century and a quarter after Marvell, the breach had become less tolerable. Separated from God, beleaguered by industry (the practical application of science), heirs to a de-spiritualization of body, landscape, and imagination, the Romantics informed us of what Thomas Carlyle in "Characteristics" calls "dis[-]ease."[17] Out to save the race, the Romantics "stole fire." They borrowed the creative power of divinity and moved, in their great odes, over the waters and above the face of earth, making of the desiccated earth a new ground for genesis.

But not only the Romantic but the metaphysical poet had to rely more and more on him*self* as a stay against change. In a classic discussion of seventeenth-century poetry Louis Martz describes the typical religious meditation as wholly preoccupied with the divine light of God.[18] But Martz's reading of seventeenth-century meditation may seriously underestimate the political, social, and psychic traumas of the metaphysical period, for "by the middle of the seventeenth century ... the customary appeal to an external authority ... was inevitably weakened, and religion, like philosophy, was constrained to look within for its certainties."[19] In migrating away from God and setting down roots instead in nature, in other words, the Romantics may have only *further developed* a forlornness that had already begun in the metaphysical period.

The defining feature of Early Modernism is the approaching absence or obscuration of God. To live without God is to live in a world where everything can be deconstructed, where every attempt at truth is at best a note written toward a supreme fiction. In this sense, the early modern dilemma brought on by what Donne calls the "new Philosophy" ("The first Anniversary," line 205) already anticipates in many ways the "forlornness" that Sartre in our own century describes as the heart of existentialism. That "forlornness" is at a far remove from the religious certainties of Martz's Augustinian meditation, for the Romantic accepts rather than rejects the world. That is, rather than reeling back toward the securities of an austere pre-revolutionary High Church poetics, the Romantic poet – and my point is to include Milton and Marvell as precursors to this category – looks forward to a Stevensian luxuriance which finds "abundant recompense" for an absent God by a fulfillment of the sensual imagination. The Romantic poet, in the male Romantic tradition at least, lives in the wasteland of his own death, but it is a wasteland he can plant, make green, and populate with the God-like fertility of his imagination. The Romantic poet, standing self-sufficiently in the plenitude of his own imagination, is an autonomous ouroboros for whom the sky is the limit.

Because he has no choice, the Romantic poet substitutes his mind for God. Both Milton and Marvell foreshadow this substitution, Milton when he asks the "Celestial Light" to "Shine inward" (*Paradise Lost* III.51–52) and Marvell when he calls for the annihilation of "all that's made" to the preferable "green Thought in a green Shade." In our own century, Wallace Stevens makes the substitution final when he writes, "We say that God and the imagination are one ... / How high that highest candle lights the dark."[20] If the substitution of mind for God brings with it potentially or inevitably the pain of alienation, it also brings the recompense both of self-reliance and of freely offered fruit. This earth and our perception of it, in other words, becomes paradise; or at least, "all of paradise that we shall know" (68).

The Romantic poet writes poems to get himself outside time, as well as to reconcile himself to death for which there is, in his theodicy, no cure but the compensating luxuries of the poem-in-the-making. The one thing that stands outside time and space for the Romantics is the poem itself. Poems, which detach themselves from historical moments much more easily than poets, are like Yeats's "golden bird" which "never takes its bodily form from any natural thing."[21] They are, like Keats's nightingale in the forest dim, "not born for death."[22] Not dying, poetry remains "a friend to man" while each human generation vanishes ("Ode on a Grecian Urn," line 48). Poetry is thus that part of the poet that manages to get outside of time both while he lives and after he dies. It is the mountain prominence from which poets view all time, and it is also, paradoxically, the urn which holds the poet's remains, the eloquent historian which allows the dead poet to be "a man speaking to men" for as long as men read.[23]

The conception of the sky as a limit, the requirement that we not go beyond the sky, describes not only the mind-as-God hovering over earth to create, but the shape of the Romantic ode. For both Renaissance and Romantic poetics, the poem is the means to wholeness. It is what the poet looks through to see "God." But for the Romantics, God is earthbound. God is generation and waste ("Ode on a Grecian Urn," line 46), the ouroboric structure of things. Keats's late odes come to accept the paradigm of life as elastic dialectic, the rising "generation" which demands "waste." This parabolic theme (generation and then waste), Wordsworth's "As high as we have mounted in delight / In our dejection do we sink as low," determines the actual curvilinear structure of the Romantic ode.[24] But it is not only Keats's "Ode to a Nightingale" but also Marvell's "The Garden" that best describes this arc of "generation and waste," the apotheotic structure which climaxes in the center and then falls away toward earth and death. With Marvell as with Keats, the poem climaxes in the center, at life's sky exhilarated height, and then falls away. But where Keats falls away into death, Marvell, like the also detached Wallace Stevens, falls away to rise again in another pleasurable "go around."

For differing historical reasons, both Marvell and Stevens partly escape Romantic dejection. A "comic" disposition permits both to ascend the ladder of the body into the heaven of the intellect until the mind becomes, like Plato's heaven, the locus of ideal forms. Balachandra Rajan has called Marvell "the most accomplished of English subversives";[25] Stevens delights in conceiving of himself as the clownish and ever-changing "emperor of ice cream." Like Stevens, Marvell preens at mind's center in the boughs of the fruit tree enjoying "the pleasures of merely circulating" (Stevens, Collected Poems, 149). In this luxuriance, Marvell, like the blind Milton who writes, perhaps ecstatically – "then feed on thoughts, that voluntary move / Harmonious numbers" (III.37–38) – anticipates Wallace Stevens's theodicy of Imaginative Man afoot in the wasteland carrying a paradise within that is greater far than the one without.

So far I have tried to provide a foundation for a closer reading of Marvell's "The Garden." I have argued that "proto-Romantics" like Milton and Marvell, and "Romantics" like Keats and Wallace Stevens, build a compromise between a no longer wholly available God and a nearly personified nature in an effort to recover grounds of knowledge and reason for being. If the typical seventeenth-century religious meditation proceeds by austerity, contracting away from the material world, annihilating self by annihilating desire until the dim light of consciousness is subsumed into the divine light of God, and if the end of such meditation is transcendence beyond earthly limits, the Romantic ode operates inversely, and by comparison it is epicurean. In the Romantic ode, self expands outward. Not by a withdrawal from, but by an intensification of bodily sense, the poet achieves a limited transcendence, one grounded on either side by birth and death. If in Renaissance meditation sensual/sexual indulgence is forbidden, in Romantic meditation, sensual/

sexual gratification is the very vehicle for spiritual transformation. The mind goes out into and inhabits nature; from this conjunction or "wedding" of the senses, mind reproduces itself but in a kind of unicorn form, a form outside of nature while suspended in it. As we shall see in the close reading that follows, Marvell's "The Garden" offers the prototype for this "Romantic" poetic. In "The Garden," as in the Romantic meditation, the poet's mind marries nature to create a state of mind which is "naturally immortal."

"The Garden" is a nine-stanza poem in iambic tetrameter which describes the same parabolic curve as the Romantic conversation lyric. Like the Romantic conversation poem, "The Garden" is cyclic rather than ascensional. It does not transcend earth, but only the formal limitations of the body. This "limited transcendence" is achieved not by Martz's Augustinian withdrawal, but rather by a full indulgence of the body's sensory apparatus.

The poem falls into three parts. The first four stanzas reject civilization (the pursuit of awards and women); the next three stanzas are climactic, describing an imaginative flight initiated by the sensual ecstasies of a seductive nature; the final two stanzas describe a "coasting to the ground," a return to earth which suggests not death but yet another flight. This three-part cycle implies the comic control of Stevens's "pleasures of merely circulating," as well as the parabolic shape of Keats's "Ode to a Nightingale." The subject of "The Garden" is characteristically Romantic. It is less about the fall, which the poet attributes to a narcissistic exploitation of nature, than the recovery from the fall by a loving, amorous return to a nature which, in response to the narrator's empathy, becomes humanized. Through a sympathetic re-engagement with nature, the narrator finds sexual, intellectual, and finally imaginative plenitude. By pursuing nature instead of self the poet metamorphoses into post-lapsarian Adam in intimate conversation with a nature from which he is no longer alienated. Through intercourse with nature Marvell relocates Eden, the language of plenitude.

The first stanza of "The Garden" wittily dismisses the public active life (the pursuit of athletic, civic, and even poetic merit), in favor of repose:

> How vainly men themselves amaze
> To win the Palm, the Oke, or Bayes;
> And their uncessant Labours see
> Crown'd from some single Herb, or Tree,
> Whose short and narrow verged Shade
> Does prudently their Toyles upbraid;
> While all the Flow'rs and all Trees do close
> To weave the Garlands of repose. (lines 1–8)

Nature, compatible with the prelapsarian state, now mocks toiling man with a slight crown "from some single Herb, or Tree" which can hardly be sufficient shade for "uncessant Labours." Man himself is to blame for this alienation. Pride separated man and nature in Eden as it does in modern England. "Vainly" is a pun: vanity (self-love) is vanity (gets you nowhere). The comically unsuccessful vain man is his own undoing, tripping on his own "amaze." Man makes a fool of himself while nature relaxes in a reference, as Anthony Hecht points out, to the biblical maxim that the lilies of the field "toil not."[26]

Vanity is the desire to see self located everywhere at nature's expense. When Narcissus bends over the pool of water he ceases to see nature; nature vanishes as the self is composed on the surface. Depth is annihilated, death inevitable, for Narcissus, pursuing his own image, becomes caught, like Alice, in a mirror from which there is almost no return. The myth that opposes Narcissus is the Christian paradox that to lose yourself is to find yourself. It is the myth Marvell tries to locate in "The Garden." Marvell will subordinate himself to nature to achieve a Wordsworth-like "wise passiveness" and a Keats-like "poetical character." By becoming himself nothing, by being "negatively capable," he will become all.

The second stanza begins with an apostrophe that calls Keats to mind:

> Fair quiet, have I found thee here,
> And Innocence, thy Sister dear!
> Mistaken long, I sought you then
> In busie Companies of Men.
> Your sacred Plants, if here below,
> Only among the Plants will grow.
> Society is all but rude,
> To this delicious Solitude. (lines 9–16)

Marvell's "delicious Solitude" away from the "busie Companies of Men" is less a Renaissance cloistering than it is a Romantic "enfolding" of the mind and body in preparation for a sensuous experience of "paradise." Similarly, the mythological interpenetration of gods and men that is more a Romantic than a Renaissance objective is here the theme.

So far, nature has been set against "rude" society – principally men. In stanzas three and four nature is set against Eve:

> No white nor red was ever seen
> So am'rous as this lovely green.
> Fond Lovers, cruel as their Flame,
> Cut in these Trees their Mistress name.
> Little, Alas, they know, or heed,
> How far these Beauties Hers exceed!
> Fair Trees! where s'eer your barkes I wound,

No Name shall but your own be found.   (lines 17–24)

Marvell courts nature, rejecting divisive woman and biologically based, merely human reproduction. The problem of Eve is the problem of the fall. Before Eve, Adam and nature stood in mutual sympathy, without threat of mortality, and linguistic intercourse was direct rather than circuitous. With Eve comes obstruction. Without Eve? "What wond'rous Life in this I lead!" the speaker exclaims, and "Two Paradises 'twere in one / To live in Paradise alone." Alone, the male magnifies himself as if expanding himself exponentially. Imaginative man reproduces upon nature to deify self: the system is circular and ouroboric, achieving something akin to the chanting men at the end of Stevens's "Sunday Morning": "The dew upon their feet shall manifest" where dew condenses against the sky of the mind and then falls in fertilizing rain to the soil (soul) out of which it rose (*Collected Poems*, 70). Marvell in the paradisal garden fashions a self-contained circulatory system.

Thus, the poem sets male and female sexuality against the self-sufficiency of the artist's mind. The artist procreates the poem, "annihilating all that's made" (a pun on maid?), and so transcends time and space, the alienating generation and waste precipitated by Eve. To have merely human intercourse is to submit to generation and waste as Keats's "Ode on a Grecian Urn" tells us. Eve is evil because she brings sexual awareness, inevitable decay. Mary Daly comments on the misogyny of such a formulation when she writes:

The myth of the Fall can be seen as a prototypic case of false naming. Elizabeth Cady Stanton was indeed accurate in pointing out the key role of the myth of feminine evil as a foundation for the entire structure of phallic Christian ideology ... the myth takes on cosmic proportions since the male's viewpoint is metamorphosed into God's viewpoint ... It misnames the mystery of evil, casting it into the distorted mold of the myth of feminine evil.[27]

Since woman is evil it is only through exorcising her that paradise can be experienced. The poem (and in some senses the history of poetry) becomes a history of finding the solaces of solitude, the potential wholenesses which, paradoxically, exclude woman. Isolated from woman, the poet is free to magnify himself in the cosmos.

In this Marvell perpetuates a medieval-seeming misogyny, and, indeed, the reader could interpret Marvell's garden as in every way exclusive, as an Eden recoverable only in the traditionally religious, and therefore de-feminized, sanctuary of the monkish poet's imagination. But Marvell's misogyny may be mitigated somewhat by his treatment of nature. Patrick Cullen tells us that in Marvell nature is unusual since it is "not the [traditional] deceiver of the soul" but "the first stage in its greater ... enlightenment."[28] Since nature has traditionally been associated with woman, and both nature and woman with evil, Marvell's conception of nature as goodly opens up at least the possibility of a feminist position, especially when contrasted with the Church doctrine of "feminine evil" as Mary Daly describes it.

But whether misogynist or potentially feminist, the more desirable sexual union for Marvell is between man and nature. This is emphasized by the fourth stanza's classical myth making. Again, the stanza as a whole sounds like Keats:

> When we have run our Passions heat,
> Love hither makes his best retreat.
> The *Gods*, that mortal Beauty chase,
> Still in a Tree did end their race.
> *Apollo* hunted *Daphne* so,
> Only that She might Laurel grow.
> And *Pan* did after *Syrinx* speed,
> Not as a Nymph, but for a Reed.   (lines 25–32)

The desire between mortal and immortal is reciprocal. The gods wish to be human, we wish to be gods. Humans have "All breathing human passion" ("Ode on a Grecian Urn," line 28); the gods have eternity. The objective is to have both, to be "naturally immortal." The pursuit of women ends in death if it does not end in poetry (Pan's reed) because through poetry flesh is taken up into immortal spirit while sexual consummation is fleshly alone and makes mortality inevitable. Poetry is the urn of immortality containing the dead body but living voice of poets. Language is the Eden from which, Marvell's narrator claims, woman has alienated man.

The rejection of "busie Companies of Men" and women prepares the narrator for the apotheosizing fifth, sixth, and seventh stanzas. The witty argument addressed half to self and half to society is abandoned as the speaker turns his sudden surprised attention to the pleasures of the bizarrely seductive garden. The fifth stanza's exuberance is as rhapsodic as Keats's "Already with thee! tender is the night" ("Ode to a Nightingale," line 35).

The progress from stanza five into stanzas six and seven is by annihilation and substitution. The speaker translates out of the real and into the ideal, out of body and into mind, out of density and into airy nothingness. The three stanzas demonstrate the cycle of ouroboric joy of the poet dallying in the solitary recesses of the garden (of his mind). Again, the fifth stanza's richness brings Keats to mind:

> What wond'rous Life in this I lead!
> Ripe Apples drop about my head;
> The Luscious Clusters of the Vine
> Upon my Mouth do crush their Wine.

> The Nectaren, and curious Peach,
> Into my hands themselves do reach;
> Stumbling on Melons, as I pass,
> Insnar'd with Flow'rs, I fall on Grass. (lines 33–40)

For Marvell, as for the Romantics, a "fall on Grass" is a fall into grace. The stimulation of this stanza is principally tactile, though all five senses are alerted. The poet is literally bombarded with sensation. The labial "p"s of "Ripe Apples drop" force the lips to press together, imitating linguistically the thud of the plump fruit falling against the speaker's head, shoulders, and the ground. Stevens's wry question in "Sunday Morning": "Does ripe fruit never fall [in paradise]?" (Collected Poems, 69), with its suggestion of the limits and frustrations of an unphysical heavenly paradise, is appropriate here, for this is a paradise of falling. The conditions of the fall are subverted in this stanza, for hapless, passive humanity does not pluck the apple. Rather, the apple falls of its own accord, responding to the presence of the luxury-minded human. The mildly pleasurable confusion of the falling fruit is made more intense by the shamelessness of this inverted fall. Nature's aggression (dropping, crushing, ensnaring) forbids moral obligation on the speaker's part. Rather, he stumbles drunkenly and helplessly over grass littered with nectarines, peaches, grapes, and apples. He has his fruit and eats it, too, in this proto-Romantic subversion of original sin.

The fifth stanza's descending motion from head to mouth to hands and finally to the "Insnar'd" feet inverts the parabolic shape of the poem as a whole. This "fall" prepares the poet for the counterpointing ascent into stanzas six and seven. "As I pass," caught between the melons-as-obstacles and the ensnaring flowers, shifts the speaker from one state to another. The speaker translates from solid and incarnate to air.

The body has been brought to rest for it is, analogous to the "busie Companies of Men," material, and at least in one sense, limited. The body is the incarnate, the caught-in-time-and-space form from which the imagination must withdraw if it is to save itself. But the body here, unlike in earlier Renaissance meditation poetry, is far from despised. Rather, the body is the ladder upon which the mind climbs into salvation. Subject to lineage, age, and decay, the body degenerates as it generates. Thus, the ripe apples dropping into the speaker's palms are objective formulae for the body's sacrifice but the body is sacrificed not to God but to the mind itself. Marvell's sacrifice is not burdened by loss, grief, and pain; rather, it escalates through pleasure. Sacrifice brings body up into mind. Thus, in the fifth stanza, the body disintegrates in the embrace of the ensnaring flowers as it reorganizes itself in the mind. The body vanishes, as if annihilated, and attention progresses to mind, the second stop on the progress to soul.

The speaker is brought to rest for a moment in the passage from the fifth to the sixth stanza. As if moving across a fulcrum, he makes his way from one pole (the body) to another (the mind):

> Mean while the Mind, from pleasure less,
> Withdraws into its happiness:
> The Mind, that Ocean where each kind
> Does streight its own resemblance find;
> Yet it creates, transcending these,
> Far other Worlds, and other Seas;
> Annihilating all that's made
> To a green Thought in a green Shade. (lines 41–48)

As the poet withdrew from "rude" society into the solitude of the garden, so now his mind withdraws from the "ruder body" into *its* solitude. Alliteration links "Mean while" and "Mind" to frustrate the balance of repose upon which the poem rests. The poet remains far from toil, in passivity, on the very verge of supernatural procreativity.

The repetition of "Mind" in the first and third lines (above) indicates Marvell's "discovery" of the mind as a subject, a discovery which leads in romanticism to the substitution of the mind for God. The repetition of the word "Mind" has the effect of holding a mirror up, as if the mind contemplates the cloud the breath creates by uttering "Mind." But this mirror more than pairs: it exponentially amplifies. This is not mind mating, but mind to the power of mind ($mind^{mind}$). This exponential curve appears elsewhere in the poem. In, for example, "Two Paradises 'twere in one / To live in Paradise alone," and in the core couplet, as we have seen, "Annihilating all that's made / To a green Thought in a green Shade." World to its own power; green to the power of green: Marvell here achieves "natural immortality" by imitating the supernatural procreation of the mind. The two lovers are the human mind and nature, but they have ceased, by the marriage in stanza five, to be equivalent.

Stanza six describes not an equivalence, but a subversion. The balance between man and nature rests on its (Renaissance) fulcrum for a moment in "that Ocean where each kind / Does streight its own resemblance find," but it then tips inward with the following couplet's "Yet it creates." Dominance has shifted from outer to inner green, from the heard melody of stanza five, to the unheard melody of stanza six's apotheosizing:

> Yet it creates, transcending these,
> Far other Worlds, and other Seas;
> Annihilating all that's made
> To a green Thought in a green Shade. (lines 45–48)

The closing couplet is as close as you can possibly get to an articulation like Keats's: "Heard melodies are sweet, but those unheard / Are sweeter" ("Ode on a Grecian Urn," lines 11–12). Both Marvell's and Keats's apotheosizing lines describe a transformation from outer to inner muse, from the sweetness of whatever is extended in time (chronological notes, ripe apples) to the greater sweetness of the random notes and apples in the process of forming. Both, in other words, describe the formlessness of the creative act itself, the presence of the mind moving like God's form over the waters of the deep. Both describe the gathering fist of the withdrawing wave of "about-to-be." The difference between God and man, then, becomes less distinct as the Coleridgean "repetition in the finite mind of the eternal act of creation in the infinite I AM" occurs.[29] As God created earth out of his own body, so man becomes body to create his mind as God. Creating out of nature, the poet comes to a "green Thought" (the marriage of nature and mind) in a "green Shade" (the ocean of possible forms). Inside the womb-like mind, moving over the waters of the deep, the Romantic poet comes, not as he has, crawling, but as he shall, "flying" out of nature.

Nature, as Keats saw, is paradoxical in that while it provides sensuous beauty and pleasure, fulfillment to the ravenous appetite desire, it also leads inevitably to decay. Indulgence expedites decay. Keats accepts decay. Marvell, like Stevens, transcends it by believing in the value of temporary pleasure. Marvell waits contentedly in the boughs of the fruit tree "till prepar'd for longer flight" as Stevens delights as "the emperor of ice-cream" (*Collected Poems*, 64). Indulgence is apotheosis, the better than Ovidian metamorphosis, the saved-by-the-bell change out of mutability into temporary but repetitive immutability, the infinite "I AM" because "I am not," Stevens's cool, snowy "One must have a mind of winter ... to behold ... Nothing that is not there and the nothing that is" (*Complete Poems*, 9–10). The act of creation, in other words, is an act of annihilation. Milton welcomes a similar annihilation when, "Presented with a Universal blanc," he is recompensed by the "Celestial Light" which he wills to "Shine inward" that he "may see and tell / Of things invisible to mortal sight" (*Paradise Lost* III.48, 51–52, 54–55). Creation must finally be at the expense of all that's already made (including nature, and the self as one knows it), including the poet's own body which, lying in the grass, evaporates into the disembodied "green Thought in a green Shade."

"The Garden," like the Romantic poems toward which it looks, incarnates the transcendent as it transcends the incarnate. The effort is to make mind supervise nature. If the mind can organize nature, it is no longer subjected to it, a mere victim of growth and decay. Ultimately, then, nature like "busie Companies of Men" and women will be subverted by the creative mind for in its attempt at identification with nature, the creative mind can not tolerate alienation. The creative mind annihilates "all that's made" so that nothing exists but the mind itself. Nothing exists outside the mind; nothing is "not me"; everything is me. Alienation is not possible in this state of temporary if delusive bliss, nor is death.

Thus, the pleasure of the "fruit bowl" (fifth) stanza is surpassed by the pleasure of the pivotal sixth stanza. The pleasures of the mind improve upon those of the body, allowing for the further transformation into the disembodied seventh stanza:

> Here at the Fountains sliding foot,
> Or at some Fruit-tree's mossy root,
> Casting the Bodies Vest aside,
> My Soul into the boughs does glide:
> There like a Bird it sits, and sings,
> Then whets and combs its silver Wings;
> And, till prepar'd for longer flight,
> Waves in its Plumes the various Light.   (lines 49–56)

The freedom declared in the "Annihilating all that's made" couplet is now possible. The soul is released from its confining body and like a bird, and with the fluidity of the watery fountain, it glides into the boughs, into the green shade itself. This higher level now mediates between earth-bound god (stanza two) and heaven-bound man, between pantheistic and Platonic, between Renaissance and Romantic on the one hand, and Romantic and modern (Stevensian) on the other. The soul, referred to as "it," now preens its silver wings. The wings are silver both because they pick up the reflected light of the sun (and mind) and because they are transformed by the soul itself which is, like an angel, silvery. The bird/soul sings and preens, waving its plumes in the many-colored light of this world. Significantly its future falls in a subordinate clause ("And, till prepar'd for longer flight"), for the waiting on earth is pleasurable and perhaps even preferable; repetition, change, and ouroboric pleasure cycles happily substitute for ascent (without change) in this proto-Romantic revision of Platonic/Christian values. The bird is at its absolute ease, as if unconscious in the boughs. The whole effect is of airy lightness – both of gravity and of color – so that we as readers are lifted through wetness into airy nothingness. The brain is blank except for cool evergreen. It is in this state of purity, of animal-like ease in "unbodied joy"[30] that the mind "becomes" God. Man as body is metamorphosed and flies toward the "God" of the mind.

The last two stanzas are a retrospective, a sailing off from the imaginative flight of the fifth, sixth, and seventh stanzas, after the lodging of the bird in the tree:

> Such was that happy Garden-state,
> While Man there walk'd without a Mate:

After a place so pure, and sweet,
What other Help could yet be meet!
But 'twas beyond a Mortal's share
To wander solitary there:
Two Paradises 'twere in one
To live in Paradise alone.

How well the skilful Gardner drew
Of flow'rs and herbes this Dial new.
Where from above the milder Sun
Does through a fragrant Zodiack run;
And, as it works, th'industrious Bee
Computes its time as well as we.
How could such sweet and wholsome Hours
Be reckon'd but with herbs and flow'rs!   (lines 57–72)

They bring the poet around to the mild regret that pleasure leaves, to the inevitable return from bliss to the more material "Garden-state" and from there to the "busie Companies of Men" and women. But Marvell's return, unlike Keats's "Forlorn! the very word is like a bell / To toll me back from thee to my sole self!" ("Ode to a Nightingale," lines 71–72) is not grievous. What had been annihilated is reestablished as in Narcissus' mirror and the transcendent fades as a mist away. But Marvell's moment of transcendence has refreshed his poet-speaker. Happily now he sees the hours not as divisive but as "wholsome." The transcendence has brought him a wholeness with "the skilful Gardner" utterly unlike the broken, jumbling "busie Companies of Men." Read in the modern, Stevensian sense, the "skilful Gardner" is the poet himself whose imagination has, at least in one sense, replaced (and therefore no longer depends absolutely upon) God.

"The Garden" shares the parabolic shape of Keats's odes. But the return from flight for Marvell, unlike for Keats, is not dejected. His fall on grass is not debilitating, for the poem, resting ultimately on its Christian/Platonic ascensional foundation, ends by preparing for yet another temporary cycle around the dial ("And, till prepar'd for longer flight / Waves in its Plumes the various Light"). Or, one could say that the poet, like Stevens's "emperor of ice-cream," ends by enjoying the almost pagan "pleasures of merely circulating," and that these particular pleasures, these circlings around and around the earth in the mind, exclude linear ascent, the straight-up-the-cross flight into the sky of Marvell's High Church predecessors.

The flight from earth to bough, from sensation to poetry, in Marvell as in Keats and Stevens, is a flight toward the God in the mind. The flight represents the constantly written poem of the mind that finds what suffices (Stevens, *Complete Poems*, 239), that *makes* Eden simply because it must *have* Eden. Like Milton's Adam and Eve who leave a garden of God's making to tend a garden of their own, Marvell's narrator finds a "Paradise within" that makes him "happier far" (*Paradise Lost*, XII.587). This internal paradise brings abundant recompense for present losses (the disruptions to faith of the new science, the English Civil War), and prepares a remedy for losses to come (industrialization, new science, capitalism, Romantic alienation). Marvell is peculiarly modern in that while he fixes his poetry in the old world vocabulary of fall and redemption, he anticipates, like Milton, the Romantic solution to loss. In this Marvell looks forward to Keats and finally to Wallace Stevens, to a comic metaphysics which accepts death itself as the fall, and therefore nature's fruits as freely offered.

NOTES

1 See especially Joseph Anthony Wittreich, Jr.'s introduction to *The Romantics on Milton: Formal Essays and Critical Asides* (Cleveland: The Press of Case Western Reserve University, 1970). For discussion of Milton and Marvell see Christopher Hill, "Milton and Marvell" and Wittreich, "Perplexing the Explanation: Marvell's 'On Mr. Milton's *Paradise Lost*,'" in *Approaches to Marvell. The York Tercentenary Lectures*, ed. C. A. Patrides (London: Routledge and Kegan Paul, 1978).

2 See John Carey, ed., *Andrew Marvell* (Baltimore: Penguin, 1969), 23: "When the eighteenth century thought of Marvell it was not as a poet but as an incorruptible patriot, the tyrant's foe."

3 For similar attention to nature and consciousness, Milton could be added to this list. Milton's relationship to nature is commented on in several studies. To take one example, Richard Mallette (*Spenser, Milton, and Renaissance Pastoral* [Lewisburg: Bucknell University Press, 1981]), argues that Milton distrusts nature, for "the beauties of natural life must be transcended" (84), but even Mallette admits that "we hear an almost melancholy note of regret from the poet over the departure of what man has found beautiful in his natural home" (98).

4 See Edmund Gosse (1885) who writes that Marvell's "sympathy with nature" is like Wordsworth's; a similar position is taken by Alexander Grosart (1872), Stopford Brooke (1876), Edward Wright (1921), and Emile Legouis (1924). See Dan S. Collins, *Andrew Marvell: A Reference Guide* (Boston: G. K. Hall, 1981), 63, 57, 59, 89, 94. Fugitive claims for Marvell's proto-romanticism continue to be made in the twentieth century. Yvor Winters, for example, writes in 1967 that "the sources of Marvell's ideas and tradition are also remote sources of Romanticism, and the poem ["The Garden"] seems to be a precursor as well as a result" (quoted in Carey, ed., *Andrew Marvell*, 176); but Donald Friedman (*Marvell's Pastoral Art* [Berkeley: University of California Press, 1970], 134), stresses that such thinking is outmoded; thus he writes that "nineteenth-century critics [mistakenly] ... saw [Marvell] as an unabashed pantheist, a worshipper of nature who had somehow hit upon the Wordsworthian mode of apprehension in the middle of the seventeenth century." For "contemporary" comparisons between Marvell and Keats see Anthony Hecht, "Shades of Keats and Marvell," *Hudson Review* 15 (1962): 50–71 and Harold Toliver, "Pastoral Form and Idea in Some Poems of Marvell," *Texas Studies in Language and Literature* 5 (1963): 83–97.

5 See three essays, "John Milton and Andrew Marvell," "Henry Vaughan," and

"Thomas Traherne," in vol. 1 of *The Collected Essays of Christopher Hill*, 2 vols. (Amherst: University of Massachusetts Press, 1985). For "Adamic pleasure" see 232. See also "Society and Andrew Marvell" in Carey, ed., *Andrew Marvell*, 73–101. According to Christopher Hill the metaphysical poets should be considered at least as modern as they are medieval; in fact, for Hill, the Romantic period did not invent but only recovered ideas generated by the English Civil War; similarly, the Romantics only further developed an "Adamic" appreciation of nature which had already begun in the seventeenth century. Hill's argument, overlooked by mainstream metaphysical criticism, is important and should be emphasized; in fact it is analogous to the case which Wittreich and Bloom have created for continuity between Milton and the Romantics, for just as New Critical and old historical prejudice argued against the relationship between Milton and the Romantics (I am thinking particularly of the violent objections on the part of Miltonists to Romantic Satanism), so also heated arguments continue against affiliations between the metaphysicals and the Romantics.

6 In "The Dead-End of Formalist Criticism" Paul de Man makes an extraordinary claim for Empson's work in *Some Versions of Pastoral*. "Under the deceitful title of a genre study," de Man writes, "Empson has actually written an ontology of the poetic" (239). For de Man, Empson located in the modern pastoral, evident generally in the seventeenth-century meditation lyric, but peculiarly in Marvell's "The Garden," the problem of the dislocation of mind and nature, a problem which de Man rather suggestively connects not only to Keats and the Romantics but to Marxism. See *Blindness and Insight: Essays in the Rhetoric of Contemporary Criticism*, Theory and History of Literature, vol. 7, 2nd edition, revised (Minneapolis: University of Minnesota Press, 1983), 229–45.

7 *Seven Types of Ambiguity* (1930; reprint, New York: New Directions, 1947), vi; see also 171–75.

8 One is much more likely to come upon comprehensive dismissals of the idea of relationship than confirmations of Empson or Hill. For a typical example, see Donald Friedman's comment in note 4 above.

9 See Ruth Wallerstein, *Studies in Seventeenth-Century Poetic* (Madison: University of Wisconsin Press, 1950), esp. 152–234; on 152 she argues that "Marvell has been no less *barbarously kidnapped* than Donne" (emphasis added). See also Rosemond Tuve, *Elizabethan and Metaphysical Imagery* (Chicago: University of Chicago Press, 1947). Tuve argues that twentieth-century critics assume the Elizabethans "wrote good Romantic poetry" (6); but, she writes, "not even the schoolboy of the sixteenth century is told to keep his eye on his object" (3). Joseph Summers ("Marvell's 'Nature'," reprinted in Carey, ed., *Andrew Marvell*, 137–50) argues that though "the similarities between the verse of Marvell and that of many modern poets are seductive" Marvell's complicated vision of nature is "finally unlike the nineteenth century's" (137, 141). John T. Shawcross, in his essay in this volume, and in "Poetry, Personal and Impersonal: The Case of Donne" in *The Eagle and the Dove: Reassessing John Donne*, ed. Claude J. Summers and Ted-Larry Pebworth (Columbia: University of Missouri Press, 1986) shares the opinion. He writes, for example, that "The false specter of Romantic effusion has blighted poetic criticism for a long time" ("Poetry, Personal and Impersonal," 57).

10 "Marvell's habit of thought," Ruth Wallerstein insists in *Studies in Seventeenth-Century Poetic*, "had deep roots not in Hegelian but in Mediaeval and Renaissance logic" (153).

In his essay in this volume John T. Shawcross writes that "what occurred in the later nineteenth century and has continued into most of the twentieth is a 'kidnapping' of Vaughan ... modern critics [have] made Donne a contemporary through a 'critical self-consciousness' which has led to reading his poetry with modern meaning."

11 Carey writes that "obscurity and misplaced erudition are pervasive faults in modern Marvell criticism" (*Andrew Marvell: A Critical Anthology*, 71).

12 *The Seventeenth Century Background: Studies in the Thought of the Age in Relation to Poetry and Religion* (1935; reprint, Garden City and New York: Doubleday Anchor, 1953), 13.

13 See "Society and Andrew Marvell" in Carey, ed., *Andrew Marvell*, 73–101.

14 "Renaissance/Early Modern Studies" in *Redrawing the Boundaries: The Transformation of English and American Literary Studies*, ed. Stephen Greenblatt and Giles Gunn (New York: The Modern Language Association of America, 1992), 41.

15 Shawcross, ed., *Complete Poetry*, 96.

16 See John Middleton Murry, "Romanticism and the Tradition" (129–45) in *Defending Romanticism* (1924; reprint, with an introduction by Malcolm Woodfield, Bristol: Bristol Press, 1989).

17 See *A Carlyle Reader: Selections from the Writings of Thomas Carlyle*, ed. G. B. Tennyson (Cambridge: Cambridge University Press, 1984), 68.

18 See *The Paradise Within: Studies in Vaughan, Traherne, and Milton* (New Haven: Yale University Press, 1964) and *The Poetry of Meditation* (1954; reprint, New Haven: Yale University Press, 1966), esp. 25–70.

19 Willey, *The Seventeenth Century Background*, 127.

20 *The Collected Poems of Wallace Stevens* (New York: Alfred A. Knopf, 1969), 524. Hereafter, quotations from Stevens's poetry will be cited by page number in the text.

21 *The Collected Poems of W. B. Yeats* (New York: Macmillan, 1976), 192.

22 "Ode to a Nightingale," line 61. Keats's poems are quoted from *The Poems of John Keats*, ed. Stillinger.

23 *Prose Works*, 1: 138.

24 *Poetical Works*, 2: 236.

25 *The Form of the Unfinished: English Poetics from Spenser to Pound* (Princeton: Princeton University Press, 1985), 35.

26 "Shades of Keats and Marvell," *Hudson Review* 15 (1962): 51.

27 *Beyond God the Father*, second edition (London: The Women's Press, 1986), 47.

28 *Spenser, Marvell, and Renaissance Pastoral* (Cambridge: Harvard University Press, 1970), 153.

29 Samuel Taylor Coleridge, *Biographia Literaria*, ed. James Engell and W. Jackson Bate, 2 vols., *Collected Coleridge*, vol. 7 (Princeton: Princeton University Press, 1983), 1: 304.

30 *Shelley's Poetry and Prose*, ed. Reiman and Powers, 226.

Selected bibliography

Abrams, M. H. *The Mirror and The Lamp: Romantic Theory and the Critical Tradition*. New York: Oxford University Press, 1953.

Natural Supernaturalism: Tradition and Revolt in Romantic Literature. New York: Norton, 1971.

Auerbach, Nina. *Romantic Imprisonment*. New York: Columbia University Press, 1985.

Ault, Donald. *Narrative Unbound: Re-Visioning William Blake's "The Four Zoas."* Barrytown, NY: Station Hill Press, 1987.

Bloom, Harold. *The Anxiety of Influence*. London: Oxford University Press, 1973.

A Map of Misreading. London: Oxford University Press, 1975.

Romanticism and Consciousness. New York: Norton, 1970.

The Visionary Company: A Reading of English Romantic Poetry. Revised edition. Ithaca: Cornell University Press, 1971.

Brisman, Leslie. *Milton's Poetry of Choice and Its Romantic Heirs*. Ithaca: Cornell University Press, 1973.

Campbell, Jane. *The Retrospective Review (1820–1828) and the Revival of Seventeenth-Century Poetry*. Waterloo, Canada: Waterloo Lutheran University, 1972.

Chandler, James K. *Wordsworth's Second Nature: A Study of the Poetry and Politics*. Chicago: University of Chicago Press, 1984.

Colie, Rosalie L. *"My Ecchoing Song": Andrew Marvell's Poetry of Criticism*. Princeton: Princeton University Press, 1970.

Crofts, J. *Wordsworth and the Seventeenth Century*. The Warton Lecture, 1940. Reprint. Folcroft Library Editions, 1974.

De Man, Paul. "The Dead-End of Formalist Criticism." In *Blindness and Insight: Essays in the Rhetoric of Contemporary Criticism*. Theory and History of Literature, vol. 7, 2nd edition, revised. Minneapolis: University of Minnesota Press, 1983.

DeNeef, A. Leigh. *Traherne in Dialogue: Heidegger, Lacan, and Derrida*. Durham and London: Duke University Press, 1988.

Di Salvo, Jacqueline. "Fear of Flying: Milton on the Boundaries Between Witchcraft and Inspiration." *English Literary Renaissance* 18 (1988): 114–37.

War of Titans: Blake's Critique of Milton and the Politics of Religion. Pittsburgh: University of Pittsburgh Press, 1983.

Donno, Elizabeth Story. *Andrew Marvell. The Critical Heritage*. London: Routledge and Kegan Paul, 1978.

Dubrow, Heather. *A Happier Eden: The Politics of Marriage in the Stuart Epithalamium*. Ithaca and London: Cornell University Press, 1990.

Dunbar, Pamela. *William Blake's Illustrations to the Poetry of Milton*. Oxford: Clarendon Press, 1980.

Selected bibliography

Eliot, T. S. "The Metaphysical Poets." In *Selected Essays*. 3rd edition. London: Faber and Faber, 1951.

Empson, William. "An Early Romantic." *The Cambridge Review* 31 May 1929.

Seven Types of Ambiguity. 1930. Reprint. New York: New Directions, 1947.

Some Versions of Pastoral. London: Chatto and Windus, 1935.

Force, James E. "The Newtonians and Deism." In *Essays on the Context, Nature, and Influence of Sir Isaac Newton's Theology*. Edited by James E. Force and Richard H. Popkin. London: Klumer Academic Publishers, 1990.

Frei, Hans. *The Eclipse of Biblical Narrative: A Study in Eighteenth and Nineteenth Century Hermeneutics*. New Haven: Yale University Press, 1974.

Friedman, Donald. *Marvell's Pastoral Art*. Berkeley: University of California Press, 1970.

Galperin, William. *Revision and Authority in Wordsworth: The Interpretation of a Career*. Philadelphia: University of Pennsylvania Press, 1989.

Geisst, Charles R. *The Political Thought of John Milton*. London: Macmillan, 1984.

Gilbert, Sandra M. and Susan Gubar, *The Madwoman in the Attic*. New Haven: Yale University Press, 1979.

Gordon, R. K. "Keats and Milton." *Modern Language Review* 42 (1947): 434–46.

Goslee, Nancy M. "'Under a Cloud in Prospect': Keats, Milton, and Stationing." *Philological Quarterly* 53 (1974): 205–19.

Granqvist, Raoul. *The Reputation of John Donne 1779–1873*. Studia Anglistica Upsaliensia 24. Uppsala: University of Uppsala, 1975.

Grierson, Herbert J. C. *Metaphysical Lyrics and Poems of the Seventeenth Century*. Oxford: Clarendon Press, 1921.

Griffin, Dustin. *Regaining Paradise: Milton and the Eighteenth Century*. Cambridge: Cambridge University Press, 1986.

Hagstrum, Jean H. "William Blake Rejects the Enlightenment." In *Blake: A Collection of Critical Essays*. Edited by Northrop Frye. Englewood Cliffs, New Jersey: Prentice-Hall, 1966.

Harvey, Elizabeth D., and Katharine Eisaman Maus, eds. *Soliciting Interpretation: Literary Theory and Seventeenth Century English Poetry*. Chicago: University of Chicago Press, 1990.

Havens, Raymond Dexter. *The Influence of Milton on English Poetry*. Cambridge: Harvard University Press, 1922.

Healy, Thomas, and Jonathan Sawday, eds. *Literature and the English Civil War*. Cambridge and New York: Cambridge University Press, 1990.

Hecht, Anthony. "Shades of Keats and Marvell." *Hudson Review* 15 (1962): 50–71.

Hill, Christopher. *The Collected Essays of Christopher Hill*. 2 vols. Amherst: University of Massachusetts Press, 1985.

Milton and the English Revolution. New York: Viking, 1978.

Hodgson, John A. "Coleridge, Puns, and 'Donne's First Poem': The Limbo of Rhetoric and the Conceptions of Wit." *John Donne Journal* 4 (1985): 190–95.

Homans, Margaret. *Women Writers and Poetic Identity: Dorothy Wordsworth, Emily Bronte and Emily Dickinson*. Princeton: Princeton University Press, 1980.

Hughes, Merritt Y. "Kidnapping Donne." *University of California Publications in English* 4 (1934): 61–89.

"The Theme of Pre-existence and Infancy in 'The Retreate.'" *Philological Quarterly* 20 (1941): 484–500.

Jacob, Margaret. *The Newtonians and the English Revolution, 1689–1720.* Ithaca: Cornell University Press, 1976.

Jacobus, Mary. *Reading Women.* New York: Columbia University Press, 1986.

Kelsall, Malcolm. *Byron's Politics.* Brighton, Sussex: The Harvester Press, 1987.

Kucich, Greg. *Keats, Shelley, and Romantic Spenserianism.* University Park: Pennsylvania State University Press, 1991.

Lams, Victor J., Jr. "Ruth, Milton, and Keats's 'Ode to a Nightingale.'" *Modern Language Quarterly* 34 (1973): 417–35

Leavis, F. R. *Revaluation: Tradition and Devlopment in English Poetry.* 1935. Reprint. London: Chatto and Windus, 1956.

Levinson, Marjorie. *Wordsworth's Great Period Poems: Four Essays.* Cambridge: Cambridge University Press, 1986.

Lewalski, Barbara K. "Milton on Women – Yet Once More." *Milton Studies* 6 (1974): 3–20.

Protestant Poetics and the Seventeenth-Century Religious Lyric. Princeton: Princeton University Press, 1979.

Lieb, Michael, and John T. Shawcross, eds. *Achievements of the Left Hand: Essays on the Prose of John Milton.* Amherst: University of Massachusetts Press, 1974.

Liu, Alan. *Wordsworth: The Sense of History.* Stanford: Stanford University Press, 1989.

Loewenstein, David, and James Grantham Turner. *Politics, Poetics, and Hermeneutics in Milton's Prose.* Cambridge: Cambridge University Press, 1990.

MacLean, Gerald. *Time's Witness: Historical Representation in English Poetry, 1603–1660.* Madison: University of Wisconsin Press, 1990.

Marcus, Leah S. *Childhood and Cultural Despair: A Theme and Variations in Seventeenth-Century Literature.* Pittsburgh: University of Pittsburgh Press, 1978.

"Justice for Margery Evans: A 'Local' Reading of *Comus.*" In *Milton and the Idea of Woman.* Edited by Julia M. Walker. Urbana: University of Illinois Press, 1988.

The Politics of Mirth: Jonson, Herrick, Milton, Marvell and the Defense of Old Holiday Pastimes. Chicago and London: University of Chicago Press, 1986.

"Vaughan, Wordsworth, Coleridge, and the 'Encomium Asini.'" *ELH* 42 (1975): 224–41.

Marilla, E. L. "The Significance of Henry Vaughan's Literary Reputation." *Modern Language Quarterly* 5 (1944): 155–62.

Martines, Lauro. *Society and History in English Renaissance Verse.* Oxford: Basil Blackwell, 1987.

Martz, Louis. *The Paradise Within: Studies in Vaughan, Traherne, and Milton.* New Haven: Yale University Press, 1964.

The Poetry of Meditation. 1954. Reprint. New Haven: Yale University Press, 1966.

McGann, Jerome J. *The Romantic Ideology: A Critical Investigation.* Chicago: University of Chicago Press, 1983.

McMaster, Helen N. "Vaughan and Wordsworth." *Review of English Studies* 11 (1935): 313–25.

Mellor, Anne K., ed. *Romanticism and Feminism.* Bloomington: Indiana University Press, 1988.

Merrill, L. R. "Vaughan's Influence Upon Wordsworth's Poetry." *Modern Language Notes* 37 (1922): 91–96.

Milner, Andrew. *John Milton and the English Revolution: A Study in the Sociology of Literature.* London: Macmillan, 1981.

Miner, Earl. *The Cavalier Mode from Jonson to Cotton.* Princeton: Princeton University Press, 1971.

Morris, Muriel. "A Note on Wordsworth and Vaughan." *Modern Language Notes* 39 (1924): 287–88.

Morton, A. L. *The Everlasting Gospel: A Study in the Sources of William Blake.* New York: Lawrence & Wishart, 1958.

Murry, John Middleton. *Defending Romanticism.* 1924. Reprint, with an introduction by Malcolm Woodfield. Bristol: Bristol Press, 1989.

Nethercot, Arthur H. "The Reputation of the 'Metaphysical Poets' During the Age of Johnson and the 'Romantic Revival.'" *Studies in Philology* 22 (1925): 81–132.

Newlyn, Lucy. *"Paradise Lost" and the Romantic Reader.* Oxford: Clarendon Press, 1993.

Nyquist, Mary. "Fallen Differences, Phallogocentric Discourses: Losing *Paradise Lost* to History." In *Post-structuralism and the Question of History.* Edited by Derek Attridge, Geoff Bennington, and Robert Young. Cambridge: Cambridge University Press, 1987.

and Margaret W. Ferguson, eds. *Re-Membering Milton: Essays on the Texts and Traditions.* New York: Methuen, 1987.

Paulson, Ronald. *Book and Painting: Shakespeare, Milton, and the Bible: Literary Texts and the Emergence of English Painting.* Knoxville: University of Tennessee Press, 1982.

Peterfreund, Stuart. "Blake and Newton: Argument as Art, Argument as Science." *Studies in Eighteenth-Century Culture* 10 (1981): 205–26.

Pointon, Marcia R. *Milton and English Art.* Manchester: Manchester University Press, 1970.

Prior, Mary, ed. *Women in English Society 1500–1800.* London and New York: Methuen, 1985.

Radzinowicz, Mary Ann. "The Politics of *Paradise Lost.*" In *Politics of Discourse: The Literature and History of Seventeenth-Century England.* Edited by Kevin Sharpe and Steven N. Zwicker. Berkeley and Los Angeles: University of California Press, 1987.

Rajan, Balachandra. *The Form of the Unfinished: English Poetics From Spenser to Pound.* Princeton: Princeton University Press, 1985.

Paradise Lost and the Seventeenth Century Reader. 1947. Reprint. London: Chatto and Windus, 1962.

ed. *Paradise Lost: A Tercentenary Tribute.* Toronto: University of Toronto Press, 1969.

Rajan, Tilottama. *Dark Interpreter: The Discourse of Romanticism.* Ithaca and London: Cornell University Press, 1980.

The Supplement of Reading: Figures of Understanding in Romantic Theory and Practice. Ithaca: Cornell University Press, 1990.

Richardson, Alan. *A Mental Theatre: Poetic Drama and Consciousness in the Romantic Age.* University Park: Pennsylvania State University Press, 1988.

Roe, Nicholas. "Wordsworth, Milton, and the Politics of Poetic Influence." *The Yearbook of English Studies* 19 (1989): 112–26.

Rollin, Roger B, and J. Max Patrick, eds. *"Trust to Good Verses": Herrick Tercentenary Essays.* Pittsburgh: University of Pittsburgh Press, 1978.

Sandler, Florence. "The Iconoclastic Enterprise: Blake's Critique of 'Milton's Religion.'" *Blake Studies* 5 (1972): 13–57.

Shawcross, John T., ed. *Milton 1732–1801: The Critical Heritage*. London: Routledge and Kegan Paul, 1972.

"Opulence and Iron Pokers: Coleridge and Donne." *John Donne Journal* 4 (1985): 201–24.

"Poetry, Personal and Impersonal: The Case of Donne." In *The Eagle and the Dove: Reassessing John Donne*. Edited by Claude J. Summers and Ted-Larry Pebworth. Columbia: University of Missouri Press, 1986.

Sherwin, Paul. "Dying into Life: Keats's Struggle with Milton in *Hyperion*." *PMLA* 93 (1978): 383–95.

Simpson, David. *Wordsworth's Historical Imagination: The Poetry of Displacement*. New York and London: Methuen, 1987.

Slights, Camille Wells. *The Casuistical Tradition*. Princeton: Princeton University Press, 1981.

Smith, A. J. "Donne's Reputation." In *John Donne: Essays in Celebration*. Edited by A. J. Smith. London: Methuen, 1972.

Stewart, Larry. "Samuel Clarke, Newtonianism, and the Factions of Post-Revolutionary England." *Journal of the History of Ideas* 42 (1981): 53–72.

Stone, Lawrence. *The Family, Sex, and Marriage in England 1500–1800*. New York: Harper and Row, 1979.

Sturrock, J. "Wordsworth and Vaughan." *Notes & Queries* 24 (1977): 322–23.

Tillyard, E. M. W. *The Metaphysicals and Milton*. London: Chatto and Windus, 1956.

Toliver, Harold. "Pastoral Form and Idea in Some Poems of Marvell." *Texas Studies in Language and Literature* 5 (1963): 83–97.

Trilling, Lionel. "The Poet as Hero: Keats in his Letters." In *The Opposing Self*. New York and London: Harcourt Brace, 1978.

Turner, James Grantham. *The Politics of Landscape: Rural Scenery and Society in English Poetry 1630–1660*. Cambridge: Harvard University Press, 1970.

Tuve, Rosemond. *Elizabethan and Metaphysical Imagery: Renaissance Poetic and Twentieth-Century Critics*. Chicago: University of Chicago Press, 1947.

Viner, Jacob. *The Role of Providence in the Social Order: An Essay in Intellectual History*. Princeton: Princeton University Press, 1972.

Wall, Kathleen. "A Mask Presented at Ludlow Castle: The Armor of Logos." In *Milton and the Idea of Woman*. Edited by Julia M. Walker. Urbana: University of Illinois Press, 1988.

Wallerstein, Ruth. *Studies in Seventeenth-Century Poetic*. Madison: University of Wisconsin Press, 1950.

Webber, Joan. *The Eloquent "I."* Madison: University of Wisconsin Press, 1968.

White, Helen C., Ruth C. Wallerstein, and Ricardo Quintana, eds. *Seventeenth-Century Verse and Prose*. Toronto: Macmillan, 1969.

Wilkie, Brian. *Romantic Poets and Epic Tradition*. Madison: University of Wisconsin Press, 1965.

Willey, Basil. *The Seventeenth Century Background: Studies in the Thought of the Age in Relation to Poetry and Religion*. 1935. Reprint. Garden City, New York: Doubleday Anchor, 1953.

Williamson, George. *The Donne Tradition*. Cambridge: Harvard University Press, 1930.

Wittreich, Joseph Anthony, Jr. *Feminist Milton*. Ithaca: Cornell University Press, 1987.

ed. *Milton and the Line of Vision*. Madison: University of Wisconsin Press, 1975.

ed. *The Romantics on Milton: Formal Essays and Critical Asides*. Cleveland: The Press of Case Western Reserve University, 1970.

Visionary Poetics: Milton's Tradition and His Legacy. San Marino, California: Huntington Library, 1979.

Woodring, Carl. *Politics in English Romantic Poetry*. Cambridge: Harvard University Press, 1970.

Index